LOVE
16½ IN. 7IN. 10½ IN.
HIGH WIDE LONG

THE RIVER SIDE
18½ IN. 6IN. 6IN.

THE SISTERS
23IN. 8IN. 8IN.

NEW FRIENDS
17½ IN. 6½ IN. 6½ IN.

LOVE
16½ IN. 7IN. 11½ IN.
HIGH WIDE LONG

STUDIES FROM LIFE
20IN. 7½ IN. 10½ IN.
HIGH WIDE LONG

CLYTIE
23 IN. 15 IN.

STUDIES FROM LIFE
20IN. 7½ IN. 10½ IN.
HIGH WIDE LONG

PROSPERITY
20IN. 6IN. 7IN.

BEATRICE
22IN. 6IN. 7IN.

PATIENCE
23IN. 13IN. 13IN.

MAIDENHOOD
21½ IN. 6½ IN. 6IN.

ADVERSITY
19½ IN. 7IN. 7IN.

PARIAN
Copeland's Statuary Porcelain

PARIAN

Copeland's Statuary Porcelain

Robert Copeland

ANTIQUE COLLECTORS' CLUB

ISBN 10: 1 85149 499 5
ISBN 13: 1 85149 499 6

British Library Cataloguing-in-Publication Data
A catalogue record for this book is available from the British Library

Printed in China
for the Antique Collectors' Club Ltd., Woodbridge, Suffolk

Frontispiece: **DANCING GIRL REPOSING** by William Calder Marshall, 1846. Ht. 18in. (45.72cm). See page 136.

Title page: **FRUIT BOY (SITTING)** by almost certainly a Derby modeller. See pages 144 and 145.

The Antique Collectors' Club

Formed in 1966, the Antique Collectors' Club is now a world-renowned publisher of top quality books for the collector. It also publishes the only independently-run monthly antiques magazine, *Antique Collecting*, which rose quickly from humble beginnings to a network of worldwide subscribers.

The magazine, whose motto is For Collectors–By Collectors–About Collecting, is aimed at collectors interested in widening their knowledge of antiques both by increasing their awareness of quality and by discussion of the factors influencing prices.

Subscription to Antique Collecting is open to anyone interested in antiques and subscribers receive ten issues a year. Well-illustrated articles deal with practical aspects of collecting and provide numerous tips on prices, features of value, investment potential, fakes and forgeries. Offers of related books at special reduced prices are also available only to subscribers.

In response to the enormous demand for information on 'what to pay', ACC introduced in 1968 the famous price guide series. The first title, *The Price Guide to Antique Furniture* (since renamed *British Antique Furniture: Price Guide and Reasons for Values*), is still in constant demand. Since those pioneering days, ACC has gone from strength to strength, publishing many of today's standard works of reference on all things antique and collectable, from *Tiaras* to *20th Century Ceramic Designers in Britain*.

Not only has ACC continued to cater strongly for its original audience, it has also branched out to produce excellent titles on many subjects including art reference, architecture, garden design, gardens, and textiles. All ACC's publications are available through bookshops worldwide and a catalogue is available free of charge from the addresses below.

For further information please contact:

ANTIQUE COLLECTORS' CLUB

www.antiquecollectorsclub.com

Sandy Lane, Old Martlesham
Woodbridge, Suffolk IP12 4SD, UK
Tel: 01394 389950 Fax: 01394 389999
Email: info@antique-acc.com
or
Eastworks, 116 Pleasant Street - Suite 18,
Easthampton, MA 01027, USA
Tel: 413 529 0861 Fax: 413 529 0862
Email: info@antiquecc.com

Dedicated to all the sculptors,
modellers, mouldmakers, potters and
firemen of Copelands who
manufactured the statuary porcelain
figures and other superb objects

Contents

The late Llewellyn A. (Comp) Compton, DFC

Llewellyn Arthur Compton was born in Sheffield and spent his youth in the Thames Valley. He joined the Territorial Army in 1938, was called up at the outbreak of war and drafted into the 250 Ack/Ack Battery. In 1942 he volunteered for aircrew duties and, after training in Canada, he became a 'Mosquito' pilot with 248 Squadron Coastal Command.

After leaving the Royal Air Force he took a course at Avoncroft Agricultural College and eventually joined an agricultural firm in Lincolnshire. There, the owner, who was a member of the Wedgwood Society, introduced him to the joys of collecting antiques.

Comp was an enthusiastic member of the Spode Society, the Wedgwood Society, and the Northern Ceramic Society, as well, I think, of the English Ceramic Circle. He contributed several learned articles to the bulletins of some of these societies including one on the Society for the Abolition of the Slave Trade and the Wedgwood cameo of 1787. He was interested in Copeland's statuary porcelain and suggested to me that he should do a series of studies of the subjects for inclusion in the *Spode Review*. This coincided with my own work for a full book on the subject so Comp agreed to devote his research to this book. It has resulted in this present volume, *Parian. Copeland's Statuary Porcelain,* and includes his research into the exploits of Austin Henry Layard during his excavations in Mesopotamia and their link with Copeland's miniature copies of some of the sculptures he discovered. He has made an enormous contribution to the completeness of this study.

Comp was always keen on research and among other subjects he sought out the original prints and paintings that were copied on to ceramic objects.

Comp died peacefully in his retirement county of Norfolk during the last week of September 2006, aged eighty-nine.

Foreword

It is generally agreed that Parian was first developed and introduced into the ceramic repertoire by Copeland & Garrett of Stoke-upon-Trent. It was launched with a display at the First Exhibition of British Industrial Art held in Manchester in December 1845 and made commercially available from 1846.

This fine marble-like porcelain was ideal for producing sculpture on a reduced scale. The influential Art Union saw in Parian an opportunity to raise the aesthetic taste of a nation and promoted its qualities. It was further promoted through displays at international exhibitions and by publication in the influential *Art-Journal.* Victorian England offered a growing new and appreciative consumer market eager to show its sophisticated artistic preferences by acquiring inexpensive art – Parian sculpture approved by the artistic establishment met all the criteria and enjoyed great success.

This book is devoted to the work of the Copeland manufactory, its search for the perfect statuary porcelain and its production of Parian Statuary. Books on ceramic subjects are usually written by collectors, dealers or auctioneers. This one is written by a collector, ceramic historian and noted manufacturer. Robert Copeland has had a lifelong interest in the ceramic arts of Staffordshire. Trained in all the ceramic processes, he brings a unique perspective and authority to his writing. His collaborator, L.A. Compton, respected for his diligent research into the historical background of ceramic subjects, makes a significant contribution to the catalogue of Copeland's Statuary Porcelain sculptures. His account of the excavations in Mesopotamia (Iraq) lends an interesting background to Copeland's models of some of the stone sculptures which were reduced examples of those in the British Museum.

Robert joined the family firm of W.T. Copeland & Sons Limited – owners of the Spode manufactory in Stoke-upon-Trent – in 1943. He worked 'at the bench' for three years before becoming manager of the bone china clay department. He later held the post of Marketing Director for ten years before becoming Historical Consultant and Curator of the Spode Museum in 1979. He retired in 1997 but continues to keep in regular touch with the Museum. His lifelong interest is in Spode and the English pottery industry. His books include *Spode's Willow Pattern and other designs after the Chinese* and *Spode and Copeland Marks and other relevant intelligence*, and four Shire publications. This book on Parian has taken twenty years to assemble and will be of value to all people interested in the subject and not just collectors of Copeland products.

Pat Halfpenny
Director of Museum Collections
Winterthur Museum
Delaware

Preface

Soon after I became Historical Consultant to Spode in 1979 with the enjoyable task of Curator of the Spode Museum, I also had the responsibility of answering enquiries about the past productions of the firm. An increasing number of these were about parian sculptures. Jean Bettaney, who acted as my secretary, told me of a box of very old photographs she had saved from being thrown away. These proved to be of a comprehensive collection of parian products: groups of figures, statuettes, portrait busts, other ornamental and functional objects. These photographs, taken in the late 1800s and early 1900s, have been invaluable. Moreover, handwritten and printed lists – some with prices – have enabled a comprehensive picture to be assembled of the extent of Copeland's Statuary Porcelain production.

L.A. Compton, a member of the Spode Society, wanted to begin a series of articles on Copeland's Parian for the *Spode Review.* I had already started to compile this book and 'Comp' agreed to collaborate with me. He has researched nearly every known subject and the bulk of the information in the catalogue section of this book is his work. Comp prepared the details of the lives of the sculptors and also researched all of the section on the Assyrian story.

My own research into the correspondence in the *Staffordshire Advertiser* of 1851, the stories of the Great Exhibitions – aided by Arlene Palmer Schwind, George Miller and the facilities of the British Library – and the Art Unions as well as the details of the manufacturing process, assisted by the mouldmakers of Spode, has resulted in a wealth of detailed information on a subject which has been rather neglected. Apart from a few magazine articles, only two hard-back books about Parian have been published: *The Parian Phenomenon,* published in 1989 by Richard Dennis, and *The Illustrated Guide to Victorian Parian China* by C. & D. Shinn, 1971. A Shire Album, *Parian Ware* by Dennis Barker, was published in 1985. So far as Copeland's productions are concerned, this new book will be an important addition.

Throughout the catalogue section reference is made to three factory records:

SPB The Statuary Price Book. A leather-bound manuscript record of statuettes, groups and busts.

NPL The Net Price List. This is a printed list but undated. For some time it was thought to have dated from c.1870. Then one or two sculptures came to my attention that were sculpted in 1881, then one in 1882, and then one c.1883. This meant that this NPL was probably printed in 1883. These estimated dates have been kept but it is important to realise that the prices were steadily reduced as the end of the nineteenth century progressed.

Making Price Books. Manuscript records of the prices paid to the makers. Although one is dated 1928, it quotes the same prices as that dated 1895. It is not known if any examples of parian were made in 1928; if they were none seems to have survived.

Reference is made to illustrations in *The Parian Phenomenon* using PP and the relevant illustration number. If an illustration does exist in the Spode MSS or elsewhere it is marked as 'Yes'.

The photographs from the Spode archives are reproduced by kind permission of the Spode Museum Trust, copyright Spode. All other images are reproduced by kind permission of the private persons who have supplied them. The author thanks them all for their considerable help.

Preface

This work concentrates on the groups, statuettes and portrait busts made by Copeland. It also includes details of the sculptors. I have not included illustrations of ornamental and functional objects made in parian because they are very numerous and only relatively few actual examples are still known. Neither have I included studies of animals.

Very many of the illustrations have only been possible because of the photographs taken over a hundred years ago on glass negatives. Over the years some of the prints have suffered some damage but have been included in order to make this catalogue as complete as possible.

Since the completion of the initial work several additional examples of busts and statuettes have come to the attention of the Spode Museum and myself. These have been included. It is always possible that other subjects might come to light after the publication of this book; if it stimulates a greater interest in Parian as well as making available a lot more information the objective of publishing will have been achieved.

Acknowledgements

My first debt of gratitude is to Spode who have allowed me unrestricted access to all the archival records and examples in the Spode Museum Trust Collection and latterly to Pam Woolliscroft, the Curator of that Collection, not least for scanning the archival photographs. Then, of course, to Comp Compton, who carried out the extensive research into the backgrounds of the individual subjects and their sculptors.

I am grateful to Her Majesty the Queen for permission to reproduce photographs of examples in the Royal Collection.

Many friends and correspondents have supplied photographs from their collections and in some cases have allowed me to photograph their treasured pieces:

Dan Chiriboga, D.W. and A.S. Delo, Maurice Martin, Mrs Anne Downs, Graham Ryan, The Harris Museum – Preston, Dorine Archer, Mr & Mrs R.K. Fisk, Mr R. Smith, Merv and Catherine Hynes, Mrs K. Beattie, Nottingham Museum, Conrad Biernacki, Margaret Durst, Mrs K. Oakes, G.D.V. Glynn, Mrs A. Dean, The Bolton Museum, Clive and Lynne Jackson, the Curator of Blair Castle, Mrs G. Gratton-Storey, Mr K.L. Allen, Mrs W. Hunka, Miss Julia Poole – The Fitzwilliam Museum, Mrs K. Rye, Mr & Mrs J.R. Copeland, Mrs A.M Oxford, Miss S. Kellond, Mrs S. Pyman, Dr Geoffrey Godden, Mrs J. Tweedale, Alfred Marshall, Dr Susan Walker – British Museum, Lichfield District Council, Mrs M. Wilton-Hayes, Miss Jill Rumsey, Mr Martin Greenwood, Dr Philip Ward-Jackson – Conway Library – The Courtauld Institute of Art, Mr George Worlock, Mr Kevin Salt, Miss Gaye Blake Roberts and Mrs Lynn Miller of The Wedgwood Museum, Mr & Mrs W. Coles, Mrs Sonia Copeland, Rodney Hampson, Dr & Mrs Maurice Hillis, The Stoke-on-Trent Reference Library in Hanley, Bill Young, Sotheby's, Mrs Thelma Seear, Mr B. Whiston, Mrs A.J. Nobes, Mrs M. Howes, Mr S.E. Hall, Mrs J. Elems, Mrs M. Nicholle, Mrs Jennifer Danks, Commander Patrick Tailyour, Keith M. Deutscher, Mr A.W. Howatson, V. Streek, Ray Hourahine, Geoffrey Fisk and Richard Thwaites.

Collectors of parian all owe a debt of gratitude to Richard Dennis for arranging the exhibition *The Parian Phenomenon* in 1984 and for the subsequent publication of the book of the same name and the author thanks Richard Dennis for permitting him to publish some of the illustrations that were used in that book.

Marks on Copeland's Statuary Porcelain

The very early statuary subjects made during the last few years of the Copeland & Garrett partnership have printed marks like that on an example of *Narcissus*, mark RC 165 in *Spode and Copeland Marks and other relevant intelligence*. Another printed mark stating

COPELAND & GARRETT'S
PORCELAIN STATUARY

will be RC 155. This mark is especially interesting as it is the only one known to describe the object as opposed to the ceramic body of which it is made. All other marks refer to Statuary Porcelain. At least three examples are known.

A similar mark to that of *Narcissus* occurs in 1847 on an example of *Innocence*, BY W.T. COPELAND. This mark has not been recorded so will be given the number RC 234d.

An embossed mark, RC 112, is found on useful and ornamental objects, but so far none has been seen on statuary subjects.

Several different marks are found on wares made during the Copeland period from 1847 onwards starting with the example RC 234b mentioned above.

Very soon, though, printed marks were discontinued and the impressed COPELAND mark RC 202 used on all groups, statuettes and portrait busts.

A quite rare mark, RC 221, has been seen on several examples of statuettes and busts, in particular on examples of bronze castings taken from moulds made from parian objects. An example of the bust of *Princess Alexandra* by Mary Thornycroft and a statuette of *Marguerite* have been seen. These examples have a thin metallic skin in which an epoxy resin material has been poured in to provide a substantial body. It is thought that these are of twentieth century manufacture and not by Copeland.

Other embossed marks do occur on hollow-ware objects, RC 227 on vintage jugs and RC 113 on a BEAUVAIS JUG.

These marks reproduced here are the copyright of Spode, a division of the Porcelain and Fine China Companies Limited.

112

113

155

165

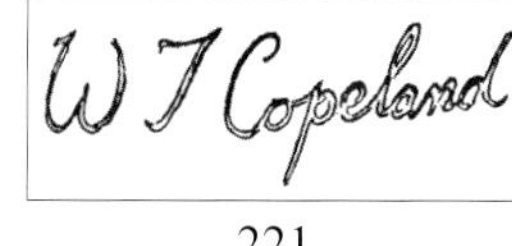

221

202

234a

234d

227

THE ORIGIN OF STATUARY PORCELAIN
Later called Parian
The material next best to marble

Ever since the 1840s there has been discussion about the origins of Parian. Although both Mintons and Thomas Boote laid claim to being first, it is now acknowledged by most authorities to have originated in the Spode factory of Messrs Copeland & Garrett. Unfortunately, there are few contemporary accounts of the event, so those that are known deserve to be studied carefully. There were also rival claims made by the employees of Copeland & Garrett: Thomas Battam, the art director; Spencer Garrett, one of the managers; and John Mountford, a figure-maker.

Maureen Batkin and Paul Atterbury in *The Parian Phenomenon*, published in 1989, whilst agreeing that the origin of parian is obscure, tend to dismiss the claims by summarising the correspondence which occurred in *The Staffordshire Advertiser* during 1851. Paul Atterbury, in his section on parian in the comprehensive volume on *Staffordshire Porcelain* in 1983, said:

> Developed first by Copeland in 1842, parian, a fine white dense material with a marble-like finish suitable for large-scale reproduction of finely detailed models, was rapidly taken up by a number of leading British manufacturers. Minton had developed their version by 1846…

There has not come to light any contemporary account of the event in 1842, when it was claimed that a specimen of a figure imitating marble was shown and purchased by His Grace the Duke of Sutherland. The reference to this early date is based on an account published in 1851 in *The Handbook to the Official Catalogues of the Great Exhibition* by R. Hunt. He states:

> The first idea of imitating marble in ceramic manufacture originated with Mr Thomas Battam, the artist directing the extensive manufactory of Mr Alderman Copeland at Stoke-upon-Trent, in the commencement of 1842. After a series of experiments he succeeded in producing a very perfect imitation of marble, both in surface and tint. One of the earliest specimens was submitted to His Grace the Duke of Sutherland, who expressed his unqualified admiration of the purposes to which it was applied, and became its first patron by purchasing the example submitted. This was on the 3rd of August 1842…

Although it is said that Hunt is not regarded as a very reliable source, he does not state that the material of which the specimen was made was called *statuary porcelain*; he calls it 'a very perfect imitation of marble'. Moreover, there is no corroboration of this statement because any evidence which may have been in the Sutherland Papers does not seem to have survived.

I try, in this chapter, to suggest an explanation of how these claims might have arisen. It is, of course, an hypothesis and, because of the scant information, the absolute truth may never be known. At the outset, however, the object of our study is the reproduction of sculpture in a reduced size, using a ceramic material to represent marble. If this is kept in mind, I think it will minimise confusion.

The first important account relating to the subject of imitations of marble appears in the January 1845 issue of *The Art-Union* magazine which included a report of the Art Union of London:

> This brings us to one of the most recent, and, as we will venture to predict, one of the most popular acts of the Committee… The Committee have constantly adverted in their reports to the connexion between Manufacturers and Art, and have felt the importance of bringing one to the aid of the other. As a first step, they have determined to reduce some fine statue to a convenient size, and to issue a certain number of copies in stone china, as manufactured by Messrs. Copeland & Garrett. Mr. Gibson, our eminent countryman, has offered any of his works for this purpose, and we have little doubt that an impetus will thus be given which will be felt throughout the whole of the Potteries and lead to much good…

A footnote mentions two examples which had been seen by the magazine's representative:

> We have been enabled to examine the material referred to, and can bear testimony to its beauty, as well as very valuable qualities for multiplying the sculptor's work… Messrs. Copeland & Garrett have already produced some beautiful examples in the material, one a statue of a Shepherd Boy by Wyatt (lent to them for the purpose by the Duke of Sutherland), and one, a copy of Marochetti's famous equestrian statue of Philibert.

This account, published in January 1845, shows that Copeland & Garrett had produced reduced size models of marble statues in 1844. Moreover, the Art-Union of London's report states that the material was to be 'stone china'. Stone china is a vitreous ceramic body used by Spode mainly for dinnerware: it was stained to a pale grey colour to match that of Chinese export porcelain and was the successor of John and William Turner's patented stone china. Spode employed a formula in 1813 which showed good translucency:

Blue (ball) clay	180 lb	20.68%
Cornwall Stone	624 lb	71.72%
Flint	46 lb	5.29%
Patent Stone (ironstone)	20 lb	2.30%
Blue Calx for stain	7 oz 2 dm	

In 1821-22 a New Stone China body was introduced which no longer showed translucency:

Blue clay	100 lb	20%
Cornwall Stone	240 lb	48%
Flint	160 lb	32%
Patent Stone	nil	
Blue Calx for stain	4 oz	

Stone china was glazed but, supposing that it was not glazed, the fine-grained body could be smoothed by polishing and, if the blue stain were to be omitted, the colour would probably be ivory in tint and might look very like marble. In 1952, to mark the fifty years' service given by Ronald Copeland to the family firm, a bas-relief plaque was modelled by Tom Barlow and made in a statuary porcelain body mixture derived from an old recipe book. After being fired, this was quite rough to the touch and was considered unsuitable; eventually the plaque was made in bone china, left in the biscuit state but polished using an abrasive cloth. The surface was very smooth.

In 1983 for the exhibition *Spode – Copeland 1733-1983, Potters to the Royal Family* in the City of Stoke-on-Trent Museum, portraits of the proprietors were mounted on the wall; the only portrait of Ronald Copeland was the rejected 'parian' plaque which I found in a disused store-room. When it was polished with abrasive cloth the surface became smooth like good quality statuary porcelain and proved very suitable for the purpose. Best quality parian did not require polishing after the final firing – it emerged from the kiln with its superb, sensuous surface.

When we made the plaques in 1952, some steps must have been wrong: raw materials were different, the recipe we followed was incomplete without process details, the firing treatment in a tunnel kiln instead of coal-fired bottle oven which would have affected the kiln atmosphere, etc.

I believe that in this reference to 'stone china' being stipulated as the material to be used lies the clue to the solution of the confusion.

Referring to Robert Hunt's account, *The Staffordshire Advertiser*, in its edition for 26 July 1851, printed a 'revised version' of his statement:

> The first idea of imitating marble in ceramic manufacture appears to have originated in 1842 with Mr Thomas Battam, the artist directing the large porcelain manufactory of Mr Alderman Copeland. The Duke of Sutherland saw the first specimen produced on the 3rd August 1842 and became the purchaser of it… .In 1844 it was seen by Mr Gibson RA and that eminent sculptor stated in a printed report that it was 'the best material next to marble', and he expressed a desire to see one of his own works produced in it… Art Union of London… Mr Gibson…gave permission for a copy to be made of his marble statue of Narcissus in the collection of the Royal Academy. The material up to this period was not, however, perfect, and in the same year Mr Battam suggested to Mr S T Garrett a series of experiments which were made and from which resulted the material at present employed. The recipe of Copeland is:
>
> | | |
> |---|---|
> | silica | 60.35% |
> | alumina | 32.00 |
> | soda | 4.16 |
> | potash | 2.55 |
>
> traces of magnesia, lime and iron.
>
> In the process of drying [*sic*] the figure contracts one-fourth.

What, then, was this 'first specimen'? It was a reduced model of Wyatt's marble sculpture of *Apollo, as the Shepherd Boy of Admetus*, which was owned by His Grace the Duke of Sutherland and was in the gardens of Trentham Hall, the one-time home of the Dukes of Sutherland.

Of what material was this reduced model made? *The Staffordshire Advertiser* explains that 'the material up to this period [i.e. 1844] was not perfect', and the Art Union of London had commissioned Copeland & Garrett to issue a certain number of copies of Gibson's *Narcissus* in stone china. I am suggesting, therefore, that the reduced statue of Wyatt's *Apollo* was made in a version of Spode's Stone China, but obviously unglazed and omitting the cobalt stain.

In October 1987 my colleagues at Spode made for my research some figurines according to the two formulae of Josiah Spode's Stone China: the ones of 1813, and that of New Stone of 1821. Both trials omitted the cobalt blue stain and the ironstone. Four pieces were made in each body and fired at different temperatures. Of the 1813 recipe pieces, after rubbing the surface with abrasive cloth, the piece fired at 2174°F (1190ºC) had a very smooth surface and was very translucent; the example fired at 2210°F (1210ºC) had softened to the point where the figure had bent over backwards, presumably in an attitude of helpfulness!

These pieces stood on my desk in the Spode Museum for several months, and many people asked if Spode was planning to re-introduce parian. The pieces made to the 1821 recipe were not so translucent, but were still smooth to the touch after rubbing with abrasive cloth. The finer examples of both recipes could reasonably be described as 'the material next best to marble'.

Now we come to the reference in *The Art-Journal* of 1859. *The Art-Union* magazine had changed its name in 1849, and it described how, in 1844, the magazine had introduced the new ware to the Art Union of London:

> When we visited the works of Mr. Alderman Copeland – then 'Copeland & Garrett' at Stoke-on-Trent, we there witnessed the first efforts to secure popularity for the new art of Porcelain sculpture. Two statuettes had been produced in it, one a graceful female bust, and the other 'the Shepherd Boy' after Wyatt, but they had not 'Sold'. The public did not show any sign of being prepared to acknowledge the real worthiness of the novelty; and it is by no means improbable that the process would have proceeded no further, had it not been for our good fortune to urge upon Mr. Garrett the wisdom of perseverance… a meeting was, in consequence, arranged by us between several sculptors, of whom Mr. Gibson was one, and Mr. T. Battam, the artist of the works. The two honorary secretaries of the Art Union of London were also present. After a careful examination of the new material an opinion was pronounced decidedly in its favour. Mr. Gibson declaring it to be 'the material next best to marble that he had ever seen' and his brothers in Art agreeing with him. A commission from the Art Union of London followed, and this new art of parian sculpture was rescued from a peril that might have proved fatal in the first infancy of its career.

The Art Union of London chose, for the first piece, Gibson's *Narcissus*. Their report submitted to the Annual Meeting on 22 April 1845 contains this statement:

> Your Committee have long borne in view the connexion between Manufacturers and Art, and have felt the importance of leading one to the aid of the other. Considering the porcelain manufacture to be of considerable consequence, and greatly dependent on Art, they propose to reduce a statue of convenient size, and to issue a certain number of copies in that material. Mr. Gibson, R.A., when in England, kindly offered the use of any of his works for this purpose, and the Committee have determined on adapting 'The Narcissus' for the first experiment, his diploma piece at the Royal Academy. Some difficulties which arose at the Royal Academy have delayed the completion of the intention, but these are now removed, and the work will be proceeded with immediately by Messrs. Copeland & Garrett.

Fifty copies were produced and were given as prizes early in 1846. The cost of these statuettes of *Narcissus* is recorded as £150, or £3 each (this is equivalent to about £250-£300 each in 2006). The November issue of *The Art-Union* magazine reported:

> Those already finished are extremely beautiful and so satisfactory that a further commission from the Society has resulted… the Committee of the Art-Union of London having awarded to Mr. Foley one hundred guineas for a reduced copy of his beautiful statue of 'Innocence' also to be executed in Statuary Porcelain.

As Geoffrey Godden points out, 'So successful were these first two models that they were included in the prize lists for many years'.

The visit to Copeland & Garrett's manufactory in Stoke-upon-Trent took place in 1844 and the commission to reproduce Gibson's *Narcissus* (which was reduced by the sculptor E.B. Stephens) was awarded in April 1845. At this time the concept was that of Thomas Battam: he had contacts in London and seems to have been an intellectual with a well-developed sense of artistic appreciation as well as an acute awareness of the value of marketing his aspirations. The Art Union of London, established in 1836, proved to be the ideal organisation to promote Battam's vision. But should Battam be accorded all the credit? It seems to me that the *original idea* of making available reduced copies of good sculpture was, indeed, Battam's.

Following the Art Union of London's commission to reproduce *Narcissus*, Copeland & Garrett employed John Mountford, a figure-maker from the Derby manufactory, to develop the porcelain-type body and perfect the process for its manufacture. Mountford came to the firm in early 1845 and by the end of that year examples of statuary of a superior quality were exhibited at the first National Exhibition of British Industrial Art held in Manchester.

The display of Copeland & Garrett at the Manchester Exhibition, 1845-6.

This display included some vases reproduced 'from the antique' as well as the equestrian model of *Emmanuel Philibert* and the statuette of *Apollo as the Shepherd Boy of Admetus;* another item was a group of *Paul and Virginia* from the original by C. Cumberworth. Extracts from the report in the January 1846 issue of *The Art-Union* testify to the good reception of Copeland & Garrett's contribution.

> The leading – indeed almost the only – contributors of British Porcelain are Messrs. COPELAND and GARRETT, of Stoke-upon-Trent. Their contributions are so numerous and so excellent, as greatly to diminish our regret that the manufacturers, generally, of Staffordshire should have given to the Exposition so little help; while those from Worcester are of no value; and there are none from either Derby, Coalbrookdale, or Glasgow. The stand (which we engrave) devoted to the productions of Messrs. Copeland and Garrett occupies the whole centre of the smaller exhibition-room;... Of statuettes there are many examples – of a character wholly distinct from the class generally known as bisque or pottery figures. The aim has been to imitate, both in material and execution, the artistic excellence and effect of sculpture; and the result has been most successful. We direct particular attention to the copy of Marochetti's statue of 'Philibert,' – not only as a fine work of Art, but as a triumph over difficulties arising from the nature of the material. Of the other statuettes, the visitor will not fail to be delighted with those of Fiamingo ('The Struggle for the Heart'), Wyatt ('The Shepherd'), and Cumberworth ('Paul and Virginia'). It is impossible to devise more apt or desirable ornaments for the drawing-room; far from being costly like bronze or marble, they are infinitely more pure and beautiful than plaster – occupying, indeed, a place between the two. Of the statuary vases we give two engravings. The vase (on the third column) is thirty inches in height, copied from a marble vase in the British Museum, with a slight alteration in the neck to adapt it for use as a flower-vase The Pompeiian 'mortuary' vases, always so exquisite in form, have supplied many valuable hints to this establishment: one of the most valuable of these copies we engrave.

In this report no name for this new material is vouchsafed, but from the accounts which were published in later years I believe that the objects displayed in this Exposition were of the material called Statuary Porcelain.

I feel sure that the material of which these pieces were made was of the porcelain newly developed by John Mountford.

The earliest reference to the name 'statuary porcelain' in connection with these productions is in the *Art-Union* of 1 November 1846 in an important feature article entitled 'Illustrated Tour in the Manufacturing Districts. Stoke-upon-Trent. The Works of Copeland and Garrett'. The vases copied from examples in the British Museum are illustrated again, but with the footnote:

> it is executed in 'porcelain statuary', of which we shall have to speak.

Later in the feature the author is as good as his word and devotes two pages to the subject, much of which repeats in different phrases what has been quoted above. One or two quotations, however, will show that later articles may have used this feature as their source.

> A new material for statuettes, vases, &c. demands our special notice, as being in many of its properties totally distinct from the 'Bisque', in which the pottery figures are generally produced. The object attempted has been to present as close an approximation to marble as the various articles available to the manufacture could realize. To this chemical task Mr. Spencer Garrett has given much attentive and

> continual study, and the result has been in the highest degree satisfactory. Statuary-porcelain, as this new form of material is called, is scarcely inferior to marble as a material for art. We may therefore fairly regard its introduction as one of the greatest additions to the bounds of artistic production which we have had to record for many a long day. Bisque itself is too opaque to satisfy the eye; the total want of reflected light is as injurious to form as the overwhelming reflection from glazed figures. The characteristic of the statuary-porcelain is lustrous transparency, and in this it rivals the best specimens of alabaster.

The feature also includes 'engravings' of *The Shepherd Boy*, that is *Apollo, Narcissus* and *Paul and Virginia*. All these engravings show the subjects in reverse, facing left instead of right. They were engraved by pottery engravers who were used to engraving the 'right way round' for transferring a tissue to a pot.

> Several of the specimens we have seen have been so perfect, as completely to deceive the eye. Mr. Gibson, R.A., the celebrated sculptor, declared it 'decidedly the next best material to marble', and was extremely anxious that one of his works should be produced in it.* This has now been effected.* This observation of the distinguished sculptor was made in our presence, when we were showing him one of the copies of the statue of his friend Wyatt. It was a comparatively early production of the Works; the material has since undergone considerable improvement. We have no doubt that Mr. Gibson will be exceedingly well pleased with the copy of his 'Narcissus'.

Another early reference to the name 'Statuary Porcelain' is a quotation in *The Staffordshire Advertiser* of 27 March 1847 from the *Report of the Exhibition of British Manufacturers* by the Society of Arts:

> …there are certainly two departments on which English pottery is likely to take a new and original position of its own. We allude to the specimens of Statuary Porcelain, exhibited by Messrs. Copeland and Garrett… It is evident that the best works of the sculptor may thus be placed within the reach of unlimited members. The material or 'body'… is very beautiful, and has only to be connected with good Art to produce a perfectly successful union.

Geoffrey Godden has suggested that 'Mountford was trying to imitate the beautiful early Derby bisque body that had been employed in the production of the graceful eighteenth-century Derby figures and groups'. This idea may have originated in the statement by Jewitt in the 1878 edition of *The Ceramic Art of Great Britain*:

> In parian, both statuary and busts, as well as other objects, are extensively made. This is another speciality of the firm, and one the discovery of which belongs to them. It is, in fact, the development of the old and ever-famous Derby biscuit ware, rendered finer and more commercially as well as artistically available by the careful attention of Messrs. Copeland, into whose hands many of the Derby models, moulds, &c., passed, and have been made available. It was introduced by Copeland about 1846, and from that time to the present has been extensively manufactured by every house.

The notion has been repeated by subsequent writers even as late as in 1977, when Catherine Landale, writing in the May 1977 issue of *Antique Collector*, stated 'More a development than an invention it came into being in an attempt to discover the recipe that the Derby factory had used, in the 18th century, for their biscuit porcelain figures and groups'.

Batkin and Atterbury also touch on this idea when they say 'The desire to reproduce the best Derby biscuit was probably one of the inspirations for Parian'. However, they recognise that other manufacturers were producing fine figurines in biscuit porcelain and bone china in the early 1800s. The early Derby figures are exquisite and are of artificial porcelain. They are full of intricate details, and these details have been achieved by individual tooling by hand so that each figure is unique. These figures were expensive and were intended for the homes of wealthy people who could appreciate them. They were not especially large, groups of figures measuring, perhaps, only 10 to 12 inches (25.5 to 30.5 centimetres) high.

Other manufacturers made bisque figures. Rockingham made figures from 1826 to the early 1830s. All the portrait busts which have been recorded are in biscuit porcelain. (Writers refer to Rockingham 'porcelain'; the paste is, in fact, of the bone china type.) Romantic figures, too, were made in bisque.

Charles James Mason made at least one fine pair of biscuit bone china figures; these depict Queen Victoria and Prince Albert and were probably issued at the time of their marriage in February 1840. Mason also made a large portrait bust in biscuit china, the identity of whom is thought to be the Duke of Wellington.

Samuel Alcock is noted for making biscuit bone china portrait busts, especially of royal persons. A letter from Samuel Alcock dated 18 May 1876 to Alfred James Copeland includes the information:

> Bisque, or Felspar, China body
> 75 lbs Ground Bone
> 45 " China Clay
> 40 " Felspar
> This is a beautifully white body, and is the one I used to make in the Bisque figures which were so successful before the introduction of Parian…

Minton had been producing china bisque figures since about 1826. According to Joan Jones this bisque body was prone to discoloration and the firm had been striving to perfect a practical body. After the introduction of parian many of the earlier models were re-introduced in the new body material.

The December 1846 *Art-Union* (page 318) states 'The bisque figures of Messrs. Minton were, until lately, the very best productions of this class of art in the potteries [i.e. the Staffordshire Potteries].' The 'until lately' indicates that Minton bisque figures had been superseded by something else which was now 'the very best production'. If Minton had shown the *Art-Union* reporter any parian figures, surely he would have mentioned them in his article.

On page 298, the *Art-Union* reporter emphasised that the Copeland & Garrett statuary porcelain figures were in a new material 'in many of its properties totally distinct from the "bisque"'.

The Staffordshire Advertiser of 5 December 1846 includes an abridged version of this comment on page 2, column 5. It describes a visit to Messrs. Minton, and mentions that 'bisque figures have enjoyed for a long time a very considerable sale', but says nothing about parian at that time (or the fact would have been commented upon rather than mentioning only 'bisque figures').

These two references seem to be good contemporary evidence that Copeland & Garrett were in the field before Minton.

Geoffrey Godden, on page 96 of his *Minton Pottery and Porcelain of the First Period 1793 – 1850* lists No. 163, *Ariadne on a Panther*, and states that it was mentioned in *The Art-Union* of 3 March 1847. This model was referred to in a letter dated 28 December 1847 where it was stated that it could be supplied in parian, rather than in bisque china, as ordered. Minton was evidently making parian by February 1847. This would have required several months of development of the body material; the moulds were probably those used for the bisque china model. However, Copeland & Garrett had exhibited many examples already in December 1846 at the Manchester Exhibition.

All the available evidence, therefore, shows that Copeland & Garrett were first. Exactly which person, as opposed to the firm for which he worked, had originated the idea will be discussed at length in the next chapter.

I am extremely grateful to Rodney Hampson for pointing out the relevance of these particular references.

In October 1987 I was shown two beautiful small figurines in biscuit porcelain, actually bone china, impressed

COPELAND &
GARRETT

At first glance they could have been mistaken for Derby, but the mark was clear. Moreover, the seam marks (which were not obtrusive) were in the wrong places for the figurines to have been from Derby moulds. Pamela Rowan, one of the most knowledgeable specialists in England in Derby figures, reminded me in 1991 that W.T. Copeland did not purchase the Derby moulds until 1852. Glazed and decorated figures by Copeland & Garrett have been exhibited in the 1983 exhibition *Spode – Copeland 1733-1983 Potters to the Royal Family* at the City of Stoke-on-Trent Museum; these two china biscuit examples are the first to be seen by me.

Few of the parian examples compare to the extreme intricacy of the Derby bisque figures and groups of the 1770s and 1780s.

It seems very much more likely that the growing affluence of the middle classes in the 1840s offered a suitable market for small sculptures in an attempt to imitate the practice of displaying objects of sculpture in the homes of the aristocracy. The leading manufacturers were seeking a new style of ceramic sculpture which, whilst resembling marble, was relatively inexpensive to produce in sufficient quantities and would fill a market desire; moreover, these sculptures would withstand cleaning regularly, unlike the plaster reproductions which one sees in some stately homes.

Having thrown doubt on a long-held notion about the inspiration for the development of parian, it is only right that an alternative suggestion should be advanced. Small size sculptures had been produced by John Turner (c.1770-80) in a white or cream-coloured stoneware. The portrait bust of Matthew Prior (in Brighton Museum) and that of Joseph Addison (in the Bevis Hillier Collection) are examples. They are unglazed, smooth, and ivory in colour.

Alternatively, an improvement of Spode's Felspar Porcelain, which had also been used for portrait busts in about 1835, seems even more likely to have been the inspiration. Busts of the Duke of Wellington and of Milton were made during Copeland & Garrett's partnership. I have seen three examples of the Wellington portrait bust, two of which are 'smear-glazed', and one which is almost free of any glaze, yet is smooth to the touch like parian. There is also a portrait bust of H.M. King George IV.

A recipe for Felspar Porcelain, recorded in July 1836, is:

felspar	360 pounds	18 98%
china clay	700	36.92%
bone	836	44.1%

stain of 27 drams cobalt calx and 27 drams of coloured magnesium.

This doubt of its Derby inspiration is justified, I think. Robert Garner, in his *Supplement to the Natural History of the County of Stafford*, published in 1860, asserts that:

> Parian, or Statuary, having a large proportion of felspar in its composition, has been invented, or rather re-invented, by a workman under the auspices of Messrs. Battam and Copeland, and improved by Messrs. Minton and others, so as to become an important article of Pottery. We use the term re-invented, as many years back, it was made at Spode's manufactory, though the result was obtained partly by the use of cawk or sulphate of Barytes in the body.

Leonard Whiter comments on some white stoneware fonts of Spode's 'which are completely unglazed and so close-textured and white that it is hard to differentiate them from Parian'.

Spode made small fonts and a recipe for these, recorded in September 1819, is:

Cornwall stone	600 pounds
Blue clay, sifted and dried,	200 pounds
banding blue for stain	2 ounces.

This gives 75% of feldspathic material. The body is very close to a 'mortar' body, that is one used for pestles and mortars.

To summarise, the manufacturers saw the possibility of a revival of interest in portrait busts and figures as ceramic sculptures, a style that had been neglected for half a century since John Turner and Josiah Wedgwood had made them in stoneware and black basalt. While a few had been made in bisque bone china in the 1820s to 1840s, production problems had caused a new approach to be investigated. It is often the case that several artists, manufacturers and others in the same field of enterprise will start to develop ideas along similar lines at the same time. It should not come as a surprise, therefore, to find several potteries working on the same idea of producing ceramic sculptures at about the same time.

If Thomas Battam really was the originator of this new 'movement' in 1842, using the stone china recipe as the basis, it would be evident to him that it would not be good economic sense to rub down every surface of the objects in order to render them smooth. He must, therefore, have realised that an 'improvement' in the body was needed. While this was being developed a major invention was introduced into the equation.

Benjamin Cheverton was granted a patent on 16 January 1844 for his reducing machine. This was, in effect, a three-dimensional pantograph which could enlarge or reduce a sculpture to a larger or smaller model.

Whereas Gibson's sculpture of *Narcissus* had been re-sculpted by E.B. Stephens to bring it down to an acceptable size for the ceramic figure, Cheverton's machine now made it possible for many large sculptures to be reduced much more easily and swiftly, and especially without losing any of the quality of the original. It was the means by which the subjects could be made available for reproduction in a pottery.

Finally, it was fashion which dictated the popularity of Greek-inspired sculpture. Undoubtedly recent archaeological excavations and a growing interest in classical art shaped this fashion, underlined by the current art and design education, and ideas encouraged by *The Art-Union* magazine. The sight of figures of *The Greek Slave* in hundreds of drawing rooms was culturally uplifting.

So there were several factors working simultaneously to advance this whole development: the market need, a new ceramic body material, the means of reproduction of large sculptures to manageable size, and the impact of fashion and style – a recipe for success which only needed to be marketed well, and this was aided by the encouragement of the Art-Union of London supported by *The Art-Union* magazine.

THE CONTROVERSY OVER WHO FIRST ORIGINATED THE IDEA OF PARIAN

The *Art-Union* in 1846 credits Thomas Battam, the Art Director of Copeland & Garrett, as the inventor of statuary porcelain in words like: 'It is but justice to Mr. Battam… to state that the original idea and introduction of this material is wholly attributable to his taste and judgement'. In the feature in the *Art-Union* of November 1846 Mr Spencer Garrett is given the credit, whilst in the *Art-Journal* of 1 October 1849 Mr Battam is given the credit again: 'Yet, beyond question, but for a very trifling accident, and, especially, the resolute perseverance of Mr. Battam, who "originated" the material, the difficulty in the way of its introduction would not have been surmounted, and it would, in all probability, have been laid aside. Other manufacturers followed the example of Mr. Copeland…'. Both Thomas Battam and Spencer Garrett were men of some importance and in a position to mention their part in any discovery to a visitor; it is not surprising, therefore, that their names are recorded in contemporary accounts of the claim.

It was not until 1851 that the controversy came into the open. On 26 July 1851, the *Staffordshire Advertiser* reprinted an article from the *Morning Chronicle*. It seems sensible to me to republish this article and all the correspondence to which it gave rise, and to give my observations on each. I think that only by doing this will the matter be laid to rest. I wish to thank Terence Lockett and Rodney Hampson for editing and augmenting the information in this section.

Staffordshire Advertiser 26 July 1857, quarterly report

STATUARY PORCELAIN, AND CHINA,…No. 111.
(From the Morning Chronicle.)

At the period when the manufacture of porcelain at Chelsea was in all its diversity the works at that place supplied chimney ornaments to the country generally. Many of the old Chelsea Porcelain figures were very finely executed, but by far the greater number were grotesque imitations of humanity, some of which are still to be discovered in the china closets of our grandmothers. Dresden was also celebrated for producing figures, and these were, not unfrequently, of a high character as works of art, but still they were all composed of the ordinary porcelain. Wedgwood, of Etruria, introduced a stone ware—a true vitrified body of a highly silicious character which he was enabled to produce either black or coloured. In this material that extraordinary man has perpetuated the works of Flaxman, and given permanence to many of the most choice relics which time has spared us of the vases of antiquity. If we examine the pottery of Staffordshire before the time of Wedgwood, we find it—with the slight exception of the red earthenware of the Elers of Nuremberg, who settled at Bradwell—to be of imperfect material and rude in form. Wedgwood saw that the work of the potter was capable of great elevation in its character ; he directed his powerful mind to the study of the chemistry of clays, and of the physical characters of earths, and the result was the production of numerous kinds of ware, all of them excellent in their varieties. He advanced a step beyond this—he sought out the beautiful where it already existed in examples of the potter's art, and copied it with surprising accuracy. His fac-simile of the Portland vase may be quoted as an example.

The genius of Flaxman was also enlisted in aid of the enlightened potter. High art was, for the first time in this country, associated with manufacture, and the result was—what it must always prove to be—eminently successful. With the death of Wedgwood, the process of improvement ceased, and, since there is no standing still, the pottery deteriorated rapidly in every way, and continued at a low point until within the past few years. The energies of a few houses in the trade have awakened general attention to the improvement of clay manufacture, and we may regard the present as the commencement of a new era in porcelain wares. Statuary porcelain and parian are exhibited by several houses, and as this manufacture is a recent introduction, and one which promises to be of high utility in many ways, a brief history of it may not be out of place.

The first idea of imitating marble in ceramic manuacture appears to have originated, in 1842, with Mr. Thomas Battam, the artist directing the large porcelain manufactory of Mr.Alderman Copeland. The Duke of Sutherland saw the first specimen produced, on the 3rd of August, 1842, and became the purchaser of it. Since that time a trade of large commercial importance to the Potteries has arisen ; and the introduction of this manufacture has materially advanced the artistic taste of ceramic wares.

Amongst the early works produced in this new material were some groups and satyrs—large caryatides for fire-places—vases and brackets. Amongst others, was a copy of the celebrated Warwick vase. The house of Copeland next introduced the parian, in conjunction with coloured and gilt decoration. The interest taken in this work by the Duke and Duchess of Sutherland tended very greatly to facilitate the progress of statuary porcelain manufacture. In 1844 it was seen by Mr. Gibson, R.A., and that eminent sculptor stated, in a printed report, that it was "the best material next to marble," and he expressed a desire to see one of his own works produced in it. Shortly after this, it was submitted to the council of the Art-Union of London, and that body was urged to adopt statuary porcelain, by commissioning a number of copies of some work of acknowledged excellence to be awarded as prizes to its subscribers. This was done, and Mr. Gibson, having expressed a great interest in the progress of this manufacture, generously gave permission for a copy to be made of his marble statue of Narcissus, in the collection of the Royal Academy. The material up to this period was not, however, perfect, and in the same year Mr. Battam suggested to Mr. S.T. Garrett a series of experiments, which were made, and from which resulted the material at present employed.

According to the classification adopted in the Exhibition, this material is divided into statuary porcelain, parian, and Carrara. This may be a refinement, but it is a perfectly unnecessary one, the materials only differing in the proportions of the ingredients employed by the manufacturer. The composition, according to analysis of the material employed by Messrs. Copeland and Co., is silica, 60.35 ; alumina, 32 ; soda, 4.16 ; potash, 2.55 ; with traces of lime, magnesia, and iron. The material is used in a liquid state, technically called "slip," about the consistency of thick cream. It is poured into moulds forming the figure or group, which, being made of plaster, rapidly absorb a portion of the moisture; and the coating immediately next the mould soon becomes of sufficient thickness for the cast, when the superfluous "slip" is poured back. The cast remains in the mould for some time, at a high temperature, by which means it is, through the evaporation which takes place, reduced to a state of clay sufficiently firm to bear its own weight when relieved from the moulds, which are then opened, and the different portions of the subject taken out. Each figure requires many moulds ; the head, arms and hands, legs, body, parts of the drapery (when introduced), and the other details of the subject are generally moulded separately. The parts, being removed from the moulds, have to be repaired ; the seams caused by the junction of the moulds must be cleaned off, and the whole put together. This is, of course, a delicate process, requiring much artistic skill ; for though all the parts may be from the same mould, it by no means follows that all the casts will be of equal merit, so much depending upon the taste and skill of the finisher—the figure maker. In the process of drying, the figure contracts *one-fourth*—so that a model which, when moist, was two feet high, becomes, when completed, not more than eighteen inches. This necessarily requires many nice adjustments on the part of the figure-maker ; and, notwithstanding every precaution, a great many of the statuettes exhibit distortions of the limbs and other parts, which arise from the unequal contraction of the clay.

Numerous examples of this manufacture, of very great beauty, are to be found in Class 25. Messrs. Minton and Co. exhibit statuettes and busts from designs by Dancker, Cellini, Thorwaldsen, Westmacott, Townsend, and Bell. In the Victoria dessert service, which has been purchased by her Majesty for a thousand guineas, and is intended as a present to the Emperor of Austria, we have the combination of parian and fine porcelain, effected with very great skill and considerable taste. The service is a full one, consisting of 72 dessert plates, 20 compotiers, and 24 other articles ; it is white, turquoise, and gold. In the wine cooler, which stands in the centre, we have the union of high art with manufacture very finely exemplified. Round the outside it has, in bas-relief, a bear hunt represented, and hunters with their dogs form a series of statuette groups round the pedestal. A streak of gold runs in and out through the design, and the whole has a very pleasing effect, the parian contrasting admirably with the glazed porcelain. The whole is crowned with an infant Bacchus pressing grapes. We are informed by members of the firm that the expense of designing, modelling, and decorating this service, far exceeded that of any service ever before manufactured in this country ; yet, with all its elaboration, it was completed within twelve months.

Another article worthy of notice is the Parnassus vase, which, like the Victoria dessert service, is a combination of parian and porcelain. It is an original design of one of Messrs. Minton and Co.'s modellers, and has many points of interest. The china is in mazarine, richly gilt—the parian bas-relief represents Apollo and the Muses. The modellings of the festoons on this vase are considered, by competent judges, equal to Sevres.

There is also a dessert centre, with parian figure-supporter. It is in turquoise and gold, with delicately painted flowers, and the cross "S," we are informed, indicates that it forms part of a service manufactured for the Marquis of Stafford. This, though a fine piece of ware, attracts less attention than it otherwise would secure, on account of its being in such close contact with the *chef d'œuvre* of the collection—the Victoria service.

In addition to these we may enumerate, as objects of especial interest, the following:—

The Cellini ewer and stand, in parian gilt—an original design by another of Messrs Minton and Co.'s modellers, and admirable in form and execution.

The equestrian statues—"Amazon" (after Feuchère) and "Theseus"—the latter original.

"Temperance" and "Flora"—copies from terra cotta statues in the collection of the Duke of Sutherland.

"Dorothea," "Clorinda," "Miranda," "Una and the Lion," "The Babes in the Wood," and some others—the works of Mr. John Bell, sculptor.

"The Distressed Mother," after Sir R. Westmacott's statue in Westminster Abbey.

"Love restraining Wrath"—an original group by Mr. Beattie, a clever artist, now resident in the Potteries.

"Atala and Chactas," also original, and suggested by a passage in Chateaubriand's celebrated tale.

The two groups of "Boys with Goats" are beautifully modelled ; they are original productions, in the style of the last century. We have also the "Greek Slave" of Mr. Power, the original of which is at the eastern end of the main avenue. Numerous other examples of parian will be found in this collection of Messrs. Minton and Co. On another occasion we shall return to a consideration of the other works from this house—particularly their encaustic tiles and tesseræ.

The statuary porcelain exhibited by Alderman Copeland's house is of very high character. The specimens are superior to many as to surface and tint. The proportions of the figures are well preserved, the contingencies of the manufacture being judiciously provided for ; and they present a more graceful fullness of contour in the outlines, especially of the arms and legs, than is usually attained. This house exhibits copies of the works of Foley, Marshall, Wyatt, Gibson, the Baron Marochetti, Mrs. Thorneycroft, and other eminent artists.

Messrs. Wedgwood and Sons, of Etruria, the descendants of the great improver of ceramic art in this country, are exhibitors of the Carrara porcelain statuary, much of which is very beautiful.

Messrs. Mayers, of Dale Hall Pottery ; Meigh and Sons, of Hanley ; T. and S. Boote, of Burslem ; Bell and Co., of Glasgow ; J. Rose and Co., of Coalbrook Dale ; and T. Hughes, jun., of Cobridge, are also exhibitors in this parian ware.

It would be difficult to over-estimate the value of this material to the manufacture of which it has become so prominent a feature. The successful position taken by the English potters in the Exhibition is due mainly to its introduction and its prompt adoption by the public. The increased love of art, which has been created by the multiplication of examples of statues of a high order through this process, is one of the most pleasing of the results which have attended it ; and Mr. Battam, to whom we are really indebted for the production of statuary porcelain, may feel pleased that his labours have produced such satisfactory consequences.

In the foreign department will be found some statuettes and busts in a similar material. Some examples from the porcelain manufactories of Copenhagen, being copies of the most favourite works of Thorwaldsen, are well worthy of attention.

Whenever the public are supplied with works of merit, they avail themselves most readily of the privilege of possessing them, if they are at all within the limits of their means. Of the salutary results of the popular cultivation of art, in a moral and a social point of view, there can be no doubt ; and on this ground, among others, we desire to see the fine examples in statuary porcelain which are exhibited largely multiplied, and, by the increased demand which must be created, brought within the limits of the humbler classes.

Much of the article repeats what had been published in earlier editions of the *Art-Journal*, including the credit to Mr Battam:

> The first idea of imitating marble in ceramic manufacture appears to have originated in 1842, with Mr. Battam…

I suppose that, with feelings running high over the forthcoming awarding of the Council Medal for the Ceramic Section in the Great Exhibition, some pottery folk wished to discredit their competitors while others wished to establish their claim to what was now a very successful product. If, indeed, this was so, then the somewhat acrimonious correspondence achieved its purpose. The awards were announced in October 1851 (*Staffordshire Advertiser,* 18 October). Following the announcement there was very considerable outrage concerning the award of the Council Medal to Minton, while only a Prize Medal was awarded to Copeland. So, on 4 September 1852, the *Staffordshire Advertiser* quoted the judges of this section, who had issued a statement:

> the Jury find that they could not recommend an award of the Council Medal for the invention of Parian without deciding on the disputed claim of priority between eminent firms, who severally advanced that claim with equal confidence. We have not felt it in our duty to come to any such decision; especially as it would appear from the statement of each party that, whichever may have actually been first in publicly producing articles in this material, both were contemporaneously working with success towards the same result.

It might seem strange to us, all these years later, that there was so much fuss, indeed acrimony, but collectors still contest the claims for the first to introduce other successful products, like bone china, or new methods and processes. When statuary porcelain was introduced first, the earliest published claim was that by Mr Battam, and, so far as I know, there wasn't a squeak of protest from Mr Boote, Mr Minton, Veritas, Spectator, FCL, or anyone else. Mr Mountford probably kept quiet either because he was unaware of such a claim, or because his employment could have been in jeopardy. Indeed, some of the anonymous writers may not have seen the accounts in the *Art-Union* (up to 1848) and *Art-Journal* (1849 onwards), but it is almost certain that the manufacturers would have read them. If the product looked as if it was going to be a failure a manufacturer would not wish to claim to be the originator; only when it proved to be a success would he wish to claim the credit.

The article of 26 July 1851 mentions:

> Amongst the early works produced in this new material (referring to that introduced in 1842) were some groups of graces and satyrs – large caryatides for fireplaces – vases and brackets. The House of Copeland next introduced the parian, in conjunction with coloured and gilt decoration…

In fact, Copeland called it Statuary Porcelain, and continued to do so for as long as the 1880s, even though Minton's name of Parian had become adopted generally. After referring to Mr Gibson's approbation, the article continues:

> The material up to this period was not however, perfect, and in the same year Mr. Battam suggested to Mr. S.T. Garrett a series of experiments, which were made, and from which resulted the material at present employed.

Reference is made to the Great Exhibition:

> According to the classification adopted in the Exhibition, this material is divided into statuary porcelain, parian, and Carrara. This may be a refinement, but it is a perfectly unnecessary one, the materials only differing in the proportions of the ingredients employed by the manufacturer.
> The composition, according to analysis of the material employed by Messrs.Copeland and Co. is:

Silica	60.35%
Alumina	32.00
Soda	4.16
Potash	2.55

> Traces of lime, magnesia, and iron.

It gives brief details of the process, at the end stating '…in the process of drying, the figure contracts one-fourth…'. There is no mention of firing, but one must assume that this large contraction takes place during the firing process from clay to biscuit rather than from mould size to the dried clay, or 'green', condition. Then the article devotes a column to describing some of the exhibits of the various manufacturers.

THE CORRESPONDENCE

9th August 1851

To the Editor of the Staffordshire Advertiser.

SIR,—*Palmam qui meruit ferat.* You inserted in your last week's paper* an article, from a contemporary, attributing the invention of that variety of porcelain which is called parian, statuary, carrara, &c., by the different manufacturers, to a gentleman, with whom much merit no doubt rests in the ceramic art, as he has well superintended the taste department at Mr. Copeland's establishment for many years, but who, we think, can scarcely claim so large an amount of honour, as an inventor, as is bestowed upon him in the article in question. Perhaps parian or statuary may not be quite the novelty which it is thought to be. Thus, *statuettes,* in composition and appearance very little different from, or inferior to, the modern statuary, were produced at the manufactory where the gentleman in question now has his *studio,* probably before he was born, and are yet in existence. In these, however, apparently, barytes or heavy spar was used, where felspar now is, but the effect is equal. We suppose that for these, and also for similar productions of other manufacturers, there was at that day little taste, and so the manufacture ceased. We believe that a workman, formerly at Mr. Copeland's, who possesses a knowledge of chemistry, and is now a small manufacturer of parian, is more entitled to the honour of reviving and improving (or of inventing if you like) this body, possibly under the auspices of Mr. Battam. Mr. Minton's manufactory, however, we believe, had the precedence in first bringing out a really beautiful article of this kind, though their parian was soon followed by the statuary of Mr. Copeland.

We believe that manufacturers and workmen in this district, with a few exceptions, commonly know as little about the chemical constituents of their ware, as they do of those of the moon, so neglected is chemistry and mineralogy in these parts, where, one would think, it ought to be the reverse. This branch of art is the result, therefore, more of numerous experiments and trials, than of the knowledge and invention of one individual ; but if not so, we may perhaps learn differently in your next week's paper from some other correspondent, and the honour will then be given where it is due.

Your very faithful servant,
PALISSY SECUNDUS.

*this letter was intended for insertion last week.

On 9 August 1851 Palissy Secundus begins the correspondence by suggesting that the material is not a novelty, for

> statuettes, in composition and appearance very little different from, or inferior to, the modern statuary, were produced at the manufactory where the gentleman in question now has his studio, probably before he was born... [that is the Spode factory] and are yet in existence. In these, however, apparently barytes or heavy spar was used, where felspar now is, but the effect is equal.

This view agrees with my own concerning portrait busts in Felspar Porcelain – see page 21. The effect is comparable, but not equal.

> We believe that a workman, formerly at Mr. Copeland's,… and is now a small manufacturer of parian, is more entitled to the honour of reviving and improving this body, possibly under the auspices of Mr. Battam. Mr. Minton's manufactory, however, we believe, had the precedence in first bringing out a really beautiful article of this kind, though their parian was soon followed by the statuary of Mr. Copeland.

The royal 'we' throughout this letter suggests that the writer hopes to show a consensus of view rather than it being that of a sole contender.

23 August 1851

To the Editor of the Staffordshire Advertiser.

SIR,— In your journal of the 26th ultimo I observed an extract from the "*Morning Chronicle*" on the discovery of that beautiful material, "Statuary Porcelain,." which has been emphatically pronounced by an eminent authority "the nearest approach to marble to which the ingenuity of the world has attained." When we remember that it has not only received the most marked commendation from the highest personage in the realm, but is also becoming one of the most generally admired, and gold-productive of all the achievements of the ceramic art, surely the merit of the discovery ought to be given to the real discoverer.

It was forcibly remarked by an ancient writer that, "the man to whom the Omniscient had entrusted one of His secrets for the advancement of the world was worthy of all honour." Admitting this principle, then, I trust, you will in this instance give the honour where it is due, and by so doing maintain that accuracy by which your journal is so generally characterized.

Your correspondent of last week, ("Palissy Secundus,") whilst taking from one gentleman the honour of discovering this body, endeavours also to take it from every one else, by stating that one slightly different in composition, but "*equal in effect,*" was produced many years ago. From the knowledge which that letter displays of the component parts of statuary porcelain, it is evident that the writer is acquainted with the subject ; and from the parenthetical sentence in his letter, it is further evident that he knows who the discoverer was.

If then, as we may reasonably suppose, he is acquainted with the subject, he cannot fail to be aware that the old stoneware or bisque china in which the statuettes were formerly produced is, for delicacy of appearance and beauty of effect, immeasurably inferior to statuary porcelain ; but with this I have nothing to do—the abandonment of one, and the general adoption of the other, is sufficiently expressive.

Let me, therefore, explain to you the facts as they are known to hundreds—in fact, to all who are engaged in the manufacture of statuary porcelain.

In the year 1845 the conductors of the Art Union of London agreed (I believe on the suggestion of Mr. Hall, of the *Art Journal*) to present a certain number of their prize-holding contributors with statuettes in bisque china (of the class referred to by "Palissy Secundus.") The figure to be given was a copy of the celebrated statue of "Narcissus," by Mr. Gibson, R.A., that gentleman liberally waiving the copyright for the purpose.

The order for the production of the statuettes was given to Mr. Alderman Copeland (as head of the then firm of Copeland and Garrett). Mr. Battam—doubtless duly appreciating the beauty of the statue—expressed his regret to the gentleman who then superintended the establishment that it could not be brought out in something more delicate than "bisque."

Previous to this Mr. Mountford, who was at that time in the employ of Mr. Alderman Copeland, observing the taste and elegance which were being introduced into the art, had been making experiments in order to discover a more beautiful body than had hitherto been used ; and receiving by this event an additional impulse to prosecute his researches, he did so with untiring perseverance, and his industry and skill were rewarded by the discovery of that material known as "statuary porcelain," or "parian."

In the latter part of the year 1845 he shewed to Mr. Spencer Garrett and Mr. Battam the sample of the body ; and it being approved of, he afterwards wrote out and gave to Mr. Garrett (as one of his employers) the receipt for its production, and in the latter end of December, 1845, the statuettes of the statuette of "Narcissus" was completed—it being the first figure produced in statuary porcelain, and it was from the receipt given by Mr. Mountford to Mr. Garrett.

I am aware, sir, that in the *Art Journals* of 1846 and 1849 the merit of this was given to others ; but as the two statements, though in the same journal, are contradictory, it is just possible that the articles (especially the latter) were contributed by some one who was not well acquainted with the subject.

The account which I have given to you is the one which is generally understood here : it was publicly stated two years ago, at a valedictory dinner given by upwards of fifty of the workmen in the employ of Mr. Alderman Copeland to Mr. Mountford, on which occasion he was presented by them with a silver snuff-box, as a testimony of their approval of that ingenuity which had introduced a new branch into their handicraft.

Hoping, sir, that you will oblige those of your readers who would give honour to skill and industry by the insertion of this letter,

I have , sir, the honour to be ,
Your obedient servant,
F.C.L.

The paper of 23 August 1851 prints a reply by F.C.L. He gives an account of the sequence of events that broadly agrees with my own understanding of what took place and accords with the account given by John Mountford, adding the details of the presentation of a snuff-box to Mr Mountford by his fellow workers in recognition of the contribution he had made to the well-being of the industry. It is worth remembering that the pottery industry at that time was having a rough passage, with many pottery workers considering emigrating to the United States of America because of lack of work, low wages and restrictive practices on the part of some of the employers. F.C.L. appears to have had an intimate knowledge of Mr Mountford's background and it suggests that he was a personal acquaintance of him and, perhaps, a fellow employee at Copelands. (See Mr Mountford's biography.)

30 August 1851

MR. ALDERMAN COPELAND'S WORKS.
To the Editor of the Staffordshire Advertiser.

Sir,—In your journal of the 23rd instant was a letter signed "F.C.L.," which letter was an answer to one that appeared in your columns the week previous, signed "Palissy Secundus," the writer wishing to know to whom was the honour due of introducing that beautiful material statuary porcelain. The answer to this enquirer places the whole honour and perseverance to Mr. Mountford ; one fact is alluded to as evidence, viz., the presentation of a silver box by his then fellow-workmen in the employ of Mr. Alderman Copeland. But we, the individuals who presented this token of esteem, while we give to Mr. Mountford the credit of producing the present material, the real suggester of the improvement and persevering gentleman to whom belongs the honour of originating the process which gave rise to it, and whose untiring energy secured its present notoriety, is Mr. Thomas Battam.

SIGNED BY THE WORKMEN REFERRED TO BY "F.C.L."

The paper of 30 August 1851 has a short letter from the workmen referred to by F.C.L. The workmen here, while giving Mr Mountford the credit of producing the present material, grant that:

> the real suggester of the improvement and persevering gentleman to whom belongs the honour of originating the process which gave rise to it … is Mr. Thomas Battam.

So here there is F.C.L. and the workmen of the manufactory of Messrs. Copeland & Garrett claiming credit for the origination and the development for the firm's employees. This, surely, sets the stage for the secondary set of claims, namely, the actual individual to whom credit should be given.

To the Editor of the Staffordshire Advertiser.

Sir,—As you have admitted into your columns two anonymous letters, in each of which I am personally referred to, and (though differing in degree of expression) my claim as the originator of porcelain statuary, and through that of the different materials which, though varying in name, may legitimately rank under that head, is either directly or inferentially questioned, I am reluctantly compelled, in vindication of my right, to enter into some details respecting its origin and progress, and of the recognition in connection with it for which I claim acknowledgement.

Loth to enter into a controversy, particularly with anonymous writers, on matters so strictly personal, still I feel necessitated to do so, lest my silence might be construed into a tacit admission of the correctness of their statements.

The first letter, signed "Palissy Secundus," I did not see till to-day, for being absent during its publication it had altogether escaped my notice. At the tenor of this I do not complain. The impressions, erroneous in many respects as they are, may but be the result of a mistaken assumption formed upon incorrect data, yet conscientiously believed to be true ; and the solicitation at the close of the letter for further information, if the writer be at fault, bears strong evidence of this, and it is only a matter of regret that, after giving publicity to his suppositions, he did not append his name as an assurance of his sincerity.

The specification which I shall include in this letter will answer that portion of his communication relating to the origin of the material, I trust. satisfactorily and conclusively.

A comparison of the present material with the old statuettes he refers to, made years since in the ordinary china bisque or stone ware, will speedily convince him of his error in asserting that *"the effect is equal."*

The letter of your correspondent "F. C. L." is of a different character, and the writer, when dealing with facts, appears a disciple of the homœopathic school, and administers truth in infinitesimal doses, and even then not in its pure integrity, but utterly neutralised and negatived by an overwhelming infusion of misconceptions and mis-statements, too apparently studied to have been accidental, and this is palpably evident from the opening statement relative to the introduction of the material down to the incident of the *"valedictory dinner of upwards of fifty,"* with which it concludes. A mistaken zeal has led to an exaggerated panegyric which must be very embarrassing to the party to whom it refers.

But my object being merely to make known the particulars of my own claim, I pass on to that, and append a copy of the statement I have had the honour to submit to the jury on ceramic manufacture in connection with the Great Exhibition.

"Particulars of claim made by Mr. Thomas Battam, of Stoke-upon-Trent, as originator and inventor of the branch of manufacture known under the generic title, as adopted in the catalogue, of 'Statuary Porcelain.'

"For having early in the year 1842 first conceived the idea of imitating statuary marble in ceramic manufacture.

"For having undertaken a series of experiments to carry out that object, and prosecuting them till it was realized by the production of very closely imitating some marbles in the possession of his Grace the Duke of Sutherland, at Trentham Hall, which had served as models for reference, both in surface and tint, and to which material this claimant gave the title of 'Statuary Porcelain.'

"Having had the honour to submit a specimen to his Grace the Duke of

Sutherland, at the manufactory of Mr. Alderman Copeland, on the 3rd of August, 1842, that nobleman was pleased to express his entire approbation of its applicability and success, and by purchasing the specimen became the first patron of this largely and increasingly important branch of manufacture.

"Having produced, in the same material, a variety of groups, statuettes, vases, pedestals, &c., &c., in 1842 and 1843.

"Having, in 1844, submitted some specimens to Mr. Gibson, R.A., that eminent sculptor declared the production to be *'best material next to marble,'* and expressed a desire to see one of his works executed in it.

"Having shortly after Mr. Gibson's visit, submitted specimens to Mr. S. C. Hall, F.S.A., the editor of the *Art Journal,* and suggested that it would form an eligible medium for the production of works for the Art Union of London to circulate, that gentleman immediately recognising the importance of the production, proffered to submit a sample to the council of that society, and advocate their adoption and patronage of it, by commissioning the execution of a number of copies of some work of acknowledged excellence, to be awarded as prizes to their subscribers. This he kindly did, and Mr. Gibson having also expressed an interest in the matter, and having generously given permission for his statue of Narcissus to be copied, that work was selected for production, and a reduced model afterwards executed, by Mr. E. B. Stephens, expressly for that purpose.

"That this commission was given to be executed in the 'Statuary' *originated by the claimant,* and that up to this time *there was no material, of process, imitating, or professing to imitate, marble in ceramic manufacture, except the 'Statuary Porcelain" referred to, and which was the sole and entire invention of this claimant.*

"That subsequently to this commission being given, and during the time occupied in preparing the moulds, it occurred to this claimant that an advantageous alteration might be made in the material by employing the components already used as a superfice in such altered proportions as should form an homogeneous body.

"That he suggested this to Mr. S. Garrett, then engaged upon the manufactory, and in accordance with these views, trials were made by that gentleman, which were submitted to the claimant, and such modifications made as were thought desirable ; and the commission, though given for the original material, was subsequently executed in the latter—and the object aimed at being the same, and the effect so similar, the original title, together with the favourable opinion of Mr. Gibson, was still retained in connection with it."

This claim in every particular, and to its minutest detail, I am fully prepared to substantiate, my principal motive for suggesting the alteration of the material was that my first process entailed some personal labour, which the other calls upon my time, consequent upon the position I have the honour to hold upon the extensive manufactory of Mr. Alderman Copeland, rendered me unable to devote to it. I am aware that to the merit of mixing the exact proportions which formed the material of 1845 there is another claimant ; but I must leave this matter to be disputed by those whom it may concern, if they think it worth the trouble—my statements are confined solely to what came under my own special cognizance, and I might be doing injustice to others by giving expressions to opinions that would be only problematical.

In conclusion, I can but most gratefully, and with the sincerest respect, acknowledge the valuable assistance rendered on the first outset of this introduction by the liberal and fostering patronage bestowed upon it by their Graces the Duke and Duchess of Sutherland—a patronage which mainly assisted to give perseverance to efforts, at first indifferently estimated, but which have finally resulted in a branch of manufacture whose influence upon the productive state of the Staffordshire Potteries has been so proudly marked in their contributions to the Great Exhibition of 1851.—I am, sir, your's very faithfully.

THOMAS BATTAM.

Stoke-upon-Trent, August 25, 1851.

A second letter published on 30 August 1851 is from Thomas Battam, who, obviously with some reluctance, feels it necessary to reply. First, he refutes the claim of Palissy Secundus that the present material is in effect the equal of earlier stoneware or china bisque. In the first paragraph he refers to his claim 'as the originator of porcelain statuary'. He criticises F.C.L. for 'an overwhelming infusion of misconceptions and mis-statements…'. He proceeds to repeat his claim

> as originator and inventor of the branch of manufacture known under the generic title, as adopted in the official catalogue, of 'Statuary Porcelain'.

I believe that there should be a clear distinction between the two terms *porcelain statuary* and *statuary porcelain.* The former describes the actual statuettes, busts, vases, etc. while the latter refers to the ceramic body material of which they are made.

In paragraph fourteen, Battam claims:

> that this commission [i.e.. to reproduce Gibson's *Narcissus*] was given to be executed in the 'Statuary' originated by the claimant…

This statement is at variance with the report of the Art Union of London, published in the January 1845 *Art-Union* (page 11), where it specifies stone china. The earliest reference to Statuary Porcelain in this connection appears in the *Art-Union* of 1 November 1846.

Battam proceeds to mention his suggestion for improving the material:

> by employing the components already used as a superfice in such altered proportions as should form an homogeneous body.

Battam's agreement that he used a 'superfice', or additional surface coating, suggests that this was an 'engobe' or clay slip, because he adds that it 'should form an homogeneous body'. This seems to preclude the 'superfice' being added after the biscuit firing, although Mountford, in paragraph twelve of his letter published on 20 September, says that 'the superfice alluded to was only submitted to an enamel heat'. I think that the matter of the 'superfice' is irrelevant and confuses the issue unnecessarily. Battam continues:

> Trials were made… and the commission, though given for the original material, was executed in the latter, and… the effect so similar, the original title, together with the favourable opinion of Mr. Gibson, was still retained in connection with it.

Battam chooses to ignore the efforts of those who actually compounded the materials and discovered the correct sequence and temperatures of firing, etc. The impression is given of Spencer Garrett and his team carrying out Battam's modifications without any input of their own. It is not surprising, therefore, that other workers felt aggrieved at this ungenerous attitude.

13th September 1851

Correspondence.

STATUARY PORCELAIN.

To the Editor of the Staffordshire Advertiser.

Sir,—The letter which I addressed to you a fortnight ago, has more than answered my expectations ; inasmuch as it has elicited, from an important quarter, a full corroboration of what I then stated : and thereby materially contributed to the advancement of the object which I had in view,—the workmen in the employ of Mr. Alderman Copeland, to whom I incidentally referred in my previous letter, having asserted, through your journal, that they "*give to Mr. Mountford the credit of producing the present material,*" i.e., statuary porcelain.

In return, therefore, let me admit that the "persevering energy" of Mr. Battam has certainly contributed in no trivial degree to give to that material its "present notoriety," for it is a fact, which is not, but ought to be, generally known, that he has, both by public and private assiduity, most industriously endeavoured to advance its importance : for this be due honour given. But Mr. Battam is not satisfied with this : he claims to be acknowledged as the "sole discoverer," even in the face of a host of evidence to the contrary. He states that "in 1842 he *conceived the idea* of imitating statuary marble in ceramic manufacture ;" this may be, and probably is, perfectly correct, but did he in any way contribute to the *development* of that idea?

Were the statuettes he produced, in the material which he states he discovered in 1842, anything but an adaption of the process which had been patented many years previously by the Messrs. Davenport, of Longport, but applied by them only to flat surfaces? And even in the adaption there was nothing new, for in the year 1841 a similar method was applied to busts and statuettes at the establishment of Mr. Charles Mason, of Longton ; and when the present body was discovered by Mr. Mountford, was not Mr. Battam's adaption at once abandoned?

It would be trite and ridiculous to state that it is not to the men who "conceive an idea" that a certain discovery would be advantageous, but to those who *develope* that idea that the world gives honour. It is the men who dive into mysteries of science and give materiality to conception that we applaud.

Who carried the bridge over the Menai Straits ?—the railway directors who conceived such a thing desirable, or Mr. Stephenson who did it ? Who built the Crystal Palace ?—the royal commissioners who felt it to be necessary that they should have a large building, or Mr. Paxton, who showed them how to build it ? The answers and application are obvious.

Apologizing for troubling you with this, I leave the matter to the public, confident that even those of your readers who have no opportunity of judging, save from what has appeared in your journal, will judge aright.

I have, sir, the honour to be
Your obedient servant,
F.C.L.

On 13 September 1851, F.C.L. states the same conclusion that Battam's claim to be the 'sole discoverer' is over-bearing. Unfortunately, he moves into deeper waters by asking if the product is no more than

> an adaptation of the process which had been patented many years previously by the Messrs. Davenport, of Longport, but applied by them only to flat surfaces.

It is uncertain to what patent he refers here. Geoffrey Godden in the book *Davenport, China, Earthenware & Glass 1794-1887* by Terence Lockett and Geoffrey Godden (page 270) refers to DAVENPORT'S PATENT in connection with china plaques, but that 'it seems certain that no such Patent was taken out by Davenport'.

I am indebted to Rodney Hampson for suggesting that the patent referred to may have been that which had been granted on 3 October 1796 to Ralph Wedgwood, Number 2137. He wonders if Ralph Wedgwood, being impecunious at some time, had sold the rights to this patent to Davenport, and that Davenport had claimed it as theirs in later years.

The abridged wording of the patent states:

> casing over inferior compositions with compositions commonly used for making cream-coloured ware, white ware, or china. Thick bats or laminae of the inferior are covered on each side with thin bats of the superior clay; if the edges of the ware are required to be cased, they are surrounded with a square piece commonly called a wad. Afterwards, the bats are beat, pressed, or rolled out to the required dimensions…

This seems to be a different process from that claimed by Battam to have been used.

F.C.L. goes on to refer to Charles James Mason's method of producing busts and statuettes. He gives no details whatsoever and is guilty of innuendo. If Battam did adapt an earlier process, then it does earn him credit for thinking of it and, as I have suggested, I believe that he did adapt Spode's own formula for stone china.

WHO INVENTED PARIAN STATUARY?

To the Editor of the Staffordshire Advertiser.

SIR,—There lately appeared in your columns several letters referring to a question of considerable interest, especially to your Pottery readers, and it was with some regret that I found the correspondence had terminated rather prematurely. I had hoped that much valuable information might have been elicited, or that, at all events, the result would have enabled the public more satisfactorily to decide to whom should be awarded the honour of having invented the new material called by some parian, and by others statuary porcelain. With your permission, I will briefly advert to the statements you have published. An article in your number of the 26th of July, copied from the *Morning Chronicle*, and in which the sole merit of inventing the new material was attributed to Mr. Battam, called forth a reply (Augt. 9) from a writer signing himself "Palissy Secundus." This writer very gently and modestly called in question Mr. Battam's claim, and asserted his belief that "Mr. Minton's manufactory had the precedence in first bringing out a really beautiful article of the kind, though their *parian* was soon followed by the statuary of Mr. Copeland." Then followed the letter of F.C.L. (Augt. 23), in which a new claimant to the honour appears in the person of Mr. Mountford, and the statements given were evidently furnished to the writer by the claimant. F.C.L. asserts that, after a series of experiments, Mr. Mountford, in the *latter part* of 1845, produced the present statuary body, and it being approved by his then employers, Gibson's Narcissus was completed in it the *latter end* of December in that year, being the first figure in statuary porcelain. In this I believe the writer is mistaken, and that he could find, on further enquiry, that the first copy of the figure was not sent for approval by the Art Union of London until February, 1846—but let that pass. Next Mr. Battam appears (Aug. 30), and characterises the statements of "Palissy Secundus" as "erroneous—the result of a mistaken assumption, formed upon incorrect data ;" but he is not so mild towards the unfortunate F.C.L., whose letter is denounced as "containing an overwhelming infusion of misconceptions and misstatements." Mr. Battam then gives a copy of the claim he had sent in to the jury of the ceramic department, and his statements therein are of such a nature that I really think had F.C.L. deigned to reply he would have been justified in giving Mr. B. a Rowland for his Oliver, or as the schoolboys say, "tit for tat." Mr. B. dates his experiments for the production of a marble-like material as far back as 1842, when he affirms that he had succeeded in closely imitating some marbles belonging to the Duke of Sutherland—that he then named it statuary porcelain, and on the 3rd of August in that year his Grace purchased the first specimen of the new material—that in 1845 the Art Union of London gave him a commission to bring out Gibson's Narcissus in the statuary originated by him ; but that subsequently (I beg your readers will mark the admission) *an advantageous alteration was made in the material!* Now, I can tell your readers what this "advantageous alteration" was. It was no less than the substitution of the Parian body of Mr. Mountford for the improved stone material in which statuary was made before Mr. Battam was born ; for prior to 1845 the Parian body had not been discovered, as is well known to all practical potters in the district. But, before proceeding further, I shall endeavour by a plain matter of fact statement, which can be easily controverted if inaccurate in any particular, to prove the correctness of the assertion of "Palissy Secundus" that Messrs. Minton are entitled to the precedence in first bringing out the beautiful material now in use for statuary. It was in February, 1845, that Minton and Co. made their first trial of Parian—a small quantity of clay only was made—and a specimen may now be seen at their works, marked in such a manner as clearly to identify it by a reference to corresponding marks in their trial books. In April and May following copies of the Portland vase, in parian, were actually sold, and the entries, "New parian," are open to inspection. On the 5th June, six copies of a bust of the Emperor Nicholas, in parian, were sent to his Grace the Duke of Devonshire. Thus, it will plainly appear, if I am correct, and I challenge disproof, that Messrs. Minton and Co's parian—the identical "body" in which their statuettes are now made—was in the market many months before Gibson's Narcissus, about which so much has been said, was completed. Now, one fact is worth a thousand assertions ; and as Mr. Battam emphatically says, that "his claim, in every particular, and to its minutest detail, he is prepared to substantiate," I make a proposition for testing the accuracy of the statements put forth by the several claimants, the equity of which can no more be called in question than the facility with which it can be accomplished. It is this—let a jury of, say three, competent practical potters be empanelled, and let the claimant who is most importunate for the honour and credit of the invention be first called upon to back his assertions by proofs. Let specimens of the statuary of 1842 be produced, and books in which it is termed statuary porcelain be accessible, and if Mr. Battam can prove that his marble-like material of 1842 is identically the same as that now termed statuary porcelain, or prove that he then so designated it by reference to his books, then the other claimants must be put out of court, and he will be in undisputed possession of the honour ; and I should be the last person to seek to deprive him of it. But I must first be in possession of those proofs, and at present I must hold the alleged invention of 1842 as "not proven." I think it would be only fair towards the public, that parties putting forth pretensions such as I have noticed, should at least be aware, when parading a novelty, of what has been done before them. Perhaps, therefore, I shall excite a little astonishment in the minds of claimants, when I state that more than fifty years ago, Mr. Turner, a contemporary of Josiah

Wedgwood (and some of whose productions are considered quite equal to those of his great rival), invented a body which he called *pearl,* which differs only in its constitution from Parian by having Cornwall stone as an ingredient instead of feldspar. A specimen of this is to be seen at the museum of the Stoke Athenæum. It was used principally for tea pots, and like parian teapots of the present day, would not well stand the test of hot water. It was soon abandoned on this account, and was not, that I am aware of, ever applied to statuary. Stone ware took its place, and was varied and improved at different times to suit the class of articles it was designed for : and up to 1845 either Bisque China or the improved stone was used for statuary. This is a notorious fact. The statuary made at Derby, many years ago, was vastly superior to the improved stone of Staffordshire, and in its composition differed but in a trifling degree from the Parian.. The Jasper of Wedgwood was also composed of the same ingredient, though in different proportions. However, as Mr. Battam says he sold the Duke of Sutherland a statuary specimen in 1842, and Mr. Minton is prepared to prove that in June, 1845, he supplied the Duke of Devonshire with *six* specimens, and as Mr. Mountford fixes December, 1845, as the date of his invention, which he disinterestedly gave Mr. Battam the advantage of, I will conclude by expressing my earnest hope that the proposal I have made for a jury to decide the vexed question be speedily adopted, which, if fairly carried out, would, amongst many others interested in the subject, give great satisfaction to your obedient servant.

September 10, 1851 VERITAS.

Also in the issue of 13 September Veritas enters the lists. After a resumé of the correspondence, he states clearly that he knows what the 'advantageous alteration' was:

> it was the substitution of the Parian body of Mr. Mountford for the improved Stone material in which statuary was made before Mr. Battam was born.

He goes on to claim that Minton & Co., in February 1845, made their first trial of Parian and that the piece could be seen at the works and corresponding 'marks in their trial book'. In April and May copies of the Portland Vase were sold and in June six copies of the bust of the Emperor Nicholas in parian were sent to His Grace the Duke of Devonshire. (There appears to be no archival support in the records at Chatsworth House, the home of the Duke of Devonshire, for any such delivery. There is a drawing, No 167, of the Emperor Nicholas in the shape book at Mintons among the items made in china bisque.)

Veritas is claiming that Minton was selling items made in the parian body 'many months before Gibson's *Narcissus*'. Why then did not Mr Minton, or one of his team, raise a voice in protest when the *Art-Union* gave so much credit to Copeland & Garrett in 1845 and 1846?

Then, like F.C.L., he moves into deep waters to claim that:

> Mr.Turner,... invented a body which he called pearl, which differs only in its composition from Parian by having Cornwall Stone as an ingredient instead of feldspar.

If my understanding of 'pearl' is correct, it was invented by Josiah Wedgwood by applying a cobalt stain to the glaze of creamware biscuit earthenware. However, this is only one use of the term 'pearl', because the name 'pearl' has been used for a dry-bodied white stoneware. Simeon Shaw in *The History of the Staffordshire Potteries* writes, on pages 225-6:

> About 1795, a new kind of Pottery, a dry body, or without glaze or smear, was introduced into the market by Messrs. Cheatham [*sic*] and Woolley, of Lane End'. [Hampson notes that nowadays this is referred to as 'Castleford'.] It is to the White Pottery, what Jasper is to the Coloured. Not being affected by change of temperature, but very fine in grain, durable in quality, and of a most beautiful and delicate whiteness, it received the name it still bears, of Pearl, from Mr. J. Spode, at that time resident in London. It is used, like Jasper, for the finest description of ornaments; and is in general estimation among all ranks of society. Very few of the different attempts made to produce Pearl of equal excellence to the inventors, have been attended with any success.

A recipe in the recipe book of Thos. Grocott, while in the employ of Josiah Spode, records:

White Jasper

32 lb of Cauk Ground fine	)	42.5%
15 lb of Blue Ball Clay	) Blunged together	19.9%
11lb of Cornwall Clay	) and sifted fine	15.3%
8½ lb of Flint	)	11.6%
7 lb of Cornwall Stone	)	9.3%
1 lb of Raw Ground Plaster	)	1.3%

(Cauk is sulphate of Barytes, Barium Sulphate, $BaSO_4$.)

Below this recipe is one for Blue Jasper:

> 70 lb of the above White Jasper, weighed dry
> 1 lb of Blue Calx Ground fine

I am grateful to Terence Lockett for drawing my attention to this reference and to the observations of George Miller, who notes that Shaw listed this dry body (that is the Chetham and Woolley body) as 'pearlware' in his *Chemistry of Pottery*, published in 1837. Shaw here lists 'Fritted Pearl Bodies and Raw Bodies... Pearl' (page 462).

William Evans also listed ten recipes of a stoneware character (page 19) in his *Art and History of the Potting Business* (1846, but extracted from pages 192-3 of *The Popular Encyclopaedia*, Volume II, Part I, published in 1836 by Blackie of Glasgow). This was written by an unidentified author. It could have been William Evans himself, but in 1836 he was only twenty years old – too young, perhaps, to have written this contribution.

The term 'pearlware', therefore, is open to much misinterpretation and should be discounted when it is clear that a stoneware is meant.

John Turner did produce portrait busts in a fine-grained stoneware, as I have mentioned earlier, but this was before 1800, while other manufacturers (page 20) were producing bisque bone china figures and portrait busts in the 1820s and 1830s. Veritas also says that Turner's pearlware was used for teapots and soon abandoned. Turner certainly made some of the finest sprigged jugs in a fine stoneware body. I am not convinced that Veritas knew enough about the earlier bodies to be able to draw correct comparisons.

20th September 1851

THE STATUARY PORCELAIN CONTROVERSY.
To the Editor of the Staffordshire Advertiser.

SIR,—I have observed with considerable interest the various letters which have recently appeared in your Journal, respecting the discovery of statuary porcelain.

In some of these my right to the discovery is asserted ; in one it is claimed in person by Mr. Thomas Battam ; and, lastly, in a semi-official manner, by a writer signing himself "Veritas," on behalf of Messrs. Minton and Co.

I would gladly have avoided entering personally into this matter, had it not been represented to me that some, who knew nothing of the subject except from the correspondence, began to think that my silence was a tacit admission of the other claimants ; under these circumstances I waive my objections, and beg to be allowed a few words on the subject.

I need not tell you, sir, that the man who is defending himself from the misrepresentations of another, must of necessity be personal and egotistical ; and personality and egotism are ever regarded with disapproval. But sir, when you remember that I cannot speak to the point without labouring under these disadvantages, I trust that they will cease to operate to my disparagement.

I will not trouble you by entering into the various letters in detail, but simply give my own statement of the case, and advert to such passages in the letters of your other correspondents as it may be necessary for me to refute in order to maintain my claim.

I am prepared to prove that in the latter part of the year 1845 I discovered, after various experiments, that material known in ceramic manufacture as "statuary porcelain ;" that I gave to Mr. S. Garrett (then of the firm of Messrs. Copeland and Garrett) the receipt for its production ; and that the first article produced therein was a statuette of Gibson's "Narcissus."

These are briefly the particulars of my claim ; and warned as I have been by the fate of another claimant, I should not have asserted them here were I not in a position to prove my assertion to its fullest extent.

And now, sir, permit me to notice briefly the claim of another correspondent.

When Mr. Battam sent to Mr. Robert Hunt the article which appeared in the *Art Journal* for January, 1849, I wrote to the editor of that publication, giving him a correct version of the matter ; but I being unknown to him, he objected to contradict a statement to which one of his regular contributors had lent his name. From that time until the present controversy arose but little has been said on the subject. On the 30th of August last I learned with surprise that Mr. Battam was not only claiming the credit of the discovery, but was also seeking tangible acknowledgement of his claim from the jury of the Great Exhibition.

Mr. Battam claims to be acknowledged as "the originator and inventor of statuary porcelain," and supports his claim by stating that "on the 3rd of August, 1842, he sold to his Grace the Duke of Sutherland the first specimen of that material." To this I give a most distinct and unqualified denial, which has also been done by "Palissy Secundus," "F.C.L." and "Veritas."

From my engagement at the establishment of Messrs. Copeland and Garrett at the period referred to, I am enabled to speak as to the nature of the material in which the statuettes sold to his Grace the Duke of Sutherland were produced ; and as I have in my possession a specimen of that material, I assert, without fear of contradiction, that it bears not the slightest relation, either in composition or effect, to statuary porcelain.

Again he states that it "occurred to this claimant that an advantageous alteration might be made in the materials by applying the *components already used as a superfice in such altered proportions as should form a homogeneous body.*" When I tell your readers that the superfice alluded to was only submitted to an enamel heat, and that statuary porcelain bears and requires a heat equal to that of an earthenware bisque oven, they will be able to draw their own deductions.

It would contribute materially to the point at issue between Mr.Battam and me, were he to answer the following questions which I respectfully submit.

Was anything invoiced by the firm of Messrs. Copeland and Garrett under the title of statuary porcelain before May, 1846 ?

Were not the goods then sold formed of the material discovered by me ?

Did Mr. Battam or any other individual intimate to me directly or indirectly the nature of that composition before I gave to Mr. Garrett, in the autumn of 1845, the receipt for its production ?

As regards the claim made by "Veritas," that Messrs. Minton and Co., "so early as February. 1845, made their first trial of parian," and that in "April and May following copies of the Portland vase in parian were actually sold," I am not in a position to refute ; but I submit, in his own words, that his position is "not proven," until he produce one of the articles then made, and it be proved to be "the identical body" in which their statuettes are now made. Any practical potter, or even ordinary observer, who will examine the statuary of Messrs. Minton and Co., in 1845, and their statuary in the Exhibition, will, I opine, be disposed to pronounce the cognomen of your correspondent a misnomer.

In conclusion, sir I will gladly agree to the proposal of "Veritas," that a jury of three or five practical potters examine the various claims. Let the statuary made by Mr. Battam, in 1842, the bust of the Emperor Nicholas, made by Messrs. Minton, in July, 1845, and the statuette of Narcissus, in which my receipt was first used by Messrs. Copeland and Co., In December, 1845, be produced ; and to the one which bears the nearest relation to the statuary porcelain now in the Exhibition, let the honour of the discovery be awarded.

I am, sir your obedient servant,
JOHN MOUNTFORD.

Stoke-on-Trent, September 17th, 1851.

[All the parties concerned having now had an opportunity of being heard, we think this discussion may now with propriety be closed.—ED.]

On 20 September 1851 John Mountford states his case. He states that he 'gave to Mr. S. Garrett… the receipt for its production' and later asserts that the figure of *Apollo* sold to the Duke of Sutherland 'bears not the slightest relation, either in composition or effect, to statuary porcelain'. In paragraph twelve he explains about the:

> superfice alluded to was only submitted to an enamel heat, and that statuary porcelain bears and requires a heat equal to that of an earthenware bisque oven…

A 'superfice' suggests that it was only a surface application, like a semi-matt paint, perhaps applied with a brush or by the ground-laying technique. See my remarks earlier on the matter of 'superfice' and Minton's letter of 11 October in which reference is made, scathingly, to 'enamelled earthenware'.

Later he asks Mr Battam to answer three questions:

1. Was anything invoiced as statuary porcelain before May 1846?
2. Were such goods sold then formed of Mountford's material?
3. Did Mr Battam intimate to Mountford the nature of the composition before Mountford gave the receipt to Mr Garrett?

He comments upon the claim by Veritas that Minton produced parian for sale in April and May 1845, but that unless Veritas could produce a specimen his case, in his own words, was 'not proven'. Lastly, he gladly agreed to submit his claim to a jury along with an example of each of the contenders' items.

The editor by now had had enough and wanted to end the correspondence, and the reader may feel the same way!

Before commenting upon this letter I will quote the receipt for 'Statuary Body for Figures, Jugs, &c for Casting' recorded in a Spode factory recipe book some time before 1860:

Fritt	100 lbs Washed Isle of Wight Sand	) Calcined
	60 lbs Felspar	) in China
	20 lbs Potash	) biscuit oven

Body	64 lbs Fritt	) Ground
	96 lbs Calc'd Felspar	) fine
	96 lbs Raw ground Felspar	) at
	192 lbs China Clay	) Mill
	32 lbs Glass	

This receipt bears little resemblance to those for stone china or the font body which I quoted earlier.

There were very many recipes for parian ware, some of which were published and are reprinted in the following chapter, but the account by Mr Battam, printed in the *Art-Journal* of 1849, differs greatly from the simple process of producing stone china. It must also be remembered that, like in cooking, a 'recipe' consists of two parts: the list of ingredients with the quantities, and the 'method'. Nearly all ceramic recipes which are published omit the method because a successful potter or colour-maker knew that it was the method which determined the success or failure of the product.

I am suggesting, therefore, that the recipe and the method of making Statuary Porcelain was the invention of John Mountford.

Without repeating quotations from even more sources, it seems to me that John Mountford, a skilled figure-maker, would not expose himself to the risk of ridicule by opposing the claim of his former employer unless he knew that his own claim could be substantiated.

John Haslam, writing in his book *'The Old Derby China Factory'* in 1876, quotes Sampson Hancock, Mountford's former employer at Derby:

> He [Mountford] was apprenticed to the Old Works in Derby, but left early in life, and came to Messrs. Copeland and Garrett's at Stoke-upon-Trent to start the figure trade there. While in their employ, he brought out the composition known to the trade as Parian… the name of this man will be recorded in time to come among those of famous potters…'.

Mountford may have come to work for Copeland & Garrett as early as 1838 and may have made the portrait busts of the Duke of Wellington, John Wesley and King George IV in the Felspar Porcelain body.

27 September 1851

Correspondence.

"PARIAN" OR "STATUARY PORCELAIN."

To the Editor of the Staffordshire Advertiser.

Sir,—We quite agree with you that the controversy on this subject has proceeded far enough ; but as we have not before addressed you, permit us to observe that after all that has been said by your correspondents, the public have a right to expect some practical result. The question is simply one of fact ; that fact being, who first discovered the "body" or material called "parian, or "statuary porcelain," now in the ceramic department of the Great Exhibition ? It must be evident to all that a question of this nature cannot be settled by argument. It must be determined by evidence. And the evidence must be of a conclusive and satisfactory nature to the impartial minds that may be called upon to decide it. Being fully satisfied that we are in a position to demonstrate our claim to the priority over all opponents,—to substantiate those facts as to the discovery and sale of parian in 1845, that Mr. Mountford admits "his inability to refute,"—and, moreover, to prove the identity of our parian of February, 1845, with the specimens now in the Exhibition. We heartily agree to the proposal that has been made by Mr. Mountford, to submit the case to a jury composed of three or more competent persons ; and we trust the other claimant will not shrink from the ordeal, but readily signify his concurrence also. In that case the truth will be easily arrived at, and the merit will be awarded where it is due. We think the subject has been invested with a great deal more importance than it intrinsically deserves ; but for that we are in no respect responsible. We can only repeat that we shall be happy to see a jury forthwith appointed, to whom we can submit the grounds on which we rest our claim, and shall cheerfully abide by their decision. We would suggest that our neighbour and friend, Mr. Wise, who is a local commissioner to the Great Exhibition, and well acquainted with the district, should be called upon to select the jury, and we feel no doubt of his kindly undertaking the office ; but we shall be quite content to leave the selection to any other equally disinterested party.

We are, sir, your obedient servants,
MINTON AND CO

The 27 September edition of the *Staffordshire Advertiser* starts with a letter from Minton & Co. Minton's use of words is rather strange:

> The question is simply one of fact; that fact being who first discovered the 'body' or material called 'parian' or 'statuary porcelain'?

Is a fact a question? Or is a question a fact?! Despite this they agree that a trial by jury should provide the answer. The editor's wish is not granted!

THE STATUARY PORCELAIN CONTROVERSY.

To the Editor of the Staffordshire Advertiser.

Sir,—With all deference to your suggestion that the discussion on this subject should now be closed, I must take leave to differ with you, for the reason that "all the parties concerned in it" have *not* had an opportunity of being heard. It will be seen on looking over again the letters of your correspondents that other claimants to the honour of having originated this material, and for very similar purposes and objects to which it is now applied, have either been incidentally named, or the claim on their behalf has been made in express terms ; and I may say, therefore, before proceeding further, that it will be only fair to these parties that they should have an opportunity, if they are so inclined, of declaring, through the medium of your columns, the part they have taken in producing this, or a similar material. Nay, with your permission, I propose to call upon them to state what they have done in it, that the statements of your correspondents may receive contradiction or confirmation, as the case may be. It is evident that the subject has been only partially discussed ; that in fact, it has been discussed with reference to the claims of the servants and managers of two eminent houses only, and it is desirable, in order that full justice may be done to all claimants, that it should receive such a thorough investigation as may at once and for ever set it at rest. The subject has excited much interest in the Potteries ; and I know that many of the older potters are watching the progress of the controversy, and the turn it is taking, not a little amused, perhaps, at the boldness of the youngsters of the present day, one of whom claims to be the "originator and inventor," and another the "discoverer" of statuary porcelain, whilst it may turn out at the end of the wordy warfare, that this material, or one so similar as not to be distinguished from it, was made now nearly sixty years ago. The object of the correspondence hitherto has been to claim the honour of its first introduction for one or the other of the eminent houses of Mr. Alderman Copeland and Messrs. Minton and Co., and the different writers have evidently been biased by their feelings in the matter, resting their claim to the supposed discovery on some little precedence in the date of their invoices. As far as the public is concerned this is a point of but little importance, it being tolerably clear that they were both simultaneously engaged in the production of divers works in this material, and the difference of a few months in the date of their respective invoices, whichever may turn out to be before the other, would not be worth the trouble of calling a jury to decide, as suggested by "Veritas" in his letter which appeared in the *Staffordshire Advertiser* of the 13th instant. The point of most interest for the public in this matter is, which of these eminent houses has brought out this material in its greatest purity ?—which has made the nearest approach to statuary marble, which parian and statuary porcelain were designed to imitate? This is a subject more worthy of emulation than a trivial dispute as to which precedes the other in the dating of the invoice.

As I am only a spectator in this controversy, whose only object in addressing the public through you is to get at the whole truth, I propose to inquire if any information can be given by any one connected with the manufacture, say 50 years ago, as to the bodies produced at that period ; then to ask those gentlemen, or some one accredited by them, who have been named in the letters of your correspondents as having produced articles in imitation of marble, as to the truth of the statements made in their behalf ; and, lastly, to review briefly the statements of the present aspirations to the honour of the discovery or invention of this material.

I myself have an article in my possession manufactured by Messrs. Cheetham and Woolley, of Longton, upwards of fifty years old, of the *pearl* body then in vogue, which is so similar to the parian or statuary porcelain of the present day as scarcely to be distinguished from it, and it would at once strike any acquainted with the trade and accustomed to examine its wares, as essentially the same. The only difference is, perhaps, in the greater purity of its components, and a slight modification in their proportions, so as to give the modern article greater delicacy in appearance. I have also seen the wares of Mr. Turner, an eminent manufacturer and experimentalist in his day, whom one of your correspondents admits was the first to produce the *pearl* body, and I can see no difference but such as I have just named.

There were other manufacturers of this kind of ware in Longton also, and I have in my mind's eye several gentlemen who could tell us something of what had been done in days long departed in the manufacture of this body, if they would favour us with their knowledge of the subject.

Will some one acquainted with the subject inform us as to the nature of the patent obtained by Messrs. Davenport many years ago, and what the patented article was intended to imitate ? Will Mr. Charles Mason state if it is true that he produced an imitation of marble by a process applied to the surface only of his goods, and that this took place as far back as 1841 ?

I might pause here and wait for replies to these questions, before proceeding to remark further upon the claims set forth in your correspondents' letters, but taking their different statements as they stand as true, and as only wanting the confirmation of the gentlemen now named, what becomes of the claim of Mr. Battam as the "originator and inventor" of statuary porcelain, and as having "in 1842 first *conceived* the *idea* of imitating statuary porcelain in ceramic manufacture," when Mr. Mason has actually *done* and *executed* the same thing in 1841 ? And what becomes of his assertion that "up to this time," i.e., in 1844, "there was no material imitating or professing to imitate marble in ceramic manufacture, except the statuary porcelain referred to, and which was the sole and entire invention of this claimant," in the face of such claims as are put forth by your correspondents on behalf of the before-named gentlemen ? We cannot, of course, suppose that Mr. Battam would have made such a claim if he had been aware that others had *done* long before what he had only *conceived the idea* of doing. We are led to believe that he must have been in entire ignorance of what had been done by other manufacturers.

After all that has been admitted by your correspondents, I think it will not be doubted that that the pearl body of half a century ago is essentially the same as the parian and statuary porcelain, and other bodies of the same kind of the present day, and that neither Mr. Battam, nor Mr. Mountford, nor any manager or servant in the employ of Messrs. Minton and Co., are the actual "inventors" or "discoverers." They are at the utmost but improvers, and the parian and statuary porcelain of to-day is only a modification, and that a slight one, of the pearl body of Mr. Turner, made sixty years ago. The fame of these eminent manufacturers rests upon higher grounds than the mere introduction of this body, and they will be remembered as the chief instruments in introducing a higher style of art workmanship into the productions of this district than had been previously attempted.

I conclude these remarks as I began, by claiming for other parties a hearing in this matter before the correspondence is closed, in order that a full knowledge of all the facts may go forth to the public, and that honour may be given to whom honour is due.

I am, sir, your obedient servant,
SPECTATOR.

Also on 27 September 1851, Spectator becomes an assailant. He suggests that other rivals should be given an opportunity to make their claims as up to that point the supporters of only two eminent manufacturers had entered the columns of correspondence. He considers that the difference in the dates of the first invoices is a point of little importance as it is tolerably clear that both manufacturers were simultaneously engaged in the production of diverse works in this material. He believes:

> the point of most interest for the public in this matter is which of these eminent houses has brought out this material in its greatest purity? – which has made the nearest approach to statuary marble, which parian and statuary porcelain were designed to imitate.

Then he discusses the pearl body, this time that of Chetham and Woolley (see my comments earlier based on Terence Lockett's notes):

> which is so similar to the parian or statuary porcelain of the present day as scarcely to be distinguished from it…

He then requires information about Turner's pearl body, Davenport's patent, and Mason's statuettes; this is only right as previous correspondents had implied that they had claims which might be relevant. In the Minton Archive Mss 1432, George Smith's receipt book of 1881 gives, for a Pearl Body, a recipe rich in fluxing material (see table on page 62). This, then, clearly does not relate to Wedgwood's Pearl White body which is an improved creamware body with china clay in the body and Cornish 'china' stone and cobalt stain in the glaze.

In short (not a strong point of Spectator, nor of some others!), he suggests that parian is but an improvement or modification of the pearl body of John Turner. He could be correct, of course; the range of ingredients for a ceramic body are limited in number, but which are used, in what proportions, and how fired make all the difference between fine porcelain and coarse earthenware.

White feldspathic stoneware is surely a better contender for the basis of parian than any of the 'pearlwares'.

4th Oct 1851

To the Editor of the Staffordshire Advertiser.

Sir.—I had determined not to occupy your columns again by prolonging a controversy, originated, and almost engrossed, by anonymous writers, chiefly for the reason that the animus evidenced in their communications sufficiently proved a "foregone conclusion," determined without either the means or the desire to form an accurate and impartial judgment. The result is, that what might have formed a legitimate subject for amicable discussion, becomes but the vehicle for the expression of ill-timed and ill- natured personality — argument has degenerated into quibbling, and instead of a fair and candid spirit, which honest inquiry would have openly assumed, we have the sorry ebullitions of petty cavil, uttered beneath the mask of anonymous signature.

As, however, two letters have appeared, bearing respectively the signatures of John Mountford and Minton and Co., each containing special reference to myself, further silence might lead to misconception ; and I am, therefore, bound to refer again to the leading points in which I am more immediately concerned.

I reiterate my readiness, as expressed in my previous communication, to substantiate *every particular of my original claim* as therein stated and implied.

For the misconception and mystification, apparently and studiously wilful, to which it is assumed to have given rise, I am in no way accountable. I am fully prepared to substantiate and defend what I *did write,* but not what I *neither wrote nor inferred.*

The challenge for a jury to examine and determine whether my original Porcelain Statuary, of 1842, is *identically the same* as that now termed "Statuary Porcelain," is simply an evasion of the question, and Messrs. Minton cannot but have been fully aware of this when they dictated or signed the letter which appeared in your last week's journal.

Will they allow me to ask the question whether their parian, stated to have been made in 1845, was not the result of specimens seen of the original statuary porcelain of 1842 ? This is a much fairer way of meeting the case than asking if the two are " identically the same."

I had nowhere stated they were "identical ;" on the contrary, most distinctly affirmed they were not ; but that I had suggested the alteration in the manner and for the reasons that I have previously stated, and to which I need only refer.

I made no further claim, and left those who might be interested to decide their respective merits, as to the actual mixing of the relative proportions of the given materials, if such a task were worth the argument.

I wrote but what *I knew,* and it would have been well if your correspondents generally had been governed by the same discretion.

The questions put by Mr. Mountford are already fully answered in my previous communication, and I cannot give them in more express and definite terms than I have used.

The different statements relative to this subject must be peculiarly bewildering and embarrassing to the majority of your readers. Left to the details of the claimants themselves, the clue, though perchance a little intricate, might have been satisfactorily unravelled, but the "explanations" of your anonymous correspondents have now wove the web into a mesh of inextricable confusion.

It brings to mind the anecdote of the Rev. Thomas Scott, who had presented a part of his celebrated biblical commentary to an old lady, and calling upon her some time afterwards, hoped she had been edified by and understood it. "Oh yes," she replied, "I understand the Bible all very well—that is very plain—and I *do* hope in time to be able to understand your explanations."

One of your correspondents states the present material was made "essentially the same" about sixty years ago, and reference is made in support of this to Mr. Turner's so-called "pearl" body. Now to the general merits of Mr. Turner's productions I will yield full and ready acknowledgement—no one more sincerely—they are such as the district may be justly proud of even at the present day ; but I will hazard the assertion, that had the purpose of that eminent potter been to imitate statuary marble he would never have thought it approached, much less achieved by the "pearl" body, and it is but little compliment to his memory thus to libel him. If this body were made with any object of specific imitation it might have been in reference to that which its name implies—indeed it must otherwise have been a misnomer.

Another writer, also anonymous, has furnished such a catalogue of other "original makers" of statuary porcelain, or something "essentially the same," with whose works he professes old and intimate acquaintance, that it seems a matter of surprise and a lamentable reflection upon his sagacity that he never thought to turn this fund of knowledge to some useful account. He brings to mind the schoolboy who knew all the birds' nests in the parish, but could neither fly, nor lay an egg, nor even incubate to life the deposits of others.

"*Biddings for claims*" have been solicited on behalf of other manufacturers, whose names are used without either their knowledge or concurrence, and therefore I withhold further allusion to them, unless personally authenticated.

Still, let these matters be settled how they may, they in no way affect the question as regards myself, viz., as being the originator of the first material to which the term of statuary porcelain was applied in 1842,—*a process which gained the cordial approval of the first English sculptor of the age,* as *"the best material next to marble,"* and was the means of securing the first commission from the Art Union of London, which commission led the way to the present material (at my suggestion), and insured its present success. Neither at the time of making the original trials, nor up to the present date, had I nor have I ever seen or heard of any imitation, even professedly, of statuary marble in ceramic manufacture.

The statuary porcelain of 1842 was the pioneer of that of 1845, for which it not only opened and cleared the path, but also bequeathed its title and credentials, which now, though turned by its successor to profitable account, yet, warped by the ungenerous influence of trade jealousies, are most ungratefully and most unjustly questioned and impugned.

In respect to the publicity given to my claim, it is but just to state that, understanding the Royal Commission would take cognizance only of introductions of recent date, I had not referred at all to the subject, till being apprized that Messrs. Minton had claimed acknowledgement from the jury on ceramic manufactures as the originators and inventors of statuary porcelain, under the title of parian (which really appeared to me incredible), and being assured that the claim was receiving favourable consideration, I was advised immediately to forward a statement of my prior invention, which accordingly I did.

If this discussion be prolonged, let us henceforth have no "fighting with shadows." Surely such a question as this may be temperately canvassed on such perfect good faith and feeling, that the *bona fide* signature to a well grounded opinion will but give it extra weight.

There are abstract subjects, in reference to which the anonymous is unobjectionable, but on matters of mere fact, involving personal allusions, it ought to be repudiated. With a good cause, and fair and honest advocacy, a writer should blush to weaken his position, and be subject to the humiliating doubts which the adoption of such a pitiful subterfuge incurs.

It is impossible to divest the mind of these doubts, whether just or not ; so many falsehoods have been attested by a "Verax" and a "Veritas"—so many foul blows by the self-styled "Fair Play"—so many roguish insinuations by "Honestas"—and so prolific a crop of sedition sown by "Patriots"—that the object of the anonymous in these days is pretty clearly understood and duly estimated.

Though not so briefly, I have been compelled to write more hastily than I could wish, as I have had little time to devote to a controversy, which must end, be it continued as long as it may, much about where it began, as far as facts are concerned ; and the more direct, satisfactory, and conclusive method of testing these is by personal investigation, for which, as I at first stated, I am perfectly prepared.

I am, sir, your's very faithfully,
THOMAS BATTAM.

Stoke-upon-Trent, Oct. 1, 1851.

On 4 October 1851 Mr Battam returns to the fray. He admits that the 1842 and 1845 materials were not identical, but astonishingly leaves to

those who might be interested to decide their respective merits, as to the actual mixing of the relative proportions of the given materials, if such a task were worth the argument.

Although he says that Mr Mountford's questions had already been fully answered in his previous letter, I cannot find such answers. He points out the mistaken notion that Turner's pearl body was intended as an imitation of marble: he asks 'if it was, why did he call it pearl?' This seems an irrelevant comment; potters often give unsuitable names to patterns, so why not to bodies?

In the fifth paragraph Battam speaks of 'evasion of the question'. But it is he who is evasive. He knew that the figures produced in 1842 were not made of the same material as those in late 1845, let alone those exhibited at the 1851 Exhibition, and that a jury would have discovered this – as Minton suggest in their next letter.

In paragraph sixteen he makes what appears to be an 'adjustment of the facts' when he asserts '...the first material to which the term statuary porcelain was applied in 1842...'. I do not believe that that term was used until 1846, at least not in any publication of which I am aware.

His claim to the Royal Commission, he says, was submitted only because an earlier claim by Messrs. Minton as the originator and inventor of parian was receiving favourable consideration.

Battam suggests that writers hiding under pseudonyms should come out with their real names. I agree, but it seems to me that he is wriggling and avoiding the issue which rests on:

a. who first thought of the idea, and
b. who perfected the formula and method of the present material.

Whilst Battam is unrepentantly claiming both, in this letter he is not substantiating either of these claims effectively.

11th October 1851

Correspondence.

THE PARIAN STATUARY CONTROVERSY.
To the Editor of the Staffordshire Advertiser.

SIR,—We were somewhat surprised to see in your last number a long letter on this subject from Mr. Battam. His protracted silence, after the manly and straightforward challenge of Mr. Mountford, led us to the conclusion that he had been fairly put *hors de combat ;* and we must retain this opinion until he, like ourselves. Is disposed to accept it. With your permission, we will, as briefly as possible, notice those few passages of his letter which are relevant to the question in dispute. This we feel called upon to do, as Mr. Battam asks us a question, and makes other direct personal allusion to us. There shall, on our part be "no fighting with shadows," nothing "bewildering or embarrassing," but simply an appeal to facts.

Mr. Battam characterises "the challenge for a jury to examine and determine whether his original statuary porcelain of 1842 is *identically the same* as that now termed statuary porcelain" as an evasion of the question—an evasion that we must have been "fully aware of." Now, we beg to ask, what the question is—what all the controversy from first to last has been about—if not to decide the question, who first made parian or statuary porcelain in the Exhibition? This was the question that occupied the attention of the jurors of the ceramic department. They saw before them a variety of statuettes and other objects in a recently introduced material, and they desired to know who first made it. They were not inquiring after another and totally dissimilar material. Mr. Battam sought to substantiate his claim as the originator of the statuary porcelain in the Exhibition, or otherwise he did nothing relevant to the point on which the jury sought information. He sent his claim before them, and instead of candidly admitting, as he has now publicly done, that his statuary of 1842 is not identical with the statuary porcelain of 1845, he merely adverts to an "advantageous alteration" that was made in its composition in the latter year. This disingenuousness, to say the least of it, places Mr. Battam in a peculiar position ; for it must be evident to all impartial persons that, should Mr. Battam's claim prove influential with the jury, they would be entirely misled, and would in fact, be deciding upon false premises, as he conceals the fact, that in 1845 one material had been *substituted* for another. And how came the question before the jury at all ? Mr. Battam states that he sent in his claim in consequence of our "claiming acknowledgement as the originators and inventors of statuary porcelain under the title of parian. Mr. Battam should have made himself better acquainted with facts before making this assertion. We can assure your readers that we never sent in any claim at all, or even thought of doing so. Information was sought for by the jury, not volunteered by us. Mr. Minton, when in the Exhibition building, was asked by the chairman the plain unmistakeable question—"Who was the first inventor of the parian material?" to which he replied, "I believe my nephew, Mr Hollins, and Mr. Copeland (in the person of Mr. Battam), both claim it. I will not, however, undertake to decide who did first make it, but it is very easy of proof." This occurred after Mr. Minton had been told that Mr. Battam's claim had been sent in. Then, but not till then, we furnished the jury with the date of our invention, but we never sent in any formal claim.

We will now define what we consider the material termed parian, statuary porcelain, and carrara, really is. It is a highly vitrified bisque hard porcelain, much more vitrified than earthenware, stoneware, jasper, the old pearl ware made forty years ago, or the hard bisque porcelain of Sevres, Meissen, or Berlin. This must be intelligible to all ; and we will now answer the question Mr. Battam puts to us, viz., "Whether our parian of 1845 was not the result of specimens seen of the original statuary porcelain of 1842?"—that is, we suppose, of Mr. Battam's alleged invention. To this we give a most direct and emphatic negative. Indeed, how could this have been the case when, as we believe, and Mr. Battam admits, no such statuary porcelain as we have above described was in existence. Before 1846, we never saw any of *his* statuary porcelain at all equal to the old stone body made 40 years ago at our works, when that clever potter. Mr. Turner, was in the employ of the late Mr. Minton ; or equal to the Derby figures, made from 60 to 80 years since. Further, we do not hesitate to express our conviction that prior to 1846 Mr. Battam did not make any "body" worthy the name of statuary *porcelain,* that of 1842 being totally different in its composition, and every experienced potter must regard it as a misnomer when designated as such. It was not a vitrified body, and was, in fact, as different from and inferior to parian or statuary porcelain as earthenware is to stoneware. It would, in our opinion, have been only fair on Mr. Battam's part to have candidly answered Mr. Mountford's question, whether he could prove that before 1846 he had ever invoiced any of his productions under the title of statuary porcelain, for it appears to be more to the name than to the merit of the material that Mr. Battam clings. In November, 1846, the *Art Journal* notices statuary porcelain as a new material, and attributes its invention to Mr. S.T. Garrett. The editor does not speak of it as an advantageous alteration. In reply to a further question from Mr. Battam, we positively deny that his statuary of 1842 was the pioneer of the parian of 1845. It is altogether incorrect to give such a degree of importance to a material which, until this controversy arose, was scarcely ever heard of, and which was so dissimilar to and inferior for the purpose to the old stone statuary we have named.

Mr. Battam laments that his invention has been, "by the ungenerous influence of trade jealousies, most ungratefully and most unjustly questioned and impugned." Whether this complaint be well-founded or not, your readers will now be fully competent to judge. It is somewhat singular that Mr. Battam should now term his invention a *process,* and not a *material,* whilst in the same breath he says that the first sculptor of the age pronounced it to be "the best *material* next to marble :" forgetting that in the *Art Journal* for March, 1848 (where the sole merit of the invention is given to Mr. Battam), this eulogium of Mr. Gibson is applied not to enamelled earthenware, but to the present statuary porcelain!

We must apologise for the length of our remarks, and will conclude by naming the following gentlemen as a jury to decide the question in dispute :—Mr. R. Brown, Mr. Rose, Mr. Alcock, and Mr. Boote, the four last-named gentlemen being manufacturers of parian, but none of them claiming the invention of it. Mr. Mountford has agreed to go to a jury ; and we trust Mr. Battam will embrace this excellent opportunity for having the merits of his alleged invention fairly tested—his proofs in support of it candidly considered—with the certainty that the decision of such gentlemen would be, like Cæsar's, not only not suspected, but above the possibility of suspicion. By this course, all "foregone conclusions" may be dispelled ; "an accurate and impartial judgment" arrived at ; and all the "mystifications and misconceptions," all "the bewilderments and embarrassments" Mr. B. has *discovered* in the controversy, may be cleared up and set at rest. We hope Mr. Battam will, as we have done, write Mr. Wise by the first post, requesting the necessary preliminaries may be arranged ; but if he shrink from our challenge, we may safely leave the public to give their own verdict, and for ever bid adieu to the subject.

We have the honour to be, sir
Your obedient servants,
MINTON AND CO.

Stoke-upon-Trent, October 8, 1851.

In the next week's issue of 11 October Minton & Co. return to the fray. They also feel that Battam is evading the true issues and say they never volunteered a claim to the Royal Commission. They define what they consider the material parian really is:

> It is a highly vitrified bisque, hard porcelain, much more vitrified than earthenware, stoneware, jasper, the old pearlware made forty years ago, or the hard bisque porcelain of Sèvres, Meissen or Berlin.

They refer to that 'clever potter, Mr. Turner, was in the employ of the late Mr. Minton'. (This was John Turner, son of the John Turner of Lane End, and brother of William; these two brothers took out the patent in 1800 for a stoneware which became known as 'Turners' Patent'. John Turner succeeded Joseph Poulson at Mintons in 1808.)

In the mid-1840s Minton was producing some fine white china biscuit china figures, groups and busts. Figure model numbers 160 onwards were also made in the new Parian body and some earlier models were re-issued in parian. Geoffrey Godden states that sales of such figures rose from £1,037.17.1 in 1845/6 to £4,733.17.1 in 1850/1.

In this letter of 11 October it is pointed out that Mr Battam termed his invention a process and not a material &c., as he claimed earlier. (I suspect that Battam was careless in his choice of words.) This is pointed out in Minton's penultimate paragraph; but this allegation is incorrect because John Gibson first commented upon the early 'stone china' examples of 1844. I believe that these really were body without any superfice.

Rather unwisely Mintons end by naming their suggestion of the names for the jury, including Mr Boote, who, despite Mintons' saying that he didn't claim the inventing of parian, in fact did claim to have been making it in 1841. (See letter of 8 November 1851.)

25th October 1851

Correspondence.

STATUARY PORCELAIN

To the Editor of the Staffordshire Advertiser

SIR,—I had determined that with my last communication the correspondence on this "vexed question," at least as far as I was concerned, should have terminated ; but the letter signed by Messrs. Minton and Co., which appeared in your last week's paper, renders some further comments absolutely necessary. These I shall make as briefly as possible. Prolonged discussion only tends to demonstrate the justice of my previous statement respecting the *animus* which commenced and has continued to mark this discussion—a spirit completely prohibitory of any possible good or satisfactory results. Argument had already degenerated into petty quibbling, and quibbling has now merged into a mere personal squabble. My so-called "protracted silence" is first alluded to. I really do not see the applicability of the comment. I had already made my claim fully and clearly—a course forced upon me by previous misstatements, in which I was personally referred to ; this caused some replies, which being anonymous, I should not again have noticed under any circumstances ; these were followed by an authenticated statement ; but as the matter to which it bore reference, and the questions which it put had been already explained and answered by the contents of my first communication, and as your appended note, which appeared at the same time, stated the discussion must then cease, I thought it waste of time to attempt to re-open the controversy merely for the purpose of reiterating what I had already written ; indeed, I had little inclination and less time to devote to so profitless a task. Messrs. Minton and Co. state the question to be decided is, "Who first made the porcelain statuary or parian, as shown in the Great Exhibition," implying, as they have before more definitely stated, that IDENTICAL material. This view may suit the purpose of interested parties, who, profiting by an idea already successfully worked out, seek, by a variation in the means of its adoption, to hide the source from whence it emanated ; but a course so narrow and restricted would have been at once rejected—no honest jury would have consented thus to limit its recognition . The mere question as to the actual *mixing* of the present material (for it is idle to assume that there is any discovery or novelty in the composition of which it is formed,) without referring to the original cause of its introduction, would have been an act of such palpable injustice, as to have been repudiated at its bare suggestion. The tragedy of Hamlet, with the part of Hamlet omitted "by particular desire," so oft referred to, would but be a parallel performance. The question was and is, *who first purposed and effected an imitation of statuary marble in ceramic manufacture?* It matters little how or by what process—whether *identical* with the means now employed or not, (though of the subsequent alteration I also claim the suggestion and direction) so that proof resting on competent authority demonstrates its success. For the conception of this purpose, and the successful achievement, as confirmed by Mr. Gibson, the first English sculptor of the age, I claim recognition—a recognition which I have long enjoyed, and of which no effort can now deprive me.

Messrs. Minton and Co., in alluding to the original process, or material, whichever they please to term it, state that they never saw any "at all equal to the old stone," &c., &c. However much I may regret the loss of their favourable opinion in this respect, I must candidly confess I feel amply repaid by having secured that of the eminent sculptor already named, which will, with allay the suffrages I am at all desirous to possess, be sufficiently conclusive as to its positive abstract merits. If evidence were necessary to establish its character, in a *comparative* point of view, with that of the present statuary porcelain and parian, I can further refer to another very distinguished foreign sculptor, who seeing them together a few months back, expressed a declaration as to the superiority of the original of 1842 over its successors, and his surprise that it should not be still continued.

Messrs. Minton and Co. remark that I had not at first stated that my original statuary was "not identical with the present material." I can but suppose that these gentlemen either have not read my claim, or that this paragraph escaped their notice when they signed the letter in which it appeared. *I have from the first distinctly deposed to this effect,*—my letters will prove this.

Again, they state "they never sent in any claim," but merely "furnished the date of their invention," after the submission of my claim. There must, on this point, be some misunderstanding. The source from which I learnt that Messrs. Minton and Co. had, if not made a claim, at least forwarded a statement, or uttered it, upon which a claim to priority of introduction was sought to be established, was one possessing direct means of personal knowledge, and above the suspicion of doubt as to its truthful expression.

I would, while making this assertion, disclaim the slightest intention, even inferentially, of casting any imputation on the correctness of Messrs. Minton as to any personal claim, as they deny such to have been made by them ; but upon conclusive authority I must again assert that such information had been furnished by some means, as caused the subject to be taken into consideration with reference to that firm only in the first instance ; and it was in consequence of this movement alone that my claim was made as I previously explained.

There is an amusing feature characterising the present aspect of the question , which is, that its bearing has become completely reversed. Originally it stood, "Who invented statuary porcelain ?" but from the vast number of veritable originators, the difficulty appears to be to decide "who did *not* invent it ?" and in the very last scene of the last act a new *debutante* makes his first appearance as a claimant. Far be it from me to dispute the position which any may justly claim. I only hold my own, and shall continue to do so.

A few words in reference to the proposed jury. And here I must remark, without purposing, or, I trust, giving the slightest offence, that there is a primitive simplicity in the idea of a party directly interested in the verdict sought , nominating the members who are to pronounce it. There arc causes in which the law admits a plaintiff or defendant to challenge or object to, but never to select, his jurors. Individually, I have every respect for the gentlemen named ; but the principle involved is such that I could not admit its wholesale adoption as thus proposed. Indeed, a verdict so gained, even if favourable, would be but of little value to the nominees.

Messrs. Minton thus promise a decision "like Cæsar's—not only not suspected, but above suspicion"—(rather an original reading of the quotation, which, as hitherto understood, referred to Cæsar's *wife,* and not Cæsar's decision.) I should, however, surmise a very different result from such a procedure, and in this opinion have met with unanimous concurrence.

I reiterate for the last time that I am prepared to prove the truth and justice of my claim, *as I have made it,* to the letter ; and if the inquiry will embody the particulars therein expressed I am ready for it. If it be restricted to the mere *mixing* of the "identical" body at the present time, I consider the question altogether evaded, and refuse to lend my name in any way to such a subterfuge, leaving it to those who may covet such a questionable honour as might be thus obtained to its full enjoyment. Others have, comparatively, but little to risk on the decision—their claims are but of recent origin ; mine, in as far as I have ever sought to establish it, has been known and acknowledged for many years by those conversant with its particulars at the time of their operation, and whose opinions are doubly valuable from these circumstances, and from the possession of those qualifications, which alone make a judgment valuable.

I must, therefore, be convinced of the just comprehensiveness of the case to be submitted, and of the perfect good faith in which it is to be canvassed, before I so far trifle with my present position as to trust it to the influence of a judgment which, as far as regards myself, can alone derive weight from my acquiescence.

Regretting thus to be completed to trespass on your space,

I remain your's very faithfully,

London, Oct. 15 , 1851. THOMAS BATTAM.

On 25 October 1851 Mr Battam returns to the 'vexed question'. In trying to justify his claim to the whole invention, and virtually rejecting a trial by jury, Battam says:

> The mere question as to the actual mixing of the present material (for it is idle to assume that there is any discovery or novelty in the composition of which it is formed) without referring to the original cause of its introduction, would have been an act of such palpable injustice as to have been repudiated at its bare suggestion.

He has not only shifted his ground but has denigrated the works, through the ages of the developers of true and artificial porcelain, all forms of earthenware and stoneware, and, of course, the person who, in performing the task of compounding the materials and the procedure for firing, produced a result which became the standard by which other parian is judged.

He refers to Minton & Co. 'alluding to the original process, or material, whichever they please to term it…'. It was, in fact, Battam who first used both terms indiscriminately! He re-affirms his contention that he submitted his claim only because Messrs. Minton & Co had 'furnished by some means' information which caused the subject to be taken into consideration. He points out, with some justification,

> that there is a primitive simplicity in the idea of a party directly interested in the verdict sought, nominating the members who are to pronounce it.

To the Editor of the Staffordshire Advertiser.

"THE QUESTION was and is, who *first purposed and effected an imitation of statuary marble in ceramic* manufacture."—Vide Letter dated London, October 15, and *signed* T. Battam.

SIR,—To decide the above question, it would be necessary to summon from their repose most of the great professors of the ceramic art who have flourished during the past two centuries. And could the aid of some witch of Endor be invoked to "call them up," how withering would be the rebuke of each and all of them to the folly and arrogance that had led any one in the year 1851 to give birth to the preposterous idea, that he had "*first* conceived and effected an imitation of statuary marble in ceramic manufacture :" What is the fact ? So early as the year 1695 the French potters attempted to *imitate marble* at St. Cloud, by the adoption of a soft paste porcelain for statuary ; after that at Vincennes ; and subsequently in hard porcelain at Sèvres, from 1750 to 1804. Indeed , such celebrity did the Sèvres statuary acquire, that from 1770 to 1774, the manufactory was almost exclusively occupied in its production. The material then used was termed "pâte de sculpture," or *statuary porcelain,* so that any modern claimant has not even left to him the merit of the name!

We are told by *Brogniart,* vol. ii., p. 268, where he is adverting to the statuary made at the commencement of the present century, that " the quality of it is white, with a tendency to a blueish tint, and imitating by that tint and its transparency *the fine marble of Carrara!!"* Yet, in the face of this, we observed the remark in your last number, from one whom we will not pain to name, that "nobody can deprive him " of the reputation of *first* doing what Brogniart says was done fifty years ago!

Amongst Mr. Copeland's collection at the Great Exhibition, was a very fine specimen, known as " The Return from the Vintage." This was copied, under the direction of your correspondent, from a splendid piece of Sèvres statuary, formerly in the possession of the Earl of Lichfield, and now of Wm. Moore, Esq., of Wychdon Lodge. We have seen this beautiful work, and we do not hesitate to give our opinion that *prior to the year* 1845, no English potter had succeeded in producing so good an imitation of marble. We say this with reverential respect to the memory of the great Josiah Wedgwood, that clever potter Mr. Turner, and to the Derby porcelain manufacturers, who all in their day, and with varied degrees of success, attempted the same thing. And with these honoured names it would be unjust not to associate those of the late Mr. Spode and Mr. Thomas Minton. It must, we think, have been upon the assumption, that the museum at Sèvres, and all the private collections containing specimens of the works we have alluded to, had shared the fate of the library of Alexandria,—that the assertion could have been hazarded that he (your correspondent) in 1842, "was the originator of the *first* material to which the term statuary porcelain was applied"—and further, that "neither at the time of making the original trials, nor up to the present date (Oct.4, 1851), had he ever *seen* or *heard* of any imitation, *even professedly,* of statuary marble in ceramic manufacture." Possibly your correspondent did not exactly mean what is here conveyed, or it follows that he must be lamentably ignorant of the history of the art he is engaged in, and singularly oblivious of the merits of that fine specimen of Sèvres statuary which we have brought under his notice.

The parian or statuary porcelain in the late Exhibition is now a well known composition. Both the French and German manufacturers have generously admitted its superiority over their own long celebrated statuary porcelain. It was for the priority in the introduction of *this* material, namely, in February, 1845, that we have been contending. We were not cognizant until your correspondent found the ground he had first taken up to be untenable that there was any other point in dispute. How could we, when your correspondent ushered forth his pretensions in these *identical* words :—"Particulars of claim made by [your readers know who] as the *originator* and *inventor* of the branch of manufacture, known under the generic title, *as adopted by the official catalogue,* of STATUARY PORCELAIN!" But now it appears that the statuary porcelain *in* the Exhibition was not here indicated. It was another and different material, which elicited the marked encomiums of the first sculptor of the age, and also of a "distinguished foreign sculptor;" and it is much to be deplored, that an invention so important should, at the beck and nod of Mr. Mountford, have been lost to the world. It was unknown in the Great Exhibition of 1851!

With respect to our "primitive simplicity" in nominating a jury, we have only to observe that it was your correspondent himself that rendered such a step necessary. Your readers cannot fail to recollect that in our first letter to you we expressed our wish to leave the selection of a jury to Mr. Wise, or to *any other disinterested party.* Mr. Mountford readily assented to our nomination ; your correspondent did not ; though, we again repeat, that the decision of a tribunal, composed of the gentlemen we named, would have been like Cæsar's *wife* [we will not make the same clerical error again], not only not suspected, but above the possibility of suspicion.

We have the honour to be, sir
Your most obedient servants.
MINTON & CO.

Stoke-upon-Trent, Oct. 29, 1851.

8th November 1851

Sir,—It seems that the matter in dispute between Messrs. Minton and Copeland has now resolved itself into the question whether the credit belongs to the discovery of the article parian or to the application of that name to statuary.

We were pleased to see such strong and constructive arguments used by Messrs. Minton & Co. in your last week's number in favour of the honour belonging to the original inventor only. They induce us to make a claim to the distinction (which we would not otherwise have done) for one of our firm, Mr. Thomas L Boote, who first made the body in the year 1841 when learning the art of potting with Mr. E Jones, and he produced a further specimen from the same receipt in the year 1843 when with Mr. Maddock which can be produced with the operative who cast the article. This last date is three years previous to Messrs. Minton's claim.

We are making the same receipt to this day. We therefore suggest that should Mr. Battam refuse to go to a jury the other claimants can do so, and the question may be as Messrs. Minton so much desire, viz. "Who produced the first piece of parian?" As far as we are concerned we shall be happy for J A Wise Esq to choose the jury—himself being chairman.

We are your obedient servants
T & R Boote

On 1 November 1851 (All Saints Day!) Minton & Co. respond and take revenge with vengeance by calling preposterous the idea that any one person in the year 1851 should claim to have

> first conceived and effected an imitation of statuary marble in ceramic manufacture.

In this letter of 29 October (published 1 November), in the second paragraph, 'your correspondent' (that is, the present writer of the letter for Minton) claims to have directed the copying of *The Return from the Vintage*. This great group was included in Copeland's Catalogue available in May 1848; it would have been in the process of being modelled and manufactured during 1847. It seems, then, that 'your correspondent' must be Spencer Garrett. It was Spencer Garrett who chaired the 'Dinner of Messrs.Minton and Co.'s workmen in Commemoration of the Firm obtaining the Council Medal' on Wednesday 22 October 1851 and reported in the *Staffordshire Advertiser* on the following Saturday 25 October.

Spencer Garrett evidently left Copelands some time before this event. I suggest that he may have gone soon after his father, Thomas Garrett, left on 30 June 1847; his son may have stayed on a short while longer. He may have left in sympathy with his father, but perhaps more likely because he had been granted a patent, No.11249, on 22 June 1847 for 'Patent Mortice Tiles'; this may have been of greater interest to Mintons than it was to Copelands. It is not without significance that the Dinner was held in the showroom of Minton's Encaustic Tile Manufactory.

But when St. Cloud in 1695 is cited as having adopted a soft paste, or artificial, porcelain for statuary, followed by Vincennes and, later, in true porcelain, by Sèvres, I fear the writer might have been carried away. The lovely figures made by the French potters are far more intricate and small in scale to be regarded as imitating marble. Perhaps the Sèvres term 'pâte de sculpture' might be translated 'statuary porcelain', but generally the delightful products using that body, paste or material are called 'figures', and I suggest that 'figure body' would be a more reasonable translation.

Now, Minton castigate Mr Battam for being presumptuous for claiming to be the originator of the first material to which the term 'Statuary porcelain' was applied. After this strong criticism, Minton & Co. proceed to explain that:

> It was for the priority in the introduction of this material, namely in February 1845, that we have been contending.

I suggest that the sequence of events may have been like this:

1842 Thomas Battam has the idea of making a reduced size statuette in unstained stone china, perhaps smoothing the biscuit surface with an abrasive stone. (Although there are several references to 'superfice' to suggest that Battam did coat his pre-1845 with 'some personal labour', could not this 'labour' have been the action of rubbing the surface and not the application of a coating of slip or enamel?)
He seeks permission from the Duke of Sutherland to reproduce one of his marble statues; *Apollo as the Shepherd Boy* is chosen and, on 3 August, Battam shows the stone china statuette to His Grace who purchases it. (No invoice or record of this event is known to exist in the Sutherland Papers.) The evidence for the occurrence hangs, initially, on the testimony of Robert Hunt, FRS, who wrote the report in *The Handbook to the Catalogues of the Great Exhibition of 1851*. This was based presumably on Battam's claim to the Royal Commission and may have been stated to Hunt by Battam himself.

1844 An example of this stone china statuette is shown to John Gibson RA by the editor and colleagues of the *Art-Union* magazine; he extols its virtues as a material for sculpture. His *Narcissus* is offered for reproduction by Copeland & Garrett to be used as prizes by the Art Union of London. This was reported in the January 1845 issue of the *Art-Union* magazine. Also in 1844, Benjamin Cheverton's patent pantograph reducing device was available, but Gibson's *Narcissus* was reduced by the sculptor E.B. Stephens.

1845 John Mountford leaves Derby in about 1838 and is employed by Copeland & Garrett. By December 1845 he has developed a recipe for a material to resemble marble more closely than anything produced hitherto; he gives the recipe to Mr Spencer Garrett, who is trained as a chemist and was in charge of Mountford's experiments. After all, Mountford, a figure-maker, would need managerial support to authorise clay mixes, preparation of fritts, firing trials, etc.

Meanwhile, Battam has obtained permission from the Trustees of the British Museum to reproduce some of their antique vases and to market them. He has also arranged to copy other sculptures like *Emmanuel Philibert*. Minton claimed (in the letter published on 27 September 1851) that parian objects had been made as early as February 1845.

The significance of this date, and Veritas' claim for Minton making reproductions of the Portland Vase in April and May 1845, is probably that the original glass Portland Vase in the British Museum was smashed on 7 February 1845. I have seen an example of a Minton Portland Vase, but I recollect that it was coloured and gilded; whilst it *could* have been glazed parian, I believe it was of bone china.

Late in 1845 the Manchester Exhibition takes place. Copeland & Garrett mount an impressive display which includes items of statuettes and vases, but the *Art-Union* report does not call the body of which they are made statuary porcelain.

1846 Reduced size copies of *Narcissus* are offered in Statuary Porcelain by The Art-Union of London.

1847 Statuary Porcelain is established. The Art Union of London commissions another statuette from Copeland & Garrett – *Innocence* by J.H. Foley. Many other subjects are added to the range and the product finds increasing favour with the public.

My conclusion, after considering all this correspondence, is that, from whatever source of inspiration, it seems that both Copeland & Garrett and Minton & Co. had been working along similar lines to develop a suitable body for moderate sized and priced sculptures. (These are distinct from the intricate studies of Sèvres, Derby, et al.)

Mr Battam, in his letters, seems to be egotistical and verbose, shifts his ground, discourteously disregards the efforts of his colleague Spencer Garrett and purposely denigrates the development of the process and mixing of the materials (which, in fact, were crucial to the attainment of the final product), and generally wriggles under the stress of Minton's self-opinionated superior knowledge of ceramic history. Despite this, it seems that he may have had the 'original' idea for reproducing sculpture, but that he allowed himself to become confused between statuary porcelain – a ceramic body material – and porcelain statuary – the actual statuettes and vases themselves.

Mr Spencer Garrett, in charge of the development, may have felt that his support and encouragement justified some recognition. John Mountford, the man to whom was entrusted the day-to-day work of finding a formula, not only a list of ingredients but also a satisfactory method of manufacture, seems to me to justify his claim to be the real discoverer of the formula for Statuary Porcelain.

It is to be noted that Mr Battam was a regular contributor to the *Art-Union* and its successor, the *Art-Journal*. He also wrote many of the explanatory notes to the exhibits in the catalogue to the Great Exhibition of 1851.

John Mountford (1817-1906) – A short biography

In *People of the Potteries. A Dictionary of Local Biography* Vol. I, edited by D. Stuart (Keele, 1985), there is a potted biography of John Mountford which draws upon the detailed information in the obituary which was published in *The Sentinel* in 1906, and which was presumably supplied by a relative. Briefly, John Mountford was born at Back Sytch, Burslem, on 13 January 1817. In that year his father took employment at Derby as enamel fireman at the Nottingham Road manufactory, and so the family moved with him. John was apprenticed as a potter making ornamental wares, but, on completing his apprenticeship (which could have been when he was twenty-one years of age), he came to Stoke-upon-Trent to work for Copeland & Garrett as a figure-maker.

Mountford left Copelands in about 1849. *The Staffordshire Advertiser* of 17 November 1849 (p.5, col.2) contains a report of a dinner given to John Mountford by forty workers at Copelands, who presented him with a gilt snuff-box etc. for his services to the trade (by the development of the formula of parian he had helped to stimulate considerable business which had been reflected in the greater opportunities for employment of many of his colleagues). He probably left at 'Martinmas', 11 November, the customary date of change or re-employment in the pottery industry, to become a partner with Samuel Keys, who had migrated from Derby in about 1830. This firm made parian ware at a manufactory in John (now Leese) Street, Stoke-upon-Trent, exhibiting as Keys and Mountford at the Great Exhibition of 1851.

The partnership survived from about 1850 to 1853, in which year it was dissolved (*Staffordshire Advertiser* 22 October 1853, p.8, col.5). The same paper on 14 January 1860 (p.8, col.1) announced a meeting of the creditors of John Mountford. At some date he returned to Derby where he worked at the Crown Derby Works until his retirement at the age of seventy-four, in 1901. He died in June 1906.

COLOUR PLATES

Colour Plate 1. **GP4. BOY WITH BEGGING DOG,** after C. MacCarthy, c.1860. Ht. 8in. (20.32cm)

Colour Plate 3. **GP13. CHRIST AND MARY,** by J.S. Westmacott, c.1855. Ht. 22in. (55.88cm), W. 15in. (38.1cm)

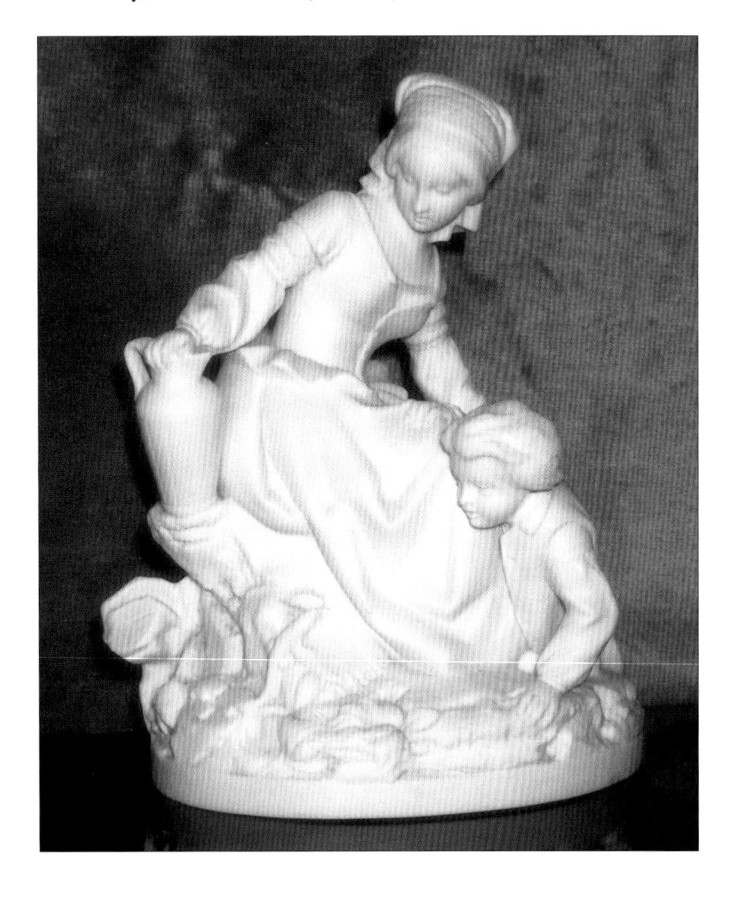

Colour Plate 2. **GP11. CHILDREN WITH LIZARD.** Ht. 9in. (22.86cm)

Colour Plate 5. **GP24. FIRST LESSON** by Owen Hale, 1884. Ht. 18in. (45.72cm)

(Left and above left) Colour Plate 4. **GP18. DUTCH SEASONS,** c.1851

Colour Plate 6. **GP48. NIGHT** by Raffaele Monti, 1861. Ht. 27in. (68.58cm)

Colour Plate 7. **GP51. PAUL AND VIRGINIA** by Charles Cumberworth, 1845. Ht. 12in. (30.48cm)

Colour Plate 8. **GP65. UNCLE TOBY AND WIDOW,** c.1870. Ht. 8in. (20.32cm), base 12 x 7in. (30.48 x 17.78cm)

Colour Plate 9. **GP66. THE AMAZON** by August Kiss, 1857

Colour Plate 10. **S9. ASTRAGALI PLAYER** or **The Dice Player,** 1851. Ht. 9in. (22.86cm), L. 11in. (27.94cm)

Colour Plate 11. **S13. BEFORE THE BALL** (companion to **After the Ball)** by Owen Hale, c.1870. Ht. 20in. (50.8cm); L. 22in.(55.88cm)

Colour Plate 12. **S20. ROBERT BURNS** by J. Steell, c.1874. Ht. 16in. (40.64cm)

Colour Plate 13. **S33. COTTAGE GIRL** by L.A. Malempré, c.1877. Ht. 15in. (38.1cm)

Colour Plate 14. **S36-C9. SLEEPING CUPID WITH BASKET** by L.A. Malempré. Ht. 9in. (22.86cm)

Colour Plate 15. **S36A-C16. CUPID VESTA HOLDER** 5½in. (13.97cm)

Colour Plate 16. **S38. DANCING GIRL REPOSING** by William Calder Marshall, 1846. Ht. 18in. (45.72cm)

Colour Plate 17. **S48. EVANGELINE** (companion to **Marguerite)** by Sarah Terry, 1869. Ht. 21in. (53.34 cm)

Colour Plate 18. **S65. GARDENER AND COMPANION.** Ht. 5⅛in. (13.02cm)

Colour Plate 19. **S80. INNOCENCE** by J.H. Foley, 1846, issued 1847. Ht. 16in. (40.64cm)

Colour Plate 20. **S99. MAIDENHOOD** (companion to **Beatrice**) by Edgar G. Papworth Jnr., 1861. Ht. 22in. (55.88cm)

Colour Plate 21. **S100. MARGUERITE** (companion to **Evangeline**) by Sarah Terry, c.1871. Ht. 21in. (53.34cm)

Colour Plate 22. **S103. MARY, QUEEN OF SCOTS** by L.A. Malempré, c.1879. Ht. 14in. (35.56cm)

Colour Plate 23. **S109. MUSIDORA** after Sir J. Reynolds (small), by W. Theed (large), 1851 and 1867. Small Ht. 7½in. (19.05cm). Large Ht. 17in. (43.18cm)

Colour Plate 24. **S121. NYMPH AT BATH** after Lorenzo Bartolini, c.1851. Ht. 9-10in. (25.4 cm), L.13in. (33.02cm),. W. 7in. (17.78cm)

Colour Plate 25. **S122. NYMPH PREPARING FOR THE BATH** (or **Nymph untying her Sandal**) by John Gibson, RA, c.1858. Marble. Ht. of the parian statuette 17⅝in. (44.77cm)

Colour Plate 26. **S126. PAUL** (companion to **Virginia**) by C. Cumberworth, c.1849. Ht. 14in. (35.56cm)

Colour Plate 27. **S134. PURITY** by M. Noble, 1865. Ht. 19in. (48.26cm)

Colour Plate 28. **S137. REBEKAH** by W. Theed the Younger, c.1851. Ht. 19in. (48.26 cm)

Colour Plate 29. **S150. SABRINA** (companion to **Comus**) by W. Calder Marshall, c.1849. Ht. 12in. (30.48 cm)

Colour Plate 30. **S153. SAPPHO** (small) by W. Theed, 1869. Ht. 16in. (40.64cm)

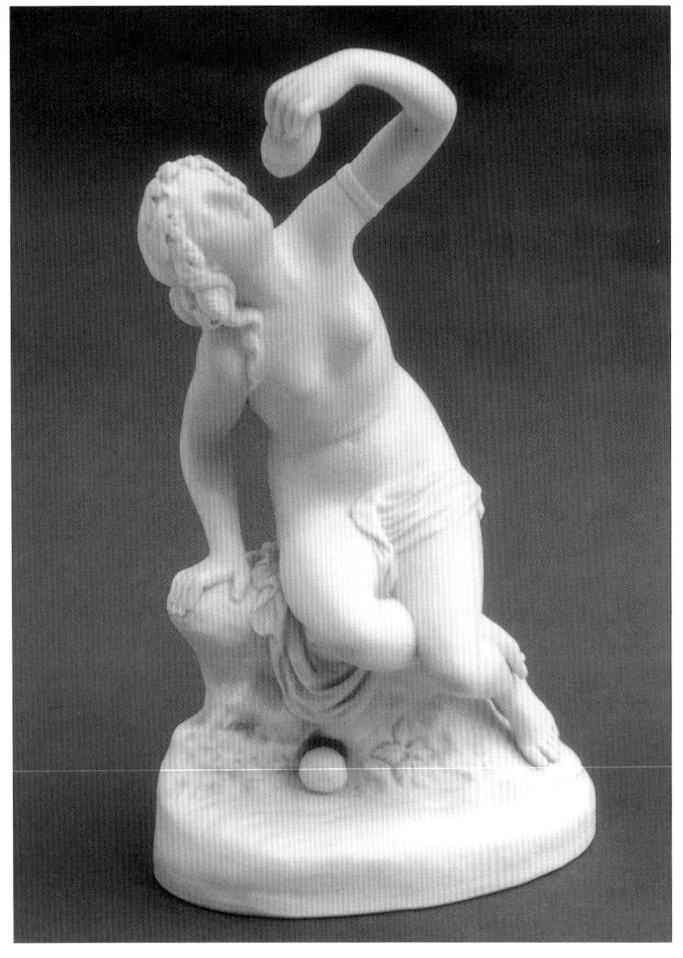

Colour Plate 31. **S154. SEA NYMPH** by J.J. Pradier, c.1850. Ht. 9½in. (24.13cm)

Colour Plate 32. **S175. THE TOILET** by W. Calder Marshall, 1861. Ht. 16in. (40.64cm)

Colour Plate 33. **S182. VENUS** by John Gibson, 1849. Ht. 16in. (40.64cm)

Colour Plate 34. **S187. VIRGINIA** (companion to **Paul**) by C. Cumberworth, c.1849. Ht. 14in. (35.56cm)

Colour Plate 35. **B15. COLIN CAMPBELL, Lord Clyde ,** possibly by Morrison, 1858. Ht. large 10in. (25.4cm), small 9in. (22.86cm)

Colour Plate 36. **B21. WILLIAM TAYLOR COPELAND** by Birks, 1838, and onwards. Ht. 22½in. (57.15cm)

Colour Plate 37. **B24. ELAINE** (or Elein) by L.A. Malempré, c.1876. Ht. 13in. (33.02cm) including socle

Colour Plate 38. **B60. OENONE by** W. Calder Marshall, 1861. Ht. 11½in. (29.21cm), on pedestal 16⅜in. (41.59cm)

Colour Plate 39. **B63. SIR ROBERT PEEL** by J.S. Westmacott, 1850. Ht. 10¼in. (26.04cm)

Colour Plate 40. **B70. SIR WALTER SCOTT,** possibly by John Steell. Ht. 17in. (43.18cm)

Colour Plate 41. **B71. THE SEASONS** by Owen Hale, 1881. Ht. 17½in. (44.45cm)

Colour Plate 42. **B82. SUTHERLAND, DUKE OF,** by John Francis, 1850.

Colour Plate 43. **B88. VIOLA SANS CHAPEAU** by F.M. Miller, 1862. Ht. 11in. (27.94cm)

Colour Plate 44. **R8. ALBERT EDWARD, Prince of Wales,** by Marshall Wood, 1863. Ht. 12½in. (31.75cm)

Colour Plate 45. **R9. ALEXANDRA, Princess of Wales,** by F.M. Miller, 1863. 12⅛in. (30.8cm)

Colour Plate 46. **R12. ALICE, Princess,** by Mary Thornycroft, 1879. Ht. 15in. (38.1cm)

Colour Plate 47. **ROYAL SEASONS – SPRING, Princess Alice**, by Mary Thornycroft, 1848

Colour Plate 48. **R24. QUEEN VICTORIA** by W. Theed, 1864. Ht. 13in. (33.02cm)

WHAT IS PARIAN OR STATUARY PORCELAIN?

It is a porcelain with a high proportion of fluxing materials, firing to a white or pale ivory colour which has a fine, smooth surface after being fired at a temperature equal to that for biscuit earthenware, about 2100°-2200°F (1150°-1200°C).

Despite what some of the letter writers said in 1851 about the relative unimportance of the proportions of the ingredients, it really is of the greatest importance and can determine the nature of the finished product.

So far as Copeland's statuary porcelain is concerned, I report the recipe recorded at some time before 1860, possibly in about 1855:

Fritt	100lbs Washed Isle of Wight sand		) Calcined in china biscuit
	60 Felspar		) oven and ground fine.
	20 Potash		)
Body	64lbs Fritt	13.3%	)
	96 Calcined Felspar	20.0%	)
	96 Raw ground Felspar	20.0%	) Ground fine at the Mill
	192 China Clay	40.0%	)
	32 Glass	6.7%	)

In July 1993 Harry Frost, Curator of the Dyson Perrins Museum at Worcester, generously sent me copies of manuscript pages from the recipe book of Thomas John Bott, the art director of Coalport, and son of Thomas Bott of Limoges enamel fame. This included the following:

Parian Copelands
Fritt

	50lb Silica, Lynn Sand or Flint	
	30 " Spa (i.e. Feldspar)	
	8 " Pearl Ash (i.e.. Potash)	
Body		
	24lb China Clay	(40%)
	24 " Calcined Spa	(40%)
	8 " Fritt	(13.3%)
	4 " Flint Glass	(6.7%)

This receipt was kindly given to James Lane by Mr. Mountford the man who first discovered this body whilst at Copeland's and the credit for which discovery was most wrongly claimed by Mr. Thos Battam. Mch 29.1862.

This recipe is virtually the same as that recorded in the Copeland recipe book. A recipe for 'Alabaster' on the same page in the Bott recipe book is dated 1855. However, if Mountford's claim is correct, this recipe must have been the one which he introduced in 1845.

These ingredients were ground on the mill and mixed with water to form a thick liquid of the consistency of cream, called 'slip'; this would be taken to the workshop and transferred into a cask or tank from which the figure-maker could draw off the slip into a jug (pitcher) so that he could pour it into the moulds of the subject which he was casting.

It will be noted that 60% of the mixture was non-clay and so would require to be constantly stirred and agitated to prevent the heavy particles from settling out to the bottom of the cask.

The moulds were made of plaster of Paris which absorbed the water from the slip to leave a deposit of clay on the inside surface of the mould. When this deposit was deemed to be of the correct thickness, the surplus slip was poured away and the 'cast' allowed to stiffen. In doing this it starts to contract and shrink away from the mould, so it requires fine judgement to decide on the correct moment when it should be released. If it remains in the mould even slightly too long cracks may be caused as some parts of the cast item are held back while adjoining parts continue to contract. Conversely, if it is released too early the clay will not be stiff enough to retain its proper shape and may even collapse.

Some subjects required fifteen to twenty moulds and the famous reproduction of the Sèvres *Return from the Vintage* needed fifty moulds. Each mould might consist of twenty or so individual sections held together in a large outer mould; this was necessary to achieve the under-cut folds of drapery, limbs, etc. When the outer mould was opened these sections were carefully withdrawn so as to avoid marking the clay. Separate moulds were needed for the head, arms and legs, as well as the main body of the figure. They were cast at the same time so that all parts had the same moisture content and were 'stuck up', or fixed to each other, in the state of 'leather hardness' so that the whole subject contracted as one piece without strains being introduced during the drying period. The pieces were 'stuck up' using a very thin smear of slip as an adhesive.

The sticking up of the figure or group required considerable skill and a knowledge of the human, and sometimes animal, anatomy. Especial care was required in putting together nude figures: lack of judgement might cause such a deviation of line as to seriously injure the beauty of the work.

When completed, the name COPELAND and perhaps COPYRIGHT

RESERVED was impressed carefully into the back of the piece. Any references to an art union, the name of the sculptor and the date of its origination was probably in the mould. After 1870 a date stamp was usually impressed also: this consists of a letter over two figures representing the month letter and the last two digits of the year in which the piece was made. In preceding years certain letters and symbols occur, and these may be a coded date mark, but the code has not been discovered.

In the *Official Catalogue to the Great Exhibition of 1851* (page 711) it is stated that:

> the shrinking that occurs before these casts can be taken out of the mould,… is equal to a reduction of one inch and a half in the height [of a figure which starts by being 24 inches high]. After the figure has been assembled, the figure-maker removes all trace of the raised seams which are caused by the joints of the moulds, and the whole worked upon to restore the cast to the same degree of finish as the original model.

This would entail 'fettling' (cutting or scraping off the clay) to render it level and then sponging the marks left by the seams.

Like all products made of clay it is essential that the object is dried thoroughly before the placing and firing stages. If there is any free moisture left in the clay it might be turned to steam in the oven and, in expanding, would cause the object to crack or even to burst.

In the case of statuary porcelain there took place a further contraction of 1½inches (3.8 centimetres) during this final drying period, making a total of 3inches (7.6 centimetres), or one eighth, of the original size.

Extreme care needed to be taken in placing parian objects, especially the statuettes and groups. The high proportion of fluxing materials meant that the safe firing range was very narrow and therefore objects needed to be 'propped'. This was performed by the figure-maker. A flat 'bat' (plate) of parian clay was made by the 'presser' and on this the statuette would be placed. Strips of parian clay were cut as needed to support the arms, and the figure itself, from the bat. A small pad of powdered flint was put on the end of the prop next to the statuette so that during the firing the two pieces of clay did not fuse together; this also served as a cushion to absorb any slight movement which might occur.

This whole assembly was taken to the 'saggar-house' where the placers put the ware into the saggars. In this case the statuette or group, on its bat, would be placed in a deep saggar and perhaps finely sifted sand might be filled in around it to ensure that it remained in a secure position as the saggar was carried into the oven for the first firing. A saggar is an oval box made of 'saggar marl', a mixture of fireclay and 'grog', broken pieces of fired saggar and pots.

On Copeland's manufactory the first firing took place in the earthenware glost oven at a temperature of about 1900°F (1050°C). This firing was important because it ensured that all the contraction had occurred. After the firing it would be seen that the seams had 'fired up', that is the clay at the mould joints had expanded; this always occurs and, while the effect is unimportant on a piece of tableware, it is not appropriate for a statuette to have a seam running down an arm or a leg. Therefore, when the saggar had been 'drawn' from the oven, the statuette and other pieces would be returned to the figure-maker, or 'repairer'. He would remove the props, if these had not been taken off by the placer drawing the oven, and proceed to rub down with an abrasive stone all the seams so that they did not show at all. He would also fill with 'stopping' any small cracks which might have occurred; if this was done carefully the subsequent firing would cause the stopping to fuse so that the original crack would not be observed.

For the second firing the statuettes, now at their finished size, were placed in saggars and embedded in fine, sifted sand and re-fired in the earthenware biscuit oven to a temperature of 2100°-2200°F (1150°-1200°C). This firing might last from sixty to seventy hours. In some cases a third firing might be needed to develop 'the extreme beauty of surface which the finest specimens present'. The bedding of sand was preferred to the use of props because it supported the figure better; besides, as all the shrinkage had taken place there was no risk of the figure being held by the sand.

The contraction during firing roughly equals that from mould to fully dried clay, making the total contraction from mould to finished fired state one fourth, or 25%.

(Reference may be made to the January 1849 issue of the *Art-Journal*, pages 17-18, in an article on *Artificial Stone – Statuary Porcelain* by Robert Hunt.)

January 1849

THE ART-JOURNAL.

ON THE APPLICATIONS OF SCIENCE

TO THE FINE AND USEFUL ARTS.

ARTIFICIAL STONE—STATUARY PORCELAIN.

THE necessities of a progressively improving taste, and the demands made by the growing desire for those luxuries which mark the advance of civilisation, have been met in a remarkable manner by inventions characterised by mechanical ingenuity, artistic skill, and scientific knowledge.

The instances already taken as examples of scientific applications are, many of them, of a striking character, and to these, as a most apt illustration of our position, we now add the rather extensive class of combinations which may be grouped under one general head—as Artificial Stones. These may be divided into five classes : Semi-vitrified bodies—as opaque glass, porcelain, stone ware, terra cotta, &c. Hydraulic cements—sulphate and carbonate of lime, including the largest number of the cements. The bituminous compounds—as Seyssel asphalte and the Trinidad mastic. Oleageneous cements—such as putty composition, Venetian cement ; and siliceous combinations—as Ransome's stone, Kuhlmann's, &c. From these it is our intention to make such a selection as will enable us to give a popular explanation of the principles involved in each class, and to show the advantages derived from a scientific knowledge in their various applications to purposes of ornamentation. This will necessarily extend itself to several papers. The art of the potter is perhaps, next to that of the agriculturist, the most ancient of all ; and the potter's wheel was evidently one of the earliest inventions of human ingenuity taxed to meet the necessities of an existence upon which rested the task of labour, as the only road to the enjoyment of being. Beyond the mere necessary utensils which almost through all time appear to have been manufactured from clays, the passion for ornament, and those strange and mysterious desires connected with the original worship of an unknown cause, which lead to the embodyment of the idea present to the bewildered mind of untutored man, have from the remotest antiquity given rise to representations of nature and imaginings of fancy in the same material. In the remains of the Assyrian temples, in the tombs of Egypt, and in the marvellous relics of a civilisation which once existed in central America, we find singular evidences of these attempts in the Plastic Art, many of which are preserved in our museums, representing, even in their grotesqueness, a rude history of the struggle of the human intellect through the night of ignorance, and affording evidence of the progress of manufacture. The history of the Ceramic Art, whether, as the Grecian Myth relates, it originated with Ceramus, the son of Bacchus and Ariadne, or with the more humble Dibutade, the sculptor, is one of far too comprehensive a character to be embraced within our limits, and we refer to it merely for the purpose of showing that from the period when the Nomadic races to the south of the Caucasus began to assemble within the rude walls of their first towns, the process of forming ornaments in artificial stone was one which occupied the ingenuity of some amongst the tribes. Passing over the Assyrian and Egyptian examples, we find in the palmy days of Athens, when the princely taste of Pericles, and the surpassing genius of Phidias, rendered that city an example of the perfection of the sculptor's art, and when every dwelling was crowded with its household gods that argillaceous compositions substituted the more expensive natural marbles ; that Phidias and Miron were pleased at directing the manufacturer, not uncommonly furnishing the form to the more humble artist.

Most of the specimens preserved to us have more the character of terra cotta than of porcelain. The Arabs appear to have been in possession of a process for glazing earthenware ; and tablets and other ornamental decorations, of this material, were employed in the celebrated Moorish palace of the Alhambra.

The production of true porcelain in Europe, with which we have more particularly to deal, dates probably no further back than 1703, when a German alchymist, Bötticher, appears to have produced a white porcelain from the clay of Aue, near Schneeberg, and founded the manufactory of Meissen. The *tender porcelain* of Sèvres, which was superseded by the discovery of Bötticher, could scarcely be regarded as other than an opaque glass, being composed of saltpetre, sea salt, alum, Alicant soda, gypsum from Montmartre, and sand from Fontainbleau.

It will be necessary before we proceed to any description of the manufacture of the porcelain statuary, that that we should give some account of the nature of the materials employed in the several manufactories on the continent and in England.

The composition of the mass of the true or hard porcelain is Kaolin, (a name very generally adopted from the Chinese,) or China clay a decomposed felspar, quartz or a pure silicious sand, and sometimes gypsum. The finest clay obtained in England, is that procured from the granite districts in the west of England, and its average composition is as follows :—

Silica	46.00
Alumina	40.00
Iron	.27
Lime	.43
Magnesia	.50
Water and Alkali	12.80

We may therefore regard porcelain as a combination of alumina (pure clay), silica (pure flint), and alkali (potash), by which the whole is fused into a semi-transparent mass. The body of the material must be regarded as clay—a porous and spongy body—into which the silicate of potash (glass) is run, by which it is rendered a dense mass. Such are the general characteristics of porcelain, the composition varying slightly in different manufactories, particularly as they are dependent upon natural productions for the substances employed, which is the cause of the varying physical characteristics of the porcelain of different districts.

The variety, however, known as Wedgwood ware, may be regarded as approaching nearer to that employed for porcelain statuary than any other ; and in it we have Cornish and plastic clay fluxed with Cornish china stone, which contains a large quantity of quartz and potash. From this kind of stoneware chemical utensils are produced, and those very interesting imitations of the celebrated Portland Vase, in which white figures are represented upon a blue ground. The heat to which the porcelain statuary is exposed is, however, very considerably greater than that required for Wedgwood ware Wedgwood, perceiving the advantages to be derived from the introduction of elegant forms, succeeded in obtaining the assistance of Flaxman, and thus furnished some very fine designs to the public in this ware. For a very complete account of the Staffordshire Potteries and of the processes of manipulation in the several departments, we must refer to the *Art-Journal* for 1846, October and November ; and in those papers will also be found some very important notices and good woodcut illustrations of the beautiful porcelain statuary of Mr. Copeland, and of the productions of Messrs. Minton and other large manufacturing establishments in the Potteries.

The Statuary Porcelain and the Parian, which in all physical peculiarities resemble each other, must be distinguished from the "bisque" china, in which a great number of figures have been produced by Messrs. Minton and others. Those pretty compositions in which net-work and lace are introduced, are of "bisque;" the delicate effect of the drapery being produced by actually dipping net in the porcelain "slip," or argillaceous mixture, from which the organic matter is afterwards burned out during the operation of "fireing."

The dead white of these figures is to many very objectionable, and it became desirable to introduce some material which should have the semi-transparency of marble. To this point Mr. Battam appears to have turned his attention, and the result of his assiduous experiments was the production of a most faithful imitation both as to surface and tint, to which he gave the name of Statuary Porcelain. Some statuettes having come under the observation of the editor of the *Art–Journal,* the value of the material was immediately appreciated ; and through his instrumentality (after being submitted by him to Mr. Gibson, and other eminent sculptors, who declared it to be "the best material next to marble,") the specimens were laid before the council of the Art-Union of London, and a commission was given from that Society for the production of a number of copies of Gibson's "Narcissus" to be awarded as prizes to its members. This encouragement gave a healthy stimulant to further exertion ; and during the time occupied by the execution of the reduced model of the figure, further experiments were made, and combinations tried, which resulted in the production of an improved material scarcely inferior to marble in appearance. This substance is of a cream-white colour, and possesses sufficient transparency of surface to reflect as much light as is agreeable to the eye. It is unaffected by the varied conditions of our atmosphere ; indeed, strong acids have no effect upon it, and when soiled it may be cleaned by washing with soap and water. Before we enter upon any of the considerations which naturally arise from so important a scientific application, we must give some description of the mode in which the manufacture of porcelain statuary is carried on in the works of Messrs. Copeland, Minton and others. We are enabled to do this through the kind attention of Mr. Thomas Battam, to whom we are indebted for the origin of the material as at present employed, having been furnished by that gentleman with the following particulars :—

The material is used in a liquid state, technically termed "slip," about the consistency of thick cream. It is poured into the moulds forming the figure or group, which, being made of plaster, rapidly absorb a portion of the moisture, and the coating immediately next the mould soon becomes of a sufficient thickness for the cast, when the superfluous "slip" is poured back. The cast remains in the moulds for some time at a high temperature, by which it is (through the evaporation that has taken place), reduced to a state of clay, and sufficiently firm to bear its own weight when relieved from the moulds, which are then opened and the different portions of the subject taken out.

"Each figure requires many moulds : the head, arms and hands, legs, body parts of the drapery, when introduced, and the other details of the subject are generally moulded separately. In one group, representing "The Return from the Vintage," consisting of seven figures, there are upwards of fifty moulds, and each of these in several divisions ; these parts being removed, have then to be repaired, the seams caused by the junctions of the mould cleared off, and the whole put together. This is a process requiring , when well executed, the greatest nicety and judgment, the fragile nature of the material in its present state rendering considerable practical knowledge necessary to form a perfect union of the different members, and also that they are so disposed as to be in strict accordance with the original model. For, though made from the same moulds, it by no means follows that all the casts will possess equal merit ; so much depending upon the taste and skill of the finisher, the 'figure-maker.'

"Peculiar care is required in putting together nude figures, in which the junction of the parts generally presenting a level circular surface, requires the decision of an educated eye to fix with accuracy. Surfaces that possess a marked and broken outline, which will only fit together at one particular point, are of course exempt from this difficulty. Want of judgment in this respect will often cause such a deviation of outline, as seriously to injure the beauty for the work. The parts are attached together by a 'slip,' similar to that used for the casting ; the surfaces to be joined together being either dipped into them, or the "slip" is applied with a pencil, and according to the discretion with which this is executed, and the neatness with which the sections of the moulds are made to fit, will be the greater or less prominence of the seams which so often disfigure pottery castings. It is possible, with care, that these seams shall be so trifling, as to be scarcely perceptible, even upon a close examination ; and it is only the want of proper precaution that the contrary is too often the rule instead of the exception.

"The 'slip' in this case is merely required to soften the surface of the clay of the members which have to be united, just sufficiently to cause adhesion. All that is used beyond that requirement is not only superfluous, but actually detrimental ; moistening the parts to which it is applied so much that the edges become pliant, and yielding to the pressure, while being attached, distort the outline, and by causing unequal shrinking in the process of firing the junctures become evident and unsightly. This fact cannot be too forcibly impressed upon those engaged in this branch of the Art, as it is of the greatest importance to their interests, for exactly in proportion to the beauty and perfection with which these objects are produced, will this novel and valuable introduction merit and obtain success.

"The figure or group being thus put together remains two or three days, when being sufficiently dry, it is supported by 'props' made of the same material, placed in such positions as to bear a portion of the weight, and prevent any undue pressure that might cause the figure to sink or yield in the 'firing.' Each end of the 'prop' is embedded in a coating of ground flint to prevent adhesion, and is thus easily removed. It is then placed in the oven, and submitted to a heat of about 50° of Wedgwood's pyrometer.

"This operation, which is gradually effected, occupies from sixty to seventy hours. The fires are then withdrawn and the oven allowed to cool ; and when sufficiently so the figures are drawn out, the seams rubbed down ; they are again placed in 'saggars' and embedded in sand, and then re-fired at a still higher temperature than they were previously submitted to. The bedding of sand is preferred in this part of the process to 'props,' as it more equally and effectually supports the figure. It could not be used in the first instance when the figure is in the clay, as by resisting the contraction, it would cause it to be shattered to pieces. It is even sometimes necessary to fire casts three times, a peculiar degree of heat being required to produce the extreme beauty of surface which the finest specimens present.

"The total contraction of the figures from the mould to the finished state is *one-fourth.* The contraction of the 'slip' with which the mould is first charged, to the state in which it leaves the mould, is one-sixteenth ; again it contracts another sixteenth in the process of drying for the oven, and one-eighth in the process of vitrification, so that a model *two feet high* will produce a fired cast of *eighteen inches only.* Mr. Minton states the contraction of their improved composition as being little more than one-fifth.

"Now let it be considered, that this contraction should in an equal degree extend through every portion of the subject to insure a perfect work ; and it will be immediately apparent that there is considerable difficulty to be overcome in its production, particularly to achieve such a result as would satisfy the requirements of a highly cultivated taste. Still, difficult as it may be and is ; with judgment in the selection of subjects, and practical knowledge brought to bear in their execution, there is no impossibility in the conclusion, that a faithful realisation of the beauties of the finest works of Art may be effected.

The chemical elements of this composition are essentially alumina, silica, and felspar, which by the action of the intense heat to which the mass is exposed, actually agglutinate so as to form the beautiful body which the finished figures present, the perfection of which is still more apparent in a fractured portion. Every manufacturer naturally employs different proportions of each substance ; and it often occurs that some material peculiar to a certain manufactory marks its character. Wedgwood, for instance, introduced the sulphate of barytes, or cauk-stone. Bone ashes are employed by many, and the steatites are used by others. During the processes of "firing," a very considerable change must necessarily take place in the chemical arrangement of the constituents, and any volatile bodies are of course expelled ; it is not therefore to be inferred that an analysis of a portion of the burnt ware represents the *actual* composition before burning, but as such an analysis is interesting the following is given, it having been obligingly undertaken for us by Mr. J. A. Phillips, of the College of Civil Engineers'.

Silica	60.35
Alumina	32.60
Soda	4.16
Potash	2.55
Lime and Magnesia, a trace	
Iron, very faint trace	
	99.66

The contraction of the composition has been spoken of as one great obstacle in the way of perfect success. This depends entirely on a peculiar physical property of alumina, which property is so obedient to certain fixed laws, as to indicate by contraction the heat to which the clay has been exposed. On a knowledge of this fact the ingenious Wedgwood constructed his pyrometer. This instrument consists of pieces of the Cornish china-clay, moulded into cylinders of a determinate size, and baked in a low red heat. These rods of clay were of such a size that they just entered between two graduated brass rods, fixed on a brass plate, half an inch asunder at one end, and 0.3 of an inch at the other ; and being exposed to any elevated heat, the degree of shrinking marked the temperature on Wedgwood's scale. Thus, the heat of melted silver so contracted the clay, that it could be passed between the rods to 23° ; that of gold allowed of its being advanced to 32° ; whilst that of cast-iron shrunk it, so that it could be pushed forward to 153°. These temperatures respectively represent 4717°, 5237°, and 21637° of Fahrenheit's scale. For practical purposes this instrument is often employed, but being liable to some errors, it has for philosophical investigations, been superseded by instruments of greater delicacy.

Such is the property of all clays, no two varieties of clay contract equally for equal heats, but the contraction is fortunately always the same for the same kind of clay. The contraction in volume on the average, for the porcelain clays, is about 38 per cent. It has been already stated to what amount the porcelain statuary contracts in each stage of its manufacture. It will of course be understood that this depends upon the manner in which the mass is formed. All bodies *cast* in a mould shrink the most, as being more liquid and less coherent ; those formed by *pressing* into a mould the least, owing to the greater tenacity of the mass. The first contractions are due to the evaporation of the water from the material, and the last to the incipient fusion of the mass, and consequently the closer aggregation of the particles.

When we regard the difficulties of the process by which the beautiful copies of the works of our best sculptors are produced in the potteries in a material closely resembling marble in its external characters, and even superior to it in its power of resisting the action of corroding substances, we cannot but regard the skill and industry to which the present state of Statuary Porcelain is due, as worthy of the highest praise.

Wedgwood appealed to high Art for assistance in making creations of the truly beautiful familiar. With Wedgwood appears to have died the spirit which actuated him ; and until a comparatively recent period, Art appeared to fancy itself degraded by any association with the economy of manufacture. By the energy, however, of several of our most extensive potters, among whom Mr. Copeland and Messrs. Minton deserve especial mention, a new style of material has been given to the public who, appreciating the improvement, have stimulated the manufacturer to further exertions ; and the spirit of Wedgwood, could it revisit the earth, would rejoice in the restoration of that union of Art and Manufacture which he made the labour of his life.

In the perfection of the sculptor's Art we have certainly the realisation of the highest powers of the creative faculty. As it is the most difficult, so is it the most sublime of human attainments, and the "mind and music" which seem to breathe from the chiselled marble exert an influence only inferior to that of the living expression. That the creations of genius, destined as they are to pioneer the way along which mankind advance in their siege upon ignorance and superstition, should remain as isolated specimens of human power in the halls of wealth is so deeply to be regretted, that we can scarcely imagine it can any longer be allowed. The painter speaks to a world through the medium of the engraver ; why may not the sculptor teach as eloquently through the agency of his elder brother the potter ?

Notwithstanding the beauty of many of the productions in porcelain statuary, the difficulties, arising in particular from contraction, at present prevent its taking that elevated ground which evidently belongs to it. But the well-known industry of the British labourer in any Art—the restless desire to excel, which distinguishes the manufacturers of Great Britain—will, we are certain, before any prolonged period, achieve that correctness which will at once place in *vraisemblance* the works of the best artists in the hands of an appreciating public.

We hope in our next article to enter carefully into an examination of the many interesting productions of Messrs. Minton, which come naturally under our consideration, together with the analogous manufactures of Messrs. Singer and others.

We feel it a duty we owe to all, to explain at once that in these articles on the Applications of Science we have the most earnest desire to give with correctness the merit of every discovery and ingenious adaption to the rightful owner of it. As this is often a subject of dispute notwithstanding our care, it may sometimes seem we err ; but ever open to correction, we trust to give offence to none. Between the merits of the productions of rival manufacturers we will not attempt any decision, but we hope fairly and honestly to represent the best points of all. To our numerous applications to manufactures connected with "Artificial Stone," we have received the most prompt replies, and, in general, the desired information. To all we express our sincere obligations, but in particular we acknowledge the assistance received from Mr. Battam and from Mr. Blashfield.

In every manufactory there is a certain amount of valuable information which may be given to the world with advantage without at all trenching on those private processes and modes of manipulation with which, as personal property, we have no concern. The manufacturer may furnish to the experimentalist many suggestive instances, and the man of science at the same time give to the manufacturer such knowledge as may serve to economise his material and increase his profits, and both supply matter of importance and popular interest to the public. Our endeavour is to unite these objects, and with the friendly aid of all parties we do not doubt of succeeding.

ROBERT HUNT.

Staffordshire Advertiser
11th October 1851
Extract from A History of Pottery

STATUARY PORCELAIN.

One of the branches of the manufacture of porcelain in which British industry and art has of late years had the start of the continent is statuary porcelain. This has been introduced within the last six or seven years by some of the enterprising Staffordshire establishments, and principally by those of Messrs. Copeland and Minton, who dispute the priority of its invention. It is now, however, fabricated in almost all the great Staffordshire works, and numerous specimens will be seen in the Exhibition among the collections exhibited by Messrs. Copeland, Minton, Boote, Meigh, Keys, and Mountford, Rose, Bell, &c. The Duchess of Sutherland, to whose magnificent patronage the local manufacture of Staffordshire is so deeply indebted, was one of the first to perceive the capabilities of this material, and to encourage its extension and use. Gibson, the eminent sculptor, having his attention attracted to it by her Grace, declared it to be the next best material to marble, and expressed an earnest desire that some of his own works should be reproduced in this new form. By the permission of the Council of the Royal Academy a reduced copy of his "Narcissus" was accordingly made at the manufactory of Alderman Copeland.

Nothing can be more interesting or beautiful than the process of producing this imitation of sculpture. Since its first introduction, like all other novelties in the arts, it has undergone great changes and improvements. The statuary material was at first limited to a thin superficial coating laid upon a more common body. At present, however, the article is composed of one homogeneous mass of statuary porcelain. In this respect it is superior to the article first fabricated, but the process is much more difficult and liable to fracture, owing to the much greater degree of contraction which takes place in the oven. The linear contraction of this material in the process of baking is about one fourth, so that a figure when moulded four feet high and put into the oven comes out only three feet high. The actual contraction of bulk corresponding to this linear contraction is more than one-half. The baked materials therefore are included in less than one-half the space occupied by the unbaked.

The process of fabrication is as follows :—The material being well mixed and rendered perfectly homogeneous, and the water combined with it being uniformly diffused through it by the most perfect kneading, it is reduced by dilution to the consistency of thick cream. This liquid, which is technically called "slip," is poured into the mould, which is formed of plaster of Paris or gypsum, and allowed to remain there long enough for the plaster, which is a porous and bibulous material, to absorb the water from that part of the slip which is in contact with the surface of the mould. The consequence is, that after the lapse of a certain time the mould is coated with a solid lining of the statuary clay of uniform thickness, within which lining the remainder of the liquid slip from which the water has not been absorbed is included. This liquid is then poured out of the mould, the solid coating of statuary clay remaining in the mould. The mould is then opened, and the hollow cast taken out of it.

Since the absorption of the water by the gypsum will be more or less, according to the length of time the slip is allowed to remain in the mould, a greater or less thickness may be given within practical limits to the solid shell of clay which forms the object produced. If the slip be immediately poured out, a coating will remain not thicker than an egg shell ; but, on the other hand, the thickness of which it is susceptible is limited by the point at which the plaster mould becomes saturated with the water imbibed from the clay.

We may observe here that a beautiful and interesting application of this process is presented in the fabrication of the extraordinary thin and light articles of porcelain called on the continent "muslin porcelain." An article, such as a cup, of this kind is fabricated in the following manner :—

A cavity corresponding exactly in form with the proposed cup is made in a block of plaster of Paris.This cavity is then filled with the creamy slip already described, which is allowed to remain in it for a few seconds, after which it is discharged from it. In this short interval, however, a certain degree of absorption has taken place, and the surface of the cavity remains covered with a thin coating of the dry porcelain clay. When this hardens, it is easily detached from the mould and forms a cup of an extraordinary degree of tenuity. The handles and other projecting parts are made in separate moulds by the means above described with reference to objects of sculpture.

To return to the subject of sculpture, it is necessary to explain that a figure or group is cast in a considerable number of separate moulds, each separate part of the figure or group being separately and independently cast. In some instances as many as fifty moulds are required for a single group.

The cast taken from each of these moulds is first retouched, the seams produced by the junctions of the mould being cleaned off by scraping the superfluous matter with a knife. The several parts of the figure or group are then united, each being placed and maintained in its proper position—a process of the greatest difficulty, and requiring the most consummate dexterity in the operator. The parts are united by applying slip to the surfaces in contact, but the clay being in this state extremely tender and friable, the weight of the projecting parts would be more than the cement used for joining them together is capable of resisting. After the figure or group is well dried in the air, it is placed in "saggars," a name given to the props which are placed under every part of it, so that it is well and evenly sustained.

All the supports are made of the same material as the object itself, so that all undergo the same shrinkage in the oven. It is evident that the slightest inequality of contraction in the baking, between the figure or group and its supports, or between different parts of the figure, compared one with the other, would destroy the nicer definitions of outline and proportion, and cause a distortion which, even though it were minute in amount, would take away all value from the article.

When it is considered that perfect uniformity of contraction not only requires homogeneity of the material, absolute uniformity in the diffusion of the water which it has absorbed, and which in the process of baking must be expelled from it, but also the most absolute uniformity of temperature round all parts of the figure or group during the process of baking, it is truly wonderful how the artistic perfection of such an object can ever be preserved. Nevertheless, such is the consummate skill brought to bear on this beautiful manufacture, that in good specimens there is not the slightest discoverable distortion or defect of form or outline.

These observations will be fully borne out by a reference to any of the finer groups presented in the Exhibition, such, for example, as the Ino and Bacchus after Foley, or the Narcissus and Venus after Gibson. Bearing in mind what has been just explained, the visitor cannot fail to regard with profound interest many of the objects exhibited in this department, which, indeed, are so numerous, that we find it difficult to select from among them those which may be considered most deserving of notice.

The group of Ino and Bacchus has been taken from an original marble by J.H. Foley, R.A., now in possession of the Earl of Ellesmere. The reduction of this statue was effected by Cheverton's process.

The figure of Sappho, three feet high, from the original marble of W. Theed, is entitled to attention, were it only for its extraordinary magnitude—a circumstance which immensely enhanced the difficulties and hazards of its execution. The original of this figure is the property of Prince Albert.

The following will also be found worthy of examination :—

The Indian Girl and the Nubian, by Cumberworth ; the Prodigal's Return and Rebecca, by W. Theed ; a Venus. by J. Gibson, R.A. ; a bust of Juno (colossal), from the antique ; the Goatherd, by R. J. Wyatt, R.A. ; Sabrina, by W. C. Marshall, R.A. ; a Dancing Girl, by W. C. Marshall, R.A. ; Innocence, by J. H. Foley, R.A. ; and Narcissus, by J. Gibson, R.A. (the three last executed for the Art Union of London as prize statuettes) ; Godiva, by M'Bride, executed for the Art Union of Liverpool ; an equestrian statuette of Emanuel Phillibert, Duke of Savoy, by the Baron Marochetti ; her Royal Highness the Princess Alice as Spring, the Princess Royal as Summer, the Prince Alfred as Autumn, and the Prince of Wales as Winter, from the original models by Mrs. Thorneycroft, executed for her Majesty.

The large tripod for a conservatory, which will be seen in Alderman Copeland's collection, claims to be the largest work hitherto attempted in statuary porcelain. It is from an original design by T. Battam, an artist connected with the establishment.

It is impossible to contemplate this collection of imitation of statuary without being struck with the value of this branch of manufacture as a means of disseminating in a suitable material the great works of ancient and modern art, and placing them under the eye of the public in a manner and to an extent which could be accomplished by no means hitherto known. It is probable that this branch of manufacture will be to sculpture what engraving has been to painting, but with a much closer affinity, colour and texture being added to design.

THE PORCELAIN IN THE EXHIBITION.

The British department of the Exhibition is extremely rich in ornamental porcelain, and although no great novelty of manufacture is present, many improvements of detail worthy of notice will be found.

A dessert service is exhibited by Messrs. Minton and Co., which is original in its design and novel in its principal features of ornamentation. The combination of statuary porcelain, which is the hard species, with the coloured and gilded porcelain, which is the tender species, is here attempted, and gilding on statuary porcelain has been also successfully accomplished.

The turquoise ground on this porcelain is very little inferior to that of the old Sèvres.

This colour resists the strongest vegetable and most of the mineral acids. The service consists of 116 pieces, the principal of which are two Sowerstands *[sic]*, with figures representing the four seasons, two wine-coolers, with hunting groups, and two oval baskets, with oriental figures. Several of the pieces are supported by figures in statuary porcelain, with fanciful designs, and the plates, 72 in number, are perforated and richly ornamented.

This service has been purchased by her Majesty, and at the close of the Exhibition is to be sent to Vienna. It is said to be intended as a present to the Emperor, and will serve as a specimen of what our manufacturers can do in this department.

Among the articles in statuary porcelain purchased in the Exhibition by her Majesty are the equestrian figures of the Amazon (after Feuchères), and Theseus, Flora, and Temperance, (from bronzes in the possession of the Duchess of Sutherland), and Love restraining Wrath, an original group.

Another striking example of the combination of statuary with painted porcelain is presented in the Parnassus vase, exhibited by the same manufacturers, the *bas relief* illustrating Apollo and the Muses.

Several vases will be observed in the Copeland collection of novel design, executed in imitation of pearls and gems, inlaid in gold, and executed in coloured enamel.

The following articles, exhibited by the same manufactory, well merit attention :—Large porcelain vase, with blue and gold enrichments and wreaths of flowers ; pair of large vases, Etruscan form, 28 inches high and 26 wide, *bleu de Roi* ground and ornamentation, with green scroll on burnished gold.

The progress made by the British manufacturers in imparting colours to fine porcelain is manifested in a striking manner by numerous services and ornamental objects, which will be easily recognised in the collections exhibited. We would especially direct attention to the following :—

A set of vases, with a Rose du Barry ground, chased gold panels, wreaths of flowers, and musical emblems.

A large copy of the Warwick vase, with *bleu de Roi* ground, the embossment in silver and gold, chased and burnished.

A pair of vases, "Queen's colour" ground, richly decorated with panels of raised and chased gold, imbedded with pearls, and having landscapes within the panels.

Several vases of novel design, executed in imitation of pearls, and gems, inlaid in gold and ornamented in coloured enamels.

Among the colours in which great excellence has been attained are, a strong and brilliant green, a cobalt blue, *bleu de Roi,* and the tint which has been denominated "Queen's colour." As illustrating these we may mention—

An assortment of dessert plates with various designs ; a set with the royal arms emblazoned in the centre, with foliated scroll border, and the royal cipher ; a set with Spanish views ; a set with turquoise band and wreath of pansies ; and a set with varieties of fruit in the centre, the blossoms and foliage forming the border. The two latter sets have been purchased by the Duchess of Sutherland.

One of the circumstances worthy of remark connected with the collection of porcelain exhibited by British industry is the various and unexpected uses to which this material has been applied—uses which will certainly be still more extended and still more varied as the improvements of the art now in progress are developed.

An example of this is presented in a chimneypiece of statuary porcelain exhibited by Messrs. Minton. The advantages of this application of the material are many and obvious, among which are extreme durability, and not being liable to stains from smoke and other causes, to which marble is subject.

There are also a variety of porcelain panels, plateux *[sic]*, and slabs for the covings of fireplaces, tops of consoles, toilet and chess tables, the panels of doors and window shutters.

Among the articles of this class exhibited are panels executed by order of Prince Albert for Osborne House, shutter and furniture panels, and toilet table, with porcelain slab and porcelain panels in the door and drawers, painted with wreathes of japonica on a rustic trellis, ordered by the Duchess of Sutherland.

Some large and costly panels of this manufacture are also exhibited in connection with Mr. Featham's display of grates, and among them some jewel designs executed for the mansion of Mr. Hope, in Piccadilly.

A great variety of slabs for washstands and tables of every description are exhibited, illustrating the admirable qualities of this material.

Lastly, some of the Copeland figures were 'tinted and gilded'. Usually this referred to the tasteful addition of a lightly printed or painted bead or beads at the edge of a garment with some gilding – perhaps head and arm bands, sandal straps or a necklace. The bead might have a second pale colour added by hand as on *Venus*, while a gilded line might also be 'chased' as occurs, for example, on both Gibson's *Venus* and on *Purity* by Noble. Indeed, Venus has a bead design either printed, or expertly painted, in brown with a pale pink wash applied on the band and a pale green filled in the patterned wave bead. The chasing consists of very many single strokes across the matt gold line.

Some few figures were coloured all over with patterns applied to garments. These varied in attractiveness. I know of *Boy with Rabbit* which my father had on his table-desk at the Spode Works; this is nice. And a figure of *Maidenhood*, donated to the Spode Museum by Jenny Derwich, is particularly beautiful. *Egeria* and *Lurline*, however, seem to lose some quality by being painted. These extra colourings had to receive one or two firings for the decoration and inevitably cost more. In the first few years that statuary porcelain subjects were being sold, printed legends were applied and these, too, had to be fired. The temperature would be about 1330°-1380°F (720°-750°C).

The various compositions of Parian and other bodies

William Burton, in his book *Porcelain – a sketch of its nature art and manufacture* published in 1906, writes:

> Some of the original Parians were made from mixtures of kao-lin, felspar and glass, and these must really be considered as hybrid forms of glassy porcelain, but the best Parian bodies have been made from China-clay and felspar alone, so that they are entitled to be considered as a variety of true porcelain even though the proportions in which the ingredients are mixed vary widely from those used in the best Chinese porcelains.

He quotes Père d'Entrecolles:

> At Ching-te-Chen the finest porcelain was made of equal parts of kao-lin and Pe-tun-tse, while for an inferior kind they used four parts of kao-lin to six parts of Pe-tun-tse, and the least that could be used was one part of kao-lin to three parts of Pe-tun-tse.
>
> For the English 'Parian' body an ordinary mixture would be one part of Kao-lin to two parts of felspar, so that it comes well within the limits which Chinese are said to have used for their mixtures.
>
> It will be understood that mixtures so rich in felspar and so poor in China clay as these would reach translucence at a temperature much lower than that needed for hard-paste (true) porcelain; as a matter of fact the Parian body is sufficiently fired at about 2100°-2200°F (1150°-1200ºC) or below the temperature that is used for English bone porcelain.

This, then, means an 'ordinary' recipe of:

China clay 33%
Felspar 67%

A comparison of different bodies, therefore, is not only interesting but revealing.

	SPODE Stone China		Spode Font Body	Spode Fel-spar	COPELAND STATUARY		MINTON					PEARL Smith's recipe 1855	Pearl white
	1813	1821			Old	1855		B348		B346	B347		
					WRB		◄--- Minton Archives					---►	WRB
CLAYS	**20.68**				**29.3**	**40.0**		**44.4**					
Ball Clay	20.68	20.0	25					5.5				7.4	36.3
China Clay				36.92	29.3	40.0	41.2	38.9	52.2	42.9	38.9		
FLUXING MATERIALS	**74.02**				**65.8**	**60.0**		**55.6**					
Cornwall Stone	71.72	48.0	75		43.9			16.7				56.8	5.3
Feldspar				18.98	14.6	40.0	58.8	38.9	47.8	57.1	55.6		
Glass					7.3	6.6						7.4	
Fritt (sand fritt)					4.8	13.4							
Ironstone	2.30												
REFRACTORY MATERIALS													
Flint	5.29	32.0											
Bone Ash				44.10							5.5		18.6
					WRB	Binns							

Although the ideal recipe is said to be Felspar 2: China clay 1, it was seldom adhered to. From the details of recipes obtained from various sources, including the Minton archives (by courtesy of Minton Limited), it seems that Copelands came closer than Mintons (even so a fair way off) in their proportions of China clay to 'Fluxing materials', but Minton's recipe does not include glass nor fritt, but it does include some ball clay.

The 'old' recipe of Copelands was taken from a published list of various recipes by W.R. Binns. Unfortunately the author has found no earlier record in the Spode-Copeland archives than that entered in about 1855.

The heydays of parian were from the early 1850s to the 1880s, by which time there was so much cheap and nasty rubbish on the market that its overall popularity waned, very few new models were introduced and the product fell into virtual obscurity by the Edwardian period.

Some wares, which may have some semblance of a parian body, were 'smear glazed' in an attempt to achieve a surface comparable to the best that the industry was manufacturing. 'Smear-glazing' could be achieved either by sponging a very thin glaze on to the object and re-firing at glost temperature, or the biscuit object could be placed in a saggar which had been coated inside with glaze. When the heat melted the glaze it vaporised and some settled on the biscuit item, but not so thickly as to cause it to become glossy. It was this sort of ware which contributed to the steady decline of demand.

For many years parian remained unpopular, perhaps also because it suffered from being of the 'Victorian' age. However, in the 1960s it began to be recognised as a superb form of sculpture. I remember hearing Arthur Negus comment on its beauty and he wondered why it was so neglected when European porcelain 'Fairings' were so popular and fetching high prices. Perhaps it was Arthur Negus who pointed the way to the return to popularity – and high prices – of parian.

The Account of the manufacturing process of Statuary Porcelain as recounted by Thomas Battam and printed in the Catalogue of the Great Exhibition of 1851

The articles under the head of Statuary Porcelain, including Parian, Carrara, &c., are produced by 'casting'. As the most direct method of illustrating this process, let us suppose the object under review to be a figure or group, and this we will assume to be two feet [61cm] high in the model. The clay, which is used in a semi-liquid state, about the consistency of cream, and called 'slip', is poured into the moulds forming the various parts of the subject (sometimes as many as fifty): the shrinking that occurs before these casts can be taken out of the mould, which is caused by the absorbent nature of the plaster of which the mould is composed, is equal to a reduction of one inch and a half [3.8cm] in the height. These casts are then put together by the 'figure-maker', the seams (consequent upon the marks caused by the subdivisions of the moulds) are then carefully removed, and the whole worked upon to restore the cast to the same degree of finish as the original model. The work is then thoroughly dried, to be in a fit state for firing, as if put in the oven while damp, the sudden contraction consequent upon the great degree of heat instantaneously applied, would be very liable to cause it to crack: in the process it again suffers a further loss of one inch and a half [3.8cm] by evaporation, and it is now but one foot nine inches [53cm]. Again, in the 'firing' of the bisque oven, its most severe ordeal, it is diminished three inches [7.6cm], and is then but eighteen inches [46cm] high, being six inches [15cm], or one-fourth less than the original. Now, as the contraction should equally affect every portion of the details of the work, in order to realise a faithful copy, and as added to this contingency are the risks in the oven of being 'over-fired', by which it would be melted in a mass, and of being 'short-fired', by which its surface would be imperfect, it is readily evident that a series of difficulties present themselves which require considerable practical experience successfully to meet.

The moulds are made of plaster of Paris which, when properly prepared, has the property of absorbing water so effectually that the moisture is extracted from the clay and the ware is enabled to leave the mould, or 'deliver' with care and rapidity. Prior to use, the plaster (gypsum) is put into long troughs, having a fire running underneath them, by which means the water is drawn off and it remains in a state of soil fine powder; and if its own proportion of water be again added to it, it will immediately set into a firm compact body, which is the case when it is mixed to form the mould.

Mould Making

One of the most skilled jobs in a pottery manufactory is the preparation of the moulds in which the clay articles are formed. It is a complicated process and involves making 'back-up' moulds so that the original **Master Block** is scarcely ever used in case the detail of the **Model** should be lost or harmed by **working moulds** being made from it.

The process of mould making begins with the senior mould maker appraising the subject. The model might be made of clay, plaster of Paris, or even of some hard substance like bronze or marble. In the case of these latter materials, in order not to destroy the original model, a special procedure needs to be followed. Lumps of plaster in its soil state are put on the 'marble' statue, one at a time. The surfaces of each piece are brushed with 'size' (a soap solution) to avoid the new plaster keying on to the surface of the piece formed earlier. Each piece, when it has hardened enough, is taken off and cut smooth at the edges with a sharp knife, or scraped to render the joints to 'butt up' accurately. The new piece is then replaced in its position on the statue and the next lump of plaster is applied to it, and this procedure is followed until the whole statue is covered with the small part-sections of the plaster mould. When this has been achieved a large piece of plaster is applied to hold the individual part-moulds in their correct places and tightly together. This is, or was, called the 'matrix', or 'mother' mould. (This is a précis of the *Art-Journal* article pages 256-7, 1854.)

In order to make working moulds of a statue or group of subjects in practice the individual elements of the original model need to be moulded separately for ease of reproduction. Into this 'mother' mould, then, would be poured clay in order to form a model which could be dissected into its component parts – legs, arms, head, objects held, etc.

The head mould maker might take many days while he studies the model and decides precisely the best places to cut it. Like a butcher, he will cut it up into its component parts, but like a surgeon he must not make any mistakes; every incision must be correct. Less like a surgeon, he has enough time to consider the operation, and the effect of cutting a limb on the final appearance of the repaired figure when it is re-assembled. Having made his decision, and in the nineteenth century I believe all highly skilled pottery mould makers were males, he will carefully sever the various parts and, if of clay, place them in a damp-box to avoid them drying out.

Next he will take one part, let us say a single limb like an arm, and proceed to make a two-part mould of it. He will lay it on a bed of modelling clay (which does not dry out as quickly as potting clay) with wooden 'cottles' (in this case, flat pieces of wood) around the four sides. Clay will be added to build it up to where the widest points are as these will be where the seams occur.

The team of modellers at Copelands c.1880. John Abraham (seated), Arthur 'Spode' Birks, Francis Xavier Abraham, George Painter. Arthur Birks joined Copelands in 1842, later becoming head modeller. He retired in 1898 after fifty-six years' service.

The clay will be rendered very smooth. An extension will be added at one point through which the clay will be poured into the 'working mould'; this is called the 'spare'. The whole exposed surface is 'sized' to prevent the poured plaster from adhering to any of the prepared surfaces.

Plaster of Paris is 'blended' with water to a creamy consistency and poured all over the arm and its surrounding bed of clay. In about a minute the plaster will have set sufficiently hard for the 'cottles' to be removed and the outside of the new plaster to be scraped to a suitable shape to be handled in use. When the plaster has hardened completely the modelling clay is removed, and shallow hollows cut into the surface at several places; these are the negative 'natches' which help to register the two halves of the mould when they are put together. The arm and plaster are sponged again with size and the cottles replaced around the plaster half-mould, and freshly blended plaster poured on to the half-mould. When the plaster has set the cottles are removed, the newer part is scraped to shape and the two parts separated. An air escape 'hole' is cut into each part of the mould at the other end from the 'spare' so that when clay is poured in the air displaced may escape.

The original clay model arm is removed, the two parts put together and placed in a drying room. This, then, is the master block mould of the arm. Its only function is to enable the master case mould to be made from it in much the same way as described above; the master case mould is used to make the working block mould, and the working case moulds are made from this, and eventually the working moulds are made from the working case mould. The process is a series of positive and negative images:

Original model +
Master block mould -
Master case mould +
Working block mould -
Working case mould +
Working moulds -
Clay objects +

If this causes admiration, consider the preparation of the multi-part mould for a figure; Battam said upwards of fifty moulds were needed for *The Return of the Vintage.*

PREPARING A MULTI-PART MOULD OF A SMALL PORTRAIT BUST

The actual work could take up to two or more weeks, so an old mould in the Spode Museum Trust's Collection was used to enable a simulated reconstruction of the process to be illustrated.

A rubber compound was poured into the existing mould in order to provide the *model*. This was laid into the lower half of the completed mould to simulate it being laid in a bed of modelling clay (Figure 1). A *cottle* of clay (like a wall) was placed around the top of the head to make a part-mould section for the top of the forehead and the front of the hair (Figure 2). A solution of soft soap and water (*size*) was applied so that the new plaster would not adhere to it nor to the existing plaster mould. Plaster of Paris was then poured in (Figure 3). When this was set sufficiently, the clay cottle was peeled away gently (Figures 4 and 5), and while the plaster was still quite soft the new section was shaped by scraping away the surplus (Figure 6).

The new section was removed very gently and replaced to check the fit (Figure 7) and then checked to see that the features of the hair were correct (Figure 8). Further scraping was necessary to ensure it fitted with the other sections (Figure 9) and it still was too big (Figure 10) so more scraping was necessary until it was of the correct size and considered a perfect fit (Figure 11). (If the model had been laid in a bed of clay in the usual way, there would not be a *rigot* at this stage. The *rigot* is the trough or ditch-like groove surrounding the bust which is provided for any surplus clay slip to escape into.) The reader is now asked to visualise the same procedure being followed for each separate mould section which would butt up to the first one, or next one until all the separate sections formed the whole side. When all the five side mould sections, or part-moulds, had been made, the top part-mould would be *run* (i.e. the plaster would be poured on to the remaining surface of the bust): at each stage the exposed parts are brushed with soft soap *size*. Figure 12 gives an idea of how this appears as this part is replaced. It will be seen that all the frontal features and the chest are included in this top part-mould. At this stage, small round hollows are carved into the lower outer casing and the top part-mould; these are called *natches*, and when the upper outer mould casing is *run,* they will be reproduced as positive *natches*, or bumps; they were to keep the various parts firmly secured together (Figure 13).

To make the other part-moulds in the other side, the whole process is repeated until the whole complex mould is completed.

After all the part-moulds have been made and both the outer mould casings completed, the *rigot* is cut into the upper and lower part-moulds (see Figure 9). When the clay slip is poured into the mould, this rigot will be filled. After the mould is taken apart, these thickened strips of clay will break off the cast bust to leave a much thinner seam than would be the case if they were not present.

A full description of *Making of Plaster of Paris repetitions of statues* is published in the *Art-Journal* of 1854, pages 256-7. This deals with large, life-size reproductions of marble statues, and is not fully applicable to the much smaller figures and busts made in statuary porcelain described above.

Figure 1. The model in half of the mould assembly.

Figure 2. A clay wall round the part of the head needing the next mould section.

Figure 3. Plaster of Paris poured into this section.

Figure 4. Removing the clay wall after the plaster has set sufficiently.

Figure 5. The newly run section revealed.

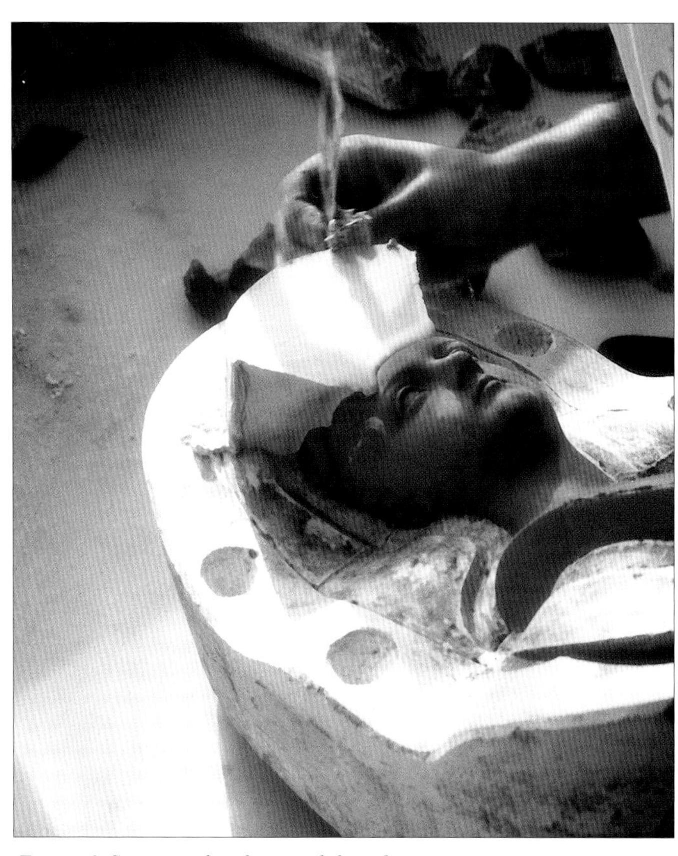

Figure 6. Scraping the plaster while soft.

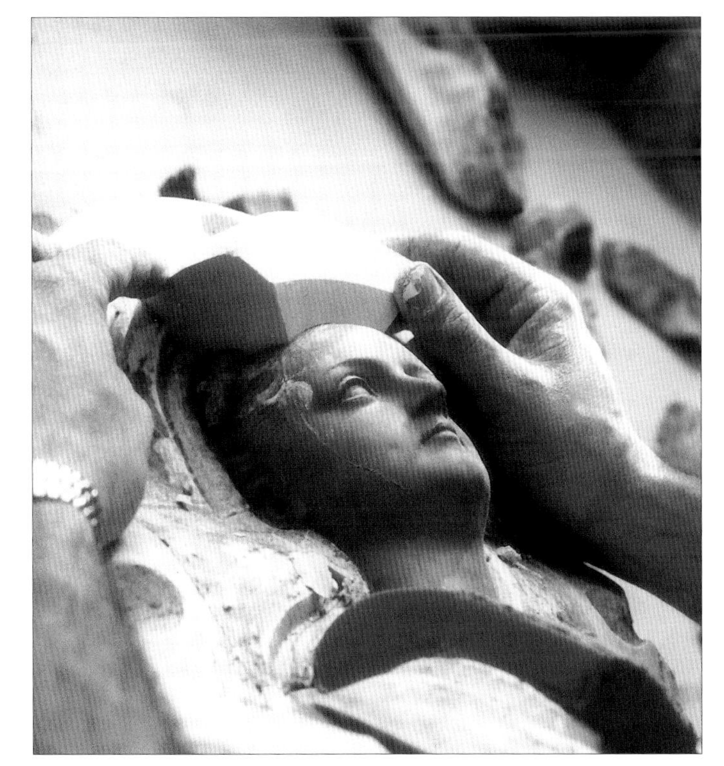

Figure 7. Checking the fit after scraping to shape.

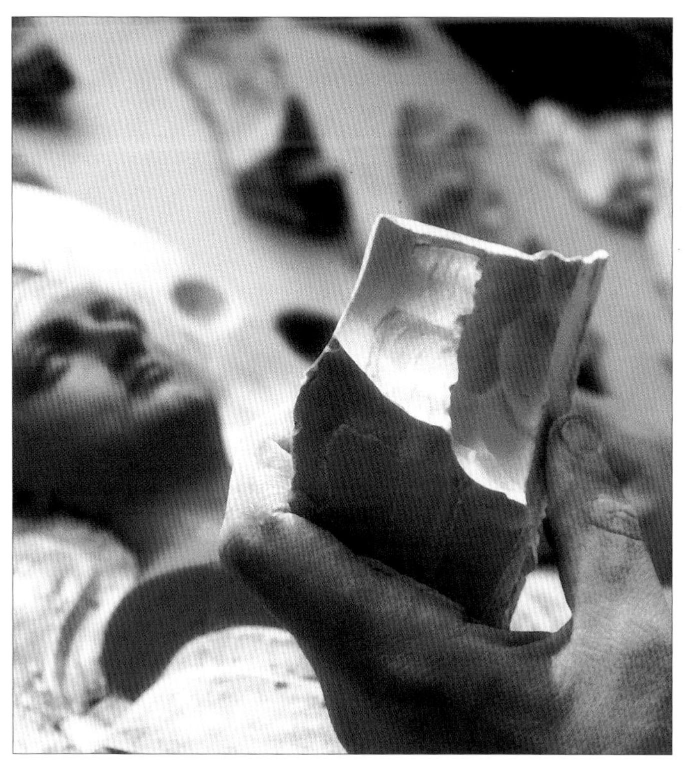

Figure 8. The new mould section.

Figure 9. The new section – still too big. Notice the 'rigot', the V-shaped trough around the bust.

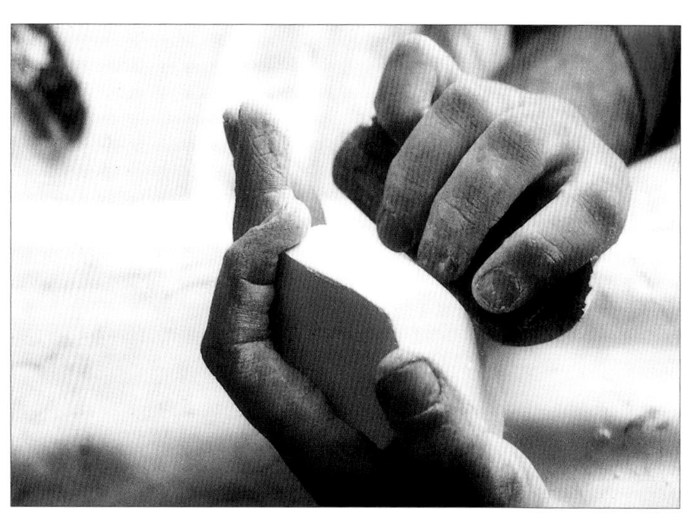

Figure 10. Further scraping to fit.

Figure 11. The new mould section in place, now the correct size and shape.

Figure 12. Placing the top, face, mould.

Figure 13. Putting on the outer casing to hold all the individual mould sections in place.

Making a portrait bust

Using a very old multi-part mould of an unidentified bust retained in the Spode Museum Trust's Collection a simulated process was re-enacted.

First, the parts of the mould were assembled (Figures 1-3). The completed mould, suitably held together with thick rubber bands, was positioned on the rack and clay *slip* poured into it through the hole left at one end (Figures 4-5). After about fifteen minutes, by which time the plaster mould had absorbed much water from the slip to form a thick deposit of clay on the inside surface, the mould was tipped so that surplus slip could be poured away (Figure 6). The mould was then left to drain (Figure 7).

Half an hour later, when the cast bust had stiffened sufficiently to be handled, the mould was taken apart, piece by piece (Figures 8-9). The front portion of the bust was now revealed (Figure 10). The mould was turned upside down, using a flat plaster *bat* to hold together the individual part moulds around the front section. This enabled the more intricately modelled hair to have its part-moulds removed very carefully (Figures 11-12). The cast bust was removed gently from the mould (Figure 13). The ceramic bust now lay beside the part of the back mould which formed the hair (Figure 14).

Figure 15 shows the rubber 'original' for comparison. Note the large *spare* at the base. This is for the hole through which the clay slip is poured and, if necessary as the water is absorbed, more slip to be added. Moreover, the hole needs to be large enough to allow surplus slip to be drained away; if too small the thickening deposit could block the hole.

The bust was then dried, the seams caused by the joins in the mould parts *fettled* (that is trimmed and smoothed level) and placed for the first firing.

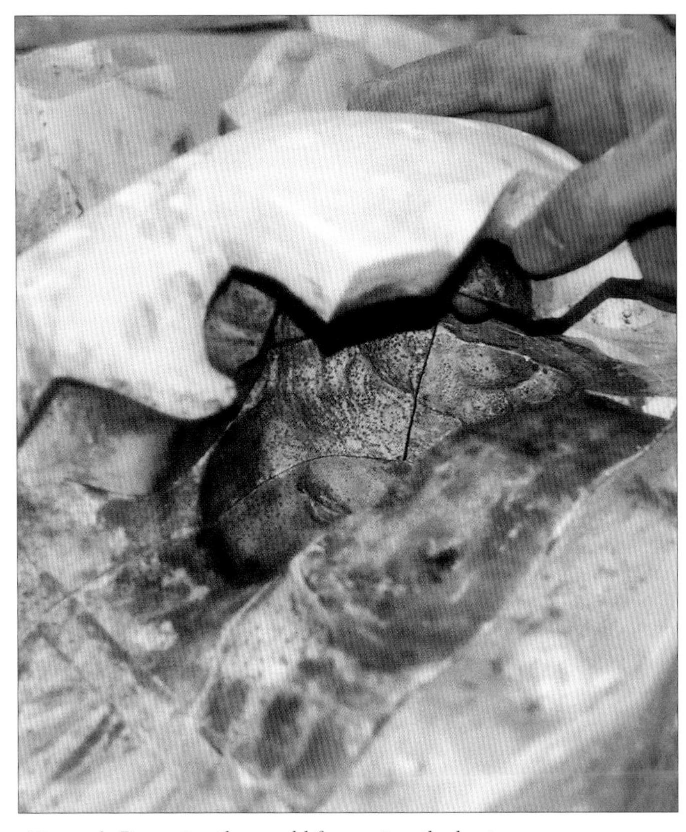

Figure 1. Preparing the mould for casting the bust.

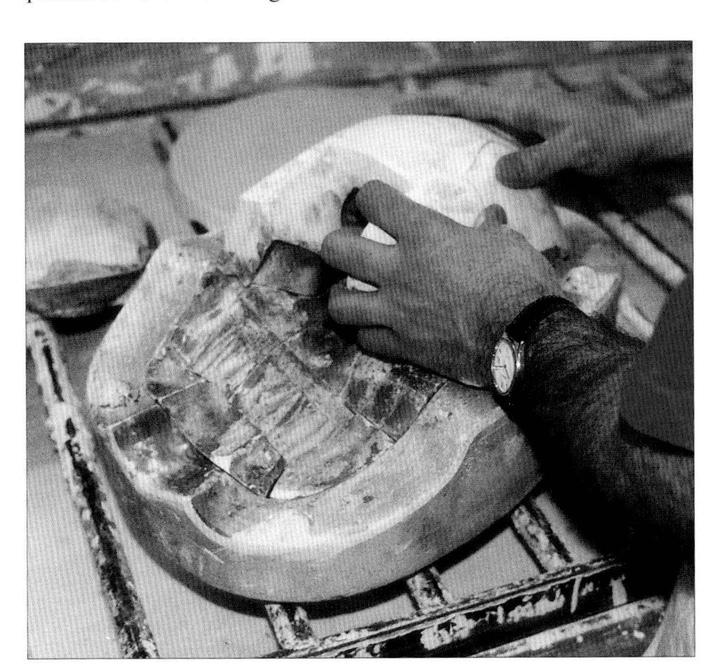

Figure 2. Placing the individual mould sections into position.

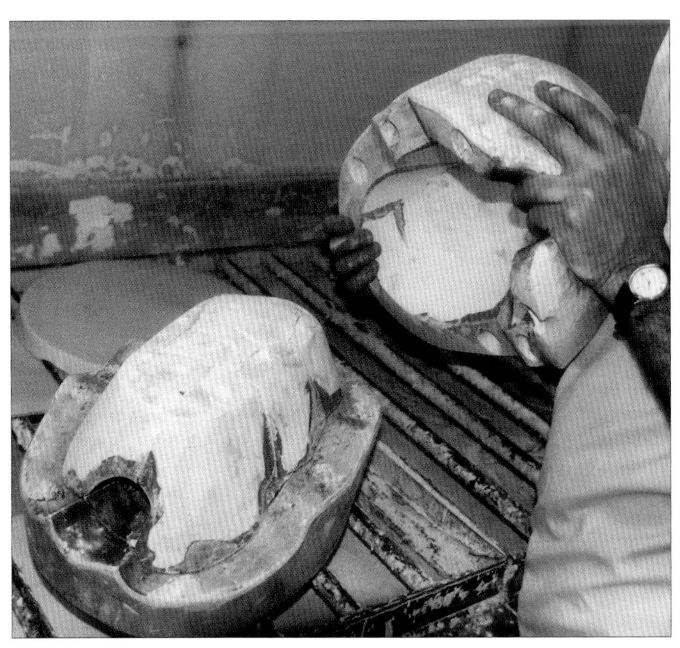

Figure 3. About to place the outer casing over the individual moulds.

Figures 4-7. Pouring in the slip and subsequent draining of the surplus.

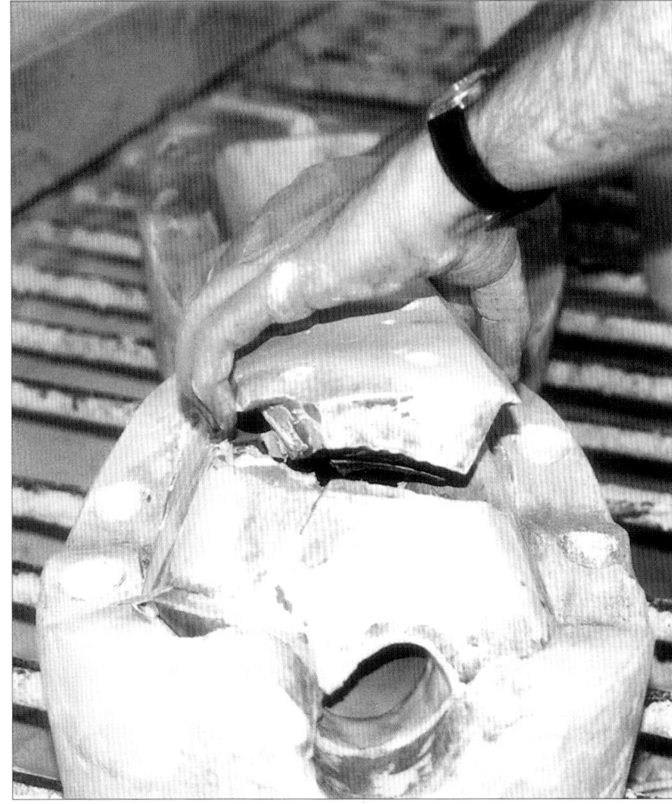

Figures 8-10. Removal of individual moulds after taking off the outer casing (Figure 8).

Figures 11 and 12. Removing individual mould sections from the back of the bust.

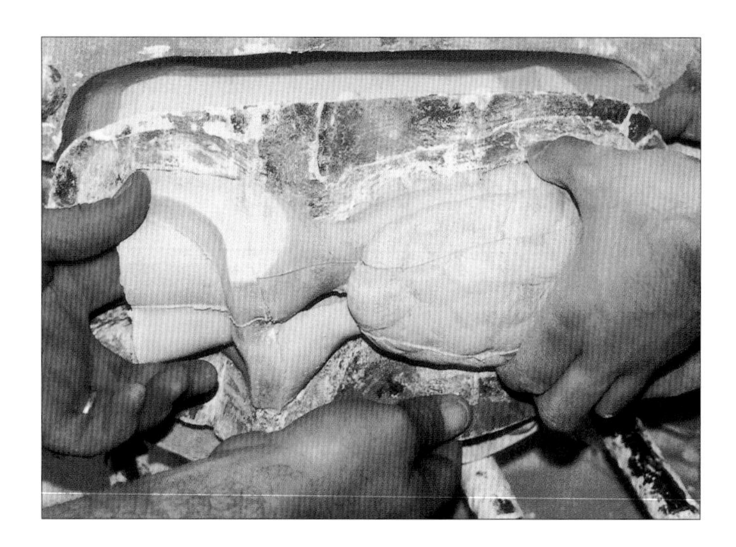

Figure 13. Gently withdrawing the case from the mould.

Figure 14. The cast bust with the mould for the back.

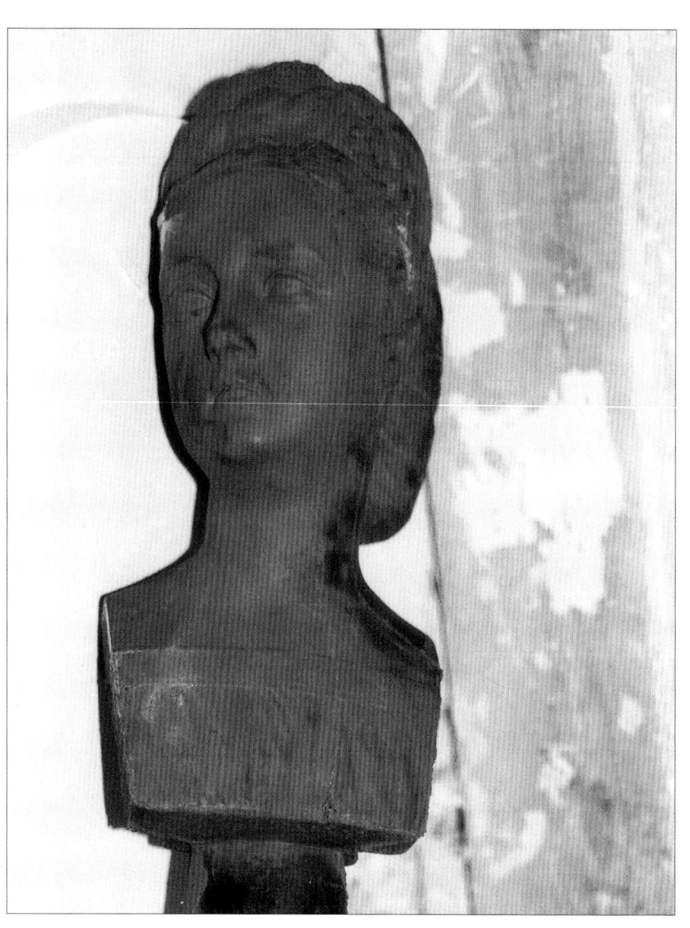

Figure 15. The 'original' bust.

The figure maker at Copelands, August 1899. Sometimes he might be called the repairer because he would rub down seams and 'stop' any cracks after the first firing.

The making of a ceramic figure

The lack of old figure moulds on the Spode manufactory has meant that it was impossible to re-enact the process of slip casting, sticking up and placing an actual figure.

However, in 1952 I took a series of photographs of the manufacturing process of making a fine bone china figure of a Derby figure (from moulds derived from those bought by W.T. Copeland in 1852). These figures are very much smaller than most parian ones but the principle is much the same.

1. A hollow plaster-of-Paris mould was filled with clay 'slip'.
2. The mould absorbed water rapidly allowing a deposit of clay to build up on the inside surface of the mould. When this deposit had acquired the correct thickness, the surplus slip was poured back into the jug.
3. Some time was allowed to elapse to permit the clay cast to stiffen sufficiently. The mould was opened and the piece removed. Each individual piece was made in its own mould by the same method. Arms, legs, head, supporting base and other parts, each required its own mould
4. All the parts which go to make up the figure had the seams smoothed and then were laid out carefully. The point of contact of each piece was trimmed to ensure a perfect fit.
5. The figure maker fitted together the various parts, using a little thick slip as an adhesive and brushing away any surplus that had squeezed out. Much of the charm of the finished figure depended upon his work: the angle of the head or the position of the arm was entirely due to his skill. The figure maker shown here was Arthur Steel.
6. Petals and leaves, if required, were moulded freely from soft clay using the fingers stroking the clay in the palm of the hand. A piece of textured fabric could give surface modelling; a piece of metal gauze could be used to give the impression of the centre of a flower.
7. Petals were assembled to form the complete flower.
8. The completed figure was allowed to dry very thoroughly. The slightest trace of moisture could cause cracking during the firing process.
9. When it came to the placing of the figure it was usually necessary to prop certain parts. The figure was placed on a 'bat', or base, of clay of the same kind as that of which the figure was made. Strips of clay were made, dried, and tipped with 'slop flint' (a slurry of flint powder and water) and fixed as props to support arms and prevent them from drooping during the firing. The flint was to prevent the props from sticking to the figure. All statuettes were placed upright; busts were placed flat and bedded in fine iron-free sand. The ware was placed in saggars for stacking in the oven.
10. The first firing would have taken place in the cooler part of the biscuit earthenware oven or, possibly, in the glost oven in which the temperature would have been about 1920°F (1050°C).
11. On the piece being 'drawn' (i.e. removed) from the oven it would be seen that the seams, that is the parts of the clay where the mould joints occurred, had 'fired up' or expanded, to form ridges. Also, the whole piece would have contracted about one fourth of its original clay size. The piece would have been taken back to the figure maker who made it and he would rub down the seams and any other excrescences with an abrasive stone so that no ridges or raised spots were apparent. This craftsman was sometimes called the 'repairer'. (A recipe for a 'rubbing stone' is 10 pounds sifted fired sand and 5 pints of slop Cornish stone fired in the earthenware biscuit oven.) Any small cracks were filled with 'stopping', a thick paste of finely ground parian biscuit with water.
12. For the second firing the piece would have been placed in the earthenware biscuit oven to be fired at about 2000°-2100°F (1100°-1150°C), and it was this extra heat that caused the feldspar to produce the exquisitely sensuous surface.

1.

2.

3.

4. 5. 6.

7. 8. 9.

13. While the clay cast was still just soft enough when removed from the mould the manufacturer's name COPELAND was impressed; also after 1870 the date mark, and possibly COPYRIGHT RESERVED. The sponsor's name, like ART UNION OF LONDON, and sculptor's name might have been in the mould so would already be impressed in the base or back of the object.

Some manufacturers might 'smear-glaze' their wares. Table ornaments, which needed to be cleaned often, might be so treated. This was achieved by placing the object in a saggar whose sides had been washed over with glaze. On being fired the glaze would vaporise and some would settle as a very thin layer upon the objects placed in the saggar.

A few ornaments were fully glazed and this glaze was very luscious in quality. Decorations were sometimes added to bottles and vases of parian. Some statuettes had added gilding in the form of bangles and the borders of drapes were 'tinted', that is a delicate pattern was hand applied in colour. Sometimes the gilded lines and bands were 'chased'; the gold was matt but a pattern of strokes was burnished to enhance the effect.

THE ART UNIONS

With special reference to Parian in general and Copeland's Statuary Porcelain in particular

If it had not been for the Art Unions in the early middle of the nineteenth century it is most probable that the introduction of parian sculpture would not have occurred. The ready availability of fine, reduced size sculptures at reasonable cost was a splendid idea. But without the publicity and promotion given, first, by the Art Union of London and followed by many others, especially the Crystal Palace Art Union, the idea could have become no more than a failed enterprise.

What was an Art Union? It was an association of people who desired to 'advance civilization by the improvement of Art'. In discussing the Crystal Palace Art Union, the *Art-Journal* in 1861 (page 53) comments:

> An Art-Union is an association which necessarily possesses, and ought always to exercise, a two-fold influence upon Art. Its office is as well to cherish and to elevate some peculiar expression of Art, as to cultivate and refine the public taste through a widely extended diffusion of genuine works of Art.

Many people enjoy a bit of a gamble and the Art Unions were really lotteries in which a member subscribed a sum of money – one guinea upwards – which entitled him or her to one chance of obtaining some work of art at the annual distribution. The Art Union purchased pictures, sculptures, lithographs and engraved prints, drawings and medals. On the evening of the distribution, subscribers assembled; their names, in alphabetical order, were each allocated a number. Round wooden tallies, each with a number inscribed upon it, were put into a large 'wheel', or wooden drum, so that there were the same number of tallies in the drum as chances in the list. Into a second drum were placed the requisite number of tallies to correspond to the number of prizes. The drums were turned and a lady from the audience drew a numbered tally from the first drum. This number was checked with the subscribers' list and the name announced to the meeting. A second lady then drew a tally from the second drum; this tally carried the value of the prize marked upon it, which was announced to the meeting.

This was the basis by which the Art Union of London was governed. It was founded in 1836, two years after The Association for the Promotion of the Fine Arts in Scotland, which was the first Art Union, founded in 1834 in Edinburgh.

Unfortunately, very little attention has been given to the history of the Art Union movement and published material is scarce. Geoffrey Godden gave a good, if brief, account in the September 1961 issue of *Apollo* (pages 68-70).

So far as Copeland's Parian is concerned, it was the initial support of the Art Union of London in commissioning fifty reduced sculptures of John Gibson's *Narcissus* in 1844 which really promoted parian and set it on its highly successful course. These statuettes were distributed at the Art Union's 1846 annual meeting, after important improvements to the formula had been made. The price paid to Messrs. Copeland & Garrett for these fifty pieces was £150, £3 each. The Art Union ordered a further fifty copies and commissioned J.H. Foley to reduce his sculpture of *Innocence* for manufacture by Copeland for the 1847 distribution. The earliest examples of these two subjects have transfer-printed inscriptions applied inside their bases, but quite soon these gave way to the impressed mark COPELAND. Whilst examples of Copeland & Garrett's Statuary Porcelain were exhibited at the National Exhibition of British Industrial Art in Manchester from December 1845 to January 1846, the pieces which really led the way were these two sculptures sponsored by the Art Union of London.

Several more subjects were sponsored by the Art Union of London from Copeland and their success encouraged the support of other art unions, as well as building the popularity of sculptures and ornamental objects which were sold directly to the public through the retail trade.

Parian subjects commissioned from Copeland by the Art Union of London:

1844	*Narcissus* by John Gibson, RA, reduced by E.B. Stephens
1846	*Dancing Girl Reposing* by W.C. Marshall
1847	*Innocence* by J.H. Foley
1849	*Venus* by John Gibson
1855	*Stepping Stones* by Edward Wyon
1857	*Venus & Cupid* after Pradier
1861	*Clytie* reproduced by C. Delpech from the Roman marble bust
1862	Bust of *Apollo* from the Roman marble
1862	*Go to Sleep* by Joseph Durham
1863	Bust of *Alexandra, HRH the Princess of Wales* by Mary Thornycroft

1865 Bust of *HRH the Prince of Wales,* after Morton Edwards
1871 Bust of *HRH the Princess Louise* by Mary Thornycroft
1873 *Mending the Net* by Edward Wyon
1879 Bust of *HRH the Princess Alice* by Mary Thornycroft

There were many other art unions founded in Great Britain, some of which commissioned Copeland to manufacture pieces for them. The Association for the Promotion of the Fine Arts in Scotland (FAA) commissioned the following:

1853 Group of *Sir Walter Scott* by John Steell
1857 *Corinna* by W. Brodie
1866 *John Wilson* by Steell
1870 Statuette of *Ruth* by Brodie

The Art Union of Liverpool commissioned a statuette of *Italian Boy* in about 1851 and an equestrian figure of *Lady Godiva*, sculpted by John McBride, in 1860. The Royal Art Union of Ireland, in 1847, had Copeland reproduce in statuary porcelain the figure of *The Return Dove*, sculpted by James Farrell.

The art union which supported ceramic enterprise in the greatest degree was The Crystal Palace Art Union. Founded in 1858 by Thomas Battam, one-time Art Director of Messrs. Copeland & Garrett, it concentrated on commissioning and promoting parian sculptures and other fictile (that is, ceramic) objects until it ceased its operation in 1882. In 1865 it changed its name to The Ceramic and Crystal Palace Art Union.

Sculptures commissioned by the Crystal Palace Art Union from Copeland were:

1858 *Nymph preparing for the Bath,* or *Nymph untying her Sandal* by John Gibson
1859 Busts of *Ophelia, Lesbia* and *Miranda* by W.C. Marshall
1860 Bust of *Purity* by M. Noble
1861 Bust of *The Bride* by R. Monti
1861 Bust of *William Shakespeare* by Raffaele Monti
1861 Bust of *Enid, The Fair and the Good* by F.M. Miller
1861 Bust of *Oenone* by W.C. Marshall
1862 *The Toilet* by W.C. Marshall
1862 *The Sleep of Sorrow and the Dream of Joy* by R. Monti
1863 Bust of *Viola* by F.M. Miller
1864 *L'Allegro* by E.H. Baily

The bust of *The Bride* is dated 1861, although *The Mother,* commissioned in 1871 as a companion to *The Bride*, was commissioned by the Ceramic and Crystal Palace Art Union. Busts are known with both CPAU and C&CPAU inscriptions.

A number of busts of members of the Royal Family were also commissioned by the CPAU:

1855 *HM Queen Victoria* and *HRH the Prince Albert* by Joseph Durham
1863 *HRH the Prince of Wales* by Marshall Wood and *Alexandra, HRH the Princess of Wales* by F.M. Miller
1864 *HRH the late Prince Albert* and *HM Queen Victoria* by William Theed

Sculptures commissioned from Copeland by the newly named Ceramic and Crystal Palace Art Union were:

1865 *Hope* by L.A. Malempré; statuette of *Purity* by M. Noble, bust of *Milton* by Noble and bust of *Juno* by Malempré
1868 Bust of *The May Queen* by Joseph Durham
1869 *The Reading Girl* by P. MacDowell; *Sappho* by William Theed
1871 *The Flute Player* by R. Monti; *The Shepherd Boy* by Malempré;
busts of *The Mother* and *Love* by R. Monti.
1873 *Girl with Rabbit,* also called *The Pets*, by F.M. Miller; bust of *The Hop Queen* by J. Durham
1874 *The First Bath of the Season* by Chesneau; *Sweet Apples* and *Wild Flowers* by Malempré
1875 *The Angel and the Flowers, Happy Dream,* and *Venus* by Malempré
1876 Bust of *Elaine* and statuette of *Mignon* by Malempré
1877 *The Cottage Girl, The Strawberry Girl* and *The Guardian Angel* by Malempré
1879 *Mary, Queen of Scots* by Malempré.

Whereas the Crystal Palace Art Union included photographs and stereographs, its principal items were of parian, both sculptures and ornamental objects being included.

The *Art-Journal*, in its article on page 53 of 1861, states that 'the number of the subscribers of the second season, which did not very greatly exceed the 5,000 of the first season...' and regrets that this first season's numbers were not increased by many more subscribers. Nevertheless, this was a good total. In 1865 the Council decided to offer only objects in ceramic and so changed the name of the organisation to The Ceramic and Crystal Palace Art Union.

However, by 1882 the number of subscribers had fallen to 224! The Council of the Art Union decided to cease operations so that the meeting on 25 November 1882 was the last. The Report to that meeting recorded *at least 20,000 examples of Ceramic Art* had been circulated during the twenty-five years of its founding in 1858.

There are some documents in the Spode Museum Trust's archives which date from August 1880 that suggest that there were difficulties arising between W.T. Copeland & Sons and the Ceramic and Crystal Palace Art Union.

A list of C & CPAU works returned to the Works in five packages, valued at £125.19.10, is dated 22 August 1880. There is no explanation for the return of these items, but it may have something to do with the relinquishment of the premises of 160 New Bond Street by W.T. Copeland & Sons who moved to 12 Charterhouse Street.

On 19 August 1881 WTC & Sons wrote to the Council of C & CPAU:

> Having referred to Mr. Copeland your letter of the 5th which states *I enclose statement of the account up to March as handed to Battam & Co. to collect* _ he writes us that *CPAU has nothing whatever to do with Battam & Co.* This is corroborated by Mr. F. Battam's letter of 1st April as also by our books here...

WTC is claiming £86.1.11 that is outstanding. Then, a note that a list of

> The following Works are wanting according to Stock taken on our removal from Bond Street as per list sent you on 7th June. Total £37.14.4. Charged to C & CPAU 23/8/81.

A list of C & CPAU Stock held at Stoke-upon-Trent Works, dated 10/11/1881, is valued at £328.2.10. It seems that the Art Union would have ordered these goods to be manufactured but that demand had been less than expected and so these items remained at the manufactory.

Copeland, having expended money on their production, which was exclusive to the Art Union, found themselves out of pocket and so decided to unload some of them in a market a long way away – New Zealand.

Battam & Co. wrote to W.F.M. Copeland on 13 July 1882 enclosing a copy of a letter received from the old agent, Messrs. Upton & Co. at Auckland, New Zealand:

> Dear Sir, A severe blow was struck at your business in Auckland towards the latter end of last year by the sale there by Auction of a number of your Society's works. Amongst others busts of Prince & Princess of Wales, statuettes Musidora & L'Allegro – as we represent to subscribers that these works are
> 1st Copyright
> 2nd only to be obtained through the Society
> 3rd That all imperfect Copies are destroyed.
> We need not do more than point out to you that the sale by Auction of your works will destroy not only your reputation & ours but will cause a fall off of subscribers, at one blow.
> The Auctioneers name was Mr Lewis, we may add that 6 copies of Musidora were sold much under the Subscribers Value & the matter was brought under our notice by some of your oldest Subscribers.
> We are, yours faithfully, Upton & Co.

15 July. W.T. Copeland & Sons' reply included the comment: 'We frequently have asked you (per Mr. F Battam) whether you could dispose of the "Imperfect" and "Ordered but not taken" works made for you. But they were always refused. We have always reserved to ourselves the right of disposing out of the United Kingdom any such works as above described, & this we have frequently done and we cannot see how the disposing of inferior works could injure you in the subscriptions for perfect articles. Will you take these seconds? Shall be glad for you to do so.'

28 Sept. Battam replied: '…it is the first intimation from you that you considered you possessed the right to disposal of the imperfect copies of the copyright works produced by you from the models furnished to you by the Society. On the contrary it was distinctly understood that all the Models were to be made exclusively for the Society and that copies of the same could only be obtained by subscribing for them direct to the Society or of the appointed agents as expressly announced on the official Prospectuses, and on the faith of this understanding the Models have been entrusted to your firm from time to time ****** the long period of over 23 years. I have to express the Council's surprise and regret that it was not evident to you that the selling of the imperfect copies of the works would prove injurious to the interests of the Society and after this expression of their opinion they trust that the sale will be discontinued as they cannot give up these exclusive rights of issue of their own copyright works.'

4 Oct. W.T. Copeland & Sons: 'In reply we can only repeat that we have always reserved the right of disposing of seconds out of the United Kingdom and we have continuously practiced it. If you will take them together with those works made to order but not taken we shall be only too glad and we think this would remove every difficulty that you may see.'

13 Nov. Battam replies: 'I am in receipt of the works you have in stock. I regret to see the number is so large. I have more than once suggested when you were in want of work to apprise me and not to have works made for stock in anticipation of orders. Am I to conclude that all the works on the list are perfect, you have only marked one of them 'Angel & Flowers' as being imperfect.'

14 Nov. Copelands reply: 'I am quite surprised at yours of 13th about these works. All have been made to your order in fact the bulk you returned from Bond Street. They are all perfect to best of our knowledge. We shall be glad to receive orders to send them all to you, it being no fault of ours they being in stock. Else what are we to do with them. Look at the money lost keeping them all these years. Reply will oblige.'

16 Nov. Battam replies: '…point out that you are under a wrong impression when you say the works in stock as list were ordered by me. For some years after the first orders have been completed I have only written for copies as they were required by subscribers; my books & letters will verify this. The Bust of 'Happy Dream' is an exception; 100 copies were ordered but 50 were to be made first, and were sent, but finding it was not selected by the subscribers I did not write for a second 50. The 100 copies of 'Wild Flowers' have been supplied and only a few ordered since as they were required. We have had about 90 of the 'Sleeping Cupid'. While I feel it is only justice to myself to mention these facts, I will of course do all in my power to send orders to work off the stock from time to time.'

17 Nov. Copeland replies: 'I cannot allow yours of 16th to go unanswered. I have before me all the documents. How could we possibly have sent to Bond Street all those works which you returned unless you had in the first place ordered them from us for no one but yourself had anything to do with the ordering of C.P.A.U goods. And as regards those we had in stock here they were made to your orders or by estimate for certain quantities as arranged by letter between yourself and ourselves. So what is to be done with them. If you don't take them we must dispose of them I suppose as seconds out of the United Kingdom.'

20 Nov. F. Battam to Richard P. Copeland: 'I can only now acknowledge the receipts of yours but as soon as I can command time I shall be able to prove to you that what I have attested is true. I enclose an order for a few works to be taken from the stock which please to have sent next week I will forward another

one. I can only repeat that I will do all in my power to work off your stock…'

3 April 1883. F. Battam writes to W.T. Copeland and Sons: 'I have the pleasure to enclose cheque £47.9.0 in settlement of the account which please to return receipted. I am desired by the Chairman of the late Ceramic & C.P. Art Union to inform you that no copies are to be produced of any of the works issued by the late Society without an order either from Mr. J.H. Battam or myself. This caution is rendered necessary by the special rule laid down by the Society at its formation 25 years ago and by which it was guided throughout *"that no person should be able to obtain a copy of any of the works issued by it except by becoming a subscriber to the Institution"*.

5 April. Copelands reply: 'We beg to note in your favor of the 3rd inst. that the Ceramic & Crystal Palace Art Union no longer exists. We are therefore at a loss to understand the purport of the rest of your letter. We conceive the Society having terminated its existence its rules and regulations are no longer in force and as our interests have not been in any way considered by the Society in its closing arrangements we shall hold ourselves at perfect liberty to supply copies of all works hitherto produced by us. I am Dear Sir, yours truly, W.T. Copeland & Sons.'

Thus ends an interesting correspondence which shows the difficulties encountered when dealing with an art union.

According to the Report of the Council for the Season 1881-82 (the last) there were 224 subscribers. Of these 82 had London addresses, 56 New Zealand and 11 Australian; 68 in England, 2 in Scotland, 3 in Ireland and 2 in Wales. So it can be seen that New Zealand might not have been the best place to unload surplus stock by auction!

It is clear that the fashion for parian sculptures had passed its peak and that the market steadily declined from about 1882, or some years before, until it ceased at the start of the 1914-1918 war.

THE GREAT EXHIBITIONS

Fairs have been a feature of communities for centuries. They provide the opportunities for traders to display their wares and to sell goods. An exhibition is a display of works of art, industrial products, or items of general interest. The sort of exhibition about which I am writing enabled manufacturers and artists to display their best items and to solicit orders for delivery later. In particular it gave the general public a chance to see a huge assembly of new things which in the ordinary course of their lives they were unlikely to see or experience.

Exhibitions of this sort had been held in France for over fifty years before England tried the experiment. This was in Trafalgar Square in London in 1828. It was not a success.

The first National Exhibition of British Industrial Art was held in Manchester at the end of 1845. Copeland and Garrett had a prominent stand on which were displayed many examples of porcelain statuary (see page 19). Among the objects were the figure of *Apollo as the Shepherd Boy of Admetus*, the equestrian figures of *His Grace the Duke of Wellington* and *Emmanuel Philibert, Duke of Savoy*. A standing figure of the *Duke of Wellington* was also displayed. Several more exhibitions were held in various parts of England.

The Society of Arts held annual exhibitions of 'Specimens of recent British Manufactures & Decorative Art' at their house in the Adelphi, London. In 1848, for instance, the report, on page 9, records:

> Mr.Copeland has produced in his beautiful material called Statuary Porcelain a number of works of Art of high merit, which have the great value of rendering familiar to us at moderate cost, works of Sculpture from the hands of the highest Artists, and mark an important advance of public taste in this direction.

On page 16:

> The most important specimen of MR.COPELAND'S Statuary Porcelain is also the greatest novelty, No.212. 'The Return from the Vintage' proves that English Pottery can successfully reproduce the greatest feats of the Dresden Manufactory, whilst 210 'Innocence' in the same material, after Mr.Foley's beautiful design, shows that there is no occasion to go abroad for models.

This exhibition, which ran from 8 March to 29 April, included very many objects by Mr. W.T. Copeland.

It was in 1849 that an exhibition for the annual meeting of the Association for the Advancement of Science was held in Birmingham. Although it is probable that Copeland exhibited at this exhibition I have not discovered the catalogue. However, Geoffrey Godden in his book *Victorian Porcelain* (Barrie & Jenkins, 1961) states that:

> The Birmingham Exhibition of 1849 followed much the pattern of that in Manchester two years earlier. The Copeland firm, which was known as W.T. Copeland and Sons from 1847, continued to exhibit their statuary porcelain, or parian, and their porcelain slabs richly decorated for fireplace panels and for table tops.

It was this exhibition of 1849 which inspired Prince Albert to promote the Great Exhibition of 1851.

The Exhibition of the Works of Industry of all Nations – the Crystal Palace Exhibition of 1851 – was a real triumph. The Official Catalogue was comprehensive. Section III, Class 25, included the ceramic wares; the first entry was for Minton, followed by the entry for Copeland. These listed in detail many if not most of the individual sculptures of each manufacturer. The entry for Exhibit 2 reads (as it applies to this subject):

COPELAND, WILLIAM TAYLOR, *Stoke-upon-Trent, and 160 New Bond Street* – Manufacturer.

Works in porcelain statuary:
Group of Ino and Bacchus, by J.H. Foley, RA, from the original model in the possession of the Earl of Ellesmere. This group is represented in the annexed engraving.
Group of The Prodigal's Return, by W. Theed. This group is represented in the accompanying Plate 35.
Sabrina, by W.C. Marshall, RA. See Milton's Comus.
The Goatherd, by the late R.J. Wyatt, RA., from the original marble in the possession of the Duke of Sutherland. [Note. The correct title of this is 'Apollo as the shepherd boy of Admetus' and the sculptor's name is Wyatt.]
Venus, by John Gibson, RA.
Sappho, by W. Theed, from the original marble.
Equestrian statuette of Emmanuel Philibert, Duke of Savoy, by the Baron Marochetti. Rebecca, by W. Theed.
The Indian Girl and the Nubian Girl, by Cumberworth.
Head of Juno, life size, from the antique. The Astragali Players. The Girl with Scorpion.
Innocence, by J.H. Foley, RA. executed for the Art Union of London.
Narcissus, by John Gibson, RA. executed for the Art Union of London.

The Dancing Girl Reposing, by W.C. Marshall, executed for the Art Union of London.
Lady Godiva, by J.P. M'Bride [*sic*], executed for the Art Union of Liverpool. (See Tennyson's Godiva.)
Sir Walter Scott; reduced copy by John Steel [*sic*], RSA., from the original colossal statue on the Calton Hill, executed for the Edinburgh Association for the Promotion of the Fine Arts.
Group of Graces, and group of Cupids, as Kanephoroi.
HRH the Princess Alice, as Spring.
HRH the Princess Royal, as Summer.
HRH the Prince Alfred, as Autumn.
HRH the Prince of Wales, as Winter. The above illustrative series from the original models, executed by Mrs Thorneycroft [*sic*], for the Queen.
'The Bride' and 'The Sea Nymph'. Group of 'Paul and Virginia' by Cumberworth.
Sir Robert Peel, by Westmacott.
Sir George Bentinck, by Count D'Orsay.
Jenny Lind, by Durham.
Shakespeare [by Raffaele Monti]
The Lady Clementina Villiers, by M'Donald.
HRH the Princess Helena, by Mrs. Thorneycroft [*sic*].
Duke of Wellington, by Count D'Orsay.
Duke of Sutherland, by Francis.
Pair of Cellini vases and pedestals.
Group of 'The Return from the Vintage' consisting of seven figures.

Then follows an account of the process of manufacture written by Thomas Battam (reproduced on page 63). After that is a list of objects of which these were in parian:

Variety of vases, garden pots, and articles of ordinary use.
Ancient font, from the original in Winchester Cathedral.
The Portland jug.
Lily of the valley jug.
The acanthus garden vase.
Two wedding plateaux for supporting a bride cake: containing appropriate mottoes, and entwined wreaths of orange blossom and passiflora.

The Council Medal was awarded to Mr Herbert Minton and the Prize Medal was awarded to Mr William Taylor Copeland. However, Mr Copeland declined to accept it because he believed that it ranked as second place to the Council Medal and he was unwilling to accept second place to Minton. A comprehensive account of the controversy was written by Vega Wilkinson and was published in the *Spode Recorder* for November 1991, 'The Medal Controversy 1851' and also in *Spode – Copeland – Spode* pages 85-8. Mr Copeland did accept a Bronze Medal 'for Services'.

The Great Exhibition was an astounding success. More than six million visitors had attended, a daily average of 43,000 people. After all costs had been taken into account, a profit of £186,437 was declared. Quoting from John Allwood's *The Great Exhibitions:*

> After much discussion it was decided to use most of the surplus – after giving an award of £5,000 to Paxton – for educational purposes and particularly the purchase of 87 acres of land at South Kensington as a site for a centre for arts and sciences. Today this site houses, among others, the Victoria and Albert Museum, Science and Geological Museums, the Royal Albert Hall, the Imperial College of Science and Technology, and the Royal Colleges of Art and Music.
>
> It also provided the sites for the 1862 International Exhibition (where today stands the Museum of Natural History). Bursaries were also provided in the arts and sciences, and scholarships which continue to be operated by the Royal Commission for the Exhibition of 1851.

The next two international exhibitions took place in 1853. W.T. Copeland exhibited at both. At the World's Fair of the Works of Industry of all Nations in New York he was awarded a Bronze Medal. At the Great Industrial Exhibition in Dublin a record of the exhibition, written by T.D. Jones, states:

> Some very fine works in porcelain statuary and several examples of the jewelled designs executed in white and colored enamels on porcelain, by W.T. Copeland, Stoke-upon-Trent, Staffordshire.

In 1854 The Universal Society for the Encouragement of Arts and Industry presented its Bronze Medal to Alderman Copeland, MP, on 31 January. In 1855 the Exposition Universelle Agriculture, Industrie et Beaux Arts was held in Paris. The report in the *Art-Journal of Industrial Art* included the comments:

> ...the exhibit of Messrs. Copeland beyond illustrating the specialité of the house in the manufacture of Parian statuettes, in which, however there is little novelty since 1851 ... some of the larger busts in parian are remarkable specimens of the successful application of that peculiar and beautiful material to works of considerable size, as compared with the ordinary production therein.

The Silver Medal was awarded to W.T. Copeland, Alderman of London for his exhibit.

A Bronze Medal was awarded to W.T. Copeland for his exhibit at the Commercial Treaty Exhibition held in Paris in 1860.

The next important event was the International Exhibition of 1862 in London. The report on this exhibition in the *The Practical Mechanics Journal* comments:

> PARIAN OR STATUARY PORCELAIN. – The trade in the material thus named has risen to a very important position in the pottery district; not indeed that we can class all the various productions under the title of art manufactures, for many persons totally unqualified have been tempted to engage in the business, and the market has thus been overrun with an immense quantity of inferior wares. Happily, however, we have a good set-off against these shortcomings – the productions of Messrs. Copeland & Minton, and a few others, being really art manufactures. Mr. Copeland has long made this branch one of the leading features of his establishment. His 'Return from the Vintage' and 'Ino and Bacchus' will be remembered by those who studied the works in 1851...

In the *Illustrated Times* of 31 May 1862, a short paragraph remarks:

> Alderman Copeland's collection of Parian figures is surpassed by that of no other exhibitor. We particularly direct attention to the statuette of Beatrice. With regal step, and look wherein disdain was pictured still proceeding, thus she said (like one who doth her bitterest taunt retain): 'Yes, I am Beatrice – regard me well!'

One of the comports from the Temple service.

Although the Catalogue entry for Copeland is non-descriptive, another publication devoted two pages to exhibits by him. The two volume work is *Masterpieces of Industrial Art and Sculpture at the International Exhibition 1862* by J.B. Waring. One page described and illustrated objects of cut glass in the Class XXXIV for which he received a Bronze Medal. Alfred Copeland, his second son, acted as a juror in this class for which he received a Bronze Medal. The other page illustrated several objects in bone china including one in what Copeland called Jewelled Porcelain. Another page illustrated the marble sculpture by Raffaele Monti, entitled Sleep of Sorrow and Dream of Joy. This sculpture was reproduced in reduced form by Copeland, and was sponsored by The Ceramic and Crystal Palace Art Union. W.T. Copeland was awarded a Bronze Medal for his exhibit in the Pottery Class XXXV.

The *Illustrated Catalogue of the Industrial Department* includes an entry for:

> **TEMPLE, EMILY,** *184 Regent Street, and Brighton.*
> Dessert service, ceramic statuary figures, supporting pierced comports, richly decorated. Dessert service, consisting of centrepiece with figures and raised comports in statuary porcelain, elaborately ornamented in mat and chased gold, the drapery of the figures enriched with tinted borders... The following is a description of centrepiece and raised comports, which have been modelled by W. Beattie, of London under the direction of and from the designs suggested by Madame Temple, expressly for the Exhibition. Upon a base of great richness arises a column worked with ivy and scrolls, the caps are composed of rich acanthus foliage, out of which springs an elaborate perforated tazza, lined with a ruby glass, to hold fruit or flowers. Upon the base, and dancing round the column are three female figures, with various insignia, expressive of joyfulness, gratitude and abundance. Among the foliage of the acanthus are three genii of the dance, hovering over and admiring the spirit and grace of the joyous, happy trio. The figures of each of the different size groups are varied in composition, although emblematical of joyfulness and abundance. The service has been manufactured exclusively for Madame Temple, by W.T. Copeland.

The Dublin International Exhibition was held in 1865:

> Messrs. Minton & Mr. Copeland have in the Exhibition works of the highest merit, presenting great originality ... Mr. Alfred Copeland, having accepted the office of juror, the firm of W.T. Copeland, 160 New Bond Street, London, was precluded, according to the rules of the Executive Committee, from receiving the medal which would have been otherwise awarded it.

In 1867 L'Exposition Universelle de MDCCCLXVII à Paris took place. The *Art-Journal* reported:

> Messrs. W.T. Copeland and Sons uphold the renown of British porcelain. The selections we have made from their contributions are limited to three leading pieces in the Dessert Service manufactured for His Royal Highness the Prince of Wales. The CENTRE-PIECE contains figures representing the four quarters of the Globe – reductions of those that form the monument to the Good Prince Albert in the gardens of the Horticultural Society, the admirable work of Joseph Durham, ARA. The compotier and cream bowl are from models by G. Halse and F.M. Miller – sculptors of recognised ability.

On another page:

> We give on this page other of the main contributions of Messrs. Copeland and Sons of London & Stoke-upon-Trent. They are universally admitted excellence: the renown of England is upheld by this eminent firm. The two statuettes are from models of the sculptor Joseph Durham, ARA. 'Chastity' and 'Santa Filomena'; ... The whole collection exhibited by Messrs. Copeland and Sons might be engraved with advantage to this work [i.e. the Catalogue] and to the satisfaction of our subscribers. The great merit – it is universally admitted – is ORIGINALITY ... To their great excellence the universal accord of 'all nations' bears testimony; one of the evidences of this sentiment is the Gold Medal awarded by the Jury. This firm has, therefore, amply justified the honour of England in this important class of Art-industry.

Copeland exhibited at the subsequent International Exhibition in London which was held in 1871. The *Art-Journal Catalogue* reviewed their exhibit in glowing terms. The Official Report, while it, too, reported favourably on Copeland's display, made some very interesting observations on the difference between the 'particularly pleasing' yellowish tint of the colour of English parian compared with the 'bluish white' colour of Continental statuary biscuit. Their comments are reproduced on page 83.

A four page report on Copeland's exhibit was included in the *Rapports des Béléques Belges.* This too was very complimentary.

Copeland exhibited at the Weltausstellung in Vienna in 1873. I was unable to locate a catalogue for this exhibition but a comprehensive account of the Copeland display occurs in the Italian report of the exhibition. Also in 1873 a good order for Copeland's Statuary was placed by the important department store J.E. Caldwell & Co. in Philadelphia – four boxes in all with a cost for the ware of £68.4s.0d.

The Exposition Universelle held in Paris in 1878 included a display by W.T. Copeland & Sons. The Illustrated Catalogue comments:

> In the specimens of parian exhibited there is the usual excellence for which the production of this House [Minton] and that of Copeland have been for some years so remarkable, and which so far surpass in colour and beauty of material the cold-toned bisque statuettes, &c., of French and German manufacture.

The *Art-Journal Catalogue* wrote:

> We have selected from the various and varied contributions of Messrs. Copeland for this page [12] only the Flower Bouquet-holders – baskets, and so forth borne by figures – in statuary porcelain, a material they were the first to introduce, and have since carried to a high degree of perfection.

The Society of Arts Artisan Report on the Paris Exhibition of 1878 regretted that the Copeland display was not as large as usual and that they did not exhibit to a greater extent.

> Only a few specimens of their Parian figures are shown: but they are as beautiful as ever. The pair of dragon vases, in blue and gold, are of Japanese design.

In 1879 Australia joined the club! The Sydney International Exhibition was well supported by English manufacturers of ceramics and glass. According to Reports of the Judges, W.T. Copeland & Sons were classified as First Degree of Merit for their Parian Statuettes. However, almost every exhibitor was either classified as this or Highly Commended! A Bronze Medal was awarded to Copeland.

The last international exhibition to which Copeland sent a display of parian ware was the 1889 Exposition Universelle in Paris. For this display a Gold Medal was awarded.

After this the popularity of parian statuettes and other objects in parian seems to have waned. Very few new models appeared and, although production continued until the beginning of the Great War in 1914, only examples of previous models were produced.

One example of a figure made after the war, in the 1920s, is in the Spode Museum Trust Collection and does not compare favourably with the pre-war ware. It is possible that the recipe for the body had got lost, or that the nature of the materials had changed, and that the correct firing procedures had been forgotten.

An extract from the Official Report on the Various Sections of the London International Exhibition 1871.
Division II - Manufactures, Part V. Pages 60- 61.
(From the Smithsonian Institute Library).

Mr. Leon Arnoux's Report.

The production of the material called parian, or statuary biscuit, introduced in North Staffordshire, not more than twenty-six years ago, by the exertions of Messrs. Minton, Copeland & Mountford, has since greatly developed, no doubt on account of the simplicity of the principles on which its preparation is founded, and the small capital it requires at the outset. This body corresponds to the hard porcelain biscuit made by the Germans and other continental nations, the best types of which are the Sèvres biscuit groups, which for finish and perfect execution have never been surpassed. The mixture is about the same in all countries, and requires only granitic materials – that is, the clay extracted from a decomposed pegmatite or felspar, which is called kaolin on the continent, and Cornish clay in England; and the undecomposed felspar, generally supplied from Sweden or America, which, containing a good amount of soda or potash, acts as a flux on the former. In Germany and France, where good fire-clays are more abundant than in England, very little felspar is used – an intense heat producing the desired effect. Here, on the contrary, the absence of a good fire-clay compels us to have the goods fired at a much lower temperature; consequently more felspar is used. Of course, parian may be made in many other ways, but for our explanation we select the simplest type. After the materials have been finely ground and mixed, the figures are cast in plaster moulds, in separate pieces, which will have to be put together by experienced workmen. A striking difference of colour is to be noticed when the English and foreign statuary biscuits are placed side by side: the English have a yellowish tint, particularly pleasing; the foreign a bluish white colour. From this contrast it might be inferred that in one of them some colouring material had been introduced, whereas the difference is entirely owing to the process of firing. In the French and German ovens great care is taken that no air should be admitted, except that which is strictly necessary to effect the combustion of the fuel; consequently the ware is fired in a reducing atmosphere with an excess of oxide of carbon, the small quantity of iron existing in the clays, combining under the influence of the heat, with the silicic acid, forms a silicate of protoxide of iron, which, like all the salts of protoxide of this metal, has a bluish or greenish colour. In the English parian ovens, air is abundantly introduced, the ware is fired in contact with an excess of carbonic acid, and as iron oxidises when heated in this gas, the result is the formation of a silicate of peroxide of iron of a reddish-brown colour. It is this salt which, spread in small quantity in the mass of the biscuit, produces the pleasing creamy colour already mentioned. This being understood, one will not be surprised at the many and unsuccessful attempts made on the continent to produce a biscuit similar to ours, without altering the construction of their ovens. Today, however, parian like ours in every respect is manufactured in France, Germany, and also in Sweden, by the Gustafsbergs Company. This Company uses the clay from Cornwall, and the appearance of their groups or figures are quite satisfactory. Messrs. Copeland, who have given a great deal of attention to their statuary biscuit, continue to exhibit a number of figures, neatly made and generally from elegant models. But, since the number of the manufacturers of these goods has greatly increased in England, parian, from the competition so created, has become a comparatively cheap article in our market.

THE SCULPTORS OF COPELAND'S PORCELAIN STATUARY

Explanatory Notes

As with the other sections of this work, it was felt that interest would be added to each entry if supporting biographical and historical information were to be included.

For the requirements of this biographical section recourse was made to readily available information to be found in standard reference works which cover nineteenth century sculptors and modellers active in the field of parian production. Moreover, other stones were turned over in attempts to unearth information on sculptors about whom little or nothing had been published and the author records his warm thanks to the many persons who have been kind enough to reply to his enquiries, often with very helpful information.

The reference works which were consulted are listed in the Bibliography and, on balance, they provide enough details. However, there proved to be a small number of artists, prominent among the Staffordshire potters, about whom there was a surprising paucity of recorded information. Where this difficulty arose resort was made to the *Busse-Compendium* (B-C), a German publication giving minimal personal details of some 89,000 internationally recorded artists who were still alive after 1806, or were born before 1880, thus effectively covering the period of this work. Of itself, *ipso facto,* the *Busse-Compendium* embraces a monumental number of authoritative reference sources. Entries gleaned from this source are marked 'B-C', followed by its index number, for example, Nelson, George (B-C 57704).

Where the artist's name is given without supporting notes it may be assumed that the individual's name is known from factory records only (FRO).

ABBOTT, GEORGE **1803-1883**

London born, Abbott exhibited a portrait bust of 'Mrs George Abbott' at the Royal Academy in 1834, but he did not attend the Academy Schools until 1839. He did so then upon the recommendation of Benjamin Wyon. In 1852 he modelled seated figures of 'Prince Albert, the Prince Consort' and the 'Duke of Wellington' for Copeland to reproduce in quantity in statuary porcelain. His 'Wellington' was produced also by Samuel Alcock and Co., and by John Rose of Coalport.

Attributed works

Prince Albert, the Prince Consort, seated figure

The Duke of Wellington, seated figure

Reference: R. Gunnis; C. & D. Shinn

BAILY, EDWARD HODGES, RA **1788-1867**

Edward Hodges Baily was born at Bristol, the son of a ship's carver. His artistic career started when he was sixteen with the execution of portraits in wax. His ability was such that he became a pupil of John Flaxman. He joined the Royal Academy Schools in 1808, becoming an Associate in 1817, and he was elected a Royal Academician in 1821. He was the second prize winner in the Nelson Memorial Competition and his statue of Nelson was placed on top of the corinthian column of William Railton's prize winning design in 1843.

Attributed work

L'Allegro, statuette

Reference: R. Gunnis

BARING – perhaps F. Baring (B-C 03989)

Details are few but it is known that he was active 1868-1881.

Attributed work

Bust of Unknown Lady

Reference: B-C (entry from Bénézit)

BARTOLINI, Lorenzo **1777-1850**

Born in Tuscany, he died at Florence. His works are to be seen in the Walker Art Gallery, Liverpool ('Venus') and at Morgan in Meneage, Cornwall ('Sir Vyell Vivien'), etc.

Attributed work

Nymph at Bath

Reference: R. Gunnis

BEATTIE, William

His exact life-span is uncertain and there appears to be very little recorded of his personal life. He was a regular exhibitor at the Royal Academy from 1829 onwards. Residing in Stoke from 1850, his skills were used widely by such pottery firms as Copeland, Minton, Adams, Wedgwood and others. His sculptures were mainly executed in the parian body.

Attributed works

The Golden Age, group
Love Story, group
References: R. Gunnis; M. Batkin

BIRKS, Arthur 'Spode' 1832-1906

He was the son of Isaac who died in 1850. He was modeller at Copelands from 1872 to 1898 and head modeller for his last twenty years. He was given a fine presentation vase by the partners and his fellow workmen on his retirement. The portrait bust of W.T. Copeland is dated 1838, three years after he was Lord Mayor of London, and it is almost certain to be a copy of the marble sculpture, which is signed (*after* Behnes 1838). Such a copy, in parian, could have been made at any time afterwards, and possibly as late as 1875, although it might have been modelled by Isaac Birks who was a modeller at Copelands. W.T. Copeland died in 1868. See photograph on page 64.

Attributed work
Alderman W.T. Copeland, portrait bust
Reference: Peter S. Goodfellow: *The Vine Pottery Birks, Rawlins & Co*

BONHAM CARTER, Miss Joanna Hilary 23 Jan. 1821-6 Sept. 1863

First cousin and a close friend of Florence Nightingale, Hilary Bonham Carter is not known generally as a sculptress, her activities being restricted by somewhat irksome commitments to her family. It was said at the time that she 'was devoured by little black relations, just like fleas'! For a short while she was secretary to 'the Lady of the Lamp' during which time she was permitted a concession to model her head and shoulders. In 1861 she executed the series of woodcuts used as illustrations for Miss Nightingale's *Observations on the Sanitary State of the Army in India.* Miss Bonham Carter's original statue 'Florence Nightingale' was exhibited at the Royal Academy in 1864. It was cast in bronze and later the family had a plaster cast made for the library; the height of these was 34in. (86cm). The plaster version, somewhat damaged, may be seen at the Florence Nightingale Museum, Claydon House, Middle Claydon, Buckingham.

Attributed work
Florence Nightingale, statuette
References: Elspeth Huxley, *Florence Nightingale,* London: Weidenfeld & Nicholson, 1975; National Trust, Claydon House

BRODIE, William 1815-1881

The son of John Brodie, ship-master, of Banff, he studied at the Trustees School of Design in Edinburgh 1847-1851. He went to Rome in 1853 to study under Lawrence MacDonald with whose assistance he sculpted 'Corinna', the Lyric Muse. Brodie was elected an Associate of the Royal Scottish Academy in 1857, becoming a full member in 1859, and being appointed Secretary of the Academy in 1876, a post he held until his death.

Attributed works
Corinna, statuette
Penelophon, the Beggar Maid, statuette
Ruth, statuette
Storm, statuette
Sunshine, statuette
Reference: R. Gunnis

BUTLER, Timothy fl.1806-1878

An eminent 'portrait' sculptor. His busts of eminent personages were particularly well received by the Victorian cognoscenti. His original portrait bust in marble of Samuel Cooper was executed for the Royal College of Surgeons.

Attributed work
Samuel Cooper portrait bust
Reference: R. Gunnis

CHANTREY, Sir Francis Leggatt, RA 1781-1841

Born near Sheffield, the son of a carpenter, Chantrey started his working life with a grocer before becoming apprenticed to a wood-carver and gilder. He moved, later on, to portrait painting before becoming a sculptor. His earlier life proved something of a struggle, but by 1815 he had become an Associate member of the Royal Academy, full membership being granted him in 1818. His success was now assured and in 1835 he was knighted by King William IV.

He achieved a prodigious output, mostly of portrait busts of a high quality of which he himself considered his study of Sir Walter Scott (1820) to be the finest. He amassed a fortune of some £150,000 which, upon his death, passed to the Royal Academy after the death of his wife. This is known as 'The Chantrey Bequest'.

Clearly, the Copeland parian copy, which seems to have appeared first in about 1880, must have been reproduced by permission from the owner; no documentation has come to the notice of the authors on this matter. It is possible, also, that Copeland's portrait bust of Byron may have been copied from Chantrey's study.

Attributed works
Sir Walter Scott, portrait bust
Lord Byron, portrait bust (possibly)
Reference: R. Gunnis

CHESNEAU, Aimé fl. mid-years 19th century

He exhibited at the Royal Academy and at the British Institution from 1863-1875. He was a specialist in bronze portrait busts, roundels and reliefs. He was born in Paris, and studied under Carrier-Belleuse and Jules Salmson.

Attributed work
First Bath of the Season statuette. This is the figure which is also known by the name of 'Flower Girl' (see S54)
Reference: Busse (from Thieme-Becker & Bénézit)

CHEVERTON, Benjamin 1794-1876

A sculptor in his own right, Cheverton sent his works to exhibitions held by the Royal Society of British Artists between 1835 and 1849. Examples of his work may be seen now in various museums and art galleries in the United Kingdom. He is best remembered, however, as an accomplished engineer who perfected a machine to reduce or enlarge with accuracy and to scale portrait busts and statues in three dimensions.

Works known to have been reduced by Cheverton's Machine
Dancing Girl Reposing by W.C. Marshall, statuette
Daniel O'Connell by J.E. Jones, portrait bust
The Greek Slave by Hiram Powers, statuette
Jenny Lind by J. Durham, portrait bust

Lady Clementina Villiers by L. Macdonald, portrait bust
The Return Dove by J. Farrell, statuette
This list is not claimed to be complete; it includes those studies which are *known* to have been reduced, but it is probable that many more were dealt with by this ingenious device. No original sculpted work by Cheverton is recorded as having been made by the Copeland manufactory in statuary porcelain.
References: C. & D. Shinn; Busse; P. Atterbury & M. Batkin in *Parian Phenomenon*, p.19.

CROWQUILL, Alfred **1805-1872**
The pseudonym of Alfred Henry Forrester, who appears to be not generally known as an original sculptor, but rather as a modeller, interpreting the original work of others. He was one of the principal designers of Samuel Alcock & Co., where he specialised in modelling hollow-ware.
Attributed work
Wellington, seated figure
He also sponsored the statuette of The Hop Girl, shown at the 1862 International Exhibition (see S76)

CUMBERWORTH, Charles **1811-1852**
Charles Cumberworth, the son of an English officer and a Frenchwoman, was born in America but arrived in France at an early age. His working life was short, but during it he suffered two unfortunate disappointments. The first occurred in 1842 when he won a Paris Academy Prize which would have allowed him to study in Rome. When it was discovered that he was not a Frenchman he was disqualified from receiving the prize. Later, in 1846, his sculpture of the group of 'Paul and Virginia' was sent to the Royal Academy only to arrive two days after the official closing date. The Museum of La Rochelle houses some examples of his work.
Attributed works
Indian fruit-girl, statuette
Nubian water-bearer, statuette
Paul & Virginia, group
Paul, statuette
Virginia, statuette
References: R. Gunnis; *Art-Journal* 1851, p.167, 1852, p.316

DELPECH, C.
It seems that Delpech was not a sculptor of original works but rather a sculptor who reduced to smaller size the works of others.
Attributed works of reduction
Clytie, bust
Apollo, bust
Daphne, bust

D'ORSAY, Count Alfred Guillaume Gabriel **1801-1852**
A London and Paris social leader with an active interest in the fine arts. It seems questionable whether the Count actually sculpted the works ascribed to him or whether, in fact, they were the work of others, chiefly Thomas Henry Nicholson. Whatever the truth of the matter, it does appear that he possessed considerable artistic talents.
Attributed works
Bentinck, Lord George, portrait bust
Nicholas, Emperor of Russia, portrait bust
Wellington, Duke of, portrait bust
Wellington, Duke of, equestrian statue
Wellington, Duke of, statuette
References: R. Gunnis; Century; *Art-Journal* 1852, p.286

DUQUESNOY, François **1594-1643**
Born in Brussels, Duquesnoy lived mostly in Italy where he was known by the sobriquet 'Il Fiammingo' (The Fleming). He was famous for his bronzes of 'putti', small boys engaged in various pursuits. These were featured extensively by many 18th century potters amongst whom Josiah Wedgwood was the most prominent. Duquesnoy's death was encompassed by his brother Jerome, also a sculptor, who poisoned him, and for which crime he was burned.
Attributed works
Struggle for the heart, 'Contending Cupids', group
References: Riley; Century

DURHAM, Joseph, RA **1814-1877**
One of the most important and prolific of the Victorian sculptors, exhibiting some 130 works at the Royal Academy between the years 1835-1878. Twenty of his works were reproduced by Copeland. Other manufacturers also availed themselves of his services. His portrait busts of Queen Victoria and the Prince Consort were commissioned directly by Her Majesty, while his statue of Prince Albert, executed in 1863, now stands in front of the Albert Hall in London.
Attributed works
Colin Campbell, Lord Clyde, portrait bust (possibly; this may have been sculpted by Morrison, after Durham)
The Hop Queen, bust
Jenny Lind, portrait bust
May Queen, bust
Peace, bust
Prince Consort, portrait bust
Queen Victoria, portrait bust
War, bust
Shakespeare, portrait bust (probably)
The Four Continents: Africa, America, Asia, Europe, seated figures
Chastity, statuette
Go to Sleep, statuette
Master Tom, statuette
Miss Ellie, statuette
Santa Filomena, statuette
On the Sea Shore – Calm, statuette
On the Sea Shore – Storm, statuette
Reference: R. Gunnis

EDWARDS, Morton
Known to have been active between 1864-1870. He was the Honorary Secretary of the Society of Sculptors, a society founded by sculptors to further their interests within the Royal Academy where, they felt, their work was not recognised sufficiently well. His portrait bust of Albert Edward, the Prince of Wales, was executed for the City of Toronto. This, together with three portrait busts of the Marquis of Zetland for the Freemasons, are the only

works known to have been sculpted by him.
Attributed work
Albert Edward, Prince of Wales, portrait bust
Reference: B. Read & Busse [B-C 23578] (from Thieme-Becker & Bénézit)

FARRELL, James **1821-1891**
Son of Terence Farrell, an eminent Irish sculptor, in whose Dublin studio he received his instruction. He exhibited first at the Royal Academy in 1836, subsequently sending works to the Royal Academy in London between 1843 and 1869. He was elected an Associate of the Royal Hibernian Academy in 1880, and he became a full member in 1882.
Attributed work
The Return Dove, or The Return of the Pet Dove, statuette
References: R. Gunnis; *The Illustrated Exhibitor*

FOLEY, John Henry RA **1818-1874**
Born in Dublin, the son of a grocer, Foley joined the Royal Dublin Society's Schools in 1831 before proceeding to London to join his brother, Edward, in 1834. He exhibited first at the Royal Academy in 1839, going on to enjoy a most successful career. He was elected a member of the Royal Academy in 1858, and a member of the Royal Hibernian Academy in 1861. His most notable work is the seated figure of the Prince Consort which forms the centrepiece of the Albert Memorial in London. Sadly, Foley died before it was finished and it was left to his pupil, G.T. Teniswood, to effect its completion.
Attributed works
Ino and the Infant Bacchus, group
Innocence, statuette
Egeria, statuette
Caractacus, statuette
References: R. Gunnis; *Art-Journal* January 1849

FRANCIS, John RA **1780-1861**
Born in Lincolnshire, Francis trained initially as a farmer, but forsook the rural life to study sculpture under the direction of Chantrey in London. He acquired the patronage of Mr Thomas Coke of Norfolk (later the Earl of Leicester) in about 1815. As a result of this he became the unofficial sculptor to the Whig Party. A favourite of King William IV, he later developed a close relationship with the Prince Consort; the statue of a greyhound on the terrace of Osborne House in the Isle of Wight is 'Eos', the Prince Consort's favourite greyhound, which was modelled by the Prince himself and cast by Francis. Francis exhibited at the Royal Academy between the years 1820 and 1857. His marriage to a relation of Lord Nelson resulted in the birth of a daughter, Mary, who was later to become the wife of Thomas Thornycroft; both were eminent sculptors.
Attributed works
Duke of Sutherland, portrait bust
Queen Victoria, portrait bust
References: R. Gunnis; B. Read (p.139, pl.166)

GIBSON, John, RA **1790-1866**
The son of a horticulturalist, Gibson arrived in Liverpool at the age of nine and five years later began his career by being apprenticed to a wood-worker. He soon acquired a preference for working in stone, so he removed to a firm of monumental stonemasons where he developed his skills as a modeller and sculptor. Gibson's abilities soon gained recognition, and he received encouragement from eminent sculptors such as Nollekens, and, later, when domiciled in Rome, from Canova and Thorwaldsen. He became eminently successful and in 1844 was commissioned by Queen Victoria to execute a statue of herself, and it was on this work that he introduced the practice of adding colour to his sculptures. In 1833 he was elected an Associate and, five years later, a full member of the Royal Academy. He exhibited there from 1816 until 1864. Gibson's burial in the English Cemetery in Rome was attended with much ceremony in recognition of his receipt of the Order of the Legion of Honour from the French President.

John Gibson, RA. is particularly important in the history of statuary porcelain. His unshakeable confidence in the material as 'the next best to marble' played a most significant role in its future as a medium for the production of works of art. See the chapter on the Art Unions.
Attributed works
Narcissus, statuette
Nymph untying her Sandal, or Preparing for the Bath, statuette
The Tinted Venus, statuette
References: R. Gunnis; C. & D. Shinn; B. Read; *Art-Journal* May 1849, pp.139-141 and April 1866, p113

GIRARDON, François **1628-1715**
The son of a metal-founder, Girardon was apprenticed initially to a sculptor and cabinet-maker. At the age of fifteen he was already an accomplished painter who became a protégé of Chancellor Seguier under whose patronage he studied in Rome and Paris. As an appointed 'Sculpteur du Roi' he supervised the decoration of the King's ships and was involved heavily in supplying architectural designs and models for the Palace of Versailles, for the Louvre and elsewhere. He was made a Chevalier in 1690.

In 1657 Girardon married a flower-painter by whom he sired ten children; his wife pre-deceased him by fifteen years. He died, a very rich man, on 1 September 1715 on the same day as King Louis XIV.
Attributed works reproduced from his originals:
Autumn and Winter, a pair of candlesticks

HALE, Owen
Floruit (alive and working) in the late 19th century and known to be active in 1884. Hale worked in London in the late 19th century, exhibiting figures at the Royal Academy in 1884. He was an Associate of the Society of British Artists. With sixteen items recorded to his name, Owen Hale was a leading sculptor for Copeland, his forte being the imaginative interpretations of romantic themes.
Attributed works
Adversity, statuette
After the Ball, seated figure
Before the Ball, seated figure
Evening Devotion, group
Companion to Evening Devotion, group
First Lesson, group
William Gladstone, portrait bust
Italian Flower Seller, statuette
New Friends, group
Prosperity, statuette
Queen Victoria, portrait bust
The Riverside, statuette
Companion to the Riverside, statuette
The Seasons, set of four busts
The Tribute of Jehu, bas-relief plaque)
The Beautiful Garden Scene, bas-relief plaque)
These are reproductions from Assyrian panels in the British Museum (q.v.)

HALSE, George
Known to have been active 1855-1888, Halse was self taught.
Attributed works
Christina Linnaeus, statuette
Trysting Tree, Boy, statuette
Trysting Tree, Girl, statuette
Young England, statuette
Young England's Sister, statuette
Reference: B-C 34356

HANCOCK, John **1825-1869**
John Hancock was a Londoner who was born at Fulham. He enjoyed only a relatively short life, during which he failed to achieve much acclaim. He was largely self-taught, although he attended the Royal Academy Schools for a short while in 1842.
Attributed work
Una, bust

HAYS, Aaron **1814- c.1890**
A full account of Aaron Hays is given in the section devoted to 'Assyria Revived'; see 'The Impresarios', page 263
Attributed works
Beethoven, portrait bust
Sardanapalus, statuette
Queen of Sardanapalus, statuette
Sennacherib, statuette
Winged Human-Headed Bull, statuette
Winged Human-Headed Lion, statuette
Nimrod's Head, vase
Lion couchant, paperweight

JONES, John Edward **1806-1862**
Born in Dublin, the son of a painter of portrait miniatures, J.E. Jones trained as an engineer, a profession in which he became most successful, being responsible for the construction of Waterford Bridge. He abandoned engineering in 1840 to become a sculptor, an occupation in which he attained a similar eminence, especially in the sphere of portraiture. A letter written by Daniel O'Connell on 14 May 1840 reads:

> My dear Jones
> The bust is admirable – as a work of art it does you the greatest credit and it is a most striking likeness – infinitely more like than any other bust attempted of me – My friends are unanimous in approving of it most highly both for execution and correct resemblance.
> Believe me to be,
> Very faithfully Yours,
> Daniel O'Connell John E Jones Esq

Attributed works
Emperor Napoleon, portrait bust
Daniel O'Connell, portrait bust

LAWSON, George A. **1832-1904**
George Lawson studied under Alexander Ritchie at the Royal Scottish Academy and in Rome where he was a contemporary of John Gibson. He is known as a contributor to the 'Sir Walter Scott' Memorial in Princes Street, Edinburgh, having sculpted the figures of Diana Vernon, Baillie Nicol Jarvie and Robert the Bruce. His statue of 'Wellington' stands outside St.George's Hall in Liverpool, while that of his 'Robert Burns' stands at Ayr.
Attributed work
Blind Boy and Dumb Fanny, group

LESLIE, Charles R. **1794-1859**
Charles Robert Leslie was a painter of historical and humorous subjects, in addition to portraits and book illustrations. There is no evidence that he engaged in sculpting, and the modeller of the group of 'Uncle Toby and the Widow' is unknown; it may have been a factory modeller. It was issued in about 1870, some eleven years after Leslie's death. Illustrated in *Art-Journal* Jan. 1853, p.33.
Work based upon his painting
Uncle Toby and the Widow Wadman, group

McBRIDE, John Alexander Paterson **1819-1890**
McBride trained initially under Sir William Spence. In 1844, however, aged only twenty-five years, he exhibited a group 'Margaret of Anjou and her Son'. Although the work attracted an unfavourable press review, Samuel Joseph was sufficiently impressed to take him into his studio, waiving his normal fee of 500 guineas. Domiciled in Liverpool, he became secretary of the Liverpool Academy and a protagonist of the Pre-Raphaelite school. His last work, a statue of H.M. Stanley, was reproduced in parian by Messrs. Minton.
Attributed work
Lady Godiva, equestrian statuette
References: R. Gunnis; C. & D. Shinn

MacCARTHY, Candelon **fl. c.1854**
Also known as 'Carletto', she was a member of the MacCarthy family of sculptors who specialised in animal subjects. She is known to have been actively sculpting in 1854. She was possibly the wife of either Sexon John James MacCarthy or of Hamilton MacCarthy (q.v.)
Attributed Works
Begging Dog, animal figure
Bone-picker Dog, animal figure
References: R.Gunnis; Mackay p.243; Busse; R. Dennis, 'The Parian Phenomenon', Catalogue of an Exhibition December 1984, attributes these two subjects, Numbers 251 and 252, to this sculptor; they were introduced in 1848.

MacCARTHY, Hamilton, and Carlton **Hamilton b.1809**
Carlton b.1817
Two brothers who collaborated in the execution of much of their work, especially in their careers. They specialised in animal figures, particularly horses; in 1846 their address is given as Tattersall's! They received commissions from well-known owners, including Colonel Alfred James Copeland (b.1837), son of Alderman W.T. Copeland.

A Hamilton MacCarthy was known to be active in sculpture.
Attributed work
Death of the Fox, animal group

MacDONALD, Lawrence **1799-1878**
Scottish born, the bulk of MacDonald's work was executed in Rome where, as a popular and prolific portrait sculptor, he concentrated on portrait busts of the noble and illustrious. His prodigious output called forth the unkindly comment: 'A patent family likeness pervades them all, a universal type reminding me of a bad dinner tasting as if every dish had been cooked in the same pot; insipid and unappetising – very!' Be that as it may, his earlier portrait busts of women flattered them sufficiently to ensure a steady stream of customers!
Attributed work
Lady Clementina Villiers, portrait bust
Reference: R. Gunnis

MacDOWELL, Patrick **1799-1870**
Born in Belfast, MacDowell became fatherless at an early age, resulting in an unsettled childhood. His mother removed to England in 1811 and settled in Hampshire, eventually lodging in the house of the sculptor, P. Chenu. MacDowell attended the Royal Academy Schools in 1830, going to Rome for a brief period in 1832. An Associate of the Royal Academy in 1831, he was elected to full membership in 1846.
Attributed works
Reading Girl, statuette
Eve, statuette (possibly)
References: R. Gunnis; *Art-Journal* January 1850

MALEMPRÉ, Louis Auguste **1819-1888**
Floruit in the late 19th century. A sculptor of French origin, Malempré was residing in London in the mid-19th century. He supported himself by working as an assistant to William Theed the Younger. He exhibited bas-reliefs at the Royal Academy from 1848-1879. He was known to have used bronze at least as one of the materials in which he produced sculptures. The late Mr D.A. Boyce carried out extensive research in an attempt to discover more about this sculptor, who sculpted about thirty-one subjects which were reproduced in the statuary porcelain body by Copeland. His efforts were unrewarded, with only the briefest mention in Bénézit's *Dictionary of Painters and Sculptors* and the record of his death in the Register of Births, Marriages and Deaths kept at St. Stephens House, Aldwych, London. His statue of the composer, Balfe, remains in the foyer of Drury Lane Theatre.

With more than thirty items registered in his name, Malempré was the sculptor who produced more works than any other that were reproduced in statuary porcelain for Copelands.
Attributed works
Angel and the Flowers (The Reaper and the Flowers), group
Autumn, statuette
Beaconsfield, Earl of, portrait bust
Bohemian Girl, statuette
Cottage Girl, statuette
Early Struggles, group
The Four Elements: Air, Earth, Fire and Water, statuettes (comports also were made with these subjects)
Guardian Angel, group
Happy Dream, bust
Hope, statuette
Ino and Bacchus, group
Juno – after the antique, bust
Lurline, kneeling, statuette
Mary, Queen of Scots, Princess Alexandra as, statuette
Mignon, statuette
Music, bust
Poetry, bust

Queen Victoria, seated figure
Salisbury, the Marquis of, portrait bust
Shepherd Boy, statuette
Sleeping Cupid, statuette
Spring, bust
Spring, statuette
Summer, bust
Summer, statuette
Sweet Apples, statuette
Venus, statuette
Wild Flowers, statuette
Winter, statuette
References: Bénézit; J. Mackay

MAROCHETTI, Baron Carlo **1805-1867**
Carlo Marochetti, Royal Academician and Baron of the Italian Kingdom, was born in Turin. He is said to have been educated in Paris at the Lycée Napoléon and at the School of Beaux-Arts. He excelled at sculpting equestrian statues and was described by John Ruskin as 'a thoroughly good sculptor'.
Attributed works
Jeejeebhoy, Sir Jamsetjee, seated figure
Emmanuel Philibert, Duke of Savoy, equestrian statuette
References: Cyclopaedia; B. Read; C. & D. Shinn

MARSHALL, William CALDER **1813-1894**
Born and educated in Edinburgh, Calder Marshall moved to London in 1834. After studying in Rome for a while, he returned to London in 1839. He was a prolific producer, whose work was used extensively by the Art Unions. However, Marshall was not considered to be a great artist, one critic being moved to comment, cruelly, that 'he was endowed with no more poetry, or fancy, or classic perceptions than a cow!' Nevertheless, he became a full member of the Royal Academy in 1852 and was nominated a Chevalier of the Legion of Honour in 1878.
Attributed works
The Bather, statuette
Comus, statuette
Cupid Captive, group
Dancing Girl Reposing, statuette
Hermione, statuette
Lady Macbeth, statuette
The Last Drop, statuette
Lear and Cordelia, group
Lesbia, bust
Miranda, bust
Oenone, bust
Ophelia, bust
Ophelia, statuette
Sabrina, statuette
The Toilet, statuette
Reference: R. Gunnis

MELI, Giovanni **b. c.1815**
Floruit in the mid-19th century. An Italian sculptor and free-lance modeller who plied his trade in England in the 1840s-1860s. He was active in the Potteries, modelling for Adams, Copeland & Garrett and Wedgwood. In about 1858 he commenced manufacturing parian ware on his own account, while at the same time assisting Sir James Duke and Nephews. This enterprise was short-lived and, after returning to Italy in 1865, Meli emigrated to the United States and established a manufactory in Chicago to make terracotta.
Attributed works
Although Meli did model for Copeland & Garrett and Copeland during the years 1840 to about 1850, none of his work has been positively identified.
References: C. & D. Shinn; M. Batkin

MÊNE, P.J. **1810-1871**
Born and died in Paris and, largely self-taught, Mêne built a reputation for himself as an animalier. He exhibited at the Great Exhibitions of 1851 and 1862.
Attributed works
Boy with Terriers, group
Terriers (Chasse au lapin), group
Death of the Fox (possibly), group
Dogs group, group (P.P. fig.578)
Reference: J. Mackay

MILLER, Felix Martin **1820- post 1880**
Losing his parents at an early age, Miller was brought up in the London Orphan School from where he moved to the Royal Academy Schools. His 'Orphans' group, carved in marble, was set up later in The London Orphan Asylum. Although his work was much respected by eminent contemporaries, he appears to have attracted rather more praise than monetary reward. He was thought very highly of by J.H. Foley and was employed by both Copeland and Wedgwood. The date of his death seems not to have been recorded but it would have been after 1880 because he was exhibiting at the Royal Academy up until then.
Attributed works
Emily and the White Doe of Rylstone, group
Enid the Fair and the Good, bust
Evangeline, bust
Prince of Wales, after Marshall Wood, portrait bust
Princess of Wales, after Marshall Wood, portrait bust
Girl with Rabbit, also called The Pets, group
Viola sans Chapeau, bust
References: M. Batkin; R. Gunnis

MONTI, Raffaele **1818-1881**
Born in Milan, Raffaele Monti studied under his father, Gaetano, at the Imperial Academy. After sojourns in Austria and England, Monti returned to Italy in 1847, where he was involved in the King of Sardinia's Italian Independence movement. He fled to England in 1848, where he remained until his death. Monti is known most particularly for his statues and busts which, although worked in the solid, appear to be covered with a transparent veil. Copeland reproduced many of his sculptures.
Attributed works
The Bride, bust
Companion to Love, statuette
Flute Player, statuette
Grief, or Sorrow, bust
Infancy of Jupiter, group

Instruction of Jupiter, group
Lady Godiva. statuette
Love, bust
Love, statuette
Morning, group
Mother, bust
Night, group
Nora Creina, statuette
Pomona, comports
Shakespeare, bust
Sleep of Sorrow and Dream of Joy, group
Reference: R. Gunnis

MORRIS, Rowland James **1847-1909**
R.J. Morris studied first at the Hanley School of Art under the instruction of Protat, before proceeding to South Kensington. He became famous for his work on the terracotta façade of the Wedgwood Institute in Burslem, in the Staffordshire Potteries. At that time, 1873, he was working for Josiah Wedgwood and Sons. Later he was to become a freelance modeller working for several Staffordshire pottery manufacturers.
Attributed works
Comedy, bust
Tragedy, bust (possibly)
Cupid at Sea, statuette
Young Naturalist, statuette)
Companion to Young Naturalist, statuette) This pair of figures is known also as Rustic Children of England.

MORRISON
There is insufficient information about sculptors named Morrison. The Busse-Compendium No.56246 lists Morrison, J., active in 1825 as a British sculptor. Dennis lists R. Morrison who exhibited at the Royal Academy between 1844 and 1857. This seems to be the sculptor of the two busts sculpted in 1858 of Sir Colin Campbell and General Havelock.

NOBLE, Matthew **1817-1876**
Born a Yorkshireman, Noble studied in London under John Francis. He first exhibited at the Royal Academy in 1845. Public attention was drawn to him by his monument of the Duke of Wellington, erected in Manchester in 1856. The decision to award Noble this commission was resented by others because of his comparative youth and obscurity. Later he became both a popular and respected artist.
Attributed works
Purity, statuette
Purity, bust
Richard Cobden, portrait bust
John Milton, portrait bust
Queen Victoria, portrait bust
Reference: R. Gunnis

PAPWORTH, Edgar George **1809-1866**
Born in London, the only son of Thomas Papworth, master plasterer to the Royal palaces. In 1834 he went to Rome on a Royal Academy Travelling Scholarship, but ill health cut short his studies. Working as a silver designer, he made the centrepiece presented by 'The Slave Population of Jamaica' to the Marquis of Sligo in 1839. Despite wide popularity, he died in penury and was buried in Highgate Cemetery.
Attributed works
Beatrice, statuette
Fairy Cap (Psyche disguised), statuette
Maidenhood, statuette
Peace, statuette
Young Emigrant, statuette
Young Shrimper, statuette
References: R. Gunnis; B. Read

PHYFFERS, Theodore **fl. 1840-1872**
Phyffers, a Belgian, who studied under Charles Geerts, initially came to London at the invitation of Sir Charles Barry to carry out wood carvings for the House of Commons. Specialising in ecclesiastical sculptures, examples of his work are to be seen in the Cathedrals of Canterbury, Carlisle and Salisbury.
Attributed works
The Heavenly Chorus, group
Miss Nightingale and the wounded soldier, group (this sculpture is known also as The Wounded at Scutari).
Reference: R. Gunnis

POWERS, Hiram **1805-1873**
An American who commenced his career by modelling busts in Washington. Removing to Italy in 1837, he remained there for life, his works being sent to the world's most important exhibitions. His famous statue of 'The Greek Slave', exhibited in New York in 1847, was shown also at the Great Exhibition in 1851. This was the first totally nude figure of a girl to be shown in public; because of its beauty and posture it was admired greatly and was reproduced by many firms, including Copelands and Mintons.
Attributed work
The Greek Slave, statuette.
References: B. Read; C. & D. Shinn

PRADIER, J.J. **1792-1852**
Pradier, the scion of an old Huguenot family, initially studied classical painting at L'École des Beaux-Arts. His serious work in sculpture started in 1820 when he specialised in busts and neo-classical statuettes. He ultimately became Professor of Sculpture at L'École.
Attributed works
Boy, Dog and Bird, group
Ondine, or River Allegory, statuette
Sea Nymph, statuette
Venus consoling Cupid, group
Reference: J. Mackay

ROBERTS, David. RA **1796-1864**
Roberts appears to have been, in the main, an architectural painter and painter of theatre scenery, etc.
Attributed work
Pair of wall brackets, moulded with flowers, scrolls and winged cherubs
See Catalogue of R. Dennis Exhibition 1984, No.365
Reference: B-C 67989

SCHWANTHALER, Ludwig Michael **1802-1848**
A German sculptor working mostly in Munich under official patronage. He left his collection of models to the Government of Bavaria; they are in the Schwanthaler Museum.
Attributed work
Lurline seated, statuette
Reference: Century

SHARP, Thomas **b.1805**
Little seems to be known of Thomas Sharp other than that he was a protégé of Sir Francis Chantrey, upon whose recommendation Sharp attended the Royal Academy Schools in 1831. He gained a silver medallion in 1834, having exhibited already in 1831. He appears to have been well regarded by the cognoscenti, not only for his sculptural work but also for his abilities as a chaser of silver.
Attributed work
Little Nell, statuette
Reference: R. Gunnis

SPENCE, Benjamin Edward **1822-1866**
Born at Liverpool, the son of the sculptor William Spence. Young Spence studied in Rome under R.J. Wyatt and John Gibson and spent the rest of his life in Italy. He was not considered to have been a great artist; his work, although pure and elegant, lacked originality and vigour.
Attributed works
Hop Queen (This may be the statuette 'Hop Girl', for which a sculptor's name is not known, but the figure was displayed at the 1862 Exhibition under the sponsorship of Alfred Crowquill. Its existence is known from a stereoscopic photograph of items at that exhibition.)
The Finding of Moses, group
References: R. Gunnis; B. Read; *Art-Journal,* 1862 p.231 and Obituary p.364

STEELL, Sir John, RSA **1804-1891**
An eminent Scottish sculptor who resided in Rome for many years before returning to live in Scotland. He was a member of the Royal Scottish Academy and was Queen Victoria's appointed sculptor in Scotland. He sculpted the seated figure of Sir Walter Scott which is located in the Scott Memorial on Princes Street, Edinburgh. He was knighted by the Queen upon the inauguration of his statue of the Prince Consort in 1876; this, too, is in Edinburgh. He built a foundry for the artistic casting of bronze, where the works by himself and others were reproduced in that metal.
Attributed works
Sir Walter Scott, portrait bust
Sir Walter Scott, seated figure
Professor John Wilson, 'Christopher North', statuette
References: R. Gunnis; B. Read

SUMMERS, Charles **1827-1878**
The son of a stonemason, Summers studied under Henry Weekes and M.L. Watson. In 1851 he achieved distinction by gaining, simultaneously, both the silver and gold medals of the Royal Academy. This had not been achieved previously. He also received a grant of £500 to continue his studies in Rome. These were abandoned, however, in favour of an unsuccessful gold-digging venture in Australia. After working as a modeller for the Australian Houses of Parliament he returned to Rome to remain there for the rest of his life. Several of his works are located in Australia.
Attributed work
Boy with Shell at ear, statuette (at present there is no certain proof of this attribution)
Reference: R. Gunnis

TENERANI, Pietro **1789-1870**
An Italian, born near Carrara, he worked under Thorwaldsen. He was a prolific sculptor, producing a vast number of works. General Director of the museums and galleries of Rome, a special museum was opened after his death to house his statues, groups, busts, etc., of which there were more than four hundred and fifty. His statue of 'Flora' sculpted in 1848 is in the Royal Collection.
Attributed work
Flora, bust
Reference: R. Gunnis

TERRY, Sarah **fl. 19th century**
A sculptress of portrait and genre subjects who worked in London between the years 1862 and 1879.
Attributed works
Evangeline, statuette
Marguerite, statuette
Reference: J. Mackay

THEED, William the Younger **1804-1891**
A Staffordshire man, born at Trentham, near Stoke-upon-Trent, son of William Theed, RA, who worked for Josiah Wedgwood from 1791-1793. William the Younger attended the Royal Academy Schools, thereafter working for a while for E.H. Baily. Later he studied in Rome under Thorwaldsen, Gibson and Wyatt. He was much patronised by Queen Victoria and the Prince Consort. In 1861 he was commissioned by the Queen to take a death mask of Prince Albert. He is known also to have worked for the pottery firm of Bates, Brown-Westhead & Moore.
Attributed works
Edmund Buckley, portrait bust
Humphrey Chetham, seated figure
Duchess of Kent, portrait bust
Princess Feodore of Hohenlohe-Langenburg, portrait bust
Juno, bust
Musidora, statuette
Napoleon, portrait bust
Napoleon I, seated figure
Prince Consort, portrait bust
The Prodigal's Return, group
Psyche, statuette
Queen Victoria, portrait bust
Rebekah, statuette
Rebekah at the well, group
Ruth, statuette
Sappho, statuettes

Seasons Figure, figure as comport
Daniel Webster, seated figure
Silvain van de Weyer, portrait bust
References: R. Gunnis; C. & D. Shinn

THORNYCROFT, Mary 1814-1895

The daughter of John Francis (q.v.), Mary was born at Thornham, Norfolk, close to the Sandringham Estate. She exhibited first at the Royal Academy at the tender age of twenty-one. In 1835 she married Thomas Thornycroft, a pupil of her father, and they lived for some years in Rome.

Impressed by her work, John Gibson (q.v.) recommended her to Queen Victoria, an introduction which resulted in the Queen's invitation to model portrait sculptures of her children. As a consequence, Mary sculpted four life-size marble statues of the four eldest children, each representing one of the four seasons. W.T. Copeland was swift to visit Mrs Thornycroft and negotiated the right to reproduce these statues as half-size statuettes at the total fee of £200. (See under Royal Seasons, pages 239-240).

Thereafter Mary Thornycroft received many royal commissions to model statues and portrait busts of members of the Royal Family, several of which were reproduced by Copeland in statuary porcelain.

Attributed works
Alexandra, Princess of Wales, portrait bust
Princess Alice, portrait bust
Princess Helena, portrait bust
Princess Louise, Marchioness of Lorne, portrait bust
The Seasons, set of four statuettes, comprising:
  Spring, posed by Princess Alice
  Summer, posed by Princess Victoria, the Princess Royal
  Autumn, posed by Prince Alfred
  Winter, posed by Albert Edward, Prince of Wales
References: R. Gunnis; R. Copeland (*Spode & Copeland Marks,* p.30)

THORWALDSEN, Albert Bertel 1770-1843

A noted Danish sculptor. In 1793 he gained the first gold medal awarded by the Copenhagen Academy. It carried with it a bursary covering three years of overseas residence. Thorwaldsen went to Italy and, excepting the years 1838-1841, remained there for the rest of his life. His mausoleum lies within the Thorwaldsen Museum in Copenhagen.

Attributed work, suggested:
Venus (such a subject made by Copeland has not been identified although suggested by Shinn)
References: R. Gunnis; C. & D. Shinn; Century

VANDE VENNE, M. fl. 1840

A Dutchman, born at Bois le Duc, he studied at the Royal Academy of Antwerp and later worked in Rome. Although little is known of him, he was thought well of by his contemporaries. His sculpture of 'The Temptation' was exhibited at the Great Exhibition of 1851, although it was sculpted in 1840. An illustration of it was published in the *Art-Journal* of 1855 opposite page 156.

Attributed work
Eve with Serpent (The Temptation), seated figure
Reference: Art-Journal

WARBURG, Eugene 1825-1861

A free-born Afro-American sculptor, Warburg studied and practised in New Orleans where he was born. His successes amongst local dignitaries aroused the hostility of local artists, and so he left to work abroad in England, Belgium, France and Italy, where he died in Rome. Whilst in England, 1852-1857, he secured the patronage of Harriet, 2nd Duchess of Sutherland for whom he executed a series of bas-reliefs based upon the novel *Uncle Tom's Cabin,* by Harriet Beecher-Stowe. The *Art-Journal* of 1857 reports on page 295:

> Statuette of 'Old Tiff', of much merit and considerable interest has been recently produced by Alderman Copeland, in statuary porcelain; it is the work of Mr. Warburg, an American sculptor of 'mixed blood', an artist of great ability and general intelligence. The group represents 'Old Tiff', the hero of Mrs. Stowe's latest novel, nursing the little maiden who is the heroine of the story. It is a striking work.

Mrs.Stowe said of it: 'It is beautifully truthful, and shows how far the expression of love and fidelity may go in giving beauty to the coarsest and plainest features'.

Attributed work
Uncle Tiff, group
Reference: Grocer & Wallace

WEEKES, Henry, RA 1807-1877

Born and educated in Canterbury, England, at King's School. He studied under Behnes and Chantrey, from whom he received a legacy upon the latter's death. He inherited Chantrey's studio, finishing many of the uncompleted works. He sculpted a figure of the 'Young Naturalist' which was shown at the International Exhibition in London in 1862. It is almost certain, however, that this was not the figure reproduced by Copeland; an example illustrated in *The Parian Phenomenon* states that it is marked 'R.J.Morris 1886', the date being that of its manufacture and not the date when it was first put into production, which is thought to have been about 1878.

WESTMACOTT, James Sherwood 1823-1900

Son of Henry Westmacott by his first wife and nephew of Sir Richard Westmacott with whom he studied sculpture. His two busts of cherubs 'Asleep' and 'Awake' are sometimes called 'Night' and 'Morning', but this is incorrect, especially as Monti's great statuettes have these titles. James Sherwood Westmacott came from a family of sculptors, none of whom attained very great distinction.

Attributed works
Asleep, bust
Awake, bust
Christ and Mary, group
Master Davy, statuette
Sir Charles Napier, portrait bust
Sir Robert Peel, portrait bust
Prince Albert, portrait bust
Queen Victoria, portrait bust
Reference: R. Gunnis

WICHMANN, Ludwig Wilhelm **1788-1859**
A German sculptor born at Potsdam, he studied under Gottfried Schadow. In 1807 he went to Paris and studied in the studios of David and the sculptor Bosio. He went to Rome in 1819 but after two years he returned to his native country and was appointed Professor at Berlin Academy.
Attributed work
The Toilet, statuette
Reference: The Art-Journal 1851, p.238 and illustration

WOOD, Marshall **d.1882**
Little is known of this British sculptor except that he worked in London.
Attributed works
Daphne, bust
Daphne, statuette
Prince of Wales, portrait bust
Reference: B-C 87700

WOOD, Shakespere **early 19th century-1886**
An Irishman from Belfast, Wood worked mostly in marble, producing medallions, relief portraits and busts. He exhibited at the Royal Academy from 1868-1871. He died in Rome in 1886.
Attributed work
Relief plaque of an unidentified gentleman, dated 10 July 1847
References: J. Mackay; *Parian Phenomenon* fig.571, p.175

WOOLNER, Thomas, RA **1825-1892**
Born at Hadleigh in Suffolk, Woolner initially studied under Behnes, the painter, whose death caused him to transfer to William Behnes, the sculptor, brother of his late master. He joined the Royal Academy Schools in 1842 and exhibited work there in 1843. He went to Australia in 1852, but returned in 1854 and established himself as a specialist in portrait sculpture. Two of his works, 'Eros', and 'Euphrosne', were reproduced in basalt and carrara by Wedgwood. In his capacity as a sculptor Woolner became a founder member of the Pre-Raphaelite brotherhood. In 1875 he sculpted a 'Blue Coat Group' for Christ's Hospital, Horsham, but the present administration of that school has no knowledge of it.
Attributed work
Red Riding Hood, statuette
References: R. Gunnis; M. Batkin

WYATT, Richard James **1795-1850**
After an apprenticeship with J.C.F. Rossi, Wyatt joined the Royal Academy Schools, after which he proceeded to Paris to study under Bosio. Then he moved on to Rome, where he entered the studio of Canova, upon whose demise he worked with Thorwaldsen. Wyatt specialised in the female figure, his work being reproduced frequently by the Staffordshire potters.
Attributed work
Apollo as the Shepherd Boy of Admetus, sometimes called The Goatherd, statuette
References: R. Gunnis; B. Read; C. & D. Shinn; *Art-Journal* 1850, p.249

WYON, Edward William **1811-1885**
Son of Thomas Wyon, chief engraver of the seals of Kings George III and IV, he joined the Royal Academy Schools in 1829 where, from 1831 to 1876, he showed nearly one hundred busts, medallions, etc. The two caryatids at the entrance to the Fitzwilliam Museum in Cambridge are examples of his work. Wyon's sculptures were used extensively by Wedgwood.
Attributed works
Fisherman's Daughter, now called Mending the Net, seated figure
Stepping Stones, statuette
References: R. Gunnis; Reilly & Savage

PARIAN WARE GROUPS

GP1

GP1 – BABES IN THE WOOD
c.1851
Ht. 5¾in. (14.6cm)
Illus: Yes

This group is listed with 'additional works are now ready' in a price list thought to have been published about 1851; it was printed in English, German and French! The price, which was probably retail, was 21/-. It was not printed in subsequent lists but it was included in the Statuary Price Book (SPB) under the title **'Children in the Wood'** at 15/- and 21/- respectively wholesale and retail; at some later date the wholesale price was reduced to 10/6. A handwritten note in the Net Price List (NPL) of c.1880 states that the wholesale price in 1884 was 5/-. The making price in 1928 was 1/6.

Based on an old English ballad of which the author is not known. The story is also known as **'Children in the Wood'** and is preserved in the collection of Joseph Ritson, an eighteenth century antiquary.

The ballad was entered in the 'Stationers' Register' in 1595. In 1601 a play, possibly of Italian derivation, was published; 'the plot centred on a young child piurthured *[sic]* in a wood by two ruffins *[sic]* with the consent of his unkle *[sic]* '.

Joseph Ritson (1753-1803) was born at Stockton. Among his known works are 'Ancient Songs' (1790); 'Scottish Songs' (1794); 'Robin Hood – a collection of Ballads' (1795).

GP2 – BLIND BOY AND DUMB FANNY
c.1867
Ht. 12in. (30.48cm). (The Copeland record photograph states 13in. high, while the c.1880 and 1876 Price Lists state '14 inches high'.)
Sculptor: G.A. Lawson
Marks: G A Lawson Sc. Aug 1867
Illus. Yes PP 538

The marble group was first exhibited at the Royal Academy in 1866. The subject is taken from 'Langley Lane', a poem by the poet Robert William Buchanan, which formed part of a collection known as *London Poems,* published in 1866. The original invoice is in the Spode Museum Trust's Collection:

6 Fitzroy Terrace, London
14 Augt 1867
Messrs W.T. Copeland & Sons
To a model of blind boy & girl taken from Buchanans poem of 'Langley Lane' with copyright £20 -
(Receipted) Geo A Lawson 21/8/67

A copper engraving in the Spode Museum Trust's Collection relates the two stanzas which are relevant to the story of 'The Blind Boy'. A print from this might have been transferred to the inside of the group.

In the 1876 Retail Price list it was £2.18.0. The wholesale price in the 'c.1882' NPL was 35/-; the retail price as written in the SPB was 52/6, but the entry was made after the original entries for other items.The making price in 1928 was 4/-.

Robert Buchanan was born in Caverswall, near Stoke-on-Trent, in August 1841. An account in *Pearson's Weekly* for the week ending 20 February 1892 opines that Buchanan is 'one of the literary giants of the present day'. Buchanan's father worked under Robert Owen as a socialist missionary. Robert Buchanan spent his early years in Scotland and was educated at the High School and University of Glasgow before travelling to London. Here he found employment on the *Athenaeum* and the *Literary Gazette.* Because he spoke Danish he went to Schleswig-Holstein and Denmark as war correspondent for the *Morning Star.*

GP2

GP4

GP3 – BLUE COAT BOY AND GIRL on double pedestal (Factory Record only)
c.1885
This group is listed in the SPB as 'Blue Coat boy & Girl on double pedestal 2/6 RV 13/6/85; ditto on single 8d'. The lack of further details suggests that these two figures were made for a private commission. Mr Nicholas Plumley, archivist of Christ's Hospital, Horsham, states that he had never come across a reference to this item (letter 16/6/1989).

There were a number of 'Blue-Coat Schools' located throughout England, the first of which, known as 'Christ's Hospital', was founded on the site of the Greyfriars' monastery in London during the reign of Henry VIII. The name 'Blue-Coat School' derives from the blue coat, or gown, worn by the scholars, often with yellow stockings (said to deter rats!). They were invariably associated with the relief of the under-privileged. Entry was normally restricted solely to male scholars; the only exception determined by the author is that of the school at Liverpool, where girls were also accepted. This school was founded in 1717 by Bryan Blundell, a 'master of a ship in the foreign trade', as a day-school. It became a boarding-school in 1718, eventually housing a hundred pupils. It was located in School Lane, Church Street, near St Peter's Church, Liverpool and is now, for boys only, to be found at Wavertree, Liverpool.

GP4 – BOY WITH BEGGING DOG
c.1860
Ht. 8in. (20.32cm)
Sculptor: After C. MacCarthy
Illus: Yes
This is listed in the NPL at 2/-, and at 3/- in the SPB. It was also issued as a vesta holder at the same prices. The retail price for either in 1876 was 3/6, while the revised wholesale price in 1884 was 1/8.
See Colour Plate 1

GP5 – BOY WITH DOG and COMPANION
c.1860
This is listed at the same prices as the Boy with Begging Dog, in both the lists quoted.

GP6 – BOY WITH FALCON companion to **Girl with Falcon**
c.1876
This item is included in the Making Lists of 1895 and 1928, but is not found in any published or manuscript price list. However, **Girl with Falcon** is included in the 1876 retail price list at 3/6.

GP7 – BOY, DOG AND BIRD
c.1850
L. 8in. (20.32cm)
Sculptor: J.J. Pradier
Illus: Yes PP 556
This group is included in the SPB where the retail price was 24/-. The retail price in 1876 was 18/-, while the NPL of c.1880 quotes it at 10/-; in 1884 the revised wholesale price was 7/6. The making price in 1928 was 1/9.

A plaster example of this sculpture is in the Museum of Art, Geneva. (Ref. Dennis Catalogue No.341.)

GP8 – BOY WITH RABBIT
c.1855
Ht. 11in. (27.94cm)
Sculptor: Raffaele Monti
Illus: Yes PP 500
The SPB lists this group with the additional note 'Greek Figure' and the prices 27/6 and 42/- respectively for wholesale and retail. The retail price in 1876 was £1.16.0. In the c.1882 NPL it is quoted at 18/-, being reduced to 12/6 in 1884. In these printed lists it is to be found under 'Statuettes'. The original marble was sculpted by Monti in 1848.

GP9 – BOY WITH TERRIERS or **CHASSE AU LAPIN**
c.1860
Ht. 11in. (27.94cm), 12in. (30.48cm)
Sculptor: P.J. Mêne
Illus: Yes PP 578
This group is a version of Mêne's sculpture 'Chasse au Lapin' which

GP7

GP8

GP9

GP10

was exhibited at the Exposition Universelle at Paris in 1855. Many small bronze versions were issued, often failing to include the boy, as indeed did another Copeland version, 'Group of Terriers' (see Miscellany). In most of the references the group is to be found under **'Terriers with Boy'.**

The SPB quotes 25/- and 37/6 as the wholesale and retail prices; the 1876 retail price was £1.16.0. The c.1882 printed NPL has £1.0.0, and this was not reduced in 1884; the 1928 Making Book lists it as 'Boy & Terriers' at 5/-. The printed lists quote the height as 12in. (30.48cm).

GP10 – BURNS AND MARY
c 1860
Ht. 19in. (48.26cm)
Sculptor: W. Beattie
Illus: Yes PP 559
The group is that of Robert Burns with Mary Campbell ('Highland Mary'), one of Burns' many mistresses, who died in October 1786. They met in the spring of that year; the relationship was something of an enigma, the truth of which may never be known. She was said by some people to be nothing more than a common prostitute. Burns claimed that she died of a malignant fever; however, there is good evidence to suggest that she died in childbirth. She lies buried in Greenock cemetery. She features in four of Burns' works: *'Will ye go to the Indies, my Mary?'*, *'The Highland Lassie'* and posthumously: *'Highland Mary'* and *'To Mary in Heaven'*. This last poem is also known as 'Thou ling'ring star with less'ning ray' and *'My Mary, dear departed shade'*. (Scots Musical Museum – Volume III).

The group is listed in the SPB at 6 guineas and 10 guineas respectively for wholesale and retail. The 1876 retail price was £9.9.0 while the NPL charge was £4.14.6, reduced in 1884 to 63/-. The making price in 1928 was 13/-.

GP11

GP11a

GP11 – CHILDREN WITH LIZARD
Ht. 9in. (22.86cm)
Marks:COPELAND and moulded mark of Samuel Alcock
Illus: Yes
This group is included in the SPB at 10/6 and 16/-; there is also a note that a turquoise and gilt version was made for the Crystal Palace Art Union at a price of 24/-. The price is printed in the NPL at 10/-, being reduced to 7/6 in 1884. The retail price in 1876 was 16/-.

With the inscribed mark, the moulds for this group had been bought at the sale of Samuel Alcock. Exactly when the moulds were sold is not known because the concern changed hands three times:

Samuel Alcock & Co	1828-1859
James Duke & Nephews	1860-1863
Hill Pottery	1863-1867

See Colour Plate 2

GP12 – CHILDREN SLEEPING IN COTS (PAIR)
c.1870
L. 6in. (15.24cm)
Illus: PP 549
They appear to be lying in a most uncomfortable posture! One wonders whether they are really asleep or dead.

These children are listed in the SPB under this title at 5/- and 7/-, with a reduction made at a later date to 3/- and 5/-. In *The Parian Phenomenon* they are titled '**Sleeping children in Cots**'. They are not listed in the 1876 retail price list. They are included in the c.1880 price list, where they are listed under 'Miscellaneous' as '**Sleeping Child in Cot (Matchbox)**'.These were available as match boxes at 3/- each and the SPB quotes a base at a third of the full price. The NPL also lists '**Sleeping Child on Cushion**'.

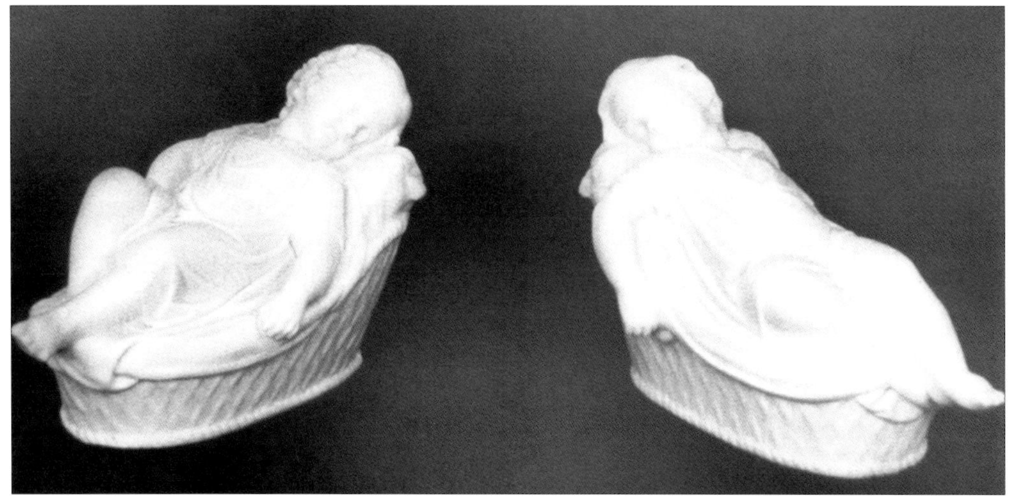

GP12

GP13

GP15 – CRITICAL MOMENT

c.1883
Sculptor: Owen Hale
Illus: Yes
A young girl is hanging on for dear life while her donkey bucks, having been frightened by a dog.

A handwritten note in the NPL quotes a wholesale price of 35/- in 1884 and the making price in 1928 was 8/6. This appears to have been a difficult subject to manufacture.

GP16 – DAVID AND GOLIATH

The group portrays the single-handed encounter between David, the shepherd boy son of Jesse, and the giant Goliath, a native of Gath and the champion of the confederate Philistine camp. David accepted Goliath's challenge and slew him by slinging a smooth pebble at him. For his success, King Saul of Israel took David into his royal household but he was jealous of him so that David had to be very careful to avoid death. Samuel had previously anointed David as the future King of Israel (1055-1015 BC). See the First Book of Samuel, Chapter 16 and onwards.

Listed in the Making Lists for 1895 and 1928; also in the SPB (c.1860) at 70/-W, 105/-R.

GP17 – DUBLIN SEASONS

Mentioned in *The Parian Phenomenon* as being a group of four figures. The source for this item is the factory Making List of 1928 in which it is entered under 'Figures: Seasons, Dublin (Set of 4) 10d (each).' No other entry is known at the moment.

GP13 – CHRIST AND MARY

c.1855
Ht. 22in. (55.88cm), W. 15in. (38.1cm)
Sculptor: J.S. Westmacott
Illus: Yes PP 524
This group was issued in two sizes, the smaller one measuring 16 x 11in. (40.64 x 27.94cm).

It portrays Christ in the house of Martha and Mary. St. Luke tells the story in Chapter 10, verses 38-42, of how Jesus was welcomed by Martha into their house. Her sister had settled down at Jesus' feet and was listening to what he said. But Martha was upset about her preparations and burst in upon them, saying, 'Lord, don't you mind that my sister has left me to do everything by myself? Tell her to get up and help me!' But the Lord answered her, 'Martha, my dear, you are worried and bothered about providing so many things. Only a few things are really needed, perhaps only one. Mary has chosen the best part and you must not tear it away from her!' (J.B. Phillips translation.)

The SPB lists this at 8 and 12 guineas respectively for wholesale and retail; the retail prices in 1876 were 12 and 7 guineas. In the c.1882 NPL the price was £5.5.0 for the larger group and £3.3.0 for the smaller one. These were reduced in 1884 to 65/- and 37/6. The 1928 making prices were 13/6 and 7/6.

See Colour Plate 3

GP14 – COTTAGE CHILDREN

c.1860
Ht. 13in. (33.02cm), L. 10in (25.4cm), W. 6in. (15.24cm).
Illus: Yes
The prices stated in the SPB are 35/- and 52/6. The retail price in 1876 was 2 guineas. The NPL quotes £1.1.0, reducing to 10/6 in 1884.

GP14

GP15

GP18a

GP18 – DUTCH SEASONS

c.1851

Illus: Yes, the factory record shows them as comports. They were not a group on one base but four individual figures.Two figures, **Spring** and **Winter**, are illustrated as single figures. In all lists they are under 'Figures' or 'Statuettes', not under 'Groups'.

These are listed in the addendum to a price list believed to have been issued in about 1851; here they appear as 'A Set of Dutch Figures, as the Four Seasons 10in. high. 5/-'. The SPB lists them as:

Dutch Seasons Set Figures 42/-W, 105/-R. Also separate 10/6 W, 17/6 R.
Dutch Season with embossed comport 14/- W, 21/- R, and with 8in. Windsor Comport, 18/- W.

There was also a version with Cov'd Cooper bucket 25/- W. The Making Book for 1928 lists the regular size at 1/6, and a large size at 1/9.

A copy of the c.1880 NPL, for the trade only, charges 10/6 each, and an annotated copy of 1884 has reduced this to 6/-.

See Colour Plate 4

GP18

GP18b

GP19

GP19 – EARLY STRUGGLES
c.1874
Ht. 17in. (43.18cm)
Sculptor: L.A. Malempré
Illus: Yes PP 539
This group is listed in the c.1880 NPL at £2.2.0, which had been reduced to 30/- in 1884. It does not appear in the SPB and in the 1928 Making Book the maker would receive 5/6.

The concept of this group is in line with the similar groups 'First Lesson', 'Happy Days', 'Happy Mother', and the two versions of 'Evening Devotion'.

GP20 – EMILY AND THE WHITE DOE
1861
Small Ht. 18½in. (46.99cm)
Large Ht. 30½in. (77.47cm)
L. 23in. (58.42cm), W. 15in. (38.1cm)
Sculptor: F.M. Miller
Marks: F M MILLER SC. NORTON OF RYLESTONE
Illus: Yes PP 557
The original marble group was exhibited by Miller in 1859 and the receipt for £8.0.0. for a plaster cast with copyright supplied to Mr Alderman Copeland is signed by F.M. Miller and dated 15 December 1860.

The theme is taken from William Wordsworth's poem 'The White Doe of Rhylestone' which tells the story of Emily, an Elizabethan Catholic girl and sole surviving daughter of a rebellious family. In her lonely bereavement she gains solace from visits by a white doe which she had reared in earlier times. The figure is based on Birket Foster's illustrations of Wordsworth's poems.

Emily Norton of Rylstone had a pet white doe; after her lover's death she visited his grave at Bolton Priory and after her death the doe

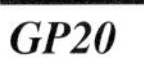

GP20

GP20a

GP21

GP21a

GP21b

continued to visit Francis' grave.

Copeland included a large version of the group in his display at the International Exhibition of 1862 in London; this is now in the collection of the Victoria and Albert Museum.

The retail price in 1876 was £5.15.6. for the small group and in the c.1882 NPL £3.3.0., which was reduced to 46/- in 1884. The SPB quotes 3 guineas and 5 guineas respectively for wholesale and retail c.1864. The large group was 25 guineas in the SPB at wholesale. The example in the Spode Museum Trust collection is extremely heavy and one can appreciate why this version was so costly.

GP21 – EVENING DEVOTION and COMPANION
c.1870
Ht. 20in. (50.8cm) both groups
Sculptor: Owen Hale
Illus: Yes
These two groups will have appealed to the sentimentally minded of the day and are in the same vein as 'Early Struggles', 'First Lesson' and 'Happy Days'. In order to distinguish between them, 'Evening Devotion' shows the child in a kneeling posture, while the companion group shows the child sitting on the stool with her arms raised.

These groups are not mentioned in the SPB, nor in the 1873 and 1876 price lists. They are listed in the NPL of c.1870, however, where they are priced at £3.13.0 each, with a handwritten note that in 1884 the prices were 70/- and 63/- respectively. In the 1928 Making Price Book they are both at 13/- each.

GP22 – FATES, A GROUP OF
c.1861
Sponsor: Rennie & Adcock
Marks: COPELAND
Illus: Yes
One example only is known of this group and this is in the Spode Museum Trust Collection; it is in two pieces. The only mention in any list is in the SPB where the wholesale price was 35/-. The modelling is of a very high quality.

The Fates, called Moirae by the Greeks and Parcae by the Romans, were three in number. Homer called them the 'thread of life' because they were conceived as the divinities of the duration of human life. Clotho was the 'spinning' fate, and is the central figure of this group, holding a spindle in her uplifted left hand; Lachesis, the disposer of lots, was the one who assigns to man his fate; and Atropos, the inevitable, or the fate that cannot be avoided. All three are said to cut off the thread when life is to end. Clotho spins the thread of life. Lachesis fixes the length and, as the figure on the right, points towards the globe. Atropos, on the left, holds a pair of scales in her left hand and a cutting instrument in her right hand (these are missing from the piece).

GP23 – THE FINDING OF MOSES
1862
Sculptor: B.E. Spence
Illus: Yes (from the *Art-Journal*, page 70, March 1864, entitled the Infant Moses)
The only evidence, so far, for this group is a stereoscopic photograph of the exhibit in the International Exhibition of 1862 in London.

Moses, the great law-giver and leader of the Israelites in their escape from bondage in Egypt and journey through the desert, was hidden, as an infant, in a basket placed among the riverside reeds of the Nile to protect him from the cruel edict that all Hebrew male children should be drowned. He was discovered by an Egyptian princess who adopted him and called him Moses, 'because', she said 'I drew him out of the water'. So he was brought up as a prince. The story is told in Exodus chapters 1 and 2.

Wedgwood, too, used the incident as source material for a parian group; this was sculpted by W. Beattie (see PP 630).

GP22

GP23

GP23a

GP24

GP24 – FIRST LESSON
1884
Ht. 18in. (45.72cm) both groups
Sculptor: Owen Hale
Marks: OWEN HALE SC. 1881
Illus: Yes
Reminiscent of 'Evening Devotion', also by Owen Hale, this group is not mentioned in the SPB, nor is it included in the 1873 and 1876 price lists, but it is listed in the c.1882 NPL where it is written in by hand with the price in 1884 of 45/-.

An attractive coloured version is illustrated, marked L 84.

See Colour Plate 5

GP25 – GIRL WITH DOVE
c.1860
Ht. 13in. (33.02cm)
Illus: Yes, as a comport
An offering, among many, to Victorian sentimentality. A romantic portrayal of sweet innocence produced in one form or another by several manufactories. Copeland's 'Girl with Dove' was issued also as a candlestick. A bust of a girl with dove was sculpted for Copelands by W.C. Marshall, RA and named 'Lesbia'.(q.v.)

This 'group' was regarded as a statuette in the Price Lists. It is listed in the SPB at 5/-, and 10/- retail. The NPL of c.1870 confirms the price of 5/-, with a handwritten note that the price in 1884 was 4/-. Here it is listed as a statuette, as it is in 1873, at 5/6, and in 1876 at 8/6 retail. The 1928 making price was 10d.

GP26 – GIRL WITH FALCON
This is really a statuette and is companion to **Boy with Falcon**. It is listed only in the Retail Price List of 1876 at 3/6, and in the 1928 Making List at 6d. It may be assumed that it is a small figure.

GP27 – GIRL WITH LADYBIRD
c.1875
Sponsor: Ceramic and Crystal Palace Art Union
Little is known of this piece. It is listed at 21/- in a list of stock held at the factory in 1881 for the Ceramic and Crystal Palace Art Union. It is probably a statuette. The 1928 Making List includes a figure called'Ladybird' at 3/3. At this price it suggests that it may be a large figure.

GP28 – GIRL WITH LIZARD
It states in PP (p132) that this figure is included in an 1870s price list, but I have not found it; it may have been confused with **Children with Lizard**. However, it is entered as a figure in the 1928 Making List at 1/6d.

GP29 – GIRL WITH RABBIT also called **THE PETS**
1873
Ht. 16½in. (41.91cm)
Sculptor: F.M. Miller
Sponsor: Ceramic and Crystal Palace Art Union
Marks: F.M.Miller Sc 1873
Illus: Yes PP 502
The *Art-Journal* in 1872 included the statement 'Mr Felix Miller has produced for the Ceramic Art Union a charming statuette entitled **The Pets**, the pets being a pretty little girl nursing a rabbit'.

The item is recorded in the SPB at 21/- and, although not listed in the other printed price lists because it was exclusive to the CCPAU, a price of 10/6 is handwritten in the NPL for 1884, three years after that Union had ceased trading. In the stock sheet of items held in 1881 for the CCPAU the price was £1.0.0. In 1928 the making price was 2/6.

GP25

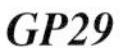

GP29

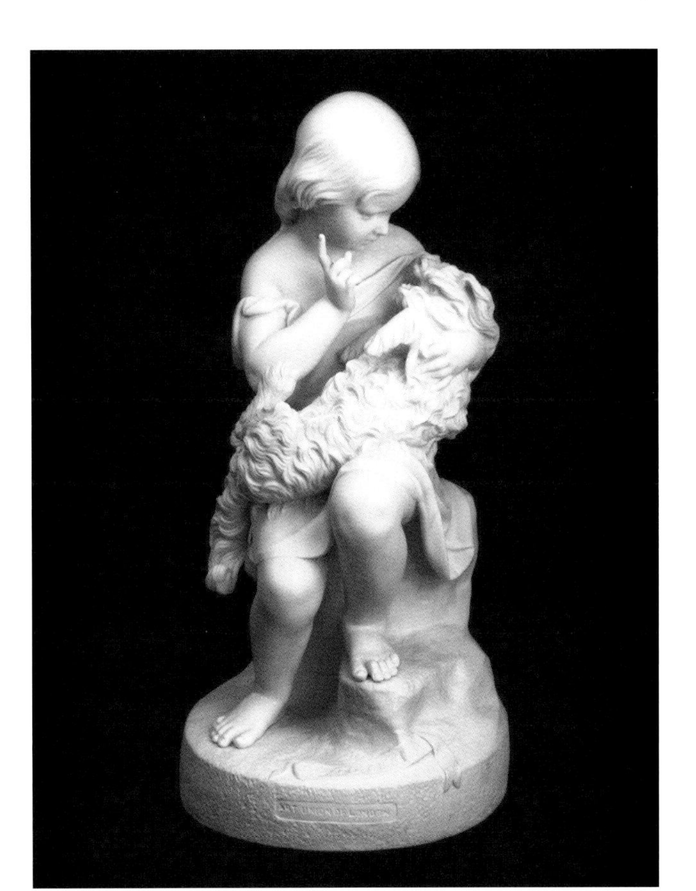

GP30

GP30 – GO TO SLEEP
1862
Ht. 19in. (48.26cm)
Sculptor: J. Durham
Sponsor: The Art Union of London
Marks: J.DURHAM Sc 1862
Illus: Yes PP 495
The original marble sculpture was commissioned by F. Bennoch Esq. and was displayed at both the Royal Academy and the International Exhibition in London in 1862. The reduced model in statuary porcelain was given by the Art Union of London as prizes in 1863, 1864, and 1865.

The price to the AUL quoted in the SPB was 35/-. There is also a reference to 61/- being charged to the AUL, but it is not clear to what this refers, nor when. It is listed as a statuette in the 1928 Making Book at a price of 4/6. It is not listed in any price book.

GP31 – THE GOLDEN AGE
c.1851
Ht. 18in. (45.72cm)
Sculptor: William Beattie
Illus: PP 564
It is said that HM Queen Victoria purchased an example at the International Exhibition in Dublin in 1853.

This is a complicated subject and is priced at 6 guineas wholesale and 10 guineas retail in the SPB. In 1873 the trade price was £5.15.6, while in 1876 the retail price was £8.18.6. The NPL of c.1882 was £5.5.0. The 1884 trade price was 4 guineas. In 1928 the making price was 16/-.

GP32 – GREAT EXPECTATIONS or **RUSTIC SPORTS – FISHING**
Ht. 8in., W. 9in., D. 6in. (20.32cm, 22.86cm, 15.24cm)
Illus: Yes

GP31

GP32

GP33

GP34

The subject is derived from the novel *Great Expectations* by Charles Dickens, which appeared as a serial story in the magazine *All the Year Round* between 1860 and 1861. The story was published in book form in 1861.

Under its title **'Rustic Sports – Fishing'** it is listed in the c.1880 NPL at 15/-, yet the photograph in the Copeland record adopts the alternative title. A trade price of 10/6 is noted in the NPL, but the item is not printed there, this price being handwritten for 1884. The SPB lists a richly gilded, raised and chased version where it is called **'Rustic Groups'** under **'Rustic Boy'**.

GP33 – THE GUARDIAN ANGEL
1877
Ht. 24in. (60.96cm)
Sculptor: L.A. Malempré
Sponsor: The Crystal Palace Art Union
Illus: Yes

The inspiration for this group came from the novel of the same name, published in 1868, by Oliver Wendell Holmes (1809-1894), an American, who was a successful novelist, poet and essayist. He was professor of anatomy and physiology at Harvard University from 1847 to 1882.

Although the sculpture was illustrated as an engraving in the *Art-Journal* in 1880 under the title 'The Guiding Angel', Copelands listed it in several places. The SPB gives a price of 28/- trade, but does not give a retail price, although there is no note that it was for the CCPAU.

In 1881 the stock list of items held for the CCPAU quoted it as a group at 50/-. The making price in 1928 was 9/-.

In the lists of statuettes in the 1873, 1876 and c.1882 price lists there is a 'Guardian Angel' but, at the prices of £1.4.0, £1.16.0, and £1.1.0 respectively, this item may be another name for a small version of 'Peace'.

Groups, busts and statuettes sponsored by art unions and others are not listed in factory price lists while they remain exclusive to their sponsors.

GP34 – HAPPY DAYS
Ht. 19in. (48.26cm)
Illus: Yes
Another group in the sentimental vein of mother and child.

It is not listed in the SPB, nor in the price lists of 1873 and 1876; it is included in the c.1882 NPL at £2.2.0 with the handwritten note that in 1884 it was 27/6. The 1928 making price was 5/6.

GP35 – HAPPY MOTHER
c.1867
Ht. 12in. (30.48cm)
Sculptor: Richard Westmacott ?
Illus: Yes
This attractive domestic theme was used widely as a decorative motif on ceramics from the 18th century onwards. One version designed by Lady Templetown, named 'Sportive Love', was modelled by William Hackwood and used by Josiah Wedgwood in the 18th century. The interpretations by Adam Buck which were used as prints on ceramics were also popular.

This particular group is the only one using this theme which is included in the SPB where it is priced at 30/- trade and 45/- retail. It is not in the 1873 and 1876 lists. It is in the c.1882 NPL at £1.1.0 with the price reduced to 18/- in 1884. In 1928 the making price was 3/3.

An example was given to the Lichfield Museum by W.T. Copeland and is available for inspection by appointment.

GP35

GP36 – HARVEST GROUP
The only reference to this item appears in the SPB where it is priced at 7 guineas, with the added comment 'flowers turq. & gold'. It is stated in *The Parian Phenomenon* that it is listed in the 1895 and 1928 Making Lists, but it is not in the 1928 list under this title; the 1895 list has it just as 'Harvest' with no price.

GP37 – THE HEAVENLY CHORUS, A GROUP OF ANGELS
Sculptor: Theodore Phyffers
Sponsor: William Taylor Copeland
Very little is known of this group; no prices and no illustration. The source for this entry is a letter from Mr Phyffers, dated 29 July 1857, to W.T. Copeland, expressing his willingness to sell his group of Miss Nightingale & the Wounded Soldier with copyright, to be published in statuary porcelain, 'also the group of Angels representing the "Heavenly Chorus" on the same terms, for six guineas, – reserving for myself the right to copy the above named modellls [*sic*] in marble and my name to be marked in full (without the address) on the copies of your publication'. This letter was followed by another paper stating:

> Mr Copeland agrees to purchase of Mr Phyffers a Group Of Angels representing The Heavenly Chorus upon the same terms for Six Guineas to be paid for on the 10th September 1857...
> Received of W.T.Copeland Esq. the sum of Six Guineas for the Group of The Heavenly Chorus as above. Thre Phyffers Septber 19th 1857.

GP38 – THE INFANCY OF JUPITER
1871
Ht. 20in. (50.8cm)
Sculptor: Raffaele Monti
Marks: R MONTI 1871

GP38

GP39

Illus: Yes

The Romans regarded Jupiter as the supreme deity; in Greek mythology he is Zeus, the son of Cronus and Rhea. Cronus had the habit of swallowing his children immediately after their birth, but when Rhea was pregnant with Zeus, she applied to Uranus and Ge (Heaven and Earth), his parents, to save the life of the child. They sent Rhea to Lyctos in Crete where, after Zeus was born, Rhea concealed him in a cave of Mt. Aegaeon, and gave Cronus a stone wrapped up in a cloth, which he swallowed as he thought it was his son. Another location was the Mt. Ida where his nurse was the nymph Amalthea who fed him on the milk of a goat. This parian group is Monti's conception of this particular myth.

The group is recorded in the SPB at 84/- trade and 126/- retail. On 27/1/72 the price was 4 guineas. Although not in the 1873 NPL, it was listed in 1876 at £7.0.0 retail. It is included in the c.1882 NPL at £4.4.0 with the handwritten note that in 1884 it was 70/-. The making price in 1928 was 13/-.

GP39 – INO AND THE INFANT BACCHUS
1851
Ht. 18in., L. 24in. (45.72 x 60.96cm)
Sculptor: J.H. Foley
Marks: J H FOLEY SCULP. PUB. MAY 1 1851
Illus: Yes PP 488

Bacchus, known by the Greeks as Dionysus, is the god of wine. He was the son of Zeus and Semele, one of the daughters of Cadmus of Thebes. Before his birth, Semele was persuaded by Hera to request Zeus to appear to her in the same glory in which he had approached his own wife Hera. Zeus unwillingly complied, and appeared to her in thunder and lightning. Semele, being seized by the flames, gave premature birth to a child. Zeus saved the child, so preserving him to grow to maturity. He is supposed to have been brought up by the nymphs of Mt. Nysa. This sculpture shows his aunt, Ino, the sister of Semele, regaling the infant god with grapes.

The group was reproduced by permission of the Earl of Ellesmere who owned the marble original. At the 1851 Great Exhibition both the original and the parian model were displayed. For this important event Copeland showed his version on an ornamental base which bore the legend 'Great Exhibition of the Industry of all Nations 1851. Manufactured by W.T.COPELAND'. Foley's original plaster model is in the collection of the Royal Dublin Society.

The entry in the SPB quotes 12 guineas trade and 18 guineas retail with the 'pedestal' (base) at 60/- and 84/-. On 2 June 1871 these prices were changed to 8 guineas and 12 guineas, with the trade price of the pedestal rising to 100/-. In the 1851 Price List the price for 'Group of Ino & Bacchus' was 16 guineas; presumably complete with base and at trade. (Firing the base absolutely level must have been difficult which may account for the disparity in the prices.) In 1873 the trade prices were 11 guineas each, while the retail prices in 1876 were 15 guineas and 17 guineas respectively. The NPL of c.1882 quotes £8.8.0 each for group and base, with the handwritten note of 75/6 for the group and 5 guineas for the base in 1884. The making price in 1928 was 13/-.

GP39A – INO AND BACCHUS
1863
Ht. 18½in. (47cm)
Sculptor: L.A. Malempré
Sponsor: Ceramic and Crystal Palace Art Union
Illus: Yes PP523

GP39A

GP40

GP40 – THE INSTRUCTION OF JUPITER
c.1871
Ht. 22in., base 16 x 11in. (55.88cm, 40.64 x 27.94cm)
Sculptor: Raffaele Monti
Illus: Yes
This is a companion piece to **The Infancy of Jupiter**, but it is not mentioned in any of the factory records apart from there being a good photograph of it.

It might be noted from the photographs of these two groups that the goat has only one horn. The myth deals with this by suggesting that it was Jupiter, that is Zeus himself, who broke off one of the horns of the goat, and endowed it with the power of becoming filled with whatever the possessor might wish. Hence this horn was often called the horn of plenty, or cornucopia, and it was used in later times as the symbol of plenty in general.

GP41 – LEAR AND CORDELIA
c.1860
Ht. 10, 11 x 12in. (25.4, 27.94 x 30.48cm)
Sculptor: William Calder Marshall, RA
Marks: W.C. Marshall RA SCULPT
PUB. MARCH 1 1860 BY W.T.COPELAND
Illus: Yes PP 491
The inspiration for the group is derived from William Shakespeare's *King Lear*, Act V, Scene III, in which Lear, in his madness, declaims his belief in Cordelia's continued existence. Cordelia, Lear's youngest daughter, had been disinherited earlier, but had returned with an army to support her father and to de-throne her sisters. Her army was defeated and Cordelia was murdered. A verse from the play is sometimes to be found printed on the base; here the group is called 'Death of Cordelia'.

Shakespearean Illustration
Lear – O, you are men of stone,
Had I your tongues and eyes, I'd see them so
That heavens vault should crack –
O, she is gone for ever! –
I know when one is dead and when one lives
She's dead as earth!
King Lear
Act 5th, Scene 3rd
COPELAND CERAMIC STATUARY

This group has the distinction of being one of the few which occurs in all the known factory lists. The SPB quotes 45/- trade and 70/- retail. In 1873 the trade price was £2.0.0. and the retail price in 1876 was £3.3.0. The c.1882 NPL gives £1.10.0 with 21/- for 1884. The making price in 1928 was 3/9.

GP42 – LEONIDAS ARMING FOR THERMOPYLAE
c.1860
Ht. 19in. (48.26cm)
Illus: Yes
Leonidas, King of Sparta (491-480 BC), was killed in 480 BC defending the narrow pass which led from Thessaly to Locris, known as the pass of Thermopylae, 'the Gate of the Hot Springs'. Leonidas' forces, composed only of 300 Spartans and 700 Thespians, were opposed by a vast army of Persians under the command of Xerxes, King of Persia. The story is told in Herodotus, book VII.

The group is priced in the SPB at 6 guineas trade and 10 guineas retail. In 1873 the price was up to 7 guineas. It was not included in the retail price list of 1876. In the c.1882 NPL it is 5 guineas, with a handwritten note that in 1884 it was 4 guineas trade. In 1928 the making price was 16/-.

GP41

GP42

In the SPB there is a reference below the entry of 'Leonidas':'Plynth Scagliola 21/- 31/6'. Scagliola is an imitation stone or plaster mixed with glue. It is not known to what this refers.

GP43 – LOVE STORY
c.1865
Ht. 9in. (22.86cm)
Sculptor: William Beattie
Illus: Yes
A romantic subject which evidently retained its popularity throughout the period.

The SPB gives three versions: the standard group was 27/6 trade and 42/- retail; a coloured version was 34/- and 52/6 respectively; a version 'with lace', and un-coloured, was 31/6 and 45/- In 1873, it was £1.4.0, with the retail price in 1876 at £1.16.0. The NPL of c.1882 quotes £1.1.0, and in 1884 it was 10/6 trade. The making price in 1928 was 2/-.

GP44 – MISS NIGHTINGALE AND THE WOUNDED SOLDIER
1858
Ht. 13in. (33.02cm)
Sculptor: Theodore Phyffers
Illus: Yes PP 546
The group is listed here under the title used in the c.1870 NPL, although the sculptor called it 'Miss Nightingale supporting the Wounded Soldier'. Although not listed by Copelands otherwise, *The Parian Phenomenon* calls it 'Florence Nightingale and the Wounded at Scutari'.

GP43

GP44

It was illustrated in the *Art-Journal* of 1858, pages 48-9, where it is called 'The Wounded at Scutari'.

The group was commissioned by Mrs Charles Bracebridge, Selina, who, together with her husband, was the intimate friend of Miss Nightingale and for a considerable time her companion and fellow-worker in the Crimea. The original marble sculpture was exhibited at the Royal Academy in 1857.

H.W. Longfellow wrote a poem 'Santa Filomena' in her honour, 'Saint Nightingale: a tribute to Florence, the saint of the Crimea'. This was published in the *Art-Journal.* A more detailed account of Miss Nightingale's life and work is given in the statuette section (page 161).

In the SPB this item is listed as 'Nightingale, Miss. Group' at 45/- trade and 63/- retail. In 1873 the price was £2.8.0 with the retail price in 1876 at £3.2.0. The c.1882 NPL quotes £1.17.6, with 35/- for 1884. The 1928 making price was 7/-. The original invoice in the Spode Museum Trust Collection is as follows:

London 1st August 1857
W.T. Copeland Esq MP
To Theodore Phyffers
To an original Group & Cast of 'Miss Nightingale supporting the Wounded Soldier', with Copyright to make same in Porcelain Statuary in England & elsewhere, Mr Phyffers name to be placed upon each Copy, and the right of producing the Group in Marble to be reserved to Mr Phyffers, who on his part agrees not to produce any in plaster – as per letter of 29th July 1857 £15.15.0.
Received fifteen guineas Thre Phyffers.

GP45 – MORNING
1862
Ht. 28in. (71.12cm)
Sculptor: Raffaele Monti
Marks: R MONTI PUB MAY 1862
Illus: Yes PP 550
The group comprises an infant at the feet of a scantily attired female discarding what might be intended as the veils of night. This might be a romantic portrayal of the awakening world greeting the new-born day. The sculpture is the companion to **Night** and both works were shown by Copelands at the International Exhibition in London in 1862 and later at the International Exhibition in Vienna in 1873. The original marble study was displayed also at the 1862 Exhibition.

In the SPB it is listed as: 'Morning, Figure of with pedestal 6 gns'. No retail price is given. In 1873 the trade price was £7.10.0 and the retail price in 1876 was £11.11.0. In the c.1882 NPL it was priced at £6.16.6. The making price in 1928 was 18/-.

GP46 – MOTHER AND CHILD
1857
Sculptor: Owen Hale
Illus: Not with this title
There is no group of this name recorded in the factory records that I have available to me. The writers of *The Parian Phenomenon* state that 'Two versions of the Mother and Child group appear in the Making Lists of 1895 and 1928, one by Owen Hale'. Having searched the 1928 lists I cannot locate it, but they are recorded in the 1895 Making List but without prices, and both **Happy Days** and **Happy Mother** are listed in the 1928 Making Price Book as well.

There are, however, several groups of a mother with child, one of which was sculpted by Owen Hale – **'First Lesson'**. The various groups which might come within this category are:

Happy Mother
Happy Days
First Lesson, by Owen Hale
Early Struggles, by Malempré
Play, Group of Play, or At Play
Evening Devotion, and Companion

See under the respective title for details.

GP45

In the SPB there is an entry for Mother, figure of, 30/- and 45/-. The cost of this suggests that it might refer to a group, but there are no further details.

A fine example in the Collection of Lichfield District Council, donated by Alderman Copeland in 1858 and catalogued under this title, corresponds to the Group called **Happy Mother**. See GP35.

GP47 – NEW FRIENDS
c.1883
Ht. 17in. (43.18cm)
Sculptor: Owen Hale
Marks: OWEN HALE 1883
Illus: Yes PP 522
An attractive piece of romanticism; a young girl with a small dog jumping up.

The only mention of this item is in the NPL of c.1880 where the group is entered in manuscript with a price of 18/6 in 1884. The making price in 1928 is given as 3/6.

GP48 – NIGHT
1861
Ht. 27in. (68.58cm)
Sculptor: Raffaele Monti
Marks: R MONTI
Illus: Yes PP 552

GP47

GP48

The companion group to **Morning**. This seems to represent the withdrawal of the world to sleep by covering up the young child with a veil so that it might re-vitalise itself in sleep. This group was displayed by Copeland at the International Exhibitions of 1862 in London and 1873 at Vienna.

The group is listed in the SPB as 'Night, figure with pedestal 6 gns' (no retail price given). The 1873 trade price list quotes £7.10.0, while the retail price in the 1876 list was £11.11.0. The c.1880 NPL quotes it at £6.16.6 with the handwritten note that in 1884 it was 6 guineas. In 1928 the making price was 30/-.

See Colour Plate 6

GP49 – PATIENCE
after 1876, possibly 1883
Ht. 28in. (71.12cm)
Sculptor: probably Owen Hale
Illus: Yes PP 485 (this reproduces Copeland's composite illustration)
Another romantic portrayal of a commonplace scene of affection shown by a girl caressing her dog.

The only references to this subject are in the NPL of c.1882 in which the handwritten price of 4 guineas is given for 1884 and a different picture of the group included on a composite illustration from a trade catalogue of about 1885, where the measurements are given as '23in. 13in. 13in.' (58.42cm. 33.02cm. 33.02cm).

An earlier accompanying price sheet quotes 4 guineas with a handwritten note of 4 guineas on 29/8/95. This price is printed on a later, undated, list with a handwritten price of 5 guineas.

GP50 No entry

GP51 – PAUL AND VIRGINIA
1845
Ht. 12in. (30.48cm)
Sculptor: Charles Cumberworth
Marks: COPELAND & GARRETT STATUARY PORCELAIN (Printed mark). Later issues after 1847 had only the impressed COPELAND mark.
Illus: Yes PP 511
The inspiration for this group stems from the novel 'Paul et Virginie' by Bernadine de Saint-Pierre, first published in 1787. The scene is set on L'isle de France (Mauritius), where two fatherless children are brought up by their respective mothers in poverty and innocence. They fall in love at an early age and become devoted to one another. After some years Virginia is recalled to France by an aunt who is wealthy, but also very harsh. Eventually Virginia returns to Mauritius and, as Paul awaits her landfall, her boat is shipwrecked before his eyes and Virginia drowns. Within a few weeks Paul dies of a broken heart.

This is one of the earliest parian groups and at first both figures and base were made by the 'pressing' process using plastic clay, before the casting method had been perfected. It was illustrated in the *Art-Union* journal in November 1846 and was exhibited at the Exhibition of Industrial Art in Manchester in 1846. In 1848 HRH the Prince Albert bought an example. The group continued to be displayed at major exhibitions including that in Birmingham in 1849 and in London in 1851.

It is listed in the earliest known price list of 1848 at £3.10.0, where it is also illustrated; these early delineations are reversed, probably because

GP49

GP51

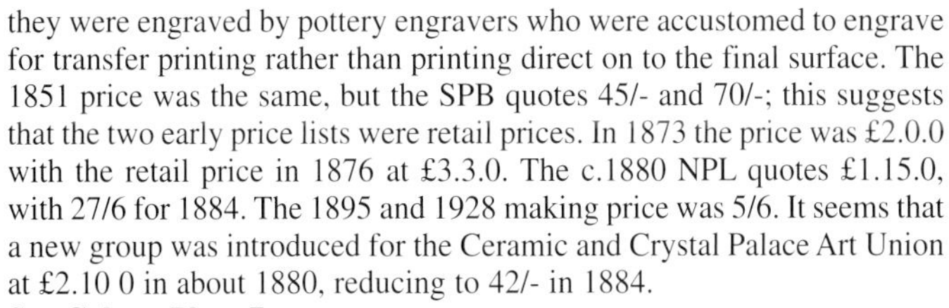

they were engraved by pottery engravers who were accustomed to engrave for transfer printing rather than printing direct on to the final surface. The 1851 price was the same, but the SPB quotes 45/- and 70/-; this suggests that the two early price lists were retail prices. In 1873 the price was £2.0.0 with the retail price in 1876 at £3.3.0. The c.1880 NPL quotes £1.15.0, with 27/6 for 1884. The 1895 and 1928 making price was 5/6. It seems that a new group was introduced for the Ceramic and Crystal Palace Art Union at £2.10 0 in about 1880, reducing to 42/- in 1884.
See Colour Plate 7

GP52 – PET BLOODHOUND
after 1867
Ht. 8in. (20.32cm)
Marks: Samuel Alcock monogram, moulded
Illus: Yes
This group and the companion piece, **Pet Lamb,** were acquired from The Hill Pottery after it closed. The Samuel Alcock monogram mark is moulded in the figure of the girl. Copeland also produced the model in majolica.

Although the photograph in the factory record album is labelled **'The Pets'**, the price lists refer to this subject as **'Pet Bloodhound'.** The 1895 and 1928 Making Books call it **'Girl with Bloodhound';** they are all the same model.

The SPB lists it at 10/6 trade and 16/- retail; there was also a version 'Ivory, col'd & gilt 24/-'. The NPL of 1873 charged 10/6, while it was retailing at 16/- in 1876. The c.1880 NPL charged 10/-, and 7/- in 1884. This subject is listed in the Making Books at 1/6, and with the 'Figures', not as a group.

GP52

GP53 – PET LAMB
after 1867
Ht. 9in. (22.86cm)
Marks: Samuel Alcock monogram, moulded
Illus: Yes
This group is a companion to **Pet Bloodhound** and is priced the same as that figure. The only variation is in the Making Books where it is included among the groups and priced at 1/9. There was also an 'ivory, col'd & gilt' version.

See note on Alcock under GP11 **Children with Lizard**.

GP53

GP53a

GP56

GP54 – PET RABBIT
This is an alternative title for **Girl with Rabbit** and another title for this group was **The Pets**. The SPB goes as far as to describe it as **'Girl with Pet Rabbit'.**

GP55 – PET LIZARD
This subject is the same as **Children with Lizard** and **Girl with Lizard**. The use of alternative titles for the same subject is very confusing. The way one can determine if they are the same item is by comparing the prices; if the prices correspond exactly the item is identical, despite its title. So far no selling prices have been found.

GP56 – PLAY or **GROUP OF PLAY**
Ht. 18in. (45.72cm)
Illus: Yes
Quite a large group, it is not listed in the SPB, but is listed as '**Play**' in the c.1880 NPL at £3.3.0, and the handwritten note quotes 50/- in 1884. The Making Books of 1895 and 1928 quote 9/6.

It is in the same class as the other groups of mother and child and may have been sculpted by Owen Hale.

GP57 – PRODIGAL'S RETURN
c.1851
Ht. 20in. (50.8cm)
Sculptor: William Theed
Marks: 'Father I have sinned'
Illus: Yes PP 558
This fine group illustrates one of the best known of Christ's parables which is related in the Gospel according to St. Luke, Chapter 15, verses 11-32; the moment caught in this group is taken from verses 20 and 21. 'And he arose, and came to his father. But when he was yet a great way off, his father saw him, and had compassion, and ran, and fell on his neck, and kissed him. And the son said unto him, Father, I have sinned against heaven, and in thy sight, and am no more worthy to be called thy son'.

It was exhibited by Copeland at the Great Exhibition in 1851, in

GP57

GP57a

which year it was also illustrated in the *Art-Journal Supplement*. Theed's original marble sculpture was exhibited also at that exhibition and is now in the Usher Art Gallery in Lincoln.

The group is included in the 1851 Catalogue where a pencilled price of 10 guineas is given. The SPB quotes 6 guineas and 10 guineas respectively.

In 1873 the trade price was £5.15.6, and the retail price in 1876 was £8.18.6. In the c.1880 NPL the price was £4.14.0, and 70/- for 1884. The making price was 14/-.

GP58 – REBEKAH AT THE WELL
c.1868
Ht. 16in. (40.64cm)
Sculptor: William Theed
Marks: OPUS W.THEED Sc
Illus: Yes
The inspiration for this group is to be found in the Book of Genesis, Chapter 24, in which Abraham sends his servant to 'take a wife for his son Isaac' from among his kinsfolk in the land of Mesopotamia. The servant sought a sign from God to show him which girl was to be chosen. When he came to the city of Nahor he halted by a well outside the city and waited for the girls to draw water. He prayed '…let it come to pass, that the damsel to whom I shall say, Let down thy pitcher, I pray thee, that I may drink; and she shall say, Drink, and I will give thy camels drink also: let the same be she that thou hast appointed for thy servant Isaac'. And so it happened that Rebekah fulfilled all that the servant had prayed for and, in due time, accompanied the servant back to Abraham, and Rebekah became the wife of Isaac.

The group is listed in the SPB at 94/6 trade and 7 guineas retail. In the 1873 NPL it was £4.14.6 and in the 1876 retail price list it was £7.7.0. In the NPL of c.1880 it was £4.4.0 and 63/- in 1884. The Making Books each quote 12/-.

GP58

GP59

GP59 – RETURN FROM THE VINTAGE
1848
Ht. 26in. (66.04cm)
Sculptor: after a Sèvres original
Illus: Yes PP 572
This group is included in the illustrated 'catalogue' of Copeland's Statuary Porcelain which was available in May 1848; here a pencil note is given of its retail price of £15.15.0. This was for the complete group which included the elaborate cover. The price remained the same in the c.1851 catalogue; again, only a pencilled note gives this information.

Although this piece was made specially for the Earl of Lichfield to act as a centrepiece for a banquet, copying a Sèvres example owned by him, the Copeland lists include it among the groups and not with miscellaneous items and centrepieces. It is said that well over fifty moulds were needed for the production of this, perhaps one of the most intricate groups made by Copeland or any other manufacturer of parian.

It was exhibited at the Great Exhibition of 1851 where the entry was:'Group of "The return from the Vintage," consisting of seven figures'.

The SPB quotes 10 guineas trade and 15 guineas retail. There is an added note that a version which was 'richly gilt in raised and chased gold 16 gns' was dated 10/2/65. I wonder where this one is?

In 1873 it was £9.9.0 trade and £14.14.0 retail in 1876. The NPL of c.1880 quotes for the complete group, 26in. high, £8.8.0, and, in a fair hand, 6 guineas in 1884. The making price was 24/- in both record books.

GP60 – RUSTIC SPORTS – FISHING
This subject is dealt with under the title of **Great Expectations** (GP32).

GP61 – SIR WALTER SCOTT WITH DOG
1850
Ht. 13in. (33.02cm); base 11 x 9in. (27.94 x 22.86cm)
Sculptor: Sir John Steell
Sponsor: Fine Arts Association of Edinburgh
Marks: J STEELL SCULP EDIN 1850
Illus: Yes PP 498
This group is after Steell's original marble sculpture for the statue in the Scott Memorial on Princes Street, Edinburgh. His favourite dog, Maida, is lying at his side, seemingly startled by the shutting of the book in his master's hand. The parian group was exhibited at the Great Exhibition of 1851 where the entry reads: 'Sir Walter Scott; reduced copy by John Steel *[sic]*, R.S.A., from the original colossal statue on the Calton Hill, executed for the Edinburgh Association for the Promotion of the Fine Arts'. This seated figure is said to be the first marble statue ever commissioned in Scotland from a native artist.

The Scotsman of 13 March 1850 contained an announcement that the Association for the Promotion of the Fine Arts intended to commission one hundred 'statuary porcelain' copies of John Steell's statue in Scott's monument. The copies were to be distributed among their members in the following July. The group was also to be re-issued at a later date.

The SPB has the price of 57/- crossed out and 45/- written by its side; it is marked 'for FAA'. It adds 'Statuette'. The NPL of c.1880 does not list it but a handwritten note prices it at 50/- trade on 27/4/11; this was sixty years after its introduction, by which date the Fine Arts Association would have relinquished its rights. The group is listed under 'Figures' in the 1895 and 1928 Making Books at 8/-.

GP61

GP62

GP63

GP63a

GP62 – THE SISTERS
c.1880
Ht. 24in. (60.96cm)
Illus: Yes PP 485
An attractive group showing a young girl playfully teasing her younger sister. Whilst this might be an original idea of the sculptor, it might have been inspired by one of the following sources:

A. 'The Sisters', a comedy written by James Shirley, and licensed in 1652, or
B. 'The sisters', an historical novel written by Georg Ebers, who was a German egyptologist and novelist. This book was published in 1880 and the scene was laid in Egypt in 164 BC.

It is not included in any known printed list of productions, but a handwritten entry and price of 35/- for 1884 occurs in the NPL of c.1880. The Making Books also include it at 9/-. It is illustrated on the trade catalogue page of about 1880.

GP63 – SLEEP OF SORROW AND DREAM OF JOY
1862
Sculptor: Raffaele Monti
Sponsor: The Ceramic and Crystal Palace Art Union
Marks: R MONTI MADE FOR THE CERAMIC & CRYSTAL PALACE ART UNION
Illus: Yes PP 507
Monti's original marble sculpture of the group was exhibited at the

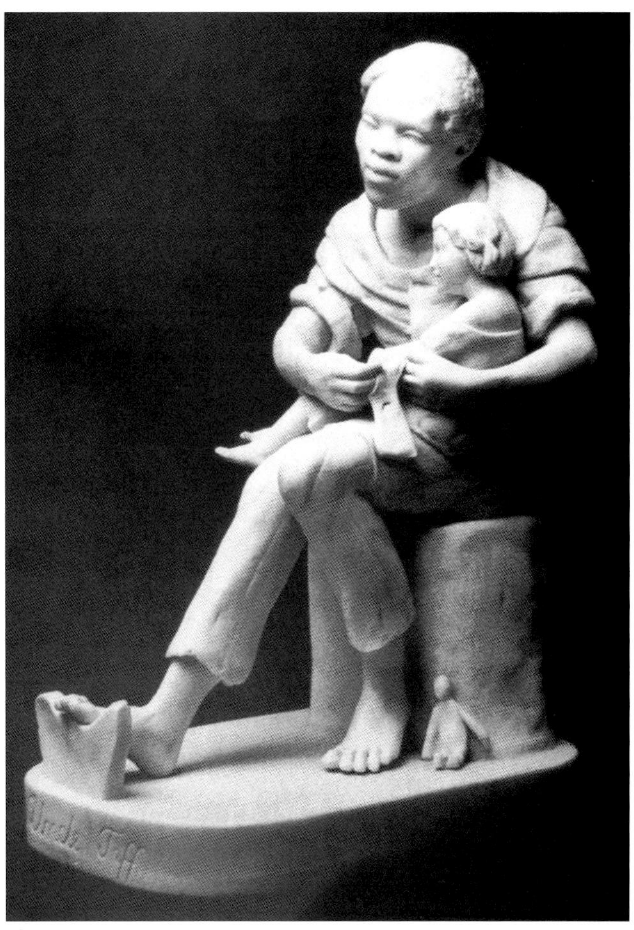

GP64

International Exhibition in London in 1862; it was also featured with a lithographically printed illustration in *Masterpieces of Industrial Art & Sculpture at the International Exhibition 1862* with text by J.B. Waring. Here it was described as 'Dream of Joy'. The original sculpture is now in the Victoria & Albert Museum.

The group is a celebrated allegorical subject of the Italian Risorgimento. The Italian title for the marble is 'Piacere e Delore' (Pleasure and Pain) showing one figure flying away in ecstasy while the other prostrates herself in despair.

Because the group was sponsored by an Art Union it was not included in the Copeland printed lists, but a handwritten entry 'Joy & Sorrow 4 gns' is found in one of the copies of the c.1880 NPL. A list of stock held at the factory for the C & C P A U dated 10/11/81 lists it at £5.0.0. The making price was 19/- in 1895 and 1928.

An example is in the Castle Museum, Nottingham.

GP64 – UNCLE TIFF
c.1857
Ht. 12in. (30.48cm)
Sculptor: Eugene Warburg
Marks: Uncle Tiff EUGENE WARBURG 1856
Illus: Yes PP 540
The derivation of 'Uncle Tiff' has not been established with absolute certainty, but it is likely to stem from the Harriet Beecher-Stowe novel *Uncle Tom's Cabin.* Whilst in England (c.1852-7) Warburg received a commission from Harriet, 2nd Duchess of Sutherland, to execute a series of bas-reliefs based on the Beecher-Stowe novels. The figure is of an elderly male negro with a small girl on his knee (perhaps 'Little Eva').

A possible explanation for the different appellation might be that Warburg, not wishing to offend the duchess by plagiarising her plaques, but at the same time selling a good figure in the round to Copelands, named it 'Uncle Tiff'. An extensive professional search of American literature failed to reveal any such character. It may well have been the name of an acquaintance of Warburg; 'uncle' or 'aunt' being a common term for an elderly negro in those days.

The authoress, in a letter to Mr.Warburg, wrote: 'It is beautifully truthful, and shows how far the expression of love and fidelity may go in giving beauty to the coarsest and plainest features' (*Art-Journal,* 1857, September. page 295).

The only mention in written records is in the SPB where the prices are 21/- trade and 31/6 retail.

GP65 – UNCLE TOBY AND WIDOW
c.1870
Ht. 8in. (20.32cm), base 12 x 7in. (30.48 x 17.78cm)
Illus: Yes PP 541
The group of Uncle Toby and the Widow Wadman is after the painting by Charles R. Leslie which is in the Tate Gallery in London. In its turn, the painting was inspired by Laurence Sterne's novel *The Life and Opinions of Tristram Shandy* (9 volumes, 1760-1767). 'Uncle Toby ... knew not so much as the right end of a woman from the wrong, and therefore was never altogether at his ease near any one of them, unless in sorrow and distress: then infinite was his pity; nor would the most courteous knight of romance have gone further, at least upon one leg, to have wiped away a tear from a woman's eye; and yet excepting once that he was beguiled into it by Mrs. Wadman, he had never looked steadfastly into one'.

The group is included in the SPB at 35/- trade and 52/6 retail, later reduced to ox/- (30/-) and 45/- respectively. In 1873, the NPL quotes £1.4.0, and the 1876 retail price was £1.16.0. The NPL of c.1880 quotes £1.0.0, with the price in 1884 being 15/-. The making price was 2/3.
See Colour Plate 8

GP66 – THE AMAZON
1857
Sculptor: August Kiss

GP65

GP66

Illus: Photograph of statue in Berlin
Although no reference has been found in the Copeland papers, the *Staffordshire Advertiser* reported on 16 May 1857 (page 4) the production by Copeland of a spirited reproduction of Amazon by Kiss. The original was sculpted and cast in bronze in 1839 and placed outside the Museum in Berlin; a copy was placed in a prominent position at the Great Exhibition of 1851. It is not known if Alderman Copeland negotiated with Kiss for its reproduction, nor whether he or another rendered the smaller version.

A group by Minton, also named 'Amazon', bears some resemblance to the study by Kiss but without the panther, without the spear, and the rider herself in a different posture. Minton's group was sculpted originally by J.J. Feuchère in 1843 and almost certainly inspired by the Kiss sculpture. Minton's example is illustrated in *The Parian Phenomenon* (Fig.102).

An illustration of the original sculpture, as an engraving, was published in the *Illustrated London News* of Saturday 21 June 1851 and was sent to the author by Dr. Philip Ward-Jackson. The photograph of the bronze statue was taken by the author in 2003.
See Colour Plate 9

GP67 – THE ANGEL AND THE FLOWERS
c.1875
Ht. 22in. (55.88cm). The Works photograph states 24in. (60.96cm); the one illustrated measured 22in.
Sculptor: Louis Auguste Malempré
Sponsor: The Ceramic and Crystal Palace Art Union
Marks: L A MALEMPRÉ Sc. 1875
Illus: Yes PP 553
The figure is sometimes known as **'The Reaper and the Flowers'** because of the last verse of Longfellow's poem of that name which accompanied the original marble sculpture; this was exhibited at the Royal Academy in 1874. The poem's opening line runs 'There is a reaper whose name is Death' thus giving a mental image of the 'grim reaper' complete with scythe. Longfellow tries to dispel the notion that death is inevitably a fearsome thing by emphasising that flowers grow amidst the 'bearded grain'. The last verse reads:

O, not in cruelty, not in wrath,
the Reaper came that day;
t'was an angel visited the green earth,
and took the flowers away.

GP67

The figure, here illustrated, shows no evidence of being concerned with a grim aspect of death, so leaving the author of this book to believe that the chosen title is to be preferred. Indeed, it is the title used by Copelands in every reference to the subject.

The group, for where it is recorded it is always as a 'group', is only mentioned in the NPL of c.1880 where the manuscript entry reads 'Angel & Flowers (as CCPAU) 60/-, (revised 1884) 50/-. It is listed in the 'stock at Stoke' of items held for the C & CCPAU on 10 November 1881, priced at £2.10.0. In the Making Books it is priced at 8/-.

PARIAN WARE STATUETTES

S1

S1 – ABSENT MAID or **NURSE IS AWAY**
Ht. 6in. (15.24cm)
Illus: Yes
Although the author prefers the title used on the factory record photograph of **Nurse is away**, the NPL of c.1880 does use the title **Absent maid**. Here the trade price was 8/- and the manuscript entry later for 1884 was 4/6. The only other mention is in the Making Books where the price was 1/-.

This charming piece is the companion to 'Washing Dolly'.

S2 – ADVERSITY
c.1870
Ht. 20in. (50.8cm). 19 x 7 x 7in. (48.26 x 17.78 x 17.78cm)
Sculptor: Owen Hale
Marks: OWEN HALE
Illus: Yes PP 485
This figure shows a poorly dressed girl, carrying a meagre basket of flowers, who is proffering a bloom with her right hand, possibly to a customer. The companion to this is the figure **Prosperity**, so the offer may be intended to be made to her. The subject was, perhaps, inspired by the activities of 'Adversity' Hume, a nickname given to Joseph Hume (1777-1855) in about 1825 on account of his predictions of imminent financial disaster.

Apart from the making price of 4/6, the only other prices occur in the NPL of c.1880 where the price was £1.11.6, with the cryptic note in handwriting of 25/- > 30/- applicable in 1884. A photograph of the figure, with her companion, occurs in the illustrated page of a catalogue of the 1880s.

S3 – AFRICA
1864
Ht. 16in. (40.64cm)
Sculptor: Joseph Durham
Illus: Yes
It is tempting to deal with this subject under the collective title of 'The Continents', but in the Copeland price lists this and the other three subjects, America, Asia and Europe, are listed individually. Each subject, therefore will be listed under its own name, but the background to their occurrence will be told under the collective name 'The Continents'. Versions were offered both plain and tinted and gilt. The SPB quotes for the plain one 2 guineas trade and 84/- retail. The trade price for the tinted and gilt version was 75/-. In the NPL of c.1880 the price was £2.2.0, while the note for 1884 was 25/- for 'Africa', and 35/- for each of the other three continents. The price in 1873 was £2.17.6 for each, and in 1876 the retail price was £4.10.0 for each. The making price for 'Africa' was 4/6, and 7/- for each of the other three; this was because 'Africa' was simpler to make, having no additional vulnerable adjuncts like a leaf or chair back.

S2

S3

S4

S4a

S5

S4 – AFTER THE BALL
c.1870
Ht. 20in. (50.8cm), L. 22in.(55.88cm)
Sculptor: Owen Hale
Illus: Yes
This is one of a pair of attractive figures reflecting the social pleasures of the time; the companion figure is entitled **Before the Ball**.

The price quoted in the c.1880 NPL was £5.5.0, with the handwritten note of 75/- for 1884. It is not listed elsewhere, but the Making Books show the price to the makers to be 15/-.

S5 – AMERICA
See text for AFRICA and 'The Continents'

S6

S6a

S6 – APOLLO AS THE SHEPHERD BOY OF ADMETUS
1842
Ht. 18in. (45.72cm)
Sculptor: after R.J. Wyatt
Marks: COPELAND'S PORCELAIN STATUARY
(on early pieces)
Illus: Yes PP 486
The background to this story is that the god Apollo had slain the Cyclops and in penance was sentenced to serve a mortal. He attached himself to Admetus, the king of Pherae in Thessaly, whom he served for nine years, looking after his flocks and herds.

In 1842, Thomas Battam, art director at Copeland and Garrett, obtained permission from His Grace the Duke of Sutherland to have a reduced copy made of a marble statue which he owned; this was to see if Battam's idea of producing a marble-like material for small sculptures would work. Evidently it did, for the Duke purchased an example. (Unfortunately this example appears to have been lost, and the whereabouts of the original marble statue which was in Trentham Park, near Stoke-on-Trent, is uncertain.

The figure is illustrated (reversed) in the 1848 catalogue with a handwritten price of £2.10.0. In the 1851 catalogue the handwritten price is still 50/-. The SPB quotes 31/6 trade and 52/6 retail. In c.1870 the trade price was £1.1.0 and in 1873 it was £1.7.6. The retail price in 1876 was £2.2.0; in 1884, the handwritten trade price was 52/6. The making price was 3/-.

Despite the continuous appearance of this subject in printed price lists it is astonishing how few examples are known. The only undamaged one known to me is in Osborne House, having been purchased by HRH the Prince Albert. Another example (with wooden stick) is in the Spode Museum in Stoke-on-Trent. This figure was exhibited at the Manchester Exhibition of 1845-6, the Birmingham Exhibition of 1849 and the Great Exhibition of 1851. It is not known why the height is shown as being 18½in. (46.99cm) on the photograph, unless the photograph is of a figure whose contraction was less than other examples of this statuette.

S7 – ARTILLERYMAN
before c.1880
No example of this statuette appears to be known at the moment. Nevertheless, it is fully recorded in the price lists. The SPB lists it at 3/- trade and 4/6 retail. In 1873 it was 3/3 trade and in 1876 it was 5/6 retail. The NPL of c.1882 also quotes 3/-. The handwritten entry in the NPL of c.1882 for 1884 prices it at 3/-. The making price was 1/-, so it was probably quite a small figure.

S8 – ASIA
See text for AFRICA and 'The Continents'

S9 – ASTRAGALI PLAYER or **The Dice Player**
1851
Ht. 9in. (22.86cm), L. 11in. (27.94cm)
Illus: Yes
The earliest dice are known to date back as far as the third millennium BC, examples having been found in the Sumerian royal tombs of Ur. The dice were made from the astragalus, the ball of the ankle-joint, and probably those of sheep were used. The Greeks played at dice during banquets, while high-born Romans set aside special rooms in which to play. American dice players sometimes refer to the game as 'Rolling, or throwing, the Bones'.

This statuette was exhibited at the 1851 International Exhibition.

The SPB quotes 31/6 trade and 52/6 retail. The NPL of c.1870 states £1.1.0. In 1873 the item was not listed. It was included, however, in the 1876 retail list at £2.5.0, and in 1884 the price was written '17/6 > 20/-. The making price was 3/6.
See Colour Plate 10

S8

S9

S10

S10a

S10 – AUTUMN
c.1872
Ht. 20in. (50.8cm)
Sculptor: L A Malempré
Sponsor:
Marks: L A MALEMPRÉ Sc. 1872
Illus: Yes PP 508
This is one of a set of the Four Seasons. It is not identifiable in the SPB, but is included in the c.1870 NPL at £1.11.0 and in the 1873 list at £2.0.0. The 1876 retail price was £3.3.0. In 1884, the handwritten price was 21/- > 25/-. The making price was 3/6.

S10A – AUTUMN
Date; late 19th Century
Ht. 15in. (38.0cm)
Sponsor:
Marks: COPELAND
Illus: Yes
A figure on an identical base to that of Winter after Girardon (S198A). No record of this figure has been found in the Copeland records.

S11 – THE BATHER
c.1851
Ht. 12in. (30.48cm)
Sculptor: William Calder Marshall
Illus: Yes
The figure seems to have been inspired by the painting of a 'Girl Bathing' by J. Lawlor, which was exhibited at the 1851 Exhibition. It was referred to on page 338 in the *Illustrated Exhibitor.* **The Bather** appears to be identical to this painting.

The SPB gives 35/- trade and 52/6 retail; there was a version 'gilt & tinted' at 42/-. This was an early entry. In the NPL of c.1870 the price had dropped to £1.1.0. In 1873 it was £1.8.0 and in 1876 the retail price was £2.2.0. In 1884 the manuscript entry in the c.1870 NPL was 12/6 > 17/6. The making price was 2/6.

S12 – BEATRICE companion to **Maidenhood**
1860
Ht. 22in. (55.88cm)
Sculptor: Edgar Papworth Jnr.

S11

S12

Marks: EDGAR PAPWORTH JN.Sc. PUB.MARCH 1 1860
Illus: Yes PP 519
Beatrice Potinari (1266-1290) featured in Dante's *Vita Nuova* and *Divina Commedia.* She is said to have been the object of Dante's affection throughout her twenty-four year life. However she married Simon de Bardi some time before 1287.

The SPB quotes 45/- trade and 70/- retail. There is also a 'gilt & tinted' version at 52/6 trade: 'Painted wreath of flowers bands gold bead border with ornamented neck in raised & chased gold'. Also 'Painted spiral wreath of flowers gold scroll & borders in raised & chased gold'. Some early examples had a verse from Dante's *Purgatory* Canto 30 printed on the underside of the base.

In c.1870 the NPL quotes £1.7.0 for the plain and £2.10.0 for the gilt & tinted version. In 1873 these were £2.8.0 and £2.15.0. The retail prices in 1876 were £3.2.0 and £4.4.0. In 1884 the handwritten prices were 25/- and 37/6. The making price was 4/6.

S13 – BEFORE THE BALL companion to **After the Ball**
c.1870
Ht. 20in. (50.8cm); L. 22in.(55.88cm)
Sculptor: Owen Hale
Illus: Yes
It does not appear in the SPB and the only printed price list which includes this and its companion is the NPL of c.1880. Here it was £5.5.0, and in 1884 the marginal note states 75/-. The making price was 15/-.
See Colour Plate 11

S13

S14– BERLIN PLAYERS, SET OF FOUR
c.1857
Ht. 6 to 7in. (15.24 to 17.78cm)
Illus: Yes
It is a possibility that these figures are copies of a set produced by Meissen; this might account for the name 'Berlin Players'. The set is also known as 'The Musicians'.

They are included in the SPB as an early entry and are priced at 3/6 each trade and at 5/6 retail. The c.1870 NPL confirms this, as does the 1873 NPL. The retail price in 1876 remained at 5/6, but in 1884 the marginal note states 3/-. The making price was 10d each.

The set of figures were reproduced in the late 1920s in bone china and painted; at that time they were included in a range of figures reproduced from the Derby moulds purchased in about 1852 by W.T. Copeland. They were called 'The Musicians' and included amongst the so-called 'Reproduction Chelsea Figures.' They were reproduced again in the 1940s and in the 1970s.

S14

S15

S15 – BOHEMIAN GIRL

c.1870
Ht. 15in. (38.1cm)
Sculptor: L.A.Malempré
Marks: L A MALEMPRÉ Sc.1877
Illus: Yes PP 509

This figure seems to have been inspired by the opera *The Bohemian Girl* by Michael William Balfe, produced in London in 1843. The libretto was by Bunn based on a ballet by St.Georges, taken, in turn, from Cervantes. It re-appeared in London in 1858 as *La Zingara.* The name 'Bohemian' here is taken to mean 'gypsy'.

Like the figures of 'Before and After the Ball' this only appears in the NPL of c.1880, where it is priced at 15/-, with the note of 10/6 for 1884. The making price was 2/-.

S16 – BOULOGNE FISHER AND COMPANION

c.1857
Ht. 7in. (17.78cm)
Illus: Yes PP 548

A charming pair of small figures; the fisher is a boy wearing a tasselled cap and carrying a net over his left shoulder while his female companion wears a head-scarf and carries what appears to be a sail. She also carries a basket on her back.

Appearing in the SPB at 4/6 and 7/- each respectively, it was 4/- in c.1870, and 4/6 in 1873. The retail price in 1876 was 7/-. In 1884 the note states a price of 3/- trade. The making price was 8d.

S16

S16a

S17

S17 – BOWLING BOY

c.1857
Ht. 10⅝in. (26.96cm)
Illus: Yes

The game known to us as 'Bowls' has two versions: an indoor version called 'Skittles' or 'Ninepins' which in North America has advanced to being 'Ten Pins', and an outdoor version sub-divided into 'Flat' green and 'Crown' green bowls.

The indoor game is played in a paved alley at the end of which stand nine 'pins' or 'skittles'. The game is won by the player whose bowls knock down the greatest number of pins with a previously agreed number of bowls – usually three – projected from a pre-determined distance. The bowls are spherical with no 'bias', that is they are evenly balanced.

The outdoor game differs in that it is played on a grass green with bowls, or 'woods' which are lop-sided, or 'biased' by shaving off a disc on either side, but leaving one side more convex than the other. The 'woods', which are usually played in pairs or multiples thereof, are aimed at a small white spherical ball, known as a 'jack'. The winner is the player with the greatest number of woods nearest to the jack. A 'flat' green, as its name implies, is played on a level surface. A 'crown' green is played on a sloping green with a 'crown' at one end; this type is mostly played in northern Britain where it is thought to be later in origin and evolved due to the difficulty in achieving flat greens in areas liable to subsidence.

'Bowls', from the Latin *bulla*, stems back to Egypt in about 5000 BC. Extremely popular in England and Scotland, it was banned from the time of King Edward III because it detracted from the compulsory military sport of archery. The statute was not rescinded until 1845 by which time it had become disregarded. Flat green bowling was well established in the 16th century, the earliest green being said to have been laid at Holyrood Palace, Edinburgh. W.W. Mitchell, a Glasgow solicitor, drew up a code of laws in 1849.

It would appear that the figure is of a boy playing the indoor game. It was quite an early entry in the SPB at 21/- trade and 31/6 retail, being reduced to 16/- and 25/- respectively. The c.1880 NPL price is even lower at 12/-; it is not included in the 1873 and 1876 lists, but a price of 10/6 > 20/- is written in the margin of the c.1880 list. The making price was 2/-.

S19

S18 – BOY WITH FRENCH HORN and COMPANION
These figures feature in most of the lists, yet, so far, no illustration or details other than prices have come to light. In the SPB the prices are 2/6 and 4/-. In the NPL of c.1870 the price was 2/6 and in 1873 it was 2/9. The retail price in 1876 was 4/6, while the manuscript note for the price in 1884 was 2/-. The making price was 6d.

S19 BOY WITH SHELL AT EAR
pre-1859
Ht. 11in. (27.94cm)
Sculptor: Possibly C. Summers
Illus: Yes PP 487
This figure might have featured in the 1851 Exhibition, but it was certainly available in 1859 when an *Art-Journal* report observed that it was on display in Copeland's 'Corridor of Statuary Porcelain' at 160 New Bond Street, London.

The prices in the SPB are 27/6 and 42/- respectively. The NPL of c.1870 shows 18/-, which rises to £1.4.0 in 1873. The retail price in 1876 was £1.16.0, and the 1884 price was 12/6 wholesale. The making price was 2/6. The high prices in the SPB do suggest that it was available much earlier than 1859.

S20

S20 – ROBERT BURNS
c.1874
Ht. 16in. (40.64cm)
Sculptor: J. Steell
Marks:COPELAND
Illus: PP 534
A biographical note on Robert Burns may be found in the 'Busts' section. The scroll at the feet of Burns is inscribed 'To Mary in Heaven'. This refers to Mary Campbell (Highland Mary), one of Burns' many mistresses, who died in October 1786. They met in the spring of that year, the relationship becoming something of an enigma, the truth of which may never be known. It was said by some people that Mary was no more than a common prostitute. Burns claimed that 'Highland Mary' died of a malignant fever, but there is good evidence to suggest that she died in childbirth. She lies buried in Greenock cemetery. She features in four of Burns' works, for details of which see the notes on the Group of Burns and Mary (GP10).

Full scale bronze versions of this figure are in the Victoria Embankment Gardens, London (1884) and in Central Park, New York (1874).

So far the only reference in the Copeland records is the entry in the Making Price books where it states 'Burns seated 7/6'.
See Colour Plate 12

S21 – CALAIS BOY companion to **Smuggler**
c.1870
Ht. about 6in. (15.24cm)
Illus: Maybe. Two figures which could be the Calais Boy and his Smuggler companion are on the same photograph as the Boulogne Fisher and Companion. It seems reasonable that these two groups should appear together. It is hard to say who is the Calais Boy and who the Smuggler!

This figure is listed only in the SPB where it, and its companion, which is listed

S21

S22

separately under 'Smuggler, compn. to Calais Boy', is priced at 3/6 wholesale; the Calais Boy is priced retail at 5/6, while the Smuggler was 5/3.

There were versions which were 'Ivory Col'd. gilt at 4/9 25/2/70'.

S22 – CALM companion to **STORM, 'ON THE SEA SHORE'**
c.1872
Ht. 19in. (48.26cm)
Sculptor: Joseph Durham
Marks: J DURHAM Sc 1872
Illus: Yes PP 495
This interesting large work is a sculpture of Saville Brinton Crossley (later Lord Somerleyton) at the age of nine years. The original marble statue remains at Somerleyton Hall, Suffolk. 'Calm' is the companion to 'Storm' which, together, are known as 'On the sea shore'. In all the price references these two figures are listed together under the collective title. The SPB quotes only the wholesale price of 42/- each. The c.1870 NPL states: 19 inches high. J. Durham R.A. £1.11.6. The 1873 does not state a height, but downgrades the sculptor to J. Durham ARA £2.2.0. The 1876 retail price list still has A.R.A. and different heights; 'Calm' at 18in. and 'Storm' at 19in. The handwritten note for 1884 is 18/6. The making price was 3/6.

If this statue was sculpted in 1872, the NPL of 'c.1870' must be later still than I thought originally! Oh dear! Why didn't and why don't producers date their price lists?

S23 – CARACTACUS
1861
Sculptor: J.H. Foley RA
Sponsor: Crystal Palace Art Union
Illus: Engraving by W. Roffe in the *Art-Journal* in 1860.
Although this item is listed in Shinn's book (page 73) 'Caractacus; sculptor J H Foley, the parian copy was chosen by the Crystal Palace Art Union', there has not been any reference found to it in any factory records. Up until now no example of a parian statuette by Copeland has been seen by the author.

Caractacus, or Caradoc, flourished about AD 50. He was the king of the Trinovantes, with his capital at Colchester. He resisted the Romans for some nine years before meeting defeat. Taking refuge among the Brigantes tribe he was later betrayed to the Romans and sent to Rome as a prisoner. However, the emperor Claudius spared both Caractacus and his family. He is often portrayed being paraded through the streets of Rome, hung about with chains; in this sculpture, however, he is shown addressing his troops as described by the Roman historian, Tacitus.

The original marble sculpture, which was exhibited at the International Exhibition of 1862, was commissioned by the Corporation of the City of London to stand in the Egyptian Hall at the Mansion House. A full account appears in the *Art-Journal* of 1860.

S24 – CHASTITY, Companion to **Santa Filomena**
1865
Ht. 24in. (60.96cm)
Sculptor: Joseph Durham
Marks: J DURHAM Sc. PUB SEPT 1865
Illus: Yes PP 521
The inspiration for this figure may have come from the poem *Comus* by Milton:

So dear to heaven is saintly Chastity and
Thou unblemished form of Chastity

A commentary on this statuette and on the subject of chastity, with longer quotations from *Comus*, appears in the *Art-Journal* of 1860.

The prices in the SPB are 3 guineas and, for retail, 5 guineas. A 'Gilt & tinted' version is priced at 73/6, which will be trade price. The c.1870 NPL quotes £2.12.6, while in 1873 the price was £3.10.0. In 1876, the retail price was £5.5.0. The manuscript note for the net price in 1884 was 30/- and the making price was 6/-.

S24

S26

S25 – CHELSEA FRUIT BOY AND COMPANION
Illus: Maybe
No illustration of these two statuettes has been found yet. However, a small figure of a boy with a hat full of fruit is in a private collection; this is extremely close to a Derby biscuit porcelain figure in the City of Derby Museum and was probably made from one of the moulds which Alderman Copeland bought in about 1852. The fact of it being called 'Chelsea' may have been due to a belief that it was one of the figures from that factory when Duesbury purchased it.

The SPB gives 4/- and 5/6. In c.1870 the NPL quotes 4/-; in 1873 this had increased to 4/3, and the retail price in 1876 was 6/6. The price in 1884 was 3/-. The making price was 8d each.

S26 – CHETHAM, SIR HUMPHREY
c.1854
Ht. 11in. (27.94cm)
Sculptor: W. Theed the younger
Illus: Yes PP 533
Sir Humphrey Chetham was born in 1580 and died in 1653. Born at Crumpsall, he was educated at Manchester Free Grammar School, subsequently being apprenticed to a linen-draper in Manchester. Later, in a London partnership with his brother, he amassed considerable wealth by selling 'Friezes, Fustians, Cottons and Haberdasherye'. In 1635 he served as High Sheriff of Lancashire. Out of his charity he maintained twenty-two boys from the Manchester district and he directed his executors to purchase Manchester Old College and convert it into a school and home for eighteen more 'male children of honest, industrious and painful parents'. The school, a Blue Coat school, was known as 'Chetham's Hospital'; it is now Chetham's School of Music. Some twenty years after Chetham's death, it was decided to mark his tomb with an inscribed marble stone. A little later it was decreed that a statue be erected to him in the hospital. Neither decision was implemented. However, in 1853, two hundred years after his death, a former pupil of the school, George Pilkington, caused a marble statue of him to be raised in Manchester Cathedral. The statue was executed by William Theed at a cost of £1,000; it shows Sir Humphrey sitting upon a chair mounted on a block of marble with at the base a college boy holding up an open book. The Copeland statuette shows only Sir Humphrey. Statuettes of personalities such as this one are uncommon, whilst portrait busts are plentiful.

An entry in the SPB quotes a trade price of 42/- and retail price of 63/-. There are no entries in printed price lists, but a handwritten note in one price list enters the item at 21/. There is no making price.

The Parian Phenomenon states the height as 11in. (27.94cm).

S27 – CHIFFONIA
1867
Up to now the only reference to this figure is in the SPB where it was offered at 8/- trade and 12/- retail. There is also a note dated 17/3/71 that a gilt version was 10/6 and 16/-, also a gilt and tinted one at 10/6.

S28 – CHRISTINA LINNAEUS
1865
Ht. 21in. (53.34cm)
Sculptor: G. Halse
Sponsor: Messrs. Piesse and Lubin
Marks: W.T.COPELAND PUB. FOR PIESSE AND LUBIN 1865 G.HALSE Sc.
Illus: Yes PP 526
Christina was the eldest daughter of Carolus Linnaeus (1707-1778), the eminent Swedish botanist and recorder of natural history, whose work was of very great importance to 18th century scientists; this was not so much for its originality but for the system of classification he introduced

S28

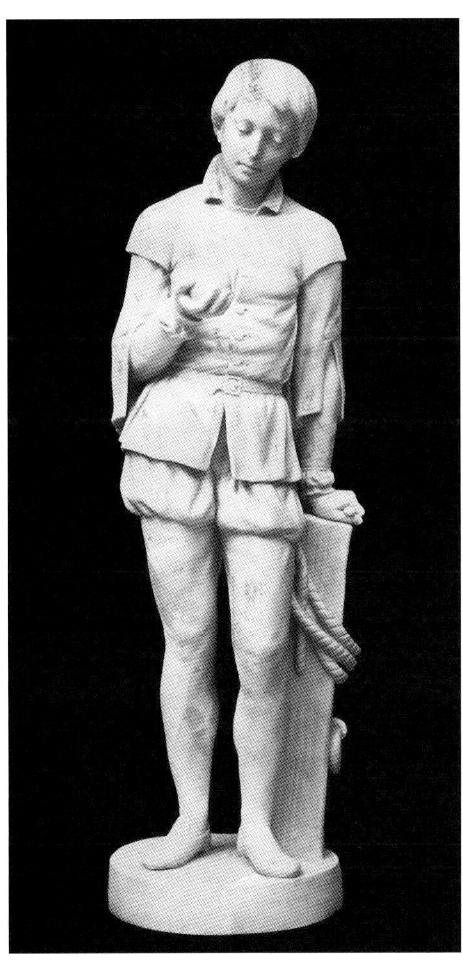
S29

concerning the definitions of genera and species, together with a uniform means of naming plants according to their nature. A learned society, The Linnean Society, was named after him, whilst Josiah Wedgwood commemorated him with a portrait medallion. Christina's paper, "Remarks on a luminous appearance of the Indian Cresses', was given before the Royal Academy of Sciences and was published in their *Transactions* in 1762. It arose from observations she had made in her father's garden at Hammarby.

The figure is listed in the NPL of c.1870, despite it being an item exclusive to the sponsors; it was £3.0.0. It is listed in the SPB at 3 guineas and £5.10.0. In the 1873 NPL its height is given as 22in. (55.88) and it was priced at £3.10.0. In 1876 the retail price was £5.5.0 and in 1884 the handwritten trade price was 42/-. The making price was 8/-, the figure, with her watering-can and the flowers on the ground, being more difficult than many, as well as being very large.

S29 – CHRISTOPHER COLUMBUS
c.1870
Ht. 15in. (38.1cm)
Illus: Yes
Columbus was born in Italy in about AD 1446 (maybe 1451) and died in Spain in 1506. The 'discoverer' of America, Columbus was of Italian origin. He went to sea at an early age, eventually arriving in Portugal where he married. He prepared plans for nautical explorations to sail westwards from Europe and attempted to gain support from the Portuguese king who declined to give him aid. Taking his plans to the Spanish king, he gained his support and, with three ships, he sailed from Spain in 1492, when he reached the Bahamas, and discovered Puerto Rico, Jamaica, and other islands (1493-96). On a third voyage (1498-1500) he reached Trinidad and the mouth of the river Orinoco in South America. On a fourth voyage (1502-04) he landed at Honduras, Costa Rica and Panama. He returned to Spain in 1504 to claim the honours and reward he had been promised, but these were not given to him and his declining years were spent in poverty and neglect.

The figure is included in the NPL of c.1870 at 12/6 and the note for 1884 gives 10/-+. The only other mention is the making price of 2/-.

S30 – COMUS, Companion to **Sabrina**
1859
Ht. 12in. (30.48cm)
Sculptor: W. Calder Marshall A.R.A.
Marks: PUBLISHED OCT 1st 1859
Illus: Yes PP 496
In classical mythology Comus is the god of mirth and is represented as a winged youth. He is also the central character in a play of that name, later printed as a poem, by John Milton, from which this figure is derived. The play was presented at Ludlow Castle in 1634 before the Earl of Bridgewater. It is thought that the play's lyrical portion was inspired by Fletcher's 'Faithful Shepherdess' and the central theme by Peele's 'Old Wives Tales'.

Inscribed on the bases of the early examples of the statuettes are the following lines by Milton:

> Come, no more – one sip of this – will bathe the drooping spirits in delight – beyond the bliss of dreams. Be wise and taste.

The SPB quotes a price of 35/- trade and another of 42/- for one gilt and tinted. The NPL of c.1870 prices it at £1.1.0. In 1873 it was £1.8.0. The retail price in 1876 was £2.2.0 and in 1884 the price was 14/- to 20/-. The making price was 3/-.

S30

S31 – THE CONTINENTS
1864
Sculptor: Joseph Durham
Illus: Yes
When His Royal Highness the Prince of Wales was to be married to the Danish princess, Her Royal Highness the Princess Alexandra, in 1863, the prince commissioned Copeland to manufacture for him a superb dessert service. The service was based upon the Festoon Embossed shape, an intricately pierced border with four panels in which are painted groups of fruit and flowers; the flowers are principally roses and the fruits are oranges with their blossom. The painting was exquisitely done by C.F. Hürten.

> The centre-piece of the service is a double assiette montee: the principal comport being supported by figures representing the four quarters of the globe, each figure with its appropriate symbol. These have been modelled by the eminent sculptor Joseph Durham, from those which support the statue of the good Prince Albert in the memorial placed in the garden of the Horticultural Society – one of the few monuments that grace the Metropolis that are really an honour to it.

So reads the account of that particular item in the April 1866 issue of *Art-Journal*. The monument referred to is now in Kensington Gardens.

Subsequent to the delivery of the complete service in 1866, individual figures of the four continents were offered for sale. This great centrepiece should be at Sandringham House with the rest of the service, but was not located when enquired about in 1983. Several of the pieces are illustrated in Arthur Hayden's *Spode and His Successors.*

S32

S33

S32 – CORINNA
c.1859
Ht. 21in. (53.34cm)
Sculptor: W. Brodie
Sponsor: Fine Arts Association of Edinburgh
Marks: CORINNA THE LYRIC MUSE W BRODIE Sc.
Illus: Yes PP 97
Corinna was a Greek lyric poetess born in the 5th century BC at Tanagra, in Boeotia, Greece. She lived long in Thebes, writing narrative poems in the Boeotian dialect. She is believed to have instructed Pindar (c.522-442 BC) and was said to be one of the handsomest women of her time. Sadly, little of her work seems to have survived, but the remains of three poems have been discovered at Hermopolis in Egypt.

The original marble sculpture was exhibited at the Royal Scottish Academy in 1855 and again in 1863.

As one has come to expect with statuary which had been specially commissioned, there are no prices in any printed lists. The SPB, however, noting FAA, gives 4 guineas. written in over a crossed-out 5 guineas. The making price was 15/-, with the complementary pair 'Before and After the Ball' the highest making price of any statuette.

S33 – COTTAGE GIRL
c.1877
Ht. 15in. (38.1cm)
Sculptor: L.A. Malempré
Sponsor: Ceramic and Crystal Palace Art Union
Marks: L.A.MALEMPRÉ Sc.1876
CERAMIC AND CRYSTAL PALACE ART UNION
Illus: Yes PP 503
The figure was inspired by Thomas Gainsborough's painting 'The

Cottage Girl with Dog and Pitcher'. The attribution sometimes made to Greuze's 'La cruche cassee' is a very unlikely one.

In a manuscript account of the items held in stock at the factory for the Ceramic and Crystal Palace Art Union this item is priced at 10/6 in 1881. The only other reference is a handwritten price of 10/6 in 1884, by which time that art union had ceased operations. The making price was 2/-.

See Colour Plate 13

S34 – CROQUET PLAYER, Companion to the **Rinker**
c.1870
Ht. 18in. (45.72cm)
Sculptor: R.J. Morris
Illus: Yes

The game takes its name from the Northern French word 'Croquet', being a dialectical diminutive of 'croche', meaning 'crook'. The true origins of the game are not known, but it is believed that they stem from the English game of 'Pall-mall', probably imported from France in the 16th century. (Pall-mall was a game in which a ball was driven through an iron ring suspended in a long alley. The street in London, Pall Mall, was developed from such an alley.) In the 1850s John Jacques made the first croquet sets and, in 1857, published a book on the game. Ten years later the first championships were organised by Walter Jones-Whitmore at Evesham, Worcestershire.

There is little reference to this figure in the factory records. A price of £1.10.0 is given in the NPL of c.1880, with a handwritten note of 25/-+ for the price in 1884. The making price was 5/-.

S34

S35

S35 – CUPIDS

Cupid, the 'god of love' in Roman mythology, and paralleled in Greek folklore as Eros, was the son of Mercury (Hermes) and Venus (Aphrodite). He is often portrayed as a beautiful boy with wings, carrying a bow and a quiver of arrows; sometimes he is shown as being blind, or possibly blind-folded.

His romantic ethos is such that, down the ages, artists of all disciplines have portrayed him perhaps more extensively than any other subject and with greater licence. The works of the Italian engraver, Francesco Bartolozzi (1727-1813), provided a fruitful source of inspiration to early and mid-19th century artists.

The burgeoning prosperity of the Victorian era, coupled with the taste for romantic 'hearts and flowers' themes, then very much in evidence, ensured a heavy demand for vicariously named armorini, cupids or putti. As usual, the potters responded with enthusiasm, and provided a flood of fat, endearing infants engaged in virtually every activity known to mankind, together with a few peculiar unto themselves!

The Copeland factory was no exception. The productions may be divided into two groups:

Group 1. Cupid engaged in a specific activity and rightly included in this section dealing with statuettes

Group 2. Cupid, or several cupids, acting as a support for some container or other object. Items in this group will be dealt with separately, but in a tabular format as for Group 1.

There is very little text that seems necessary; footnotes will be appended where extra explanation is needed. A tabular format is adopted for this difficult range of subjects.

S36 – CUPIDS, Group 1, as Figures or Groups engaged in a specific activity

No.	Title	Note	Height	Retail Prices 1848	1851
C 1	Cupid as Blacksmith at anvil	1	71½in. (19.05cm)		
C 2	Cupid at Sea		9in. (22.86cm)		
C 3	Cupid Captive	2	19½in. (49.53cm)		
C 4	Cupid Chained, or Love Chained	3	7⅞in. (20.26cm)	15/-	20/-
C 5	Cupids Contending	4	14in. (35.56cm)	£3.10.0	75/-
C 6	Cupid Sharpening Arrow	5	11½in.(29.21cm)		
C 7	Cupid Sharpening Blade	6	7½in. (19.05cm)		
C 8	Silent Cupid		9in. (22.86cm)	15/-	15/-
C 9	Sleeping Cupid with basket	7	9in. (22.86cm)		
C10	Writing Cupid		8½in. (21.59cm)		
C11	Venus and Cupid	8	8in. (20.32cm)		
C12	Sporting Cupid				
C13	Four Cupids as the Seasons			£1.11.6ea	

C1.

C2.

C3.

NOTES

1. **Cupid as Blacksmith** was sculpted by R.J. Morris. It has a number D268.
2. **Cupid Captive** is classified as a Group in the NPLs. It was sculpted by W.C. Marshall c.1862. Illus PP 528.
3. **Cupid Chained** is so called in the 1848 and 1851 catalogues, in which the retail prices are entered in pencil in the margin. The figure is re-named **Love Chained** in the SPB and subsequent price lists. The Making Book describes it as **Cupid Bound** at 1/- and **Love Chained** at 1/2. It is almost certain that it is the same item.
4. **Cupids Contending** is also called **Struggling Cupids**. It is one of the earliest subjects to be produced, but in the 1848 and 1851 catalogues it is called **The Struggle for the Heart** and is claimed to be after the sculpture by Il Fiammingo. It is doubtful whether this should be ascribed to François Duquesnoy (Il Fiammingo) who was reputed to be the sculptor most skilled in depicting them. The cupid on the right is about to stake his claim by standing on the heart, and this may have upset some people and resulted in the change of name. Illus PP 551.
5. **Cupid Sharpening Arrow** has a number D4852.
6. **Cupid Sharpening Blade** has a number D269.
7. **Sleeping Cupid** was commissioned by the Ceramic and Crystal Palace Art Union and was sculpted by L.A. Malempré. It is always found with the basket of fruit on which cupid is leaning.
8. **Venus and Cupid** is classified as a Group in the SPB. It may have been after the model by Pradier; it was sponsored by the Art Union of London.

S36 – CUPIDS, Group 1. Price details after 1851

No.	SPB. Trade	Retail	NPL 1873 Trade	1876 Retail	NPL c1882 Trade	1884 Trade	Making
C 1							2/6
C 2					£1.1.0	12/6	
C 3	3 gns	5 gns	£3.10.0	£5.5.0	£2.12.6	42/-	8/-
C 4	10/6	16/-		15/-			1/-
C 5	50/-	75/-	£2.15.0	£4.4.0	£2.10.0	35/-	7/6
C 6	15/-	15/-	16/6	£1.5.0	15/-	10/-	2/-
C 7							
C 8	8/-	12/6	6/6	10/-	6/-	4/-	10d
C 9	3/-	4/6				7/-	1/9
C10	10/6		9/-	14/-	8/-	6/6	1/3
C11	35/-					21/-	
C12	2/-	3/-		3/6			
C13					18/-ea	12/6ea	

C5.

C6.

C7.

C9.

C10.

S36A
CUPIDS, Group 2, as supports for containers or other objects

No.	Title		Note	Height	Retail Prices 1848	1851
C14	Group of Cupids supporting tazza					
	or basket	S/S		18in. (48.26cm)	£3.3.0	63/-
	" " "	M/S			£3.15.0	75/-
	" " "	L/S		24in. (60.96cm)	£5.5.0	5 gns
C15	Sitting Cupid with basket	L/S			£1.10.0	30/-
C16	Cupid Vesta Holder,					
	or with torch		9	5½in. (13.97cm)		
C17	Cupid, Winter, Lucifer		9			
C18	Cupid Kneeling with pierced basket		9			
C19	" " plain "		9			
C20	Cupid Sitting with pierced basket		9			
C21	" " plain "		9			
C22	Cupid Flower Stand with					
	pierced basket on his head			11in. (27.94cm)		
C23	" " china basket, gilt					
C24	Cupid with Cornucopia		9	6in. (15.24cm)		
	" " " gilt & chased					
C25	Cupid Flying with Hanging					
	Orchid Pan					
C26	Virgins Tormenting Cupid		10			
C27	Cupid Porter		11			
C28	Cupid Inkstand		11			
C29	Cupids Rose Basket		12			
C30	Cupid Comport, pierced Top		13			
	" " plain Top					
	" " Lucerne Top					
C31	Cupid Bound Flower Holder					
C32	Cupid Flower Stand		12			
C33	Cupid & Shell Flower Stand		13	12in. (30.48cm)		
C34	Cupid with Bulrush Basket		9			
	" " " gilt & chased					
C35	Cupid with Sutherland Baskets		9			
	" " " gilt & chased					
C36	Cupid Centre Piece		13			
C37	Cupid Season Dessert Tray		13			
C38	Elements, Figure supporting					
	Comport, Set of 4		13	14in. (35.56cm)		
C39	Lucerne Centre Piece,					
	(Cupids and Shells)		13			
C40	Cupid with Swans & Shell		12			
C41	Cupid Candelabrum, 3 light			12½in. (31.75cm)		

NOTES

9. These items are usually classified as Statuettes.
10. **Virgins Tormenting Cupid** is classified as a Statuette but the only illustration known shows a pierced basket supported on a tree above the group.
11. These items are classified as Miscellaneous.
12. These subjects were commissioned by the Crystal Palace Art Union
13. These items are classified as Dessert Comports.

S36B
CUPIDS, Group 2. Price details after 1851

No.	S.P.B.	NPL 1873		1876	NPL c1880		1884	Making	CPAU
	Trade	Retail	Trade	Retail	Trade		Trade		
C14	40/-	63/-	£2. 5.0	£3.10.0	£1.17.6		25/-	5/-	
	50/-	75/-	£2.15.0	£4. 4.0	£2. 8.0		30/-	6/-	
	73/6	105/-	£4. 4.0	£6. 6.0	£3.10.0	45/-	9/-		
C15				£1. 0.0	£1.10.0	18.0	12/6	1/-	
C16	4/9	6/6		4.0	6.0	4.0	4/-	8d	
C17	2/-	4/6		2.0	3.0	2.0	2/-		
C18	4/-	6/6		4.3	6.6	4.0	3/-	1/-	
C19	3/6			3.6	5.6	3.0	2/6	10d	
C20	3/-	4/6		3.3	5.0	3.0	2/6	1/-	
C21	2/6	4/-		2.6	4.0	2.6	2/-	5d	
C22	20/-								
C23	25/-								
C24	4/-	6/-		4.3	6.6	4.0	3/6		
C25	42/-								
C26	94/6	7 gns	£5.5.0	£7.17.6	£4. 4.0		63/-	9/-	
C27	7/6	11/-		8.0	12.0	7.6			
C28	10/-			12.0	18.0	10.0			
C29									10.6
C30	18/-			£1.0.0	£1.0.0	18.0		1/-	
				14.0	£1.1.0	12.6			
C31	10/6 gilt & chased								
C32	10/6								
C33	18/-					18.0			
C34				5.6	8.6	5.0	4/-		
				8.6	13.0				
C35				5.0	7.6	4.6	3/6		
				7.6	12.0				
C36				£1.14.0	£2.12.0	£1.10.0			2/-
C37					£1.10.0ea	18.0 ea			
C38	7/-	10/6	£3.3.0	£4.14.0		14.0 ea			
C39	57/6		£2. 8.0	£3.12.0	£3.13.6				
C40	22/-								
C41									

There are three items for which no examples have been seen, nor any illustration.

See Colour Plates 14 and 15

C14.

C16.

S38

S39

S39a

S37 – DALTON, JOHN

The only evidence, so far, that Copeland made this figure is a manuscript price of 21/- dated 1884 in a copy of the NPL.

John Dalton was born in 1766 at Eaglesfield, Cumberland, the son of a poor weaver. John became an eminent chemist and natural philosopher, having educated himself by private study. In 1793 he was appointed professor of Mathematics and Natural Philosophy at New College, Manchester. In about 1804 he perfected the atomic theory which he propounded in 1810 in a new work entitled *A New System of Chemical Philosophy*. Dalton suffered from colour blindness and in 1794 he read a paper to The Manchester Literary and Philosophical Society in which he gave the earliest recorded account of that condition, which became known as 'Daltonism'. He died in 1844.

S38 – DANCING GIRL REPOSING

1846
Ht. 18in. (45.72cm)
Sculptor: William Calder Marshall
Sponsor: Art Union of London
Marks: Marshall Fect Cheverton Sculp ART UNION OF LONDON 1848
Illus: Yes PP 518

Marshall was awarded £500 for this design by the Art Union of London. The marble version was exhibited at the Royal Academy in 1848, and a figure entitled 'Dancing Girl' (almost certainly the same one) by Marshall and valued at £700 was selected by that Art Union as the principal prize in the distribution of 1863. (Ref. *Art-Journal* 1862, page 193).

Copeland displayed the parian figure at the Great Exhibition of 1851.

References in the records are the entry in the SPB of 35/- AUL (when an item was specially commissioned by an Art Union it was not listed in the factory's printed price lists) and the making price of 5/6 in both the 1895 and 1928 books.

See Frontispiece and Colour Plate 16

S39 – DAPHNE

c.1862
Ht. 22in. (55.88cm)
Sculptor: Marshall Wood
Illus: Yes PP 565

Daphne, the daughter of the river-god Peneus, in Thessaly, was pursued by Apollo, who was charmed by her beauty. She did not care for his attentions so, as she was on the point of being overtaken by him, she prayed for help and was metamorphosed into a laurel, or bay, tree (daphne) which, in consequence, became the favourite tree of Apollo. Some scholars consider that this attractive mythological nymph was the daughter of Ladon, an Arcadian; however, Ladon seems to have been the dragon who helped the Hesperides, the guardians of the golden apples, to keep watch over them.

The statuette shows Daphne being gradually transformed into the tree which bears her name.

The SPB quotes 70/- trade and 6 guineas retail. In the c.1870 NPL she is priced at £2.12.6, and at £3.0.0 in 1873. The retail price in 1876 was

S40

S41

£4.10.0, while the trade price in 1884 is noted as 31/6. The making price was 6/- in 1895 and 1928.

S40 – DAVID COPPERFIELD
c.1850
Ht. 12in. (30.48cm)
Sculptor: J.S. Westmacott
Illus: Yes
This subject is recorded in Copeland's records under the title of **Master Davy**, under which name it will be dealt with in detail.

S41 – DIANA
c.1880
Ht. 16in. (40.64cm)
Sponsor: Ceramic and Crystal Palace Art Union
Marks: from the antique sculpture
Illus: Yes
Diana is the Roman name for the Greek goddess, Artemis, and in their mythology she is deemed to have been the daughter of Jupiter of Latona. In the Greek mythology she was the daughter of Zeus and Leto and the twin-sister of Apollo. Artemis cured and alleviated the sufferings of mortals and was especially the protectress of the young and of the female sex. She was never conquered by love; she slew Orion because he attempted her chastity and changed Actaeon into a stag because he had seen her bathing. She is a huntress and the goddess of the moon. This Greek Artemis is not to be confused with the Ephesian Artemis, or 'Diana of the Ephesians' who was an ancient Asiatic divinity.

The SPB lists one price of 21/-, with a gilt and tinted version at 28/-. A note states '31/6 RPC' (an increase made by Richard Pirie Copeland, undated).

The value of stock in 1881 was 21/- each; three were in stock at Stoke and one was returned to Stoke from the C & CPAU. A note in the NPL of 1880 puts a price in 1884 of 18/- > 23/-.

S42 – DRESDEN FRUIT BOY AND COMPANION
There are two versions of these figures; one pair is standing, the other sitting. The prices for the boy and girl are the same, but the sitting versions are slightly less in price than the standing ones. Photographs exist for the standing figures, but it is not certain what the sitting figures look like.

The origins, too, are uncertain although it is likely that they are derived, if not actually made, from the Derby moulds purchased by W.T. Copeland.

An example of the Dresden Fruit Girl occurs on a stand with two baskets, one on either side, and ornamented with green and gilded lines.

No dimensions are readily available for the sitting version, so the details refer to the standing figures.
pre-1870: perhaps c.1851
Ht. 6¾in. (17.15 cm)
Sculptor: Probably a Derby modeller
Illus: Standing figures – Yes

S42

The c.1851 price list gives 'Pair of Fruit and Flower Figures' in the list of additional works, 5in. (12.7cm) high. at a price of 9/- each. These could refer to the sitting pair. The SPB lists 'Fruit & Flower Boy or Girl, Dresden ea.5/- 7/6. The c.1870 NPL quotes:
Dresden Fruit Boy and Companion each 4.0
- - - - - - sitting 3.6
The 1873 NPL quotes:
Dresden Fruit Boy and Companion each 4.0
- - - - - - sitting 4.0
The 1876 Retail Price List quotes:
Dresden Fruit Boy and Companion each 6.0
- - - - - - sitting 5.6
The handwritten note for 1884 quotes 3.0 for each figure, with 3/6 CP Goode as extra.

A small figure of a boy with a hat full of fruit may be the Sitting Boy; height 5in. (12.67cm). It is remarkably close to the similar one in Derby porcelain. This figure is illustrated as S64, Fruit Boy (Sitting).

S42a

S42b

S45

S43 – DRESDEN FLOWER GIRL AND BASKETS
Sponsor: Crystal Palace Art Union
This item is listed, first, in the SPB where it adds 'on plynth' and the item is 'tinted & gold 10/6'. Against this entry are the initials 'CPAU'.

The other reference is in the handwritten list of 'Stock retd to Stoke' from the Ceramic and Crystal Palace Art Union, and dated 10/11/81. Here there were: '2 Dresden Flower Girls & Baskets, Turq & Gold @ 10/-...£1.0.0'.

S44 – DRINKING BOY AND COMPANION
c.1851
Ht. 6in. (15.24cm)
At the end of an edition of the list of c.1851 there is a page entitled 'COPELAND'S STATUARY THE FOLLOWING ADDITIONAL WORKS ARE NOW READY. Here is included this item at a price of 7/- each. Moreover, the SPB quotes a group with this title at 14/- (trade) and 21/- (retail). There is also an entry for single figures at 5/- and 7/6 respectively.

S45 – EGERIA
c.1857
Large: Ht. 28in. (71.12cm), small: Ht. 23in. (58.42cm)
Sculptor: J.H. Foley, RA
Marks: J.H. FOLEY
Illus: Yes PP 506
In Roman mythology Egeria was one of the four prophetic divinities known as the Camenae; these were fountain nymphs belonging to the religion of ancient Italy and Egeria lived beside her fountain which was situated between the old Appian Way and the road to Naples. Her name may also be spelt Aegeria. (The group take their name from the most important of these goddesses, Carmenta, who had her temple at the foot of the Capitoline Hill.) Egeria is featured both by Ovid and by Lord Byron in his 'Childe Harold'. She, like Carmenta, was a protector of women in childbirth and women made sacrifices to her to seek her assistance in such matters.

Foley sculpted the original marble statue for the Mansion House in London in 1855 as one of sixteen literary subjects commissioned from contemporary sculptors. The work was exhibited at the Royal Academy in 1856.

The two sizes have different designs of bases. They are well documented in the price lists:
SPB: Large 8 gns. Gilt & Tinted 12 gns. Small 4 gns-10 gns
c.1870 NPL: Large £7.7.0. Small £2.12.6
1873 NPL: Large £9.9.0. Small £3.10.0
1876 Retail Price List: Large £4.14.0. Small £5. 5.0
1884 Trade Price (Manuscript): Large 63/-. Small 35/-
1895 and 1928 Making Prices: Large 12/-. Small 7/-

S46 – EMMANUEL PHILIBERT, DUKE OF SAVOY
1845
Ht. 16in. (40.64cm) without plinth. Plinth: 11¼ x 6⅝ x 7⅞in. (28.5 x 17 x 20cm)
Sculptor: Baron Marochetti
Sponsor:
Marks:
Illus: A representation of the figure appears on the illustration of the display by Copeland & Garrett at the 1845 Exhibition in Manchester, and reviewed in the *Art-Union* magazine in 1846.

It seems extraordinary that Copeland should attempt to make such a complicated study of an equestrian subject in the first year that the statuary porcelain body had been evolved.

Dr Philip Ward Jackson supplied me with a photograph of the original bronze statue which stands in a square in Turin. This enabled me to identify the figure shown in the *Art-Union* illustration. Two equestrian subjects are shown, the one on the right remaining to be identified; no other such figures were made during the rest of the period in which parian was produced. The reviewer in the *Art-Union* observed that 'in the production [of this group] the greatest mechanical difficulties have been most successfully overcome.'

The explanation may be that the group was copied at the express wish of His Grace the Duke of Sutherland; no parian example has come to the author's attention, but a plinth for it is in the Spode Museum Trust's Collection.

Emmanuel Philibert of Savoy, Prince of Oneglia, acted as the Viceroy in Sicily for the King of Spain. Born in 1588, he died in Palermo of the plague on 3 August 1624. His portrait by Sir Anthony van Dyck is in the Dulwich Art Gallery.

S46

S46a

The price in the c.1848 price list was £4.10.0. The SPB quotes 4 guineas, with the 'plynth' extra at 21/-. In the c.1851 price list the price was still 90/-.

The subject is recorded as having been exhibited at the Great Exhibition of 1851.

The inscriptions on the plinth are:

EMMANVELI FILIBERTO	EMMANUEL PHILIBERT
CAROLI III F	SON OF CHARLES III
ALLBROGVM DVCI	LED ALLOBROGUS (A region of France near the Rhone, now Savoy)
REX CAROLVS ALBERTVS	KING CHARLES ALBERT
PRIMVS NEPOTVM	FIRST NEPHEW
ATAVO FORTISSIMO	WITH THE BRAVEST FOREFATHER
VINDICI ET STATORI	DEFENDER AND MESSENGER
GENTIS SVAE	OF HIS PEOPLE
AN M DCCC XXXVIII	ERECTED IN THE YEAR 1838
VICTOR AD AUG	CONQUEROR TO AUGUSTUS
VEROMANDVOR	VEROMANDUOR (A region of France, now Vermandos)
SVBALP REGIONE	IN THE REGION LYING NEAR THE ALPS
IN VIRTVTIS PRETIVM RECEPTA	HE GAVE BACK THE PRICE OF WORTH
VRBEM INGREDITVR	TO THE CITY WHICH HE ENTERED
IVRE VITERIS PRINCIPATVS	BEGINNING WITH AN OLD LAW
ET CIVIVM STVDIO SVAM	HE BROUGHT BACK THE PEACE
POPVI IS PACEM REDDITVRVS	TO HIS CITIZENS AND PEOPLE
XIX KAL.IAN.AN.M.D.LXII	19 1ST JANUARY 1562

S47 – EUROPE

See text for AFRICA and 'The Continents'

S47

S48

S48 – EVANGELINE, Companion to **Marguerite**
1869
Ht. 21in. (53.34 cm)
Sculptor: Sarah Terry
Marks: S.TERRY Sc. 1869
Illus: Yes PP 515
Full biographical details will be found in the section dealing with portrait busts (B27). The statuette shows this Nova Scotian girl wearing a cross and carrying a pitcher, thus casting her in the role of a 'ministering angel'. The statuette was displayed at the 1871 International Exhibition in London. Some examples have a quote from Longfellow's poem.

The prices in the SPB are 31/6 and 50/- respectively. In c.1870, the net price was £1.10.0, and in 1873 was £1.15.0. The retail price in 1876 was £2.12.6. The price was revised in 1884 to 18/- to 21/- A gilt and tinted version in August 1888 was 31/6.
See Colour Plate 17

S49 – EVE WITH APPLE
1847
Ht. 10in. (25.4cm)
Sculptor: P. MacDowell
Illus: Yes
According to the Book of Genesis, in Chapter II, verses 21-25, Eve was the first woman, mother of the human race. In this study she is contemplating the apple which she has picked from the tree of the knowledge of good and evil, and is about to eat thereof and to give it to Adam, and he did eat thereof (Ch. III).

In the 1848 Price List an Eve is listed at £1.0.0, and in the SPB the prices for Eve are 15/- and 21/- respectively. Eve then 'hides herself' until a handwritten note in 1884 lists 'Eve with apple 7/6.' It seems probable that the two are really the same figure.

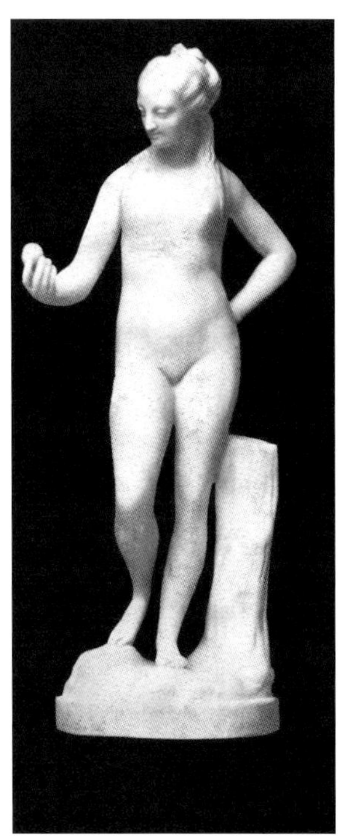
S49

S50 – EVE WITH SERPENT
c.1856
Ht. 9in. (22.86cm). L. 12in. (30.48cm)
Sculptor: after M. Vande Venne
Illus: Yes PP 489

S50

An illustration of this subject appeared in the *Art-Journal* of 1855, under the title of **Temptation**, and one wonders if Copeland then requested the sculptor to permit the reduced size model to be produced in statuary porcelain.

It is priced in the SPB at 42/- and 63/- respectively. It is not dated. The only other reference is a handwritten note in 1884 of the price at 21/-.

S51 – FAIRY CAP or **Psyche Disguised**
c.1865
Ht. 13in. (33.02cm)
Sculptor: E.G. Papworth
Illus: Yes PP 505
For biographical details see 'Psyche'. The SPB quotes a trade price of 42/- and a retail price of 63/-, but by 1870 the trade price had been lowered to £1.7.6. In 1873 it was £1.18.0, while the retail price in 1876 was £3.0.0. In 1884 the manuscript note quotes 18/-.

S52 – FALSTAFF IN A BASKET
L. 8in. (20.32cm)
Illus: Yes
Sir John Falstaff (originally Sir John Oldcastle) was a celebrated character in two of Shakespeare's historical plays, *Henry IV* and *The Merry Wives of Windsor.* He is portrayed as an obese, sensual, but witty, ageing knight. He is also a drunkard, swindler, jovial liar and a coward. Down the years Falstaff's activities have been featured by many a Staffordshire potter. This figure depicts Falstaff hiding in a basket as happened in *The Merry Wives of Windsor,* Act III, Scene III. The cover is in the form of a jumble of linen.

The item is not included in any published list, but the SPB quotes 21/- trade, and 30/- retail. The item was also issued in the majolica form as shown in the illustration. The subject appears also as a 'sprig' on a smear-glazed jug, examples of which are not rare; one is in the collection of the Fitzwilliam Museum, Cambridge. These jugs are usually marked 'COPELAND & GARRETT LATE SPODE'. They may be in a buff or grey body.

S53 – FEMALE STUNG BY A SCORPION
1851
Ht. 10in. (25.4cm)

S51

Sculptor: after Lorenzo Bartolini
Illus: see 'Nymph at Bath'
This item under this name occurs only in the SPB where it is priced at 31/6 trade and 45/- retail. Under the title 'Nymph at Bath' in the SPB the prices are different, viz. 31/6 and 52/6. For further details see the entry for 'Nymph at Bath', S121.

S54 – FIRST BATH OF THE SEASON
c.1874
Ht. 17⅛in. (43.5cm)
Sculptor: A. Chesneau
Sponsor: Ceramic & Crystal Palace Art Union
Marks: A.CHESNEAU Sc. PUBd Jan 1874 CERAMIC AND CRYSTAL PALACE ART UNION
Illus: Yes PP 536
Although there is plenty of information about this figure, there is no certainty about its correct title. Dennis lists it as **'Flower Girl**. Also called French Flower Girl'. There does not appear to be the latter description referring to a parian figure, although there was one in white china in the Copeland lists. The Making Book does list a figure as 'Flower Girl CPAU' 2/6' which probably refers to this subject. The girl is holding a very small bunch of flowers, but she does seem to be holding a towel, and Chesneau is credited with having sculpted such a subject and titled it as this is titled now. Could this have been the figure called 'Modesty' by Shinn? (See S108.)

Although not printed in the 1870 NPL, the handwritten price of 10/6 is given for 'French Flower Girl. W.China (as for CPAU).'

There is no Flower Girl of any complexion or nationality in the SPB.

S52

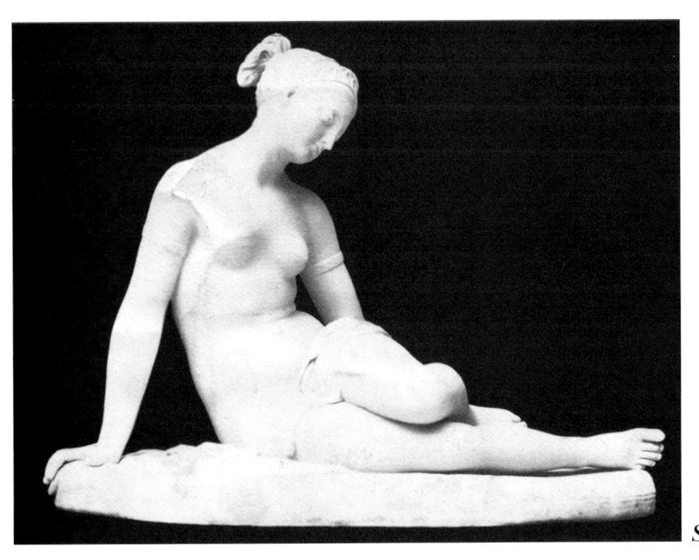
S53

S54

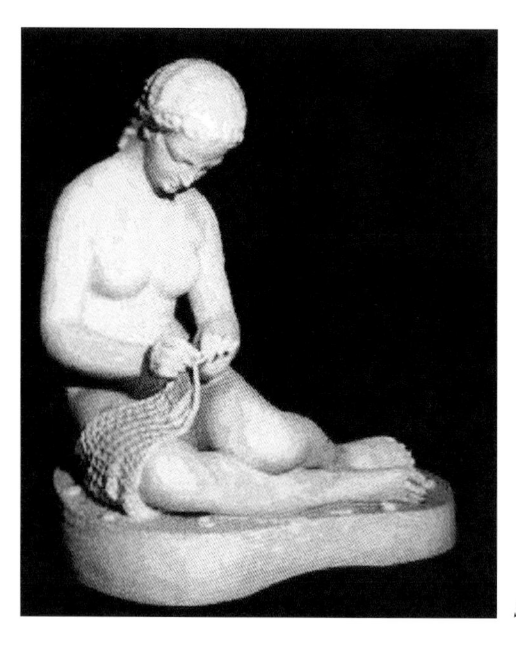
S55

S55 – FISHER GIRL – RECLINING
1861
Ht. 13in. (33.02cm)
Sculptor: John Rogers, after William Randolph Barbee
Sponsors: New York Institute of Fine Arts
Marks: COPELAND A PREMIUM AWARDED BY THE COSMOPOLITAN ART ASSOCIATION
Illus: Yes
This figure is recorded in the SPB as being made for the New York Institute of Fine Arts at the price of 3 guineas and dated 10/3/61. It is described as Fisher Girl; there is no mention of the posture that she is adopting.

In 2002 an example was sold on the Internet Auction eBay for $21,400 (£15,200). The illustration is from that auction, and shows the girl mending a net. The pose is restful and may be compared with S118, **Mending the Net**, in which the girl appears to be looking at something or somebody.

In one copy of the c.1870 NPL, it is entered in handwriting as **Fisher Girl Reclining** at the price of 20/-. Another copy of the c.1870 NPL also records it, but the price is 25/- in 1884.

S56 – FISHERMAN (SITTING) and COMPANION
1870
Ht. 7in. (17.78cm)
Illus: Yes
The SPB lists these two figures and dates them 25/2/70; the prices are 4/6 trade and 5/9 retail. This confirms the NPB of c.1870 which also quotes 4/6 each. The price in 1873 was 5/- trade and in 1876 the retail price was 7/6. The manuscript entry for 1884 is 3/6 each and there is no reference in the Making Books.

The illustration is entitled 'Companion to Sitting Fisherman' and not 'Fishwife', a name that does not occur in the records.

S57 – INDIAN FISHERMAN WITH NET
c.1849
Ht. 25½ (64.8cm) [28in. (71.1cm) with basket]
Sculptor: C. Cumberworth
Illus: Yes
The only references to this subject are in the SPB – where it is priced only at wholesale at 31/6; at this price it must be a statuette of fair size, say about 21in. (53.3cm) – and in the NPL of c.1882 in the section dealing with 'Copeland's Porcelain Dessert Comports' where it is listed as **Indian Fisherman Centre Piece** and it has as its companion the **Indian Girl Centre Piece.** They are priced as 'White £3.3.0, and China, Turquoise and Gold £3.3.0'. On their bases at 28in. high they would be dramatic in appearance on a dinner table.

The basket has been added to an otherwise straightforward figure of an Indian fisherman carrying some fish in his right hand and holding a long bamboo stick with his left hand, and this might be some form of net.

The figure is not listed among any of the Parian statuettes. Only in 2002 has an example without the basket come to my attention and in 2003 an example together with his companion Indian Girl, all coloured and gilded, was purchased by a friend.

In the case of the latter they are each mounted upon an elaborate base which is glazed before being decorated richly. Monochrome photographs of c.1880 show both figures with the baskets and measuring 28in. high.

It seems clear that these figures are NOT of parian body but are of bone china.

The **Indian Girl,** S79, on her own, without the decorated base, is listed as of porcelain statuary and is the companion of the **Nubian Girl,** S116.

The bone china figures are included here because of the confusion which has occurred in advertisements on the Internet auction website, eBay.

S56

S56a

S57

S58

S59

S58 – FISHERMAN'S DAUGHTER
c.1880
Ht. 15in. (38.1cm)
Illus: Yes
There is confusion concerning this statuette and its name. There were two different figures which began by being given the identical name. There was the seated figure sculpted by Wyon in 1873 which is now re-named **Net Mender**, but more accurately **Mending the Net** (S118), and an upright figure of a girl shading her eyes so that she may see her father's boat approaching. This latter item will be discussed under this title.

The upright, or standing, figure of the Fisherman's Daughter is not listed in the SPB, but is quoted in the c.1880 NPL at 15/-. It is omitted from the 1873 and 1876 price lists, but the price of 10/- is handwritten for 1884 in the c.1880 NPL.

The most telling evidence is the photograph of the figure. The making price is given as 2/-.

S59 – FLUTE PLAYER
1871
Ht. 13in. (33.02cm)
Sculptor: R. Monti
Sponsor: Ceramic and Crystal Palace Art Union
Illus: Yes
A delightful study of a peasant boy playing the flute; this figure may have been intended as a companion to the **Reading Girl** sculpted by MacDowell a year or so earlier (q.v.). The general concept of a boy playing a flute or other instrument in the company of a girl reading a book was used by many 18th and 19th century factories, either in porcelain or earthenware, singly, as a pair, or as a group.

Flute Boy is listed in the SPB at 10/-, on 13/1/71, and for C & CPAU. In the list of stock at Stoke held for the Ceramic and Crystal Palace Art Union there are ten Flute Players at 10/- each. Only after the closing down of that Art Union did Copelands list this item, in manuscript, at 10/- in 1884. The making price was 2/-.

S60 – FLOWER GIRL or **French Flower Girl**
A statuette of a girl with a demure expression is in the Spode Museum Trust's Collection. It has the marks as those given under 'The First Bath of the Season'. The only reference to 'French Flower Girl' is a handwritten note of the price, in 1884, for a figure in 'W [White] China as for CPAU'.

Please see notes for S54.

S61 – FRENCH FIDDLER AND COMPANION
c.1870
Ht. 5in. (12.7cm)
Illus: Yes, Fiddler only
The figure illustrated is of the version published with majolica glazes. In the SPB the parian version is priced at 5/- trade and 8/- retail respectively. An ivory and gilt version was priced at 6/- on 15/7/70. The pair are listed in the NPL of c.1880 at 4/- and, in 1873, at 5/6 each. They are priced at 8/6 each retail in 1876. In 1884 the trade price was back to 4/-.

In all the written and printed records the item is listed as 'Fiddler and Companion' and it is only on the caption to the illustration that it is called 'French Fiddler'.

S61

S62

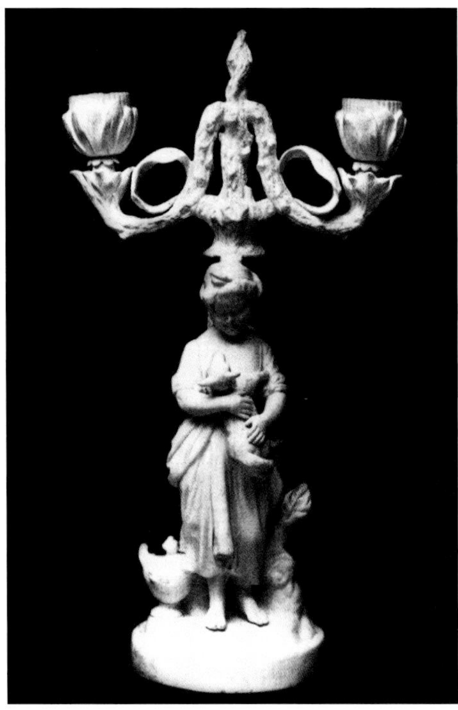

S62a

S62b

S62 –FRENCH SHEPHERD AND COMPANION
pre-1870
Sculptor: after Derby Figures
Illus: Only as candelabra and as comport
Shepherds and shepherdesses, with fruit boys and girls, are almost as confusing as Cupids when it comes to trying to make clear identifications.

The SPB records 'French Shepherd & Compn.' initially as 12/- and 18/-, but later crossed out and new prices of 8/- and 12/6 written in. The NPL of c.1880 gives each one priced at 7.0. In 1873 this had risen to 7/6 each, with the retail price in 1876 at 11/6 each. The trade price in 1884 was down to 4/-, and the making price was 1/- each.

Dennis lists them as 'French Shepherd and Companion, pair of figures also executed as candelabra'; he also lists them as 'Shepherd and Shepherdess, French'. It is as candelabra that the figures will be identified and illustrated here.

In 1933 figures of the French Shepherd Boy and the French Shepherd Girl were made in bone china and painted. These were from the Derby moulds bought by W.T. Copeland in 1852, and are virtually the same as those made in statuary porcelain.

S63 – FRUIT BOY (KNEELING) AND COMPANION
pre 1870
Sculptor: possibly a Derby modeller
Illus: not at present
A detailed discussion of the Fruit Boy and Companion sets is made at S42 when trying to explain the difficulty with the Dresden Fruit Boy and Girl. The kneeling boy and girl have to be identified and this might be possible from any illustration of them as basket supports that might be found.

The NPL of c.1880 quotes the price of 8.0 and, in manuscript, 5/- in 1884. The SPB does not list the kneeling Fruit Boy but does list three fruit boys: Dresden (S42), Sitting (S64) and Chelsea (S25).

S64 – FRUIT BOY (SITTING) AND COMPANION
Sculptor: almost certainly a Derby modeller
Illus: Yes
Like the kneeling fruit boy, this figure must be the subject of conjecture. However, I have a delightful seated figure of a boy with a few items of fruit in his hat and this is almost identical to a Derby porcelain figure in the City of Derby Museum. It is 5in. (12.7cm) high and is probably the figure described as the Sitting Fruit Boy.

The SPB gives prices of 3/6,trade, and 5/6, retail, for each figure. The companion has not yet been identified.

S65 – GARDENER AND COMPANION
Ht. 13in. (33.02cm), L. 9in. (22.86cm)
Illus: Yes, as supporters of flower holders
These two pieces are known only from the entry 'D20' in the photograph record; apart from the reference to D20 and the sizes no other detail is given. The SPB does list Gardener and Companion and gives prices: 3/6 trade and 5/6 retail, also color'd at 5/6 and 8/6. It is not clear if these items were, in fact, of parian, or of bone china; my opinion is that they were either white china or decorated china.

I acquired in 2001 another entirely different pair of **Gardener and Companion**. The gardener is 5⅛in. high (13.02cm) and his companion is 4¾in. (12.07cm) high. The man holds a flowerpot in his right hand and supports a spade with his left hand, while he is resting against an ornamental pillar. The girl stands besides a small water spout on which rests a watering can, while she holds some flowers in her skirt. The gardener is marked COPELAND. These are of parian and may be the correct ones referred to in the SPB.
See Colour Plate 18

S66 – THE GLEANER, companion to **The Reaper**
c.1851
Ht. 6in. (15.24cm)
In a supplementary list published about 1851, there is the item **Reaper and Gleaner**, a pair, and the price was 7/- for each 6 inch figure.

The SPB gives the prices as 5/- trade and 7/- retail, so the 1851 price seems to be retail. A making price of 7d is entered.

S64

S67 – GOATHERD
1846
Ht. 17in. (43.18cm)
Sculptor: R.J. Wyatt
Illus: Yes PP 486. See Apollo, S6
This figure is the same as Apollo as the shepherd boy of Admetus. The 1851 Exhibition catalogue, page 711, identifies this figure in the following words: 'The Goatherd, by the late R.J. Wyatt, RA. from the original marble in the possession of the Duke of Sutherland'. In no other place does the name Goatherd appear.

All printed references give the height as 17in. so the height of 18in. (45.72cm) written beneath the factory photograph may be wrong, or include a thicker base.

S68 – GREEK BOY
Apart from the entry in the SPB, where the prices are 27/6 trade and 42/- retail, there seems to be a dearth of information about this figure. No illustration is known.

S69 – GREEK SLAVE
1852
Ht. 19in. (48.26cm)
Sculptor: Hiram Powers
Illus: Yes
The American sculptor Hiram Powers executed the original marble statue in 1844 during his stay in Florence. He had the idea in 1840 and in his studio there Captain Grant saw a small model of the Greek Slave in plaster and was so struck with the beauty of the subject that he immediately gave a commission to the sculptor to execute it in marble. It was exhibited first in 1845 in the rooms of Messrs. Graves in Pall Mall, London. It toured in the United States of America during 1847-1849, where it scandalised society. A replica was exhibited at the Great Exhibition of 1851. The *Illustrated Exhibitor* wrote of it:

> For beauty of design and delicacy of execution this exquisite statue is inferior to nothing in the Great Exhibition. It represents an historical fact in all but the chains, for it was the custom to expose female slaves in the bazaar of Constantinople.

Examples in marble may be seen at Raby Castle, County Durham, and at the Newark Museum in New Jersey.

It was copied in 1849 by Minton and in the *Art-Journal* for May 1852 (p.162) the following announcement was made:

> THE GREEK SLAVE. Mr.Copeland is about to add to his series of beautiful porcelain statuettes, one of Powers' well-known figures, which will doubtless rival, if not exceed, in popularity many that have preceded it. A mould was made by Signor Brucciani, from the original, when it stood in the Crystal Palace, and casts have been taken from it, one of which may now be seen at Mr. Copeland's establishment in Bond Street; it is a highly successful copy. The cast is to be reduced by Mr.Cheverton's instrument to the size proposed for the statuette.

The sculptor realised that it might raise objections, so he had it 'washed clean' by the Church fathers! The Reverend Orville Dewey stated from

S69

S65

the pulpit and in print that the Greek Slave was 'clothed all over with sentiment' which therefore protected it 'from any profane eye'.

The SPB quotes 70/- and 105/- with the chain costing 3/-. The c.1880 NPL quotes £2.2.0; in 1873, £2.18.0. In 1876, £4.10.0. In 1884, 25/-. Making 5/-.

S70 – GORILLA FIDDLER
An entry in the SPB quotes 1/2 and 1/9.

S71 – GRIEF
The SPB includes this item at 12/6, dated 11/10/74 and for R & A. (It clearly states 'Figure of' and is written separately from 'Grief, Bust'.)

S72 – GUARDSMAN
The only mention is in the Making Book where it is priced at 3/3. There is also the price of 2/- when made in earthenware.

S73 – GUITAR GIRL
c.1851
Ht. 7in. (17.78cm)
In the Supplementary price list of c.1851 this figure is listed. The SPB quotes 8/- trade and 12/6 retail. The NPL of 1880 has it for 6/- and in 1873 for 6/6. The retail price in 1876 was 10/-. In 1884 the trade price was 5/- and the making price was 1/-.

S74 – HAMPSTEAD FLOWER HOLDER
1882
Sculptor: Owen Hale
Marks: OWEN HALE Sc.1882
Illus: Yes
This is an attractive item as a table decoration, with a girl riding a donkey, the basket panniers on either side being for flowers.

S74

It is listed in the c.1880 NPL at £1.1.0. It is not listed elsewhere, but there is a price of 18/6 for 1884. The c.1880 list includes it with the Statuettes and not Miscellaneous.

Note of relevance to the date of the Net Price List
This date of 1882 marked on an actual piece in the Spode Museum Trust's Collection as the date of its sculpting suggests that the un-dated Net Price List of c.1880 may in fact be in or after 1882.

S75 – HERMIONE
1860
Ht. 17in. (43.18cm)
Sculptor: William Calder Marshall
Marks: W.C.MARSHALL RA Sc. PUB JUNE 1 1860
Illus: Yes PP 536
In Greek mythology, Hermione was the daughter of Menelaus and Helen. She had been promised in marriage to Orestes before the Trojan War, but Menelaus after his return married her to Neoptolemus. He was the son of Achilles and Deidamie and was one of the heroes concealed in the wooden horse. After his marriage he was slain by Orestes, who then married Hermione.

S

Hermione is the 'Bellaria' of Greene's play *Pandosto,* the story from which Shakespeare derived his *A Winter's Tale*; in this she is portrayed as the wife of the jealous Leontes and the mother of Perdita. Shakespearean plays were a favourite source of inspiration for William Calder Marshall.

A version of this figure was issued with gilt and tinted borders.

The prices quoted in the SPB are 30/- trade and 52/6 retail; the gilt and tinted version was 40/- and 63/- respectively. In the c.1880 NPL the price was 18/- with the 'G & T' at £1.11.6. In 1873 these were £1.6.0 and £2.2.0. In 1876 the retail prices were £2.0.0 and £3.0.0. By 1884 the trade prices had dropped to 10/6 and 24/-. The making price was 2/-.

In 1859 W.C. Marshall signed an agreement with W.T. Copeland for the supply of some statuettes and a group with the reward of 15% of the trade price of each item sold. It is probable that the same consideration would have applied in the case of Hermione.

On early examples some lines from Shakespeare's *The Winter's Tale* are printed on the base:

Leontes.- Oh! thus she stood,
Even with such life of majesty (warm life
As now it coldly stands) when first I woo'd her.
* * * * * * * * * * * * *
See, my lord!
Would you not deem it breathed, and that those veins
Did verily bear blood?

Polixenes. Masterly done!
The very life seems warm upon her lip.
Winter's Tale

S76

S76 – HOP GIRL
c.1862
Sponsor: Alfred Crowquill
Illus: Yes
The only reference to this figure is a stereoscopic photograph of the item displayed in the International Exhibition of 1862.

Alfred Crowquill (1805-1872) is the pseudonym of Alfred Henry Forrester. He sculpted several parian subjects for Samuel Alcock.

S77

S79

S77 – HOPE
c.1865
Ht. 19in. (48.26cm)
Sculptor: L.A. Malempré
Sponsor: Ceramic and Crystal Palace Art Union
Marks: L.A.MALEMPRÉ Sculp CERAMIC AND CRYSTAL-PALACE ART UNION
Illus: Yes PP 520
'Hope' was the name given in later years to the Greek Muse Polymnia or Polyhymnia, Muse of the sublime hymn who usually appears in a pensive or meditating attitude. She was one of the nine female goddesses of song or divinities presiding over the different kinds of poetry and over the arts and sciences. As 'Hope' she was a popular figure with ornamentors of ceramics, appearing as sprigs (relief mouldings), prints and paintings, as well as figures. Sometimes, as here, she is seen wearing an anchor pendant as a symbol of steadfastness.

The figure is listed in the SPB at 28/- and the gilt and tinted version at 31/6. The stock list of the C & CPAU in 1881 prices it at 21/-. In 1884, after the closure of that Union, the price was 42/- for the gilt and coloured version; this was held in 1896. The making price was 5/-.

S78 HURDY – GURDY BOY
c.1870
This figure is featured in the SPB at 3/- trade and 4/6 retail; a version which was 'Ivory col'd & gilt' was 3/9 and dated 25/2/70. It is listed in the c.1880 NPL in the Miscellaneous section at 2/-. The making price was 6d.

S 79 – INDIAN FRUIT GIRL, companion to **Nubian Water-bearer**
c.1849
large, ht. 21in. (53.34cm), small, ht. 18in. (45.72cm)
Sculptor: Charles Cumberworth
Illus: Yes PP 535
This figure, also called **The Indian Girl**, together with her companion, **The Nubian Girl**, was exhibited at the Great Exhibition in 1851, and a line illustration of it was included in the *Art-Journal Exhibition Supplement.*

The figure is known as **The Indian Fruit Girl** by some authors, although what she is carrying are some shells in a carapace, the hard upper shell of a tortoise or a crustacean.

In a different form, on a tall base and with basket upon her head, she is listed as **Indian Girl Basket** and is the companion to the **Indian Fisherman Basket**. It seems possible that the latter may have been available as a figure without the deep base and basket, but it is not listed; an example in bone china is known. The **Indian Girl Basket** measures 28in. (71.12cm). It is listed under Dessert Comports.

The 1851 Price List quotes Indian Girl and Negress 2½ guineas each; these must be the small size.

	Large	Small
SPB	94/6 – 7gns	48/-
NPL	£4.4.0	£2. 8.0
1876 Retail Price List	£6.6.0	£3.12.0
c.1880 NPL	£4.4.0	£2. 2.0
1884 Trade price (MMS)	50/-	30/-
Making price	10/6	6/6

S80

S80a

S80 – INNOCENCE
1846, issued 1847
Ht. 16in. (40.64cm)
Sculptor: J.H. Foley
Sponsor: Art Union of London
Marks: Printed mark (on early examples) INNOCENCE BY J.H.FOLEY Executed in STATUARY PORCELAIN BY W.T.COPELAND FOR THE ART UNION OF LONDON 1847. Impressed mark ART UNION OF LONDON 1846
(*The Parian Phenomenon* records an impressed mark J.H. Foley Sc.London 1846)
Illus: Yes PP 536
A romantic portrayal by J.H. Foley of a cardinal virtue. The original life-size marble was exhibited at the Royal Academy in 1839; the Statuary Porcelain reduced size figure was commissioned by the Art Union of London in 1846 as a result of the favourable reception given by the public to 'Narcissus' in the previous year. The Copeland figure was introduced in 1847, exhibited at the Birmingham Exhibition in 1849 and at the Great Exhibition in 1851. The marble statue was illustrated in the *Art-Journal* of 1851.

The figure is not included in the 1848 and 1851 lists, nor in the NPL, as it was exclusive to the Art Union of London, for which the price was 30/-, recorded in the SPB. The lists of stock held at Stoke in 1881 for the Ceramic and Crystal Palace Art Union include two examples at 21/- each, and a note in one copy of the c.1880 NPL quotes 17/4 in 1884, while in another the price was 22/-. The making price was 5/-.

The Making Books list another figure as INNOCENCE (NEW) at 2/6. So far no other information about this figure is known.

The entry in the SPB reads: 'Innocence AUL only, 30/- Tested 10/6/82 CPAU'. The significance of this later tested price is not clear in the light of the price of 21/- as the stock value in 1881. Perhaps the stock value was a marked down value, as is customary in accounting practice, and the price of 30/- was what was going to be charged after the contract with the C&CPAU had terminated.
See Colour Plate 19

S81 – ITALIAN BOY
c.1851
Sculptor: A. Clerget
Sponsor:The Liverpool Art Union
The only reference in the Copeland records is the making price of 2/3 for **Italian Flower Boy.** The information at the moment rests on that given in *The Parian Phenomenon*.

S82 – ITALIAN FLOWER BOY
See S81, above

S83 – ITALIAN FLOWER SELLER
c.1885
Ht. 15in. (38.1cm)
Sculptor: Owen Hale
Illus: Yes

S83

S88

This figure is a man with two baskets and, apart from the photograph in the Copeland records, is recorded in manuscript in two copies of the c.1880 NPL: the information given above is in one, but with no price quoted, while in the other the price of 12/6 is dated 1885.

S84 – ITALIAN FLOWER GIRL
Although well documented in price lists, it is a pity that so far no illustration has been identified. The SPB lists this as: '
Italian Girl Figure 25/- 37/6 Color'd 30/-
ditto extra lace 31/6
All other references are to Italian Flower Girl.

The later prices were a lot lower so it was probably an early introduction; it was the first item to be listed under I in the SPB. The c.1880 NPL gives 18/-, in 1873 it was £1.0.0, and the retail price in 1876 was £1.10.0. The 1884 price was 10/6, while the making price was 2/-.

S85 – JOY
The only reference to a figure of Joy is in the SPB where a price of 12/6 RP is quoted on 4/10/73 for Rennie and Adcock. An earlier price of 16/- has been crossed out.

S86 – LADYBIRD, syn. **GIRL AND LADYBIRD**
Sponsor: Ceramic and Crystal Palace Art Union
Besides being included in the Making Price Books of 1895 and 1928, at 3/-, six figures were in the C&CPAU stock being returned to Stoke, at a value of 21/-.

S87 – LADY GODIVA, Equestrian Figure
1850
13in. (33.02cm)
Sculptor: John P. McBride
Sponsor: Art Union of Liverpool
A legend, going back to the eleventh century, tells the story of how Leofric, Earl of Chester, sought to raise revenues in the City of Coventry by the imposition of extra burdensome tolls. His wife, the Lady Godiva, a woman of great beauty, interceded with her husband on behalf of the citizens, begging him to grant them relief. This he agreed to do provided Godiva rode naked through the market place. This she did, but preserved her modesty by the skilful arrangement of her very long hair. In some versions of the legend the citizens were ordered to remain indoors; all but one obeyed; this was one now known as 'Peeping Tom', who was then unaccountably struck blind. Tennyson wrote a poem 'Godiva'.

This sculptured version of the Godiva legend shows the lady riding her horse, which is reputed to have been a white (? grey) one.

Copeland's statuette was displayed at the Great Exhibition of 1851 and the price given in the SPB is 42/-. However, no mention is made of the figure being an equestrian model.

S88 – LADY GODIVA, Standing Figure, companion to **Nora Creina**
c.1870
Ht. 22in. (55.88cm
Sculptor: R. Monti

S89

S90

S90a

Marks: R.MONTI 1870
Illus: Yes PP 515
The stance for the figure derives from Tennyson's poem *Godiva*, lines 42-49. For biographical details, see S87, above.

The figure is listed in the SPB at 52/6 trade and 84/-, which might be the highly decorated one, gilt and chased, for if the other Lady Godiva figure listed is not an equestrian but a standing one, then the SPB price of 42/- accords with the c.1880 NPL of £2.2.0. In 1873 the price was £3.0.0 and the retail price in 1876 was £4.10.0. In 1884 the noted price was 31/6 and the making price 6/-.

S89 – LADY MACBETH
1859
Ht. 16in. (40.64cm)
Sculptor: W. Calder Marshall
Illus: Yes
This statuette was one of the three which were the subject of an agreement made 17 January 1859 between William Calder Marshall RA of 47 Ebury Street and William Taylor Copeland of 160 New Bond Street. The other two statuettes were Comus and Ophelia. The 'royalty' was to be 15% of the trade price.

It is another of Calder Marshall's sculptures taken from the works of Shakespeare. Lady Macbeth, wife of the King of Scotland after her husband had murdered Duncan, was a principal character in Shakespeare's tragedy *Macbeth*. She was described by Samuel Taylor Coleridge thus:

> Lady Macbeth, like all in Shakspere *[sic]*, is a class individualized: of high rank, left much alone, and feeding herself with day-dreams of ambition, she mistakes the courage of fantasy for the power of bearing the consequences of the realities of guilt. Hers is the fortitude of a mind deluded by ambition: she shames her husband with a superhuman audacity of fancy which she cannot support, but sinks in the season of remorse, and dies in suicidal agony.

The subject is listed in the SPB at 30/- trade, and a gilt & tinted version at 40/-; there are no retail prices. In the c.1880 NPL the prices were 18/- and £1.11.6. In 1873, they were £1.5.0 and £1.18.0. The retail prices in 1876 were £1.17.0 and £3.0.0. In 1884, the trade prices were 10/6 and 25/-. The making price was 2/-.

S90 – L'ALLEGRO
1864
Ht. 16in. (40.64cm)
Sculptor: E.H. Baily
Sponsor: Crystal Palace Art Union
Marks: Printed on early examples: L'ALLEGRO by E.H.BAILY RA and CRYSTAL PALACE ART UNION. Impressed BAILY Sc. CRYSTAL PALACE ART UNION.PUBLISHED MARCH 1ST 1864
Illus: Yes PP 513
The theme is derived from John Milton's poem *L'Allegro,* which was written in c.1632. It might just as easily have been named 'Joi de vivre' or 'Blithe Spirit', for the semi-nude figure portrays both freedom and activity. No original source is known for it, and *L'Allegro's* companion poem, *Il Penseroso* (The Thinker), personifying the meditative or reflective life, does not appear to have been one of Baily's works.

This was commissioned by the Crystal Palace Art Union and thus does not appear in the NPL; however it is listed in the SPB at 21/- and a gilt and tinted version at 31/6. In 1881 the stock valuation was 21/-. After the closure of the C&CPAU the trade price in 1884 was 18/-, with the elaborate one at 23/-. The making price was 3/6.

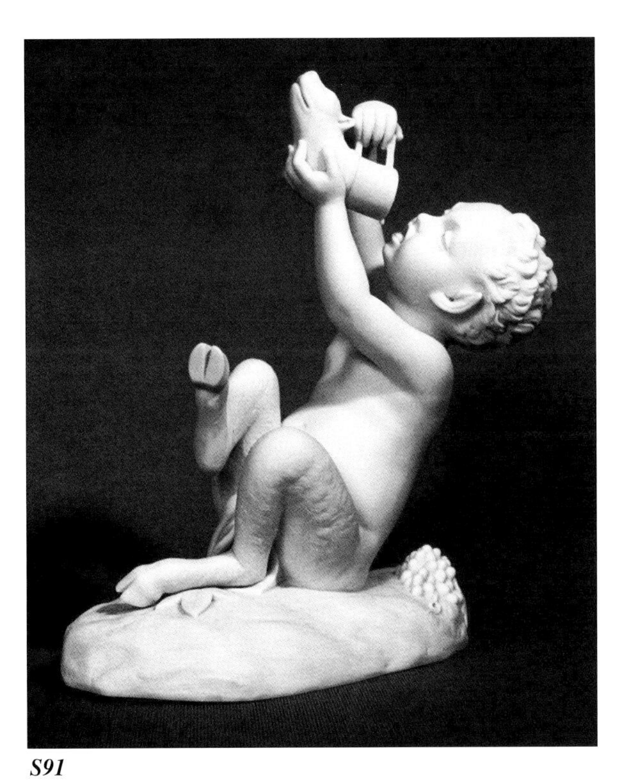

S91

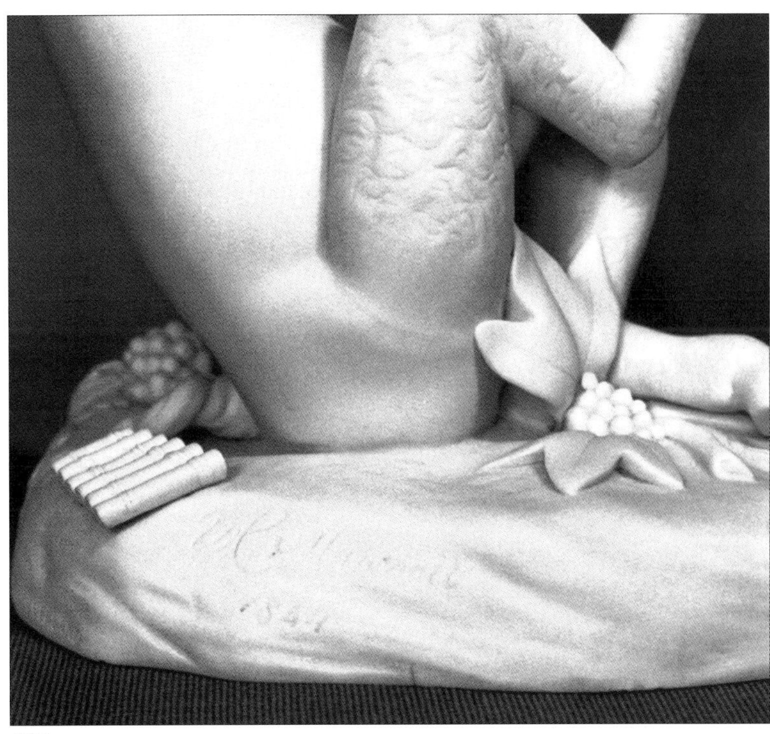

S91a

S91 – THE LAST DROP
c.1849
Ht. 9in. (22.86cm)
Sculptor: W. Calder Marshall
Illus: Yes, of the original marble figure.
This item is included in the Supplementary Price List of about 1851 where it has a hand-written retail price of 35/-. The SPB also lists it at 22/6 trade and 35/- retail. The only other reference is the Making Book price of 1/9.

S92 – LEISURE HOUR
Ht. 4in. (10.16cm)
Illus: Yes
This item consists of two children, each set on a circular base, to act as letter weights. Their attire suggests that they are children from humble backgrounds. They appear to be playing marbles or some other simple game.

The SPB quotes them at 2/- trade and 3/- retail each, while there was an ivory and gilt version at 2/9 trade dated 25/2/70. The 1873 trade price was also 2/- and 3/- retail in 1876. The c.1880 NPL quotes 2/- each. In 1884 the price was 1/6 each trade. The making price was 4d each.

S92

S93

S93 – LITTLE NELL, companion to **Master Davy**
c.1848
Ht. 12in. (30.48cm)
Sculptor: Thomas Sharp
Illus: Yes PP 566
A child character from the novel *The Old Curiosity Shop* by Charles Dickens. *The Parian Phenomenon* states the sculptor as Westmacott, who certainly sculpted the companion figure of Master Davy; however, the receipt in the Copeland records is:

> 27 Burton Crescent
> Oct. 20th 1848
> W.T.Copeland Esq
> To Thos. Sharp
> Model of Little Nell £10.10.0
> Received by Cheque Thomas Sharp.

A date of 1855 is given by Shinn.

The SPB gives the prices as 21/- trade and 31/6 retail. The 1873 NPL quotes 13/6. In 1876, the retail price was £1.1.0. By c.1880 the trade price had dropped to 12/6 and in 1884 the trade price was 10/-. The making price was 1/10.

S94 – LITTLE RED RIDING HOOD
1848
Ht. 11¾in. (29.85cm)
Sculptor: T. Woolner
Illus: Yes PP 500
On 23 December 1847 Thomas Woolner wrote to Copeland:

> Sir – On considering the time it would need to work out the design of Little Red Riding Hood, I feel it only fair to you and myself to say, that I could not undertake to model it for a less sum than £15. I think you will not call this too large a sum when you consider that it will require close upon 5 weeks to work out this design in a manner to do it justice.
> I am, Sir, your obedient servant,
> Thomas Woolner.
> This offer accepted 23 Dec 1847
> W.T.Copeland.

This letter sent and received on 23rd December (in the days before facsimile machines!). The model was paid for on 5 February 1848.

In the 1848 and 1851 retail price lists the figure is described as Little Red Riding Hood and was priced at £1.5.0. The SPB and subsequent lists enter it under R as **Red Riding Hood** at 18/- trade and 25/- retail and, in 1873, at 14/-. The retail price in 1876 was £1.1.0. The NPL of c.1880 has it at 12/-. The handwritten trade price for 1884 was 8/6 and the making price in 1895 and 1928 was 1/9.

See also S94A **Red Riding Hood** under the subjects beginning with the letter R (page 170).

S94

S95

S95 – LAMP FIGURE
An entry in the SPB records 'Lamp figure 42/-'

In 1848 an agreement was made between William Potts, a metal manufacturer of Birmingham, and W.T. Copeland, by which Copeland would supply to Potts figures made of statuary porcelain for Potts to mount into lamps, brackets, inkstands, candlesticks, candelabra and similar articles. The *Art-Journal* of 1849 carried a whole page feature on this enterprise, illustrating several of the items. The negotiations began in November 1848, when William Potts was seeking the collaboration of Copeland and showing samples of his work to Mr. Battam. On 18 November Potts wrote to complain that he had not received Copeland's reply, but by 2 December he wrote to Copeland:

> I have the pleasure of receiving your note stating your intention of supplying me with Statuary Porcelain exclusively as applicable to metal work, on the condition that I have all Figures and other subjects in that material exclusively from you this restriction on myself I always contemplated and willingly promise to strictly adhere to, and likewise undertake to endeavour to introduce the material in the most expensive and general use I can devise. I think I see a prospect of employing it for many other purposes than figures which subject I hope to have the opportunity of discussing with Mr Battam of Stoke as I hope to be there in a few days.
>
> I am beginning to sell the articles in which the Figures are introduced the general/may all/ opinions are highly commendatory. Mr Hall of the Art Journal considered them the best goods of their kind yet made in this country. Mr Cundall of Bond St is very sanguine of their being quickly saleable. Both Morrell & James & Mr Barry (of Piccadilly) have ordered them, and I see no reason to doubt the ultimate effect being satisfactory but I need not state to you, Sir, that after so flat a period in business as the last two years, buyers of fancy goods are disposed to be cautious. However I pledge myself to energetic action – I called in Bond St during yr absence to show two of the Clock Stand designs which I much wished you to notice, but as I hope to show a large number of them to Mr Battam next week, he will probably report to you of their claims. My clerk Mr Philip will soon be ready to send you the samples of Ink & Flower Stands, Candlesticks, &c. which I hope will receive from yourself and your visitors the same applause they have hitherto invariably gained.
>
> I have the honour to be etc.
>
> William Potts
>
> William Potts, 16, Easy Row, Birmingham

S96 – LOVE, Female Figure
c.1882
Ht. 15in. (38.1cm)
Illus: Yes PP 485
This figure and her companion are noticed first in a handwritten price for 1884 of 15/-. Then, there is an illustrated sheet of figures published in about 1885; a Net Price sheet was printed to accompany this where these figures are each priced at 15/-. A second Net Price sheet was published in 1895, where the price for Love had increased to 18/- each.

S97 – LOVE, Male Figure
c.1882
Ht. 15in. (38.1cm)
Illus: Yes
See the preceding entry, S96

S96

S98

S98 – LURLINE, Seated
1855
Ht. 12in. (30.48cm)
Sculptor: after Ludwig Michael Schwanthaler
Illus: Yes PP 505
The marble was sculpted by Schwanthaler (1802-1848) of Munich in 1841 for Prinz Schwartzenberg of Vienna. It is now at Castle Anif, Salzburg. A version is at Somerleyton Hall, Suffolk, and another, in bronze, at the Hofgarten, Munich.

Lurline was a legendary siren said to have lived at the foot of the Lorelei (or Loreley or Lurlei), a dangerous cliff, 430ft. (131m) high, on the River Rhine between St.Goar and Oberwesel. The legend tells of how she lured boatmen to their death in the river by playing sweet haunting music. This legend inspired a number of poems, including one by Heinrich Heine, published in 1823. Felix Mendelssohn and Lachner wrote operas, while another opera called *Lurline*, produced by Wallace at Covent Garden in 1860, was no doubt the reason behind the introduction by Copeland of a set of Kneeling Lurlines as dessert comports; these were sculpted by L.A. Malempré and will be listed in the section dealing with those items.

The figure was produced in plain statuary porcelain and its price in the SPB was 35/- trade and 52/6 retail. There was also a gilt and tinted version at 42/- and 63/- respectively. In 1873 the prices were £1.10.0 and £2.0.0. The retail prices in 1876 were £2.5.0 and £3.0.0. In the c.1880 NPL the prices were £1.7.6 and £1.16.0. In 1884 the trade prices were 15/- and 23/6. In 1895 and 1928 the making price was 3/-.

In the Spode Museum Trust Collection the example appears to have been rubbed with iron oxide because it has a somewhat mottled effect of that reddish-brown hue.

The original was portrayed in the *Art-Journal* of 1855.

S99 – MAIDENHOOD, companion to **Beatrice**
1861
Ht. 22in. (55.88cm)
Sculptor: Edgar G. Papworth Jnr.
Marks: Printed verse of poetry, and EXECUTED IN COPELAND'S CERAMIC STATUARY
Illus: Yes PP 519
This was inspired by Longfellow's poem of the same name, i.e., *Maidenhood.* The original marble statue was exhibited at the 1860 Royal Academy. Beneath the base of early examples a verse of Longfellow's poem was printed:

Standing with reluctant feet,
Where the brook and river meet,
Womanhood and childhood fleet.

Gazing, with a timid glance,
On the brooklet's swift advance,
On the river's broad expanse.

Longfellow's Poems

The SPB quotes for the plain figure 45/- trade and 52/6 retail. A version with gilt and tinted borders was £2.10.0. By 1873 these prices had

S99

S100

increased to £2.8.0 and £2.15.0 respectively. The retail prices in 1876 were £3.12.0 and £4.4.0. In the c.1880 NPL the price was £1.17.6. By 1884 the trade price had dropped to 25/- and 37/6. The making price was 4/6.

In the Spode Museum Trust Collection is a very fine example which is tinted all over in delicate colours. I am not in favour of statuary being coloured but this particular example is beautiful. It was donated to the Spode Museum in 1984.

See Colour Plate 20

S100 – MARGUERITE, companion to **Evangeline**
c.1871
Ht. 21in. (53.34cm)
Sculptor: Sarah Terry
Marks: Printed verse of poetry, and EXECUTED IN COPELAND'S CERAMIC STATUARY
Illus: Yes PP 561

The character is taken from *Faust*, a tragedy by Goethe (1749-1832), probably Germany's greatest poet-dramatist. Faust is portrayed as a charlatan who practises necromancy, but who eventually comes to see the error of his ways.

Marguerite is shown as a Christian maiden carrying a prayer-book. On the base of the early examples a verse from the poem was printed:

This girl is fair indeed.
Virtue she hath and modest heed
Her cheeks soft light her rosy lips
No length of time will e'er eclipse
Her downward glance in passing by
Deep in my heart is stamped for aye.
Faust.

The French composer, Charles François Gounod (1818-1893), used Goethe's tragedy as the basis for an opera, *Faust*, which was produced at the Théatre Lyrique in Paris in 1859.

The first price recorded in the SPB was 31/6 trade and in 1873 £1.15.0. In 1876 the retail price was £2.12.6. The c.1880 NPL has £1.10.0. The revised price of 18/- trade and 31/6 retail was initialled RP 31/8/84. The making price was 3/6.

See Colour Plate 21

S101 – MARKET BOY, companion to **Market Girl**
after 1880
Ht. 11in. (27.94cm)
Illus: Yes

A charming study which could have been used to arrange very small flowers like violets or pinks. The boy and his girl companion were adapted as dessert comports.

The NPL of c.1880 includes a handwritten price for each figure of 7/-. In the Making Price Book, however, they do not appear as Figures but are noted, in pencil, in the Group section where it reads: 'Market Boy & Girl 1/7'.

Although in *The Parian Phenomenon* it states 'Market Boy and Girl as a group', this intelligence was gleaned from this making price book and I opine that they are two separate figures, but that the making department regarded them as inseparable companions! The price of 1/7d might have been for the two! This would accord with the relationship between the making and 1884 trade price of other groups.

S102 – MARKET GIRL, companion to **Market Boy**
The details are exactly the same as for S101, her companion **Market Boy**.

S101

S102

S103

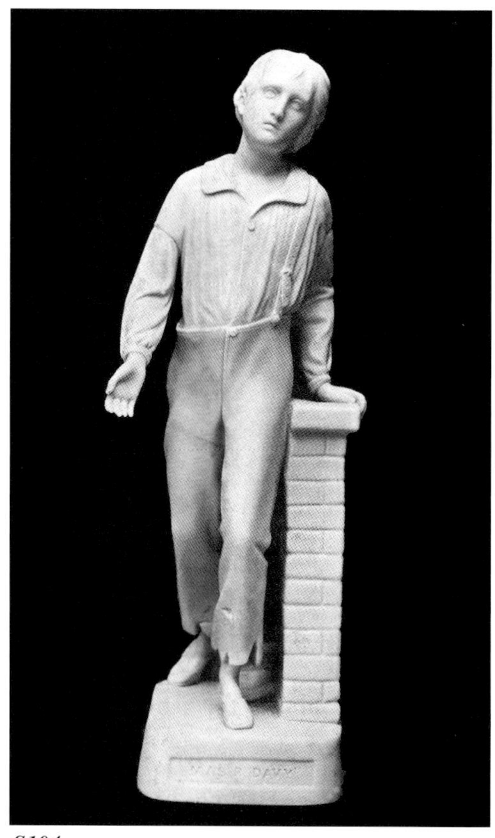

S104

S103 – MARY, QUEEN OF SCOTS
c.1879
Ht. 14in. (35.56cm)
Sculptor: L.A. Malempré
Sponsor: Ceramic & Crystal Palace Art Union
Marks: L.A.MALEMPRÉ Sc. CERAMIC AND CRYSTAL PALACE ART UNION
Illus: Yes PP 547

The figure is of HRH the Princess of Wales, Princess Alexandra, dressed as Queen Mary, Queen of Scots (1542-1587). The Queen was the daughter of James V of Scotland and Mary Guise. On the death of her father she was crowned queen in 1543. Educated in France, she married the Dauphin, Francis II, in 1558. Consequent upon the death of Mary Tudor, Queen of England, Mary Stuart laid claim to the throne of England on the grounds that she was the great-granddaughter of Henry VIII and that, Elizabeth being illegitimate, she was the true heir. Her claim failed. She was widowed in 1560. In 1561 she returned to Scotland and married Lord Darnley. He was murdered, having himself had Rizzio, Mary's private secretary, assassinated. Mary then married Darnley's murderer, James Hepburn, Fourth Earl of Bothwell (1536-1578).

In 1567 the Earl of Murray raised a rebellion and defeated Mary at Carberry Hill. She was taken prisoner and compelled to abdicate in favour of her son, James VI. Murray was appointed Regent for Scotland. She escaped from Loch Leven Castle and again took the field, but was defeated at Langside and took refuge in England where she was detained a prisoner and, because of her plotting against Elizabeth, she was executed in 1587.

The only references are the stock list held at Stoke for the Ceramic & Crystal Palace Art Union on 10 November 1881, when there were '6 figures Princess of Wales @ 10/- £3.0.0'. The other reference is a handwritten note in a c.1880 NPL quoting 10/-, again for the figure of the Princess of Wales. There is no mention in lists of Mary, Queen of Scots.

See Colour Plate 22

S104 – MASTER DAVY, companion to **Little Nell**
c.1850
Ht. 12in. (30.48cm)
Sculptor: J.S. Westmacott
Illus: Yes

David Copperfield, the title of Charles Dickens' favourite work, was issued in twenty monthly parts, the first appearing in May 1849. It is said that parts of the story were taken from episodes in the life of the author himself.

In the SPB the figure is written as **Master Davy Copperfield** and was priced at 21/- trade and 31/6 retail. In 1873 the price was 13/6 and in 1876 the retail price was £1.1.0. In the c.1880 NPL it is 12/6. The trade price in 1884 was 10/-, while the making price was 1/10.

S105 – MASTER TOM, companion to **Miss Ellie**
c.1873
Ht. 21in. (53.34cm)
Sculptor: J.Durham
Illus: Yes

Master Tom and Miss Ellie are the principal characters in Charles Kingsley's epic fantasy *The Water Babies: A Fantasy for a Land Baby.* Tom makes his appearance as one of the unfortunate urchins exploited by Victorian chimney-sweeps. He first becomes acquainted with Miss Ellie through losing his way in a labyrinth of flues and ending up

S105

S106

S107

standing on her hearth. Miss Ellie, asleep, is awakened and, seeing Tom, screams. Tom takes flight only to eventually fall into a river and is drowned.He then turns into an eft (a newt). Miss Ellie, too, comes to an untimely end by slipping off a rock. She and Tom meet again in sub-aqua circumstances and become attached to one another only to part, and then to meet yet again.

The marble was shown at the 1873 Vienna Exhibition. A review in the *Art-Journal* of 1875 remarks: 'The parian worker has been eminently successful in giving the artist's vigorous treatment and happy expressiveness to the reduced figure'.

The figure is priced at £2.10.0 in 1873 in the NPL. The retail price in 1876 was £3.15.0. The 1880 trade price lists it at £1.10.0. In 1884 the trade price was 21/-. The making price was 4/-.

S106 – MISS ELLIE, companion to **Master Tom**
c.1873
Ht. 21in. (53.34cm)
Sculptor: J. Durham
Illus: Yes
The outline of the story of *The Water Babies* may be seen above, at S105. The price details are the same as those for Master Tom.

S107 – MIGNON
c.1876
Ht. 15in. (39.1cm)
Sculptor: L.A. Malempré
Sponsor: Ceramic and Crystal Palace Art Union
Marks: CERAMIC AND CRYSTAL PALACE ART UNION L A MALEMPRÉ Sc. 1876
Illus: Yes PP 505
Mignon is the mysterious Italian maiden in Goethe's novel *Wilhelm Meister's apprenticeship,* published in 1795. Mignon loves Wilhelm and dies in despair when her love is not returned. She is, unknowingly, the daughter of an old harpist who also is tied to Wilhelm by bonds of love and gratitude. Together they wander the continent in a twilight of mystery.

Wilhelm Sherer, in his *History of German Literature,* comments: 'None of Goethe's creations appeal more strongly to the depths of the human soul than these two characters with their touching songs'. Sir Walter Scott included Mignon, as Favella, in *Peveril of the Peak,* while Ambrose Thomas produced the opera *Mignon* in Paris in 1866 and in London in 1870, the words being by Carre and Barber.

The figure is based on a painting by Ary Scheffer.

The only mentions found so far in the Copeland records are, first, the stock taken in November 1881 of the goods held for the Ceramic and Crystal Palace Art Union, when nine figures in total were in stock, and these were at a value of 10/- each. The second reference is in the Making Price Books where 2/- was paid.

S108 – MODESTY
The only reference to a figure of this name is in the list published in *The Illustrated Guide to Victorian Parian China* by Charles and Dorrie Shinn, where, on page 72, it is listed as having been introduced in 1851. Could this be a title suggested by Shinn for the figure shown as S54, **The First Bath of the Season**? (This figure, however, was dated 1874.)

S109

S109 – MUSIDORA
Date: Small 1851; Large 1867
Dimensions: Small Ht. 7½in. (19.05cm). Large Ht. 17in. (43.18cm)
Sculptor: Small: after Sir J. Reynolds. Large: W. Theed
Sponsor of the large figure: Ceramic and Crystal Palace Art Union
Marks on large figure : MUSIDORA W THEED SCULPT CERAMIC AND CRYSTAL PALACE ART UNION Pubd. 1867
Illus: Yes (large figure)
Musidora is the coy sweetheart of Damon, with whom she features in James Thompson's *The Seasons*, published in 1730. They meet by chance when Musidora is bathing and inadvertently is discovered by Damon. He writes love lines to her in the river sand, thus capturing her affections.

She is the subject of a painting by Gainsborough, now in the National Gallery, London, and Theed's figure bears some resemblance to a book illustration for Thompson's *The Seasons,* executed by Richard Westall early in the 19th century. The attribution of the small figure to Sir Joshua Reynolds is from the Supplementary Price List published in 1851. Theed's original marble statue was sculpted at the request of the Prince of Wales in 1866, and it was shown at the Royal Academy Exhibition in that year. The large figure is said to be the companion to the Shepherd Boy by Malempré.

The 1851 price list, retail, quotes 12/- for the small figure. The SPB lists both figures: the small one at 5/- trade and 8/- retail; the large one, 'CPAU Musidora, New, Figure 21/- Gilt 30/-'. Only the small one is printed in the NPL: 5/6 in 1873. The retail price in 1876 was 8/6. The NPL quotes 5/- in c.1880. The Stock value of the large one in 1881 was 21/-. In 1884, small 3/6, large 21/-, with a 'col'd & gilt' at 52/6 on 10 February 1897. Making prices were 10d and 4/6 respectively.
See Colour Plate 23

S110 – NAIADS or **SEA NYMPHS**, a pair
1865
Ht. 18in. (45.72cm)
Illus: Yes
These two figures were copied from marble statues in the garden of Trentham Hall. On 17 June 1865, Henry Wright wrote to Alderman Copeland:

> Dear Sir, The Duke of Sutherland has much pleasure in granting you permission to make copies of the figures at Trentham representing Naiads, or Sea Nymphs, in accordance with your request addressed to the Duchess, Dowager of Sutherland.
> I am Yours Truly, Henry Wright.

Copeland replied on 19 June 1865:

> To His Grace The Duke of Sutherland
> My Dear Duke, I beg to thank you for your note allowing me to manufacture copies of the figures at Trentham. And I am
> Yours faithfully, W T Copeland.

Naiads were temple deities who presided over springs and streams in Greek mythology. They were usually portrayed as beautiful young girls, their heads wreathed with flowers, they are light-hearted, musical and beneficent. Portrayals of Naiads were mostly the figments of a particular artist's imagination. Descriptions of naiads have varied from time to time and from list to list, but this pair seem to identify with the following:
SPB
Sea Nymph (or Naiad) 63/-
Naiad (or **new Sea Nymph**) 63/-
1873 NPL
Naiad and Companion each £2.18.0
1876 Retail
Naiad and Companion each £4.10.0
c.1880 NPL
Naiad and Companion each £2. 5.0
1884 MSS note 'each 31/6'
Making List
Naiad with Harp & Companion 6/6

S110

The figure on the right of the photograph looks as if she is playing a harp, but that the instrument is missing; a metal one might have been supplied when the figure was sold. Only in the Making Book are they described as Naiad with Harp & Companion, but the making price of 6/6 would accord with the large size and difficult nature of the figures.

For other naiads see Sea Nymph (S155), Water Nymph (S189), and Naiad, kneeling (S111).

S111

S111 – NAIAD, Kneeling
A 5½in. (13.97cm) high figure which might answer to this description is in a private collection, but there may be another, correct, title. When such a title is discovered more information may be applied to it.

S112 – NAIAD on DOLPHIN AND SHELL
c.1848
15½in. (39.37cm) long
Sponsor: William Potts
The subject bears a resemblance to the marble statue in the parish church of Barmouth, Wales. This was one of the many objects made for mounting in metal by William Potts, Manufacturer of 16 Easy Row, Birmingham. See notes under S95, Lamp Figure.
It is listed in the Making Price Book at 4/6d.

S112

S113

S113 – NAPOLEON 1st, companion to seated figure of **Wellington**
1853
Ht. 11in. (27.94cm)
Sculptor: W. Theed
Sponsor: ? A. Crowquill
Marks: an early example impressed OPUS W THEED Sc.PUBLD. FEBy 1st 1853
Illus: Yes PP 498
This seated figure of Emperor Napoleon is taken from the painting by Hippolyte Paul Delaroche (1797-1856). The painting, in the Musée de L'Armée in Paris, is the best known seated portrait of Napoleon. It is called 'Napoleon at Fontainbleau: The First Abdication 1814'. It is signed Paul Delaroche 1840.
The SPB has two entries:
Napoleon Statuette 42/- 63/-
Napoleon (Seated) 42/- 63/-
It is unusual for two items like this to have identical prices, yet the entries are separated only by the entry for Narcissus, so there may indeed be two figures – but there is no other record known to me of a second study of him.
In 1873 the trade price was £1.10.0; the retail price in 1876 was £2.5.0. The figure is included in the c.1882 NPL as 'Napoleon I (from the celebrated Fontainbleau Picture) £1.5.0.' The handwritten note for 1884 was 16/6. The Making Price Book titled the figure 'Napoleon Burnaparte [*sic*] 3/6'.

S114

S114a

S114b

S114 – NARCISSUS
1846
Ht. 12in. (30.48cm)
Sculptor: John Gibson, RA, adapted for reduced copy in parian E.B. Stephens
Sponsor: Art Union of London

S114c

Marks: Printed inside base of figure: NARCISSUS BY GIBSON RA Modelled by E.B. STEPHENS and executed in STATUARY PORCELAIN BY COPELAND & GARRETT FOR THE ART UNION OF LONDON 1846

A character from Greek mythology, Narcissus is known as a beautiful youth, the son of Cephissus and the nymph Liriope. He was insensitive to the feeling of love. Nemesis caused him to see his own image reflected in the water of a fountain pool, whereupon he fell in love with it but, unable to grasp it, he pined away until he was metamorphosed into the flower which bears his name. The nymph Echo, who had kept talking to Hera while Zeus was sporting with the Nymphs, was discovered by Hera and punished by being changed into an echo. In this state she fell in love with Narcissus, but as her love was not returned she died in grief, so that only her voice remained.

The original Greek standing statue was found at Pompeii. Gibson's version, exhibited in 1838 at the Royal Academy, is now in the Academy's collection at Burlington House; a marble copy is displayed in the Art Gallery in Sydney. A Copeland & Garrett Statuary Porcelain reduced copy is in the collection of the Victoria & Albert Museum, London.

Although John Gibson had suggested that Copeland & Garrett should use his sculpture as the first model to be sponsored by the Art Union of London, the Trustees of the Royal Academy would not allow a mould to be made from the original, so E.B. Stephens modelled a reduced size one; his was an exact copy, but the officers of the Art Union required a fig leaf to be added. It is said that the only parian example without the leaf was kept by Stephens! Please see page 18 for the great importance of Narcissus in the story of parian.

The figure was executed exclusively for the Art Union of London, so it does not feature in any published list except that of 26 May 1848, but with no price.

The SPB states: 'AUL Narcissus AU only 30/-. 40/- RP Mr Battam's letter 18/1/78'. The above have been crossed out and '25/- tested 10/6/92' inserted. I believe that RP stands for Mr Richard Pirie Copeland who would need to authorise a change of price. Presumably the new lower price was in line with the lower prices being charged on all other parian items. The Making Book price was 3/3 in 1895 and 1928.

S116

S117

S115 – NEAPOLITAN GIRL
The only reference to this is in the SPB where a price of 31/6 trade is given. At this price it can be expected to be quite large.

S116 – NEGRESS, companion to **Indian Girl**
Also called **NUBIAN GIRL** or **WATER-BEARER**
c.1849
Large ht. 21in. (53.34cm). Small ht. 18in. (45.72cm)
Sculptor: C. Cumberworth
Illus: Yes PP 535
A fine study, which, with her companion, would look very well at either end of a Victorian buffet or sideboard. Introduced in about 1849, it was displayed with her companion, the **Indian Girl**, at the 1851 Great Exhibition; the price for her was 2½ guineas, i.e. £2.12.6. (In the price list for 1851 she is listed as **Negress**, so it is this name that is adopted here.)

The prices for this figure are substantially lower than those for her companion, despite the similarities of size and sculpture. Only in the 1851 list are they at the same price, retail. These will be for the smaller 18in. size. The NPL give the height as 17in. (43.18cm).

The SPB also lists her as **Negress**. The various prices are as follows:

	Large	Small
Statuary Price Book	52/6 W 84/-R	36/- W 52/6 R
1873 Net price List	£2.10.0 W	£1.10.0 W
1876 Retail Price list	£3.15.0 R	£2. 5.0 R
c.1880 Net Price List	£2 5.0	£1. 7.6
Making prices	5/6d	3/6d

S117 – NIGHTINGALE, MISS FLORENCE
c.1864
Ht. 17in. (43.18cm)
Sculptor: J. Hilary Bonham Carter
Marks: J. HILARY BONHAM CARTER
Illus: Yes PP 545
Born in Florence, Italy, on 12 May 1820 and died in London on 13 August 1910, Florence Nightingale became imbued with a keen social conscience at an early age. This led her to pursue a vigorous campaign to improve the quality of life for mankind both at home, in Europe and in India. That campaign was to endure throughout the whole of her active life. The main thrust of her endeavours was directed towards improving the standards of public health through better sanitation, greater attention to personal hygiene and, above all, the institution of a system for the selection, training and certification of qualified nurses.

She is remembered best for her work among the soldiers of the Crimean War (1854-56), particularly at the Scutari Hospital where she became known as 'the Lady of the Lamp'. Later she was to write a number of treatises on matters pertaining to public health, mainly for the benefit of the government. Despite her public activities, she was a shy and modest person, albeit determined and demanding. She shunned public acclaim or any form of advertisement, as a result of which permission to reproduce her likeness in any medium was given only rarely.

One exception was the statuette sculpted by Hilary Bonham Carter, around whose neck it was to become something of an albatross, perhaps because it stretched her modelling skills too far for she was dissatisfied

S118

with its development and became increasingly reluctant to complete it. Having done so, Miss Bonham Carter was still unhappy and embarked upon a second attempt, but this too failed to please her, causing her further anguish and distress.

Finally, by uniting the head of the first attempt with the body of the second, re-modelling the face and seeking the assistance of Thomas Woolner, RA, the work was finally completed and exhibited at the Royal Academy in 1862. It was not liked by Miss Nightingale's mother, who wrote to her elder daughter: 'I have seen our F. in the Royal Academy and am shocked at the poor little Finniken Minniken they call Florence!' However, in 1866 a contemporary wrote to Florence: 'There are photographs of the statuette which are more characteristic of you than the actual portraits, none of which give a real idea of what you were ten years ago!'

Florence Nightingale was awarded many honours, including the Order of Merit. Before her death she had become totally incapacitated, blind and unable to speak. Her family refused a national ceremonial funeral in Westminster Abbey and her remains lie buried in the family grave at East Wellow, Hampshire. Her memorial consists of a simple inscription on the family tombstone: 'F.N. Born 1820. Died 1910.' It is as she instructed.

The SPB records: 'Nightingale, Miss. Figure (private work) 25/- to LH 31/6 W general'. The NPL of 1873 gives £1.15.0, the 1876 Retail List £2.12.6, and the c.1880 list £1.1.0. The 1884 trade price was 12/-. There is no recorded making price.

S118 – MENDING THE NET or **Net Mender**
c.1873
L. 18in. (45.72cm)
Sculptor: E.W. Wyon
Sponsor: Art Union of London
Marks: MENDING THE NET EDWARD W WYON. SCULPTOR 1873. ART UNION OF LONDON
Illus: Yes PP 490
Richard Dennis believed this figure was originally known as 'The Fisherman's Daughter', but an example in a private collection is clearly marked 'MENDING THE NET' on the side of the plinth, cast in the mould, indicating that this was the correct title, even though the item in the Making Price Book is entitled 'Net Mender 10/-'. This suggests that this is a latter name and was the factory title for this figure, and not that by which it should be known. However, the original sculpture which was displayed at the Royal Academy in 1865 was called 'The Fisherman's Daughter'.

So far, apart from the reference in the Making Price Book, where it is priced at 10/-, I have not found any other entry in the Copeland records.

S119 – NORA CREINA, companion to **Lady Godiva**
c.1871
Ht. 22in. (55.88cm)
Sculptor: R. Monti
Marks: R. MONTI 1870
Illus: Yes
Nora Creina features in the poem *Lesbia hath a beaming eye* by Thomas Moore (1779-1852), the eminent and much revered Irish poet. The character is presented as the epitome of virtue and modesty in contrast to the flaunting physical flamboyance of Lesbia. *Lesbia hath a beaming eye* is but one of a collection of poems by Moore that was published over a period of twenty-eight years (1807-35) under the heading 'Irish Melodies'.

In 1792 lovers of traditional Irish music organised in Belfast a festival of antiquarian harp music. During the festival the music of ten 'Harpers' *(sic)* was written down by a young musician named Edward Bunting.

S119

S120

His scores became known as the 'Irish Melodies' and it was for these airs, suitably adapted by Sir J. Stevenson, that Moore was engaged by the publishing house of the Powers Brothers to provide the lyrics.

The authors have been unable to establish from whence Moore took his inspiration for Nora Creina despite the active interest and assistance of both the Departments of 'Irish' and 'English' at University College, Dublin. It seems fairly certain that the character is not historical in origin, but literary, possibly springing from Moore's own imagination. The name surfaces again in Bernard Shaw's *John Bull's other Island* (1904) as Nora Creena *(sic)*. Moore's usage of the name is something of a paradox for, while he portrays Nora Creina as being young and innocent, in literal truth the name means 'old and wise', from the Irish 'Criona'. The mystery deepens in that Nora is not an Irish name, but is a diminutive for Honora.

The last entry under 'N' in the SPB quotes a trade price of 52/6 and retail of 84/-. In 1873 the price was £3.0.0. The retail price in 1876 was £4.10.0. In the c.1880 NPL the price was £2.2.0. In 1884, the trade price was 25/6, which rose to 30/- in 1909. The making price was 5/-.

S120 – **NURSE IS AWAY** or **ABSENT MAID** – See also S1
c.1880
Ht. 6in. (15.24cm)
Illus: Yes
The record photograph is titled 'Nurse is Away' and the author has chosen this title rather than Absent Maid which is what the item is called in the NPL of c.1880. This figure is not included in the 1873 and 1876 price lists, nor is it in the SPB. In the c.1880 NPL it is listed as: **'Absent Maid (Companion to "Washing Dolly")** 8.0'. The 1884 price was 4/6d, the making price 1/-.

S121 – NYMPH AT BATH
c.1851
Ht. 9-10in. (25.4 cm), L.13in. (33.02cm),. W. 7in. (17.78cm)
Sculptor: after Lorenzo Bartolini
Illus: Yes
The original marble sculpture by the Italian sculptor Lorenzo Bartolini, which is known as 'Nymph with a Scorpion', was produced c.1837 and is at the Château de Beauvais, near Nancy, in France. It was exhibited at the Paris Salon in 1845. A plaster model is in the Pitti Palace, Florence. The scorpion is invisible in the picture, but it has just bitten the girl's foot and is retreating to the rear. I am grateful to Philip Ward-Jackson for this information and for the photograph of the plaster model; the Copeland version varies slightly from this. In all the Copeland records this item is listed as 'Nymph at Bath'.

The SPB lists this as the second under the 'N' items at the prices of 31/6 trade and 52/6 retail. The NPL of 1873 prices it at £1.10.0. The retail price in 1876 was £2.5.0. The c.1880 NPL has £1.7.6 and the note in the margin states 1884 21/-. The making price was 4/-.
See Colour Plate 24

S121

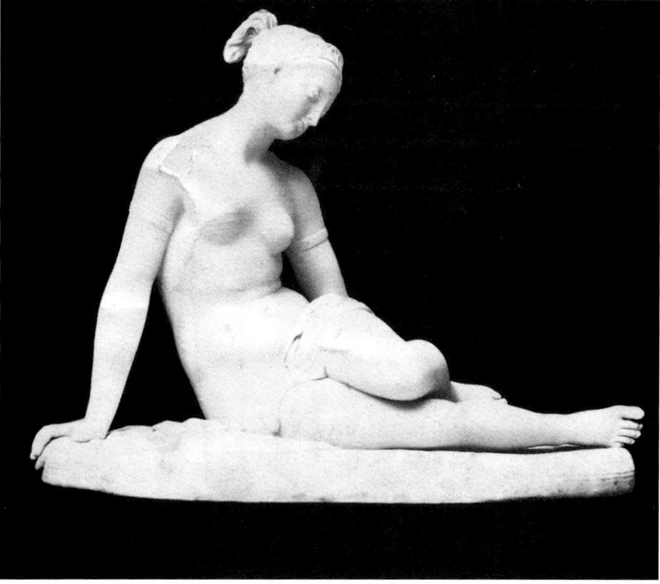

S121a

S122

S122 – NYMPH PREPARING FOR THE BATH or **Nymph untying her Sandal**
c.1858
Ht. 17⅝in. (44.77cm)
Sculptor: John Gibson, RA
Sponsor: The Crystal Palace Art Union
Marks: CRYSTAL PALACE ART UNION
Illus: Yes
The original sculpture of what has become known by some as 'Gibson's Nymph' was completed in 1831. It was owned by the Earl of Yarborough who later presented it to the Usher Art Gallery in Lincoln, where it may be seen. The figure is sometimes called **Nymph untying her Sandal**.

It is a most delightful study and first came to my notice when an owner wrote to enquire about its name and history. I, in turn, consulted Dr.Philip Ward-Jackson at the Courtauld Institute because I could not find any record of it. I am greatly indebted to him for answering this enquiry (and many more besides) by telling me the name of the sculptor and the name of the subject. I later visited the owner who permitted me to take the photograph which accompanies this account.

In 1984 there was a court case in Vancouver in which a plaintiff alleged that the figure she owned of this subject was of marble; this was the second example of the figure of which I had any knowledge.

The example in the picture has gilded and tinted highlighting to the straps and arm bangles.

A copy of the statuette was bought by Queen Victoria when she visited the Crystal Palace Art Union in 1859. A fine print of the sculpture was included in the September issue of the 1860 *Art-Journal*.

There does not appear to be any record of it in the Copeland records.
See Colour Plate 25

S123 – ONDINE
1847
Ht. 9in. (22.86 cm)
Sculptor: after Pradier
Marks: Printed – COPELAND'S PORCELAIN STATUARY
Ondine, or Undine, is the name given by Copelands to an allegorical figure, one of four, by Pradier representing rivers found on the 'Fontaine Pradier' in Nimes, France. The statue represents a famous local spring, or water-course, known as the 'Fontaine de Nimes'. The original work is also known as the River Allegory.

The figure, sitting above an over-turned water jar, should be holding a mirror in her right hand; this is shown in the illustration in the 1851 Copeland catalogue.

The retail price in 1848 was £1.10.0, while in 1851 it had reduced to 20/-. In the SPB, wherein Ondine is the first entry under the letter O, the trade price is 21/- and the retail 30/-. (This does suggest that the SPB was begun very early in the production of Statuary Porcelain.) A coloured and gilded version was priced at 42/- on 27/9/1861, while a 'gilt & tinted' one was 21/-.

The NPL of 1873 includes this figure at 16/6. The retail price in 1876 was £1.5.0. The c.1880 NPL quotes 10/6. The 1884 handwritten note shows a price of 8/6 advancing to 12/6. The making price was 1/9.

S124 – ON THE SEA SHORE. CALM and **STORM**
c.1872
Ht. 19in. (48.26cm)
Sculptor: J. Durham ARA
Marks: J DURHAM Sc. 1872 and ON THE SEA SHORE
Illus: Yes PP 495 Calm.
The companion figures of Calm and Storm are grouped together in the Copeland price lists under the title **On the Sea Shore**. The figure of **Calm** has been included as a single figure at S22. It is said to be from the marble statue of the young Saville Brinton (? Savelle Brenton) Crossley at the age of nine, which Durham sculpted in 1866. This young

S123 *S123a*

S124

boy later became Lord Somerleyton and the statue may still be found at Somerleyton Hall in Suffolk.

The companion figure of **Storm** must not be confused with the figure of Storm (S167), the companion of Sunshine, by W. Brodie. (q.v.)

The figures of **On the Sea Shore** were displayed at the Vienna International Exhibition in 1873.

The prices for both figures are the same. The SPB gives only the trade price of 42/- each. The 1873 NPL also quotes £2.2.0, The retail price in 1876 was £3.3.0 each, but the c.1880 NPL quotes £1.11.6. By 1884 the trade price was 18/6. The making price was 3/6 each.

The catalogue of Messrs. Silber & Fleming of 56-71 Wood Street, Cheapside, London, published in c.1885, illustrates both figures, the captions stating 'Parian Figure, "On the Sea Shore-Storm" (or Calm) by Durham RA. Height 19 in. diameter of base 8 inches [20.32cm]. (Nos.8309 and 8313 form a pair)'.

S125 – OPHELIA
c.1863
Ht. 17in. (43.18cm)
Sculptor: W. Calder Marshall
Marks: W.CALDER MARSHALL RA PUB JUNE 1 1863
Illus: Yes PP 522

Ophelia is the daughter of Polonius, the Lord Chamberlain, in Shakespeare's play *Hamlet, Prince of Denmark.* She is fond of flowers and, in Act IV, scene v, she says to her brother Laertes, *'There's rosemary, that's for remembrance: pray you, love, remember: and there is pansies, that's for thoughts'.* Ophelia's mind becomes unhinged when she is abandoned by Hamlet. She meets an untimely death by drowning when gathering flowers by a stream. In Act IV, scene vii, the Queen announces to the King and Laertes *"..your sister's drown'd, Laertes." "Drown'd! O, where?"*

There is a willow grows aslant a brook,
That shows his hoar leaves in the glassy stream;
There with fantastic garlands did she come
Of crow-flowers, nettles, daisies, and long purples,
That liberal shepherds give a grosser name,
But our cold maids do dead men's fingers call them:
There, on the pendent boughs her coronet weeds
Clambering to hang, an envious sliver broke;
When down her weedy trophies and herself
Fell in the weeping brook.

This statuette was one of three which Calder Marshall agreed that Copeland should reproduce in Parian; the agreement was made on 17 January 1859 and the compensation was to be 15% of the trade price. Comus and Lady Macbeth were the other two statuettes.

The SPB gives only a trade price of 30/- for a plain figure, but 40/- trade and 63/- retail for a gilt and tinted version. In 1873 the trade prices were £1.6.0 and £1.18.0. The retail prices in 1876 were £2.0.0 and £3.0.0, and the trade prices in c.1880 18/- and £1.11.6. By 1884, these were 12/6 and 26/-. The making price was 2/6.

S125

S126

S127

S128

S126 – PAUL, companion to **Virginia**
c.1849
Ht. 14in. (35.56cm)
Sculptor: C. Cumberworth
Illus: Yes PP 512
The story of Paul and Virginia is told in brief in the Groups section, GP51. The two separate figures were displayed at the Great Exhibition of 1851 and were illustrated in Copeland's catalogue published in that year.

A handwritten price of 35/- each is in the margin of a copy which came into my hands. The SPB lists them in second place at 25/- trade and 35/- retail. (Interestingly, the group, which was published in 1845, comes tenth on the SPB page.) In 1873 the trade price was £1.0.0. The retail price in 1876 was £1.10.0. and in c.1880 18/-. In 1884 the trade price was 13/6 and what might be the retail price was 25/-. The making price was 2/9.

See Colour Plate 26

S127 – PEACE
c.1852
Ht. 12¾in. (32.39cm)
Illus: Yes
The figure of an angel to personify 'Peace' might be thought to have a connotation of death, but there are many occasions quoted in holy scripture where an angel appears to a person to calm their fears or to bring good tidings. This figure seems to imply the peace of God which passes all understanding.

It comes sixth in the list of objects on the 'P' page in the SPB, so it may be presumed to have been an early figure. Here the trade price is 28/- and retail 42/-; there is also a 'Slightly Gilt & chased 31/6, & 50/-' version which is not mentioned in later lists. By 1873 only the plain figure is quoted, at £1.2.6. The retail price in 1876 was £1.14.0. The NPL in c.1880 quotes £1.1.0 and a note for 1884 of 12/6. The making price was 2/-.

S128 – PEACE
1866
Ht. 24in. (60.96cm)
Sculptor: E.G. Papworth, Junior
Illus: Yes PP 553
This figure is one of the largest made by Copelands and presents a rather different interpretation of Peace from the earlier, smaller figure. In the figure's left hand a palm or olive branch should be held, so symbolising the spirit of goodwill and reconciliation.

It is one of the later entries in the SPB, being priced at 63/- trade and 94/6 retail; there is a tinted version at 84/- trade with a pencil note of '6', presumably £6.6.0 for the retail price. In 1873 the trade price was £3.10.0 for the plain figure; in 1876, £5.5.0 retail; in c.1880, £2.12.6, and in 1884, 40/-. The making price was 5/-.

S129 – PENELOPHON, THE BEGGAR MAID
1867
Dimensions: Ht. 26¾in. (67.9cm)
Sculptor: W. Brodie
Marks: W BRODIE RSA Sc EDIN. 1867
Illus: Yes PP 516
Penelophon, the Beggar Maid, featured in a ballad which was included in *The Reliques of English Poetry* of which Thomas Percy (1729-1811) was the editor. In the one entitled 'King Cophetua', this legendary King of Africa cared not for womankind until he saw a beggar maid 'all in grey' with whom he fell in love. Penelophon also appears in works by Shakespeare, Ben Jonson, and in Tennyson's poem *The Beggar Maid*. The first edition of Percy's *Reliques*, which contained 176 poems or ballads, was published in 1765.

This figure is huge, some 2¾in. (7cm) higher than 'Peace', by Papworth. It must have presented considerable difficulties to the maker and in the placing and firing. It was not, however, the largest figure; Egeria is 28in. (71.12cm) and Sappho is 32in. (81.28cm) tall.

S129

S130

The SPB lists this as: 'Penelophon or Beggar-Maid trade 86/- AFAE'. These initials may stand for the Association of Fine Arts Edinburgh. This may be an association linked to the FAA, or Fine Arts Association, which was an Edinburgh institution, or it may just be a clerical error for FAA. Nevertheless, it was exclusive to an Edinburgh Association and it does not feature in any printed price list. The Making Price Book gives 8/6.

S130 – PICKWICK, companion to **Weller**
c.1880
Ht. 4¾in. (12.07cm)
Illus: Yes
Samuel Pickwick is an endearing, fictitious character created by Charles Dickens; he is 'General Chairman-member of the Pickwick Club', from the posthumous papers of whom Dickens took the title for his *The Pickwick Papers*.

The parian figure is taken from the book illustrations of Robert Seymour (1798-1836) who supplied the first seven out of a total of forty-three sketches in all, including the frontispiece. Robert Seymour committed suicide on 20 April 1836 in a fit of depression following a rift with Dickens.

The NPL of c.1880 quotes 4/6, while the handwritten price for 1884 was 4/-. The making price was 1/-.

S131 – POMONA, companion to **Flora**
c.1880
Ht. 14in. (35.56 cm)
Sculptor: R. Monti
Illus: Yes, as Dessert Comport
This figure, and her companion 'Flora', are not listed as statuettes but only under the category of Dessert Comports in the c.1880 NPL. Here the subject of 'Flora' is printed 'Flora Figure, by Monti, supporting Comport, 14 inches high. white 12/-'. Both 'Pomona Comport ..white 12/-' and Flora are in white china in the Copeland's Porcelain section, and not in the Statuary Porcelain section.

Pomona is listed in the SPB as 'Pomona (for fitting) Figure 9/-'. A

S131

S131a

S132

S133

similar entry for her companion reads: 'Flora (for fitting) Figure by Monti ..9/-'. The making price for either was 1/6.

S132 – PROSPERITY, companion to **Adversity**
c.1881
Ht. 20in. (50.8cm)
Sculptor: Owen Hale
Marks: OWEN HALE Sc
Illus: Yes PP 527
'Prosperity' is symbolised by a lady of means taking money from her purse, presumably to purchase a flower from 'Adversity', her companion figure, who is shown as a bare-footed flower girl (see S2).

In a similar vein to 'Adversity', the work may have been inspired by the activities of 'Prosperity' Robinson, the name applied to Frederick Robinson (Lord Goodrich) on account of his lauding of the British economy shortly before the financial crisis of 1825.

There is a reference in the NPL of c.1880 to both figures at £1.11.6, with a note of 25/- for 1884. Both figures were included on the catalogue sheet (see PP 485). An 'Accompanying [Price] Sheet' to this page, which may date to 1885, quotes 25/-, with a handwritten price of 30/- on 29/8/95; a later price sheet, undated, prints the price of 30/-, with a handwritten amendment, again undated, of 33/-. These two price sheets will be designated APS when abbreviated. The making price was 4/6, as for 'Adversity'.

S133 – PSYCHE
1846
Ht. 16in. (40.64cm)/17in. (43.18cm)
Sculptor: W. Theed
Illus: Yes PP 565a
'Psyche', 'the soul', occurs in late antiquity as a personification of the human soul. Psyche was the youngest daughter of a king and her beauty drew the jealousy of Aphrodite, called Venus by the Romans. The goddess told her son Cupid (Eros) to inspire Psyche with a love of the most contemptible of men, but Cupid himself fell in love with her. Unseen and unknown, he visited her every night in the dark and left her before the light of day dawned. Her jealous sisters made her believe that she was embracing a hideous monster and once, while Cupid was asleep, she took a lamp and drew near to him, only to find that he was the most lovely of the gods. A drop of hot oil fell from her lamp on to his shoulder, awakening him; he was cross with her for mistrust, and fled. Psyche's happiness went with him and she wandered about from temple to temple inquiring for him, until she came to the palace of Aphrodite. The goddess kept her a prisoner, making her carry out very arduous tasks; indeed, she would have perished had not Cupid, who still loved her, invisibly comforted and assisted her. With his help she at last overcame the hatred of Aphrodite and was granted immortality, and so was united with him for ever.

In this version of the story, Psyche represents the human soul, which is purified by passions and misfortunes and thus prepared for happiness. Psyche was portrayed with the wings of a butterfly, the butterfly being her symbol.

S134

Copeland and Garrett introduced this figure in 1846; in the November issue of the *Art-Journal* this porcelain statuary figure was illustrated on page 300:

> Next in notice is a most charming figure of Psyche. We have never seen any delineation of that most poetic of all conceptions of the Orphic mythology, which more completely realized the idea of the strength, and, at the same time, the weakness of the most delicate of the passions. The shade of suspicion is just beginning to cloud that sunshine of confidence with which she at first received the advances of her celestial lover.

A version had coloured and gilt borders at 28/- trade and 42/- retail in 1848; the SPB gives 25/- and 37/6 for the plain one. In 1873 and in the c.1880 NPL these became £1.7.6 and £1.0.0 respectively. The retail prices in 1876 were £2.2.0 and £1.10.0. The trade prices in 1884 were 27/6 and 15/- rising to 20/-. The making price was 3/-.

S134 – PURITY
1865
Ht. 19in. (48.26cm)
Sculptor: M. Noble
Sponsor: Crystal Palace Art Union
Marks: M NOBLE Sc. 1864 CRYSTAL PALACE ART UNION Pubd.Feby 1 1865
Illus: Yes PP 513
For a controversial view on the intention of the sculptor to change the name of this study from Aphrodite to Purity, see Purity in the section dealing with Busts (B65), which Noble based on this statuette.

A full size statuette in marble stands outside the Council Chamber in Stoke-on-Trent Town Hall. The *Art-Journal,* in which an engraving appeared in July 1859, page 224, commented on this work:

> The representation must combine the natural and the ideal; grace of form and simplicity of expression appear to be essential qualities demanded of the sculptor, and these Mr. Noble seems to have realized, far more successfully too, it may be added, than we could have expected from him, seeing that the majority of his works, and those by which he is best known, are portrait sculptures of men. His 'Purity', holding a lily in her hand for a symbol, is, however, a refined and elegant example of Mr. Noble's ability to grapple with a subject in which the spiritualism of Art and its poetical feeling enter largely.

The statuette was sponsored by the Crystal Palace Art Union. The SPB enters a trade price of 31/6, which is crossed out and 28/- written above it: this was for a 'gilt & tinted' version. A 'white' one was 21/- and this is the price at which the figures held in stock at the Stoke Works on 10 November 1881 were valued. There were two of them. By 1884, after the CPAU had ceased to trade, a handwritten note in the NPL of c.1880 gave the trade price as 15/-. The making price was 2/6.
See Colour Plate 27

S135 – READING GIRL
1869
Ht. 13in. (33.02cm)
Sculptor: P. MacDowell, RA
Sponsor: Ceramic and Crystal Palace Art Union
Marks: P.MACDOWELL RA SCULPT 1869 CERAMIC AND CRYSTAL PALACE ART UNION
Illus: Yes PP 504
Although 'Reading Girl' and 'Flute Player' were sculpted by different sculptors, it seems that they could have been intended as a pair. Both were commissioned by the Ceramic and Crystal Palace Art Union, this figure in 1869, when it was offered as a prize, and the 'Flute Player' in 1871.

The original marble statue, commissioned by Lord Ellesmere, was completed in 1838, entitled 'A Girl Reading', and was placed in Bridgewater House. (A replica was at Brynkinalt, Denbigh.) An engraving of the marble statue was included in the July 1860 issue of the *Art-Journal*, page 216, with an article on the origins of sculpture. The original marble was shown at the International Exhibition in 1862 in London.

S135

MacDowell's sculpture was an early example of a new style of sculpture 'which unites the ideal with the natural, and which recommends itself rather by its simplicity and truth of character, than by any stirring attribute of action or passion.'

The SPB quotes 10/- and this was the value accorded the nine figures held in stock in November 1881 at the Stoke Works. The handwritten note for 1884 in the NPL of c.1880 also gives 10/-. The making price was 1/10.

S136 – THE REAPER, companion to **The Gleaner**
c.1851
Ht. 6in. (15.24cm)
There is more detail in the SPB about this figure than its companion. It is the second item on the page for R, and the early prices were 5/- trade and 7/- retail. Then, these have been crossed out and 3/- and 5/- substituted, with the addition of 7/- and 10/6 for a coloured version. Although the making price of 7d is entered in 1895 and 1928, the pair of figures is not included in any printed price list other than the supplementary list published about 1851.

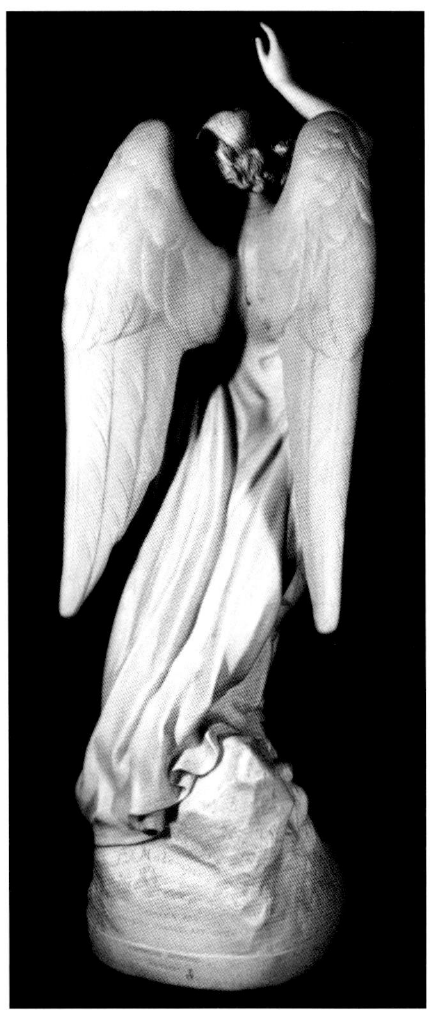

S136A

S136A

S137

S136A – THE REAPER AND THE FLOWERS

This item in the Copeland records is always listed as 'Angel & Flowers' and it is always described as a Group. Details will be found under GP67, page 119.

The Parian Phenomenon states, under 'The Reaper and the Flowers', that the original marble was exhibited under this title at the Royal Academy in 1874. It also states that: 'Another issue of this model was called The Angel and the Flowers. Both were inscribed.' Certainly the example which I was privileged to photograph was inscribed on the front of the plinth THE ANGEL AND THE FLOWERS.

S137 – REBEKAH

c.1851
Ht. 19in. (48.26 cm)
Sculptor: W. Theed the Younger
Marks: on some, OPUS W THEED Sc
Illus: Yes PP 514

Abraham sent his trusted servant to his own kindred to find a wife for his son Isaac. The story in Genesis Chapter 24 tells how the servant sought God's guidance in identifying the right girl at the well when he arrived. It was Rebekah, the daughter of Bethuel, son of Milcah, the wife of Abraham's brother Nahor, who came to the well to draw water for her flocks, and lowered her jar into the well to draw water for the camels of Abraham's servant. Rebekah answered the invitation by going straightaway with the servant and became the wife of Isaac and later the mother of Esau and Jacob.

The original marble statue was exhibited at the Royal Academy in 1850 and displayed at the Great Exhibition of 1851. It was also shown at the British Institution Exhibition in 1852.

Copeland showed the Statuary Porcelain figure at the 1851 Great Exhibition; this was illustrated, Plate 36, in the *Official Catalogue* to that exhibition. A plaster copy of the original is in the Mansion House, London, and this was featured in the London County Council Exhibition 'Sculpture 1850-1950' in Holland Park in 1957.

The retail price for this figure in 1851 was 5 guineas; the SPB confirms this and adds the trade price of 70/-. In 1873 the NPL quotes £2.18.0 and in c.1880 £2.12.6. (The factory record copy has this crossed out and 50/- inserted, but no date for the alteration is given.) The retail price in 1876 was £4.10.0. The reduced trade price in 1884 was 40/-. The making price was 9/-.

See Colour Plate 28

S94A – RED RIDING HOOD

This figure is discussed under the title **Little Red Riding Hood** (S94) because this was what the sculptor, Thomas Woolner, called it when he corresponded with W.T. Copeland in 1848.

Red Riding Hood or, more properly, 'Chaperon Rouge', was the heroine of a fairy story by Charles Perrault (1628-1703). He was a

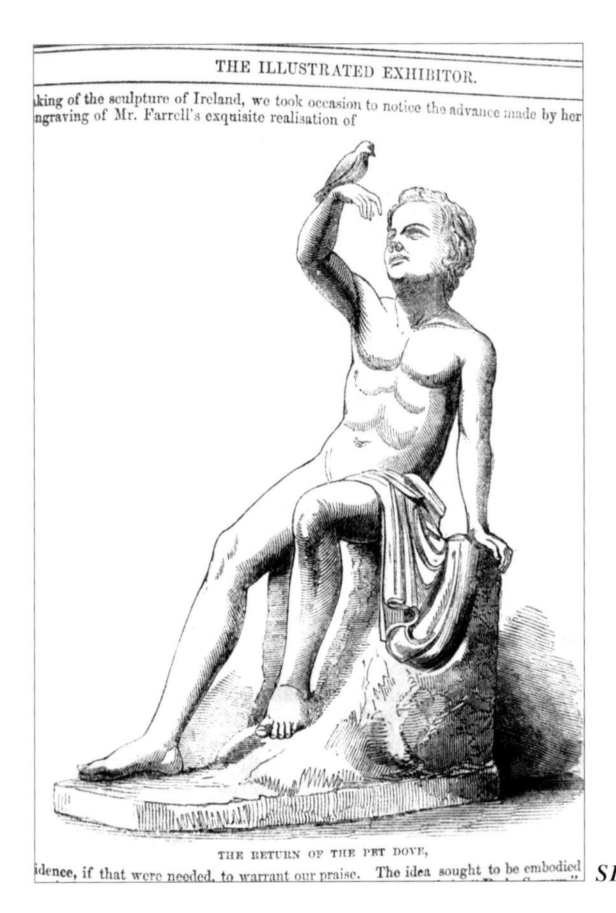
THE ILLUSTRATED EXHIBITOR.

king of the sculpture of Ireland, we took occasion to notice the advance made by her
ngraving of Mr. Farrell's exquisite realisation of

THE RETURN OF THE PET DOVE,

idence, if that were needed, to warrant our praise. The idea sought to be embodied

S138

French writer of great distinction, whose literary fame rests upon two works: *Les Hommes Illustres qui ont paru en France pendant ce siecle* (1696-1701), and *Les Contes de ma mere L'Oye* (1697). They are collections of tales known simply as *Les Contes de Perrault* and include 'Mother Goose', 'Cinderella', 'Bluebeard', 'Little Red Riding Hood', 'Puss-in-Boots', and others. The stories probably long pre-date Perrault, but to him we owe a lasting debt for giving them a simple, engaging expression still well loved by children of all ages. Sadly, Perrault died in obscurity.

S138 – THE RETURN DOVE
1847
Sculptor: James Farrell (reduced by Cheverton)
Sponsor: The Royal Irish Art Union of Dublin
Illus: Engraving in *The Illustrated Exhibitor*
Perhaps the title given to the engraving, 'The Return of the Pet Dove', furnishes a more appropriate explanation of the inspiration behind this figure than the stark factory title.

SKINDLE
THE RETURN DOVE
Reduced by CHEVERTON
EXECUTED IN
W.T. COPELAND'S
STATUARY PORCELAIN
for the
Royal Irish
ART UNION OF DUBLIN
1847
From the PRIZE STATUE
BY
JAMES FARRELL
SCULPTOR

Knowledge of this statuette rests upon the record of an engraved inscription intended to be printed upon the base of this figure. Unfortunately, so far, no museum or library in Ireland that we have asked has been able to locate either a marble, plaster or Statuary Porcelain example. It is only due to our friends, Mr and Mrs Pulver, who told me of the illustration in *The Illustrated Exhibitor*, that it is possible to show what the figure looked like.

S139 – RIFLEMAN
c.1855
This figure is recorded in the price archives, but no example has been seen by the authors. Because it occurs early in the 'R' list in the SPB, it is safe to assume that its introduction may be dated to about 1855. The SPB quotes 3/- trade and 4/6 retail. In 1873, the trade price was 3/3, while in c.1880 it was back to 3/-, as it remained to be in 1884. In 1876, the retail price was 5/6d. The making price was 10d.

S140 – THE RINKER, companion to **The Croquet Player**
c.1880
Ht. 18in. (45.72cm)
Sculptor: R.J. Morris
Illus: Yes
The figure shows a young lady on roller-skates. Roller-skates are said to have been invented first in 1760 by Joseph Merlin of Huy, in Belgium, but a whole century was to pass before they became accepted as appropriate for use as a sporting pastime. This was due to the development work of James L. Plumpton of New York. In 1884 roller-skates were available with the Richardson ball-bearing. The sport boomed in the years 1870-1900.

This statuette only appears in the NPL for c.1880 at £1.10.0, with the price dropping to 22/- in 1884. The making price was 4/6.

S140

S142

S142a

S143

S141 – RIVERS OF FRANCE
The SPB lists this as a Centrepiece Statuary & China at a price of 9 guineas and dated 7/10/70. It is probable that the item is like a large comport supported or flanked by three or four figures representing four of the rivers of France. Against the entry is the name 'Rives'.

S142 – THE RIVERSIDE, AND COMPANION
1881
Ht. 18in. (47.72cm)
Sculptor: Owen Hale
Illus: Yes PP 501 (Riverside only)
Two young maidens, modestly draped in towels, about to step into the river to bathe – a 'rural charm' theme which was used extensively by Victorian artists.

Illustrations of the figures were included in the catalogue of Messrs. Silber & Fleming (see S124 On the Sea Shore). The c.1880 NPL has £1.5.0 each and, in 1884, the note reads '21/- > 35/-' (which is probably the retail price.) The making price was 3/-.

S143 – ROBINETTE
1860, or earlier
Ht. 13in. (33.02cm)
Illus: Yes PP 505
A popular Victorian 'fancy' picture; the subject was produced in various bodies by several potters. There is no similarity between this figure and the 'portrait' of Robinetta by Sir Joshua Reynolds; moreover, Reynolds painted his picture as a 'fancy subject' and not as a portrait of an actual sitter. (The Reynolds picture is in the Tate Gallery, London.)

The price in the SPB is 25/- trade and 37/6 retail. By 1873 the trade price in the NPL was £1.0.0 and the retail price in 1876 £1.10.0. The figure was 18/- in c.1880, with a further reduction to 10/6 in 1884. The making price was 2/-.

S144 – ROMAN PIPER, AND COMPANION
1848
The Piper Ht. 11in. (27.94cm); The Tambourinist Ht. 10in. (25.4cm)
Marks: Printed COPELAND STATUARY PORCELAIN
Illus: Yes
In 1848 Copeland issued two figures which were called 'Roman Contadino and Companion'. These were re-named 'Roman Piper and Companion' in the 1851 Supplementary List. A Contadino was the name for an Italian peasant and perhaps it was thought that, because the figures were playing a pipe and tambourine respectively, they would sell better with the new title.

It is suggested that the apparel of the figures was inspired by the people using the Rhaeto-Romanic dialect of Grisons, the largest and most easterly canton of Switzerland, where this dialect is commonly referred to as 'Romansh'.

The prices are the same for the 'Roman Contadino and Companion' as those for the 'Roman Piper and Companion' in the SPB and the 1851 Supplementary list at 25/- trade and £1.17.6 retail, each. In 1873 the trade price was £1.4.0 each, in c.1880 £1.1.0, and in 1884 13/6 each. The retail price in 1876 was 16/-. The making price was 2/9 each.

S144

S144a

S145

S145 – ROMAN SEASONS (Set of Four)
c.1851
Ht. 9in. (22.86cm)
Illus: Yes PP 555
The Supplementary List of 1851 lists these as: 'A set of Roman Figures, as the Four Seasons, 10in. 5 gns'. The SPB quotes for the set, 42/- trade and 70/- retail. In 1873, the trade price in the NPL was 10/6 each and in c.1880 it was 9/- each. By 1884 this was 6/- each and 8/- with altered pedestal. The retail price in 1876 was 16/- each.

S146

S146
THE ROWER
1877
Ht. 18½in. (46.99cm)
Sculptor: R.J. Morris
Marks: COPELAND
Illus: Yes

A distinction is made between 'rowing' and 'sculling'. Rowing is when a crew of two or more oarsmen each manipulate a single oar. Sculling, a word of unknown origin, is when each oarsman operates two lighter, shorter oars.

The general history of rowing, both as a form of commercial transport and as a pleasant pastime, covers an area wider than it is possible to cover in a short account such as this. Rowing is a sport developed from a universal and age-old method of transport.

Many other sports emerged from basic human needs, of course. The date of the first race is unknown, but the Egyptian King Amenhotep (c.1566 BC) is recorded as 'being the tireless stroke of a 200 man crew'.

Copeland's figure, seemingly of an artisan oarsman, is shown wearing the round, or oval, plaited-straw hat with low, flat crown, known as a 'boater'; it was, and still is, much favoured by the fresh and salt-water boating fraternity, possibly because it is virtually unsinkable.

Annual competitive rowing events, termed a 'Regatta', now form some of the major sporting occasions of the social round. The first of these was held at Henley-on-Thames (Oxon.) in 1839. It remains the premier regatta in the world to this day.

The earliest reference to the figure is in the NPL of c.1882, where it is priced at £1.10.0, with the price in 1884 at 21/-. The making price was 4/-.

An example of the figure, but without the oar, has been reported inscribed 'CAPTAIN WEBB'. Captain Matthew Webb was the first person to swim the English Channel from Dover to Calais, a distance of 17.75 nautical miles (33km) in 1875.

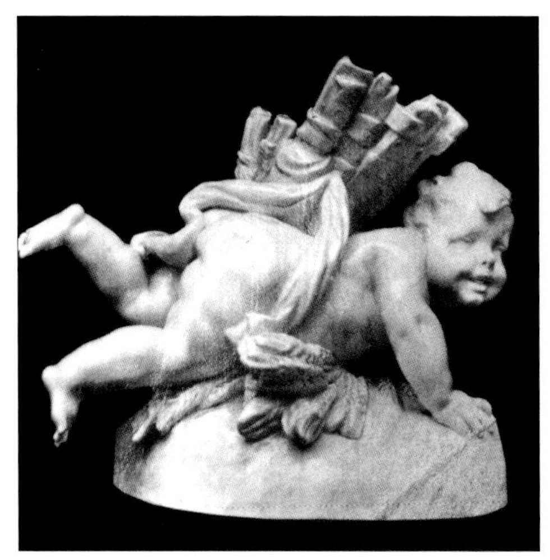

S147

S147 – RUSTIC BOY
c.1858
L. 9in. (22.86cm)
Illus: Yes

This figure is listed in the SPB at 14/- trade and 21/- retail. In 1873 it was at 16/- and in c.1880 14/-, reducing to 5/- in 1884. The retail price in 1876 was £1.6.0. The making price was 1/2d.

RUSTIC CHILDREN OF ENGLAND
See YOUNG NATURALIST (S205)

S148 – RUTH
1870
Ht. 29in. (73.66 cm)
Sculptor: W. Brodie RSA (Royal Scottish Academy)
Sponsor: Fine Arts Association of Edinburgh
Marks: W.BRODIE RSA Sc.
Illus: Yes PP 516

The name in Hebrew means 'a friend'. Ruth was a Moabitess, about whom the Book of Ruth was written and included in the Holy Bible. When Naomi's husband died, she decided to return to her own country of Israel and tried to persuade her two daughters-in-law to remain with the family of her late husband. Ruth, however, would not leave her mother-in-law and so they both travelled to Bethlehem together, where Ruth met Boaz, and later married him. It is a touching story of loyalty and fidelity.

Brodie exhibited his marble statue at the Royal Scottish Academy in 1869, a bronze version appearing later in the Aberdeen Art Gallery.

The figure is priced at 90/- in the SPB, and the making price was 11/6.

S148

S149

Sabrina fair lettering:
Listen where thou art sitting
Under the glassy, cool, translucent wave
In twisted braids of lilies knitting
The loose train of thy amber dripping hair
Listen for dear honour's sake
Goddess of the silver lake
Listen and save.
"Milton's Comus"
Illus: Yes PP 496
Sabrina was the legendary daughter of Locrine, a mythical King of England, who, together with her mother, was drowned in the River Severn by Locrine's widow, thereby becoming its nymph. Milton features her in his poem *Comus*, while her transformation is also related by Drayton in the *Polyolbion*, and by Fletcher in *The Faithful Shepherdess*. Marshall's original marble statue was exhibited at the Royal Academy in 1847. It depicts Sabrina listening to Thyrsis' invocation to her to rescue a victim of Comus. A plaster model, dated 1847, is in the collection of the Royal Dublin Society. Copeland showed the statuary porcelain figure at the Great Exhibition of 1851.

In 1851 the retail price was 52/6, with the trade price of 35/-. The SPB lists also a gilt & tinted version at 42/-. In 1873, the NPL quotes £1.8.0, and in c.1880, £1.1.0, dropping to 14/- in 1884. The retail price in 1876 was £2.2.0. The making price was 3/- for a large size and 1/9 for a small size. Nowhere else is there a hint of there being two sizes.

However, there was a centrepiece called Sabrina which measured 17in. (43.18cm) long, 10in. (25.4cm) high and 9in.(22.86cm) wide. The figures bear no similarity to Marshall's figure. This item featured in Silber & Fleming's catalogue.
See Colour Plate 29

S149 – RUTH, companion to **Rebekah**
c.1857
Ht. 20in. (50.8 cm)
Sculptor: W. Theed
Marks: OPUS W THEED Sc
Illus: Yes PP 516
Theed's sculpture shows Ruth holding sheaves of corn standing beside an overturned vessel on the ground. It serves to illustrate the events described in the Book of Ruth, Chapter II, whereby Ruth, in time of famine, is permitted to glean barley in the field of Boaz, a kinsman of her mother-in-law, Naomi.

Although Ruth was sculpted six years later than Rebekah, the original being exhibited in Manchester in 1857, Copeland issued the statuary porcelain figure as the companion to the earlier subject. In the SPB the two figures are listed next to one another at 70/- trade and 5 guineas retail. In 1873 Ruth was offered at £2.18.0, in c.1880 at £2.12.6. This was reduced to 50/- and later, in 1884, was reduced to 35/- and 57/6 (presumably retail). The 1876 retail price was £4.10.0. The making price was 7/-.

S150 – SABRINA, companion to **Comus**
c.1849
Ht. 12in. (30.48 cm)
Sculptor: W. Calder Marshall
Marks: Marshall Fect. Printed in brown, copper plate

S150

S151

S152

S151 – SANTA FILOMENA, companion to **Chastity**
1865
Ht. 24in. (60.96cm)
Sculptor: J. Durham
Marks: J DURHAM Sc Pub Sept 1865
Illus: Yes PP 521
The figure was inspired by Longfellow's poem *Santa Filomena*, which was written by him on behalf of the American people as a tribute to Florence Nightingale. The figure is wearing a chaplet of leaves and flowers, carries a spear in her right hand while holding aloft an oil-lamp with her left hand. Longfellow's poem* closes with the verses:

A lady with a lamp shall stand
in the great history of the land,
A noble type of good,
Heroic womanhood.

Nor even small be wanting here
The palm, the lily, and the spear,
The symbols that of yore
Saint Filomena bore.

Santa Filomena is the Italian for Saint Nightingale. Copeland showed the figure at the Exposition Internationale in Paris, 1867.

The SPB gives only trade prices of 3 guineas and 73/6 for a gilt and tinted version. In 1873 the NPL quotes £3.10.0, and in c.1880 this was reduced to £2.12.6, while in 1884 it was 42/-. The retail price in 1876 was £5.5.0 and in 1884 57/6. The making price was 8/6d.

* The poem, with a long feature on Florence Nightingale, appears on page 40 of the February 1858 issue of the *Art-Journal*, while discussing Phyffers' group of The Wounded at Scutari (see GP44).

S152 – SAPPHO, Original
c.1851
Ht. 32in. (81.28cm)
Sculptor: W. Theed
Illus: Yes
The original marble statue was acquired by His Royal Highness the Prince Albert and remains in the Collection of Buckingham Palace. Copeland reproduced this huge figure and showed it at the Great Exhibition of 1851; the catalogue describes it as 'Sappho, by W. Theed, from the original marble'. This figure was illustrated in the *Art-Journal* of January 1855, page 30. It will be observed that this Sappho wears no garment above the waist, and looks down towards her right.

Sappho, a lyric poetess of the Aeolian School, was a native of Mytilene on the island of Lesbos. She was born before 600 BC. At Mytilene Sappho appears to have been the centre of a female literary society; ancient writers expressed great admiration for her poetry. She wrote nine books of poetry, remains of the first, second and fourth books, together with fragments of the fifth book, having survived. Her ode to Aphrodite is thought to be complete.

She is said to have been accepted by Aristotle as being the equal of Homer and Archilochus. In the Phaedrus she is mentioned by Plato as the tenth muse.

The SPB quotes 'Sappho Large 12 Gns. and 18 Gns'. In 1873, the NPL gives £14.0.0 and in c.1880 £10.10.0; in 1884, the price was 6 guineas. The retail price in 1876 was £21.0.0. The making price was 24/-.

S153

S153 – SAPPHO, Small
1869
Ht. 16in. (40.64cm)
Sculptor: W. Theed
Sponsor: Ceramic & Crystal Palace Art Union
Marks: W THEED Sc.Pubd.1869 CERAMIC AND CRYSTAL PALACE ART UNION
Illus: Yes PP 522

This figure has a similar but not identical stance to the earlier one; also, she wears a short-sleeved shirt-like garment, the lower drapes are different and she looks forward.

In *The Parian Phenomenon,* after discussing the parian reproduction of the original marble, it states that 'The figure was reissued in 1869'. On page 134 it states '...and published again in the smaller size...' It would have been more accurate to say that Theed sculpted a smaller figure in 1869. It will be seen by comparing the original photographs of the two figures that the second, small figure of Sappho is significantly different from the earlier one.

This smaller figure is priced in the SPB at 21/- for the C.& C.P.A.U. There is a price of 30/- for a gilt and tinted one. Against this is an added note 'Gilt & chased as for W Litherland' but no price. In 1881, when that Art Union was ceasing to trade, the stock included four figures of Sappho valued at 21/- each. By 1884 this figure was included in a copy of the NPL of c.1880, in which a handwritten note quotes the figure at 16in. and at 15/- and 22/6 (?retail). The making price for this smaller figure was 3/6.

See Colour Plate 30

SCOTCHMAN, INFANTRY

Although included in the list of statuettes in *The Parian Phenomenon,* the Making Price Book clearly states that this is Earthenware and dated 2/2/16. It is a figure, but not made in Statuary Porcelain.

S154 – SEA NYMPH
c.1850
Ht. 9½in. (24.13cm)
Sculptor: J.J. Pradier
Illus: Yes PP 517

Copeland showed this figure at the Great Exhibition of 1851. It is included in the SPB which quotes 21/- trade and 30/- retail; there is a price, also of 21/- for a gilt and tinted one, with the price of 28/- for a gilt and chased version. A later entry in the SPB lists 'Sea Nymph (or Naiad) Figure of 63/-'. It is probable that this refers to those which have been included as Naiads.

In 1873, the NPL quotes 16/6 and in c.1880 12/6, reducing to 8/6 in 1884. The retail price in 1876 was £1.5.0. The making price was 1/9d.

It was illustrated in the 1851 catalogue as Nereid at 30/-. This figure by Pradier shows the nymph holding and looking at a sea shell, as if about to drink from it. The point is made in *The Parian Phenomenon* that in other versions of the design of a sea nymph she is shown with a snake (or could it be an eel?) in her left hand. It states that these are attributed to Malempré with the title of 'Cleopatra'.

Like the Naiads (see S110) the original marble of the Sea Nymph was to have been found at Trentham Hall, Staffordshire. It is uncertain if many, if any, statues remain after most of them were removed by John Broom when he left the estate in the late 1980s.

In the SPB there are mentions of several other adaptations of the Sea Nymph:

Sea Nymph & Shell (Kneeling) 18/6
Sea Nymph with inch hole as used for Oxford Comport 12/-

In the section listing Dessert Comports there will be found examples of Naiads used to support comports.

See Colour Plate 31

S154

S155

S155 – SEASONS FIGURES, various

The SPB includes several references to Seasons Figures and there are details of making prices. Here is a list of the mentions in the SPB:

Seasons Figure with basket pierced	21/-	31/6	
white & gold	27/6	40/-	
grds & gilt	30/-	45/-	
New Seasons Figure with china basket & pedestal			
	4Gns	3½ Gns*	5¼Gns
Figure only		21/-	
Seasons boy Summer fitted to a Windsor Comport			
	2Gns	63/-	+ 36/-
If painted outside only 3/- less	D955	D1411	
Seasons boys with china comports	45/-	40/-	
Dutch Seasons figure with plain Russell Comport			
	14/-	21/-	
Ditto with embossed comport	14/-	21/-	
ditto with Windsor Comport	18/-		
Summer Figure of as used for Rivers of France			
Dessert set	15/-		
Spring — " —— ditto	15/-		
Seasons Figure (Theed's) with new pedl			
& small oval pierced basket	9/-		
Seasons centre piece (New) with figures as in			
'Rivers of France'	42/-		
Basket only	14/-		
Spanish Seasons Figure with china pierced			
Basket & pedestal Turq Grd & raised & chased			
		4½Gns	
Seasons Figure (Theed's) with small round Windsor			
pierced comport as for CPAU	10/6		
Seasons Centre (Statuary & China)	47/6		C & CPAU
" Comport " "	28/-	47/6	
" Centre Staty	35/-		
Summer (from P of W's set) Figure	21/-		

* It is not clear whether these prices are trade, or some variation of the figure which is not mentioned; the 5Gns price is probably retail.
+ This price, too, is not explained.

In the Making Price Book there are the following:

Season boys		1/6	
Seasons or Months		4/6	
" Dutch (Set of Four) old way Flowering 7/6		1/6 Ea	Large 1/9
" Dublin "		10d Ea	
" Roman "	Spring & Autumn	1/8 Ea	
	Summer & Winter -	1/6 Ea	
" Theed's	Spring 1/4 Summer 1/- Autumn 1/- Winter 10d		

There are the four Royal Children representing the four seasons by Mary Thornycroft, Autumn by Malempré (S10), and the other seasons by Malempré. There are the Cupid seasons (see S36, C37), and a figure of Autumn by Monti which *The Parian Phenomenon* states was exhibited in Vienna in 1873 with its companion, Spring. The four Theed Seasons are illustrated in *The Parian Phenomenon*, 554.

S156 – SHEPHERD BOY, companion to **Musidora**
1871
Ht. 17in. (43.18cm)
Sculptor: L.A. Malempré
Sponsor: Ceramic and Crystal Palace Art Union
Marks: L A MALEMPRE MADE FOR THE CERAMIC AND CRYSTAL PALACE ART UNION
Illus: Yes

The figure is entered in the SPB on 23 March 1872 at 21/- for the C & CPAU. There were no figures of 'Shepherd Boy' in the factory stock when this was taken and evaluated on 10 October 1881. The making price was 4/-.

S156

S157 – SIR JAMSETJEE JEEJEEBHOY
c.1861
Ht. 15in. (38.1cm.)
Sculptor: Baron Marochetti
Sponsor: thought to have been privately sponsored
An Indian Parsee who became a noted philanthropist. Born in Bombay in 1783, the son of impoverished parents, Jamsetjee Jeejeebhoy went on to become a successful merchant, amassing a fortune of several million pounds which he used for the benefit of the Indian people.

His public benefactions included the release of all debtors from Bombay gaol by paying off their debts. A hospital bearing his name was founded in 1848, the same year in which he endowed schools in Bombay, Surat, Odepore, and other places.

In 1845 he financed the building of a causeway between Mahim and Bandora in order to reduce casualties occasioned by the sea between

S157

those two places; this was done at the behest of his wife. Similarly he arranged the building of the waterworks at Poona.

His public service was recognised by a knighthood in 1842, followed in 1857 by a baronetcy; he was the first Parsee baronet.

Marochetti's marble statue was shown at the 1859 Royal Academy exhibition. Sir Jamsetjee is said to have visited England in 1861 when this parian statuette was probably produced.

The figure is included in the SPB where the prices are in code: v/2 Gns and h Gns; this may be 4½ guineas and 10 guineas. It was probably made in only very small numbers, and it is not included in the making lists.

S158 – SITTING GARDENERS

S158

S161

S163

S163a

S159 – SLEEPING CHILD ON CUSHION
c.1850
L. possibly about 6in. (15.24cm)
This item is listed early in the SPB at 3/- trade and 5/- retail. In 1873, and in subsequent price lists, it is listed under 'Miscellaneous' at 3/4d. In 1876 the retail price was 5/-. By c.1880 the trade price had returned to its initial price of 3/-. No entry for the making price.

S160 – SLEEPING CHILD IN COT (Matchbox)
uncertain, but perhaps c.1855
L. 6in. (15.24cm)
Illus: Yes PP 549
It is not included in the SPB but in other lists it is the same price as S159

S21 – SMUGGLER, companion to **Calais Boy**
See **Calais Boy**

S161 – SPRING, companion to **Autumn**
c.1872
Ht. 20in. (50.8cm)
Sculptor: L.A. Malempré
Marks: L A MALEMPRÉ Sc 1872
Illus: Yes PP 508
The records list figures of Spring (S161) and Autumn (S10) as companions of 20 inches in height by Malempré. There are listed also figures of Summer and Winter, each of 18 inches (45.72cm) in height, but no name of a sculptor. It is not known by whom these were sculpted, but entries in the SPB on 22/7/1870 quote 21/- for each figure with the added note in brackets 'from P.of W's set'. However, more proof that a set of Seasons was produced for that dessert service is needed. Jewitt does not include 'Seasons', only 'Elements', and 'Months', as well, of course, as 'Continents'. But as there are only four seasons it is probable that Jewitt's account, 'The four raised fruit-dishes are elevated upon groups of three figures each, typical of the twelve months of the year, admirably modelled by F. Miller', are indeed meant to represent the seasons.

Spring, by Malempré, then, is not listed in the SPB, but is included in the 1873 NPL at £2.0.0, and, in c.1880, at £1.11.6, with a further reduction to 21/- in 1884, rising to 25/- (no explanation). The Making Price Book records 'Spring New 3/6d'.

S162 – SPRING, companion to **Autumn**
c.1873
Sculptor: Possibly by R. Monti
According to *The Parian Phenomenon,* this figure and its companion, both by R. Monti, were displayed by Copeland at the International Exhibition in Vienna in 1873.

There is a figure of 'Spring' with its companion 'Summer' listed in the SPB 'as used for Rivers of France Dessert Set' at 15/- each trade. (No Autumn or Winter are listed under their respective Letters.)

More information is needed to unravel the different figures of the Seasons.

S164

S165

S166

S163 – SPRING FLOWERS and **Companion**
c.1875
Ht. 14in. (35.56cm)
Sculptor: after C. Cumberworth
Illus: Yes
These romantic figures are based almost entirely on the group of Paul and Virginia (see GP51), although the size of them has been increased and some slight changes effected.

The earliest reference to these figures is in the retail price list of 1876 where they are priced at £1.17.6 each. The trade price in the c.1880 NPL is £1.1.0, reducing to 10/6d in 1884. The making price was 2/- each.

S164 – STELLA, figure only
c.1883
Illus: Yes, as comport
Lamps and comports with the figure 'holding up' the top were made in china, but this parian figure was introduced late in the 19th century.

The name may be derived from a play of that name by Goethe, first published in 1776, but which he altered in 1806. Stella was also the name given to Penelope Devereaux (later, Lady Rich, Countess of Devonshire) by Sir Philip Sidney. Much loved by him, she was celebrated in his sonnets, and perhaps by Shakespeare as 'The Dark Lady'. Stella was also the name given to Esther Johnson, whom Jonathan Swift may have secretly married in 1716; she died in 1728.

The only price quoted is a manuscript entry for 1884 of 21/- trade. No making price has been found, even for candlestick, comport or lamp.

S165 – STEPPING STONES
1855
Ht. 19in. (48.26cm)
Sculptor: Edward W. Wyon
Sponsor: Art Union of London
Marks: EDWARD W.WYON Art Union of London
Illus: Yes PP 566a
This figure of a young girl, carrying a small bundle of corn in her left arm, shows the sculptor's skill in depicting movement as she steps carefully but swiftly from stone to stone. It was offered as a prize by the Art Union of London in the years 1856-8.

The SPB quotes the trade price of 70/- AUL. An example in the Bolton Museum was made in 1879, showing that it remained popular for twenty years.

S166 – STORM, companion to **Calm, 'On the Sea Shore'**
c.1872
Ht. 19in. (48.26cm)
Sculptor: J. Durham
Illus: Yes
See S22, Calm and S124 for full details.
Both figures were illustrated in Silber & Fleming's Catalogue.

S167

S167a

S168

S167 – STORM, and her companion **SUNSHINE**
1858
Ht. Storm 19½in. (49.53cm.); Sunshine 20in. (50.8cm)
Sculptor: W. Brodie
Sponsor:
Marks: WM. BRODIE ARSA Sc 1858
Illus: Yes PP 508 and 510
Both these figures in marble were exhibited at the Royal Academy in 1862 and at the Royal Scottish Academy in 1859, 1863 and 1869. It was one of Brodie's favourite works. Brodie was the son of a Banff-based ship-master which may have provided the inspiration for these two works.

They were copied very closely by an unidentified foreign manufacturer who made them in porcelain and tinted them.

Their appearance in the SPB among the earlier works which are known to have been produced in 1858 points to these two figures being made in statuary porcelain in the same year that they were sculpted in marble. The SPB quotes 48/- trade and 73/6 retail. In 1873 the trade price was £2.6.0 and in c.1880 it was £2.2.0, with a further reduction in 1884 to 30/-. The retail price in 1876 was £3.10.0. All prices 'each'. The making price was 6/- each.

S168 – STRAWBERRY GIRL
c.1877
Sculptor: L.A. Malempré
Sponsor: Ceramic and Crystal Palace Art Union
Illus: Yes
The figure is modelled after the picture by Sir Joshua Reynolds. The only figure known to the authors is in the Nottingham Castle Museum Collection to whom credit is given for the photograph.

The stock at Stoke taken on 10 November 1881 of the goods reserved to the Ceramic and Crystal Palace Art Union showed that fourteen figures had been returned to the factory and these were valued at 10/- each. The making price was 2/-. There is no other record of this figure known in the Copeland papers.

S169 – STUDIES FROM LIFE, a pair
c.1883
Ht. 20in. (50.8cm)
Illus: Yes PP 485
A pair of loosely-draped maidens resting in contemplative mood on tree trunks.

In 1884, the trade price was 30/- each, this rising to 32/6, handwritten in pencil on 29 August 1895. This detail is found on the 'Accompanying Sheet' to a page of photographs of several items of parian published in the 1880s, the later price being in pencil. Then, a reprint of this sheet confirms that price of 32/6 and another pencil note revises the price up to 35/- each; this is undated. The Making Price Book records two prices: 6/- for the Study from Life and 4/6 for her companion.

S169

S169a

S170 – SUMMER
c.1870
Ht. 18in. (45.72cm)
The Seasons figures present problems of identification because too few illustrations are known at present and where one or other of the seasons is listed little information is vouchsafed, sometimes only the height.

In the SPB there is an entry for '22/7/1870 Summer (from P of W's Set) Figure 21/-'. This might be the same figure as that in the NPL of 1873, which is 18 inches high and priced at £1.4.0. Moreover, in both the SPB and the 1873 NPL there are the same details for Winter; same height, same source and same prices. It certainly seems that these two are complementary. In the c.1880 NPL the price for each was £1.1.0 and this was reduced to 15/- in 1884. The retail price in 1876 was £1.16.0. The making price was 3/-.

The Dessert Service made for the Prince of Wales
There is insufficient information about the composition of the great dessert service commissioned by HRH the Prince of Wales in 1863 to be certain that there was a set of seasons as supports for fruit dishes or comports.

A congratulatory column is devoted to this service in the April 1866 issue of the *Art-Journal*, where the details are given of the assiette montée being supported by figures representing the four quarters of the globe. (See S31 Continents, and individual figures of Africa, America, Asia and Europe.)

In addition, there were four raised fruit dishes elevated upon groups, each consisting of three figures representing, in all, the twelve months of the year; these were of parian and sculpted by F. Miller. It is probably these four fruit dishes which are otherwise described as 'seasons' in the SPB. There were four smaller comports, each dish supported by a figure symbolic of one of the four elements, Fire, Air, Earth, and Water; these were the work of G. Halse.

S171 – SWEET APPLES, companion to **Wild Flowers**
1874
Ht. 14in. (35.56cm)
Sculptor: L.A. Malempré
Sponsor: Ceramic and Crystal Palace Art Union
Marks: L.A.MALEMPRE SCULP 1874 CERAMIC AND CRYSTAL PALACE ART UNION
Illus: Yes PP 503
A charming Victorian fancy which, with his companion 'Wild Flowers', would grace any romantic's mantel shelf.

The list of stock at Stoke, taken on 10/11/81, includes six figures at a valuation of 10/6d each. The making price was 2/-.

S172 – SWISS SHEPHERD AND SHEPHERDESS
c.1858

S171

S171a

S173

S172

Ht. 10½in. (26.67cm)
Illus: Yes
Entered in the SPB with others known to have been introduced in 1858, and priced originally at 10/- trade and 15/- retail, but these have been crossed out and 8/- and 12/6 substituted, possibly in the 1860s. The 1873 NPL quotes 7/6 and the c.1880 NPL quotes 7/-, remaining at 7/- in 1884 but dropping to 6/- CP (the meaning of this 'CP' is not known). The making prices were 1/- each, and 1/6 with pillar.

S173 – TAMBOURINE BOY and **Companion**
1851
Ht. 8in. (20.32cm)
Illus: Tambourine Girl only
The first entry on the 'T' page of the SPB, where the prices are 10/- and 15/-, and there was a coloured version at 12/6 and 18/-. The pair was included on the 'Supplementary list' issued in 1851, where the pencilled price was 10/-. All prices were 'each'. The making price was 1/2d each.

THE PETS
See **Girl with Rabbit** GP29. In the records it is known variously as 'Girl with Pet Rabbit' (SPB and Making Book), 'Girl & Rabbit', or 'Pet Rabbit' (the Stoke stock-take lists of the Ceramic and Crystal Palace Art Union).

S174 – TOILET FIGURE
c.1851
Ht. 14½in. (36.83cm)
Sculptor: L. Wichmann
Marks:
Illus: Yes
A nymph, draped from the waist down, sits upon a rock performing

S174

S175

some aspect of her toilet; in her left hand she holds a small bottle, while with her right hand she anoints her hair.

This figure is second on the list of statuary porcelain under the letter 'T' in the SPB at a trade price of 46/- and 73/6 retail. In 1873 it was £1.17.6 and in c.1880 £1.15.0, dropping to 25/- in 1884. The retail price in 1876 was £2.18.0. The making price was 5/-. (The Making Price Book records it as 'Toilet, The (old)'.)

S175 – THE TOILET

1861

Ht. 16in. (40.64cm)

Sculptor: W. Calder Marshall

Sponsor: Crystal Palace Art Union

Marks: W C MARSHALL RA SCULPT CRYSTAL PALACE ART UNION PUBD JANUARY 1ST 1861

Illus: Yes

Information about this figure is derived from *The Parian Phenomenon,* page 134. The only reference found in the Copeland records up to now is the entry in the SPB, where it is stated:

CPAU Toilet (The) figure		50/-
" " "	with tinted borders	52/6
	mirror 1/- RP 6/3/74	

The figure is not listed in the stock at Stoke in 1881 of the Ceramic and Crystal Palace Art Union.

This Art Union changed its title in 1865, so if it was produced in 1861 it would have been for the Crystal Palace Art Union, and not for the Ceramic and Crystal Palace Art Union as suggested in *The Parian Phenomenon.*

See Colour Plate 32

S176 – TOM THUMB

c.1855

This figure is recorded in the SPB at 10/6 trade; no retail price or any other information. At that price it could be expected to have been 7-8in. (18-20cm) high. There is no making price and no other references.

A record of the inscription is in the Copeland factory engraving book: 'CHARLES S STRATTON known as General Tom Thumb THE AMERICAN DWARF Born Jany 11th 1832. 23 INCHES HIGH AND WEIGHS 15 LB.'

'Tom Thumb' was the sobriquet of Charles Sherwood Stratton (died 1883), an American dwarf who was exhibited around the world by P.T. Barnum. When first exhibited his height was approximately 24in. (61cm), but he eventually grew to a height of 40in. (101.6cm). In 1863 he married another dwarf, Mercy Lavinia Bump (Lavinia Warren). The character appears to derive from Henry Fielding's burlesque *Tom Thumb* (1730). It was partially plagiarised by Henry Carey in his own burlesque *Chrononhotonthologos* (1734). Theodore O'Hara turned it into an opera which may have been the immediate source for Stratton's sobriquet.

S177

S177a

S177b

S177 – TRYSTING TREE and **Companion**
1874
Ht. Boy 21in. (53.34cm); Girl 20½in. (52.07cm)
Sculptor: G. Halse
Marks: G.HALSE Sc. Pub.1874
Illus: Yes PP 537
A charming pair of figures. The boy has just put his love-letter into the bark of a tree stump; his left hand points to it. The girl seems to be walking past the tree stump having casually plucked the envelope from the bark; she looks away so as not to draw attention to her action.

Being so late in the 19th century, it is not included in the lists before 1876; in the retail price list of that year Trysting Tree is quoted at £3.3.0. No companion is mentioned.

In the c.1880 NPL Trysting Tree and Companion are quoted, each at £1.16.0. The handwritten note for 1884 shows the trade price to be 25/-. The making price was 5/- each.

Both figures are illustrated in the Catalogue of Silber & Fleming (where the height of both is given as 20in. (50.8cm).

In an illustrated brochure of the late 19th century entitled COPELAND'S CERAMIC STATUARY the boy is called Reuben and the girl Rosetta, while both are called Trysting Tree.

S178 – UNDER THE PALMS, a pair
c.1883
Ht. probably about 22in. (55.88cm)
Illus: Yes
The only written record is the trade price of 35/- in 1884. (Theed's 'Ruth' was 20in. (50.8cm) and in 1884 was priced at 35/-, although in the case of these figures the palms look quite difficult to make and fire correctly.)

Contemporary photographs have survived to show how these two figures appeared. One is a scantily clothed female figure holding a large fruit in her left hand, and standing beside what appears to be a banana palm. The caption to the illustration reads 'Companion to Palm Centre for Electric Height 22inches'. The other figure is also a female with even fewer clothes holding on to a similar palm tree stem with her left hand while holding a pitcher in her right hand.

S179 – VENUS
Venus was originally a Latin goddess of the spring; the month of April was sacred to her. Her worship seems to have been established at Rome at an early time and the worship of Venus in various guises was encouraged by different emperors.

Several versions of statues were made by Copeland and it is not certain exactly which some of them are meant to represent. Shinn, on page 75, mentions that about seven figures of Venus were made and issued by Copeland; among them he listed the following:

Venus at the Bath
Venus de Milo
Venus de Medici
Venus of the Capitol

Shinn stated that 'they were after Canova, John Gibson and Thorwaldson' [*sic*].

The Tinted Venus, by John Gibson, was an original work by that eminent sculptor, although derived from a classical model; it is described separately.

S178

S178a

S180

Venus at the Bath is an alternative title for the figure called 'Nymph at Bath' which was after the sculpture by Bartolini (see S121), but this is an entirely different statuette from that shown in *The Parian Phenomenon* as being sculpted by P. Falconer for Minton (PP 100).

Venus by Malempré may be an original or derived from an earlier sculpture (S180).

Venus de Milo was produced by Copeland as a bust (B86).

Venus de Medici. No Copeland model has been identified yet. The marble sculpture in the Louvre is somewhat different from the Minton parian figure shown at Fig. 266 in *The Parian Phenomenon.*

Venus of the Capitol is also not known as a Copeland figure.

'Venus going to the bath' is a statue by M. Kessels (1784-1836). Kessels was a Danish sculptor, a favourite pupil of Thorwaldsen, and his Venus may well be 'after Thorwaldson'. The figure also bears some resemblance to the figures by Owen Hale of 'The Riverside and Companion'. (The illustration is taken from a catalogue of 'Musée Royal des Beaux-arts de Belgique. Bruxelles. Sculpture Moderne'.) No Copeland figure corresponds to this title.

The Parian Phenomenon also includes other statuettes of Venus:

By Minton:	Fig. 100	Venus at Toilette
		Venus at Bath
	Fig. 125	Venus after the Antique Cnidiau Venus
	Fig. 266	Venus de Medici
	Fig. 267	Venus de Calipyges after the antique.
By Belleek	Fig. 791	Venus
By Worcester	Fig. 718	Venus
By Wedgwood	Fig. 638	Venus Crouching, and Venus and Cupid

S180 – VENUS, by Malempré
c.1875
18½in. (46.99cm)
Sculptor: L.A. Malempré
Sponsor: Ceramic and Crystal Palace Art Union
Illus: Yes
This figure is scantily clad with her right arm raised and her hand resting upon her head; her left arm is bent with her hand pointing to her neck.

At present the only details available are the record of the 1881 stocktake at Stoke where nine figures were listed at a value of 20/- each and the making price of 3/9d.

S181 – VENUS OF THE CAPITOL

There is no evidence at present to show that Copeland produced this version, which, presumably, was a reduced copy of the original statue by a Greek sculptor and which resides in the Capitoline Museum in Rome. This Museum was founded in 1471 by Pope Sixtus IV and built by Giacomo della Porta approximately after the designs of Michelangelo (della Porta altered the design of the windows).

The statue depicts the goddess in an undraped state with her arms held out before her. Her garment is thrown over a vase beside her. The style of the sculpture is a variation of the Venus of Cnidus, an ancient Greek city of Caria in Asia Minor (Turkey).

A marble statue in the Louvre, titled Venus of the Capitol, shows her much as Minton's Venus de Medici, except that a plaintive child is in place of the dolphin.

S182

S182 – VENUS, by John Gibson
1849
Ht. 16in. (40.64cm)
Sculptor: John Gibson RA
Marks: Printed, ART UNION OF GREAT BRITAIN
Illus: Yes PP 513
This famous statuette is also known as 'Gibson's Venus' and 'The Tinted Venus'. Gibson's original sculpture of Venus was executed in marble and was known as 'Venus Verticordia' which, in turn, derived from the antique sculpture called 'Venus de Milo'. It was completed in 1833, while other versions came later; the one reproduced by Copeland was introduced in 1849 and was included in the display at the Great Exhibition of 1851.

Venus is shown holding an apple in her left hand. The marble statue at Liverpool bears on the apple the inscription 'TO THE MOST BEAUTIFUL'. The drapery which she holds over her left arm is, in fact, the 'tunic mantle' worn by Greek women. The tortoise at her feet carries a Greek inscription 'Gibson made me in Rome'. These inscriptions do not occur on the statuary porcelain figures.

The so-called 'Tinted Venus' was the outcome of Gibson's conviction that the Greeks coloured their statues with paint. His 'Tinted Venus' was exhibited at the International Exhibition of 1862 and is now in the Walker Art Gallery in Liverpool. Gibson described the work as 'the most carefully laboured work I ever executed...I tinted the flesh like warm ivory, scarcely red, the eyes blue, the hair blond, and the net which contains the hair golden'.

Copeland's reproductions were issued as plain versions, at 42/- trade and 63/- retail in 1851, and 'Gilt & tinted at 52/6' trade. The example of the latter known to the authors has a delicate border of pale blue and pink with a fine 'spot line' of raised gilding around the hem of the garment and gilded bangles on her arms. It has no other inscription than COPELAND.

There is no mention in the Copeland records of this figure being made for the Art Union of Great Britain and by 1873 it was included for general sale by being included in the NPL at £2.0.0, that with gilt and tinted border being £2.10.0. In c.1880 these prices were £1.11.6 and £2.2.0.respectively; in 1884, 22/6 and 33/-. The retail prices in 1876 were £3.0.0 and £3.15.0. The making price was 4/6d.
See Colour Plate 33

S183 – Other models of Venus
No other figures of Venus are known to have been produced by Copeland, despite the list surmised by Shinn, but a bust of 'Venus de Milo' was made, sculpted by F.M. Miller after the antique. See Section on Busts (B86). Moreover, it is not thought that Canova modelled any item for Copeland.

Venus de Medici – Minton produced a figure after the antique, Shape 173, illustrated in *The Parian Phenomenon* at Fig. 266. The Greek marble statue, produced at the time of Augustus, is in the Tribuna of the Uffizi Palace in Florence. The graceful figure is nude, with her right arm holding her left breast and her left arm held down in front of her. She has a dolphin by her left side.

Minton produced several other statuettes of Venus including 'Venus de Calipyges', 'Venus at Bath' and 'Venus at Toilette', the two last by P. Falconet.

S184 – VILLAGE MAYOR
c.1871
Ht. 4in. (10.16cm)
Illus: Yes
Whilst the seminal source of inspiration for this small grotesque figure cannot be identified with absolute certainty, it lies within the bounds of credibility to ascribe its origin to the election of 'The Mayor of Garratt'. The elections for this position were burlesques, embodying political parodies, held in the hamlet of Garratt, which lay between Wandsworth and Tooting, near London. The area is known now as 'Garratt's Lane'. The earliest recorded election was held in 1747 and they were held thereafter at varying intervals until the late 19th century, possibly in parallel with general elections, although the evidence for this is slim. The event, which could attract 100,000 people from the London area, was the scene of much merry-making and carousal.

There are a number of accounts of how the event came into being, but all supporting evidence is ethereal to say the least! The most acceptable reason given is that the people of Garratt, wishing to prevent the enclosure of their common land, formed a part-social, part-fund-raising society with a view to accumulating sufficient money with which they could protect their interests. It is thought that the society's chairman was referred to jokingly as 'The Mayor'.

The eventual scale of the event may be judged by the action of the playwright Samuel Foote who is said to have paid nine guineas to rent a room in Wandsworth High Street from which to view the proceedings. The candidates, representing neither Whigs nor Tories, were drawn from the ranks of street-wise London scallywags endowed with a ready wit and, preferably, a physical handicap. They assumed outlandish names which they embellished with wholly spurious titles as, for example, Sir John Blow-me-down, Lord Twankum, Sir Trincalo Boreas, Admiral Christopher Dash'em or Dashwood, and suchlike. Their ceremonial dress varied from the slightly outré to the outrageously bizarre. Candidates' backgrounds were equally varied: publican, cobbler and gravedigger, cryer of fish, setter of colours, inkle-weaver and cobbler, old wig dealer, fruiterer and oyster merchant, and so the motley throng presented itself.

The most notorious mayor was one John Anderson of Wandsworth, alias 'Sir John Harpur', described in 1781 as a breeches maker, brick-dust merchant and itinerant fiddler. Another was 'Sir' Jeffrey Dunstan, a 4ft. (122cm) high second-hand wig dealer, now buried in St.Mary's Churchyard, Whitechapel. He died in 1797 from an overdose of alcohol, his corpse being rescued by friends from body-snatchers.

The last recognised mayor was a muffin-seller, 'Sir' Harry Dimsdale, elected in 1796. From then on interest waned. Prior to election each candidate was required to swear, on a brick-bat, the election oath. This was a masterpiece of double entendre which was eschewed by many Victorian historians. The oath ran as follows:

> The 'Oath of Qualification' for the Ancient Borough of Garratt, according, and as it stands on the old record, handed down to us by the Grand Volgee, by order of the Great Chin Kaw Chipo, first Emperor of the Moon, Anno Mundi 68. That you have admitted peaceably and quietly, into possession of a freehold thatched tenement, either black, brown or coral, in hedge or ditch, against gate or stile, under furze or fen, on any common or common field, or enclosure, in the high road, or any of the lanes, in barn, stable, hovel, or any other place within the Manor of Garratt, and, that you did (bona fide, in good faith) keep (ad rem, to the point) possession of that said thatched tenement (durante bene placito, whilst well pleased) without any let, hindrance, or molestation whatsoever; or, without any ejectment or forcibly turning out of the same; and that you did then and there and in the said tenement, discharge and duty pay and amply satisfy all legal demands of the tax that was at time due on the said premises; and lastly, did quit and leave the said premises in sound, wholesome and good tenable repair as when you took possession and did enter therein. So help you.
>
> Sworn (coram nobis, in our presence) at our great hall on Garratt Green, covered with the plenteous harvest of the goddess Ceries *[sic]* and dedicated to the jovial Comus.

Having sworn the oath, each candidate then mounted the platform to deliver his election address. In the 1761 election, speeches were written by John Wilkes (reformer), David Garrick (actor) and the aforementioned Samuel Foote, who wrote a short two act comedy named *The Mayor of Garratt,* satirising contemporary politics and politicians; it was performed first in 1763 at the Haymarket Theatre. After the new mayor had been elected by general acclaim, the festivities commenced.

An attempt in 1826 to revive interest in the elections came to nothing. The last election of note was in 1871, being the Centenary of the Wandsworth Common Act. It was, perhaps, for this event that the small Village Mayor figure made its appearance.

The foregoing information was drawn exclusively from *The Mayor of Garratt* by Anthony Shaw, Wandsworth Historical Cameos Number 1, published by Wandsworth Borough Council in 1980. Other sources: *The Century Cyclopedia Names; London City Suburbs* by P. Fitzgerald (Leadenhall Press 1893); *The Skirts of the Great City* by Mrs A.G. Bell (Methuen & Co.1908).

The figure is priced in the SPB at 1/- and also in the 1873 NPL at 1/-. In 1876 the retail price was 1/6d. The wholesale price remained at 1/- in the c.1880 NPL and in 1884. The making price was 4d.

It may be that several of these figures are in private homes in the Wandsworth area.

S185

S185 – THE VIOLET SELLER
c.1876
Length 5¾in. (14.61cm)
Illus: Yes
This 'figure' is really a flower container, but in the c.1880 NPL it is included among the statuettes at 4/6d. In 1876 the retail price was 7/6d. It is described in the SPB as 'Violet Stand', but at 4/6d trade it is almost certain that it is the same item. In 1884 the trade price was 3/- and the making price was 8d.

S186 – VIOLIN PLAYER AND COMPANION
The only references to these two figures are in the 1895 and 1928 Making Price Books where they are listed as 1/2d each.

S187 – VIRGINIA, companion to **Paul**, q.v. S126
c.1849
Ht. 14in. (35.56cm)
Sculptor: C. Cumberworth
Illus: Yes. PP 512
The biographical details will be found in the Groups Section, GP51.

An early figure, it is listed in the SPB at 25/- trade and 35/- retail, and it is at 35/- that it is priced in the 1851 catalogue. By 1873 the trade price had dropped to £1.0.0 and the retail price in 1876 had fallen to £1.10.0. The trade price in the c.1880 NPL was 18.0 and only 13/6 in 1884. The making price was 2/9.
See Colour Plate 34

S188 – WASHING DOLLY, companion to **Nurse is Away,** q.v.
c.1880
Dimensions: Ht. 6½in. (16.51cm), L. 7in. (17.78cm)
Illus: Yes
Together with its companion piece, 'Nurse is Away', Washing Dolly projects an amusing and familiar occurrence – a happy, mischievous small girl thoroughly enjoying herself.

Priced at 8/- in the c.1880 NPL, it was 3/- in 1884, while in 1895 and 1928 the making price was 1/-.

S187

S189

S189a

S188

S189 – WATER NYMPH
c.1860
Ht. 14in.(35.56cm)
Illus: Yes PP 528
An example is in the Collection of the Spode Museum Trust; it is coloured as if to see how it might look.

The SPB quotes 46/- trade and 73/6 retail; this is undated but, with the next quoted price of £1.18.0 in the 1873 NPL, it suggests that the figure was introduced many years before 1873. In 1876 the retail price was £2.18.0. The NPL of c.1880 quotes £1.15.0, which falls to 27/6 > 35/- in 1884. The making price was 4/6d.

S190 – JAMES WATT
c.1870 or earlier
Sculptor: possibly F. Chantrey
Sponsor: probably a private commission by a learned society
James Watt was born at Greenock in 1736 and died in Birmingham in 1819. He was an eminent 18th-19th century civil engineer and inventor. In 1757, when only twenty-one years of age, he was appointed mathematical instrument maker to Glasgow University. In 1765 he patented the condensing steam engine, which was to be developed later in collaboration with Matthew Boulton. While in partnership with Boulton, the Birmingham decorative metal manufacturer, Watt met Josiah Wedgwood – probably in the Lunar Society – and they were to become closely associated in the following years.

Among Watt's many patents was that for a reducing machine; this pre-dated those of Benjamin Cheverton in 1844 and T.B. Jordan in 1847. Watt once remarked that 'without a hobby horse, what is life?' The sculpture copying machine became his favourite hobby horse during his later years.

He built two machines: one made reduced copies, while the other made equal-sized copies of portrait busts and the like. Both machines embodied a controlled 'feeler' which moved over the contours of the original model. Watt used these machines to make copies in alabaster, mahogany, marble, ivory, jet and plaster of Paris of busts, medallions and small statues. A reduced copy of Francis Chantrey's bust of Watt sadly was left unfinished.

The 'Watt Room', a reconstruction of his workshop at Heathfield, Watt's house at Handsworth Heath, was donated in 1926 by Major Watt to the Science Museum in London, subsequent to the demolition of the house.

Over Watts' vault in Handsworth Church is a monument by Chantrey. A larger one, also by Chantrey, is to be found in Westminster Abbey; such was his eminence. A portrait bust of Watt was sculpted by E.W. Wyon for Wedgwood in 1879 (PP 655)

In the SPB there is one price of 42/- against 'Watt figure'. In a copy of the c.1880 NPL there is the handwritten price of 21/- in 1884.

S191 – DANIEL WEBSTER, seated figure
c.1860
Ht. 18in. (45.72cm)
Sculptor: W. Theed
Illus: Yes

Webster was born in 1782 and died in 1852. He was an eminent American lawyer and statesman, a member of Congress and the Senate for various States from 1813 until his death. During this time he was an extremely active politician, holding high government office on a number of occasions. He was three times an unsuccessful candidate for the Whig Presidential nomination.

The SPB quotes 58/- trade and 84/- retail. By 1873 the trade price was £2.5.0 and in 1876 the retail price was 5 guineas. In the c.1880 NPL this figure was £3.3.0, with a note of 45/- for 1884. The making price was 9/-.

S191

S192

S192 – WELLER
c.1880
Ht. 5in. (12.7cm)
Illus: Yes

Although listed as Weller, this is surely meant to represent Toby Weller, a principal character in Charles Dickens' novel *The Pickwick Papers.* Toby is Mr Pickwick's coachman and father of Samuel Weller, Pickwick's man-servant. The small parian figure catches the very essence of a coachman.

Toby Weller appears as an apoplectic man with a pimpled nose, but also good-natured and kindly. He entertains great admiration for his son Sam and Mr Pickwick, together with a dread of 'widders' (widows). The parian figure derives from the book illustrations by 'Phiz', the pseudonym of Hablot Knight Browne (1815-1882), a well-known caricaturist of the time, who completed the thirty book illustrations left unfinished by Seymour. (See note under 'Pickwick' in Statuette Section, S130.)

In the NPL of c.1880 the price was 4/6, with a note for 1884 of 3/-. The making price was 1/-.

S193 – WELLINGTON, Duke of, standing
c.1845
Ht. 16½in. (41.91cm)
Sculptor: possibly the Count D'Orsay
Illus: Yes PP 563

The first National Exhibition of British Industrial Art, held in Manchester in the winter of 1845-1846, was reported in the *Art-Union* of January 1846. An engraved view of the display of Messrs. Copeland and Garrett includes the standing figure of His Grace the Duke of Wellington. Until the publication of *The Parian Phenomenon,* in which a photograph of this statuette appears, the identity of the figure in the engraving was not recognised.

The SPB lists it as 'Wellington Pedestrian Statuette 31/6 45/-'. The figure is listed, but not illustrated, in the 1848 catalogue at £2.5.0, and again in the 1851 catalogue also at 45/-; these are retail prices and accord with the price in the SPB. There are no other details.

See the section on Busts for biographical details of the Iron Duke. (B92).

The *Official Catalogue* to the 1851 International Exhibition lists: 'Duke of Wellington, by the Count D'Orsay.' It is not known if this is the figure referred to or if it is the equestrian statue, or both.

S194 – WELLINGTON, Duke of, Equestrian Statue
c.1848

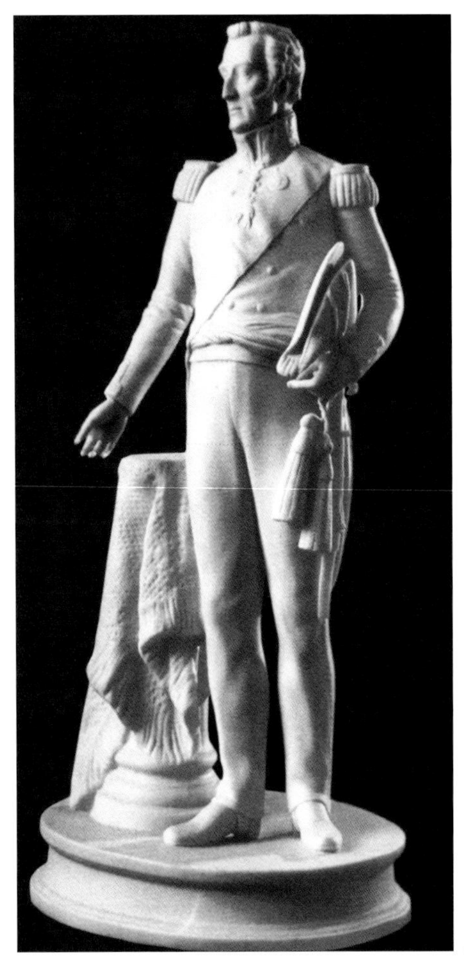

S193

Sculptor: possibly the Count D'Orsay
So far the only reference to the existence of this model is in the SPB where it lists: 'Wellington Equestrian Statue 60/-90/-'. This entry is the first on the page for letter W and comes before the statuette above (S193).

The equestrian statuette on the left of the picture of the 1845 Manchester display is almost certainly of this subject. It is next to the standing figure.

A small bronze statuette closely similar to this illustration has been noticed in ? Leeds Castle, Kent.

S195 – WELLINGTON, Duke of, seated figure, companion to **Napoleon**
possibly 1852 or 1853
Dimensions: Ht.11½in. (29.21cm)
Sculptor: A. Crowquill, after G. Abbott
Sponsor: A. Crowquill
Illus: Yes PP 499
The likelihood is that this seated figure was published at about the time of the Iron Duke's death in 1852 and that that of his great adversary was published at about the same time by the same sponsor. It is probable that the moulds for this seated figure were acquired when the Successors to Samuel Alcock, The Hill Pottery, closed in 1867.

William Taylor Copeland, when Lord Mayor of London in 1835, invited the Duke to be his guest of honour at the Lord Mayor's Banquet. Copeland had a very great respect for Wellington, which explains why three different sculptures were manufactured and also a dinner and dessert service illustrating some of the battles in which the Duke had excelled himself as a commander (WTC died in 1868).

The first reference in a price list is that for 1873 at £1.10.0. The retail price in 1876 was £2.5.0. The NPL of c.1880 quotes £1.5.0, with a note of 18/6 for 1884. The making price was 3/6.

S195

S196 – WILD FLOWERS, companion to **Sweet Apples**
c.1874
Ht. 14in. (35.56cm)
Sculptor: L.A. Malempré
Sponsor: Ceramic and Crystal Palace Art Union
Illus: Yes
A charming companion for the boy carrying apples in the crook of his arm. Had he plucked them from a neighbour's tree or are they windfalls? Does it matter now? No!

The only records of prices are the stock-take of the Union's goods held by Copelands, which in 1881 was 10/6 (there were twenty-two figures in stock on 10 November 1881) and a handwritten note that in 1884 the trade price was 7/-; this price was to clear the stock after the Union had ceased to trade. The making price was 1/10d.

S196

S197 – JOHN WILSON
1866
Ht. 17in. (43.18cm)
Sculptor: J. Steell R.S.A.
Sponsor: Royal Association

S197

S198

Edinburgh; Fine Arts Association
Marks: Jn. Steell RSA Sculpt.Edin. 1866. Royal Association Edinburgh
Published 1866
Illus: Yes PP 562, also in Shinn, Fig.34
John Wilson (1785-1854) was born in Paisley and educated in Glasgow and at Magdalen College, Oxford. Graduating in 1807, he went on to become Professor of Moral Philosophy at Edinburgh University in 1820. He also was a member of the Scottish Bar. He is remembered best as an essayist, poet and novelist who wrote under the pseudonym of 'Christopher North'. From 1817 onwards he was a principal contributor to *Blackwood's Magazine.*

The SPB records: 'F.A.Assn. Wilson Professor 2 Gns.' This suggests that when Copelands were asked to produce this figure the Edinburgh society was still known as the Fine Arts Association, and that it was granted royal status during the development stages of modelling.

S198 – WINTER
c.1870
Ht. 18in. (45.72 cm)
Sculptor: possibly L.A. Malempré
This will be the companion figure to Summer and the other seasons of which illustrations are available: Spring PP 508 (see S161) and Autumn PP 508

S198A – WINTER
Ht. 15½in. (39.37cm)
Sculptor: after Girardon
Marks: COPELAND
Illus: Yes
This statuette is after the figure by Girardon at Versailles. It may have been taken from the engraved illustration of the statue in Simon Thomassin's book *Receuil des figures, groupes, thermes, fontaines,*

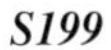
S199

S200

S201

S199a

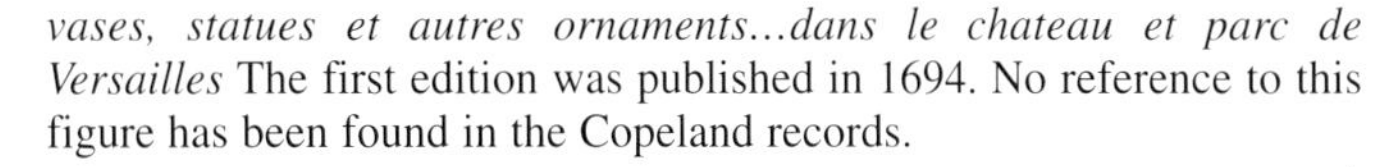

vases, statues et autres ornaments...dans le chateau et parc de Versailles The first edition was published in 1694. No reference to this figure has been found in the Copeland records.

S199 – YOUNG ARTIST AND COMPANION
c.1878
Dimensions: Ht. 7½in. (19.05cm)
Illus: Yes
Two statuettes of the same small personage occupying itself with a vase, one holding it, and the other contemplating the vase lying upon the floor.

Mention of it occurs first in the c.1880 NPL at 8.0 each and in 1884 this had fallen to 5.0 each. The making price was 1s.2d. each.

S200 – YOUNG EMIGRANT, companion to **Young Shrimper**
S201 – YOUNG SHRIMPER, companion to **Young Emigrant**
1863
Ht. 20in. (50.8cm)
Sculptor: Edgar G. Papworth Jnr.
Marks: Edgar G. Papworth Sc. Pub. June 1st 1862
Illus: Yes PP 492
The 'Young Emigrant', in marble, was exhibited at the Royal Academy in 1861 and, together with its companion, 'Young Shrimper', at the International Exhibition in London in 1862. The growing interest in travel and the practice of taking summer holidays by the sea may have inspired these figures.

The NPL quotes £1.7.0 in 1873 with the retail price in 1876 being £2.2.0. In the c.1880 list the price was £1.1.0 and 1884 it was only 15/- trade. The making price is not given. These prices were for each figure.

S202 – YOUNG ENGLAND
S203 – YOUNG ENGLAND'S SISTER
c.1871
Ht. 14½in. (36.83cm)
Sculptor: G. Halse
Marks: G. Halse Sc.
Illus. Yes PP 494
This pair of figures, epitomising the flower of English youth, would have appealed very much to the middle and upper levels of society. The

S202

S202a

S202b

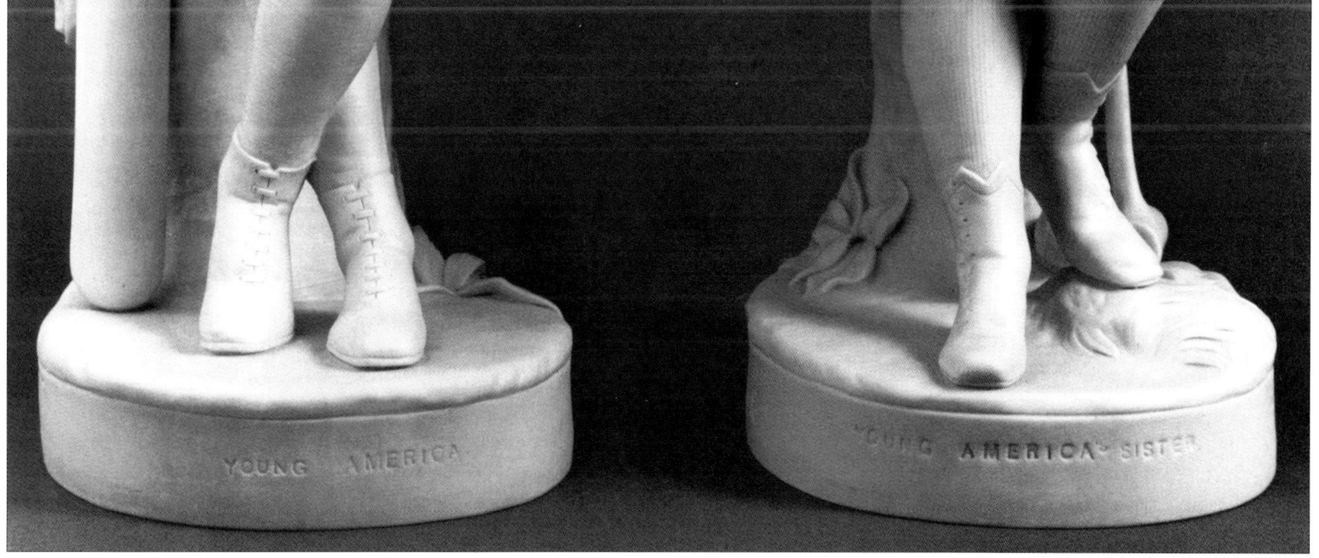

S202c

figure of Young England, in marble, was exhibited at the Royal Academy in 1870. Young England, while reading a book, has his cricket bat by his right side; Young England's sister has her finger marking the place in her book and has a croquet ball and mallet leaning against the tree stump. This pair of figures was illustrated in the catalogue of Silber and Fleming.

The author saw in a Toronto antique dealer's shop a figure of the boy but clearly marked in the base 'Young America'!

In the NPL of 1873 the figures were priced at 18.0 each, with the retail price in 1876 of £1.8.0. In c.1880 the trade price was 16/6d, falling to 12/6 > 15/- in 1884. The making price was 2/6 each.

S204

S204a

S205

S205a

S204 – YOUNG FLORIST and **COMPANION**
Dimensions: Ht. 14½in. (36.83cm)
Illus: Yes
Apart from the photographic record in the factory archive there is no other information available at present.

The Young Florist is standing behind three shallow bowls for the arrangement of small flowers; he is ready with a syringe poised to spray the flowers to freshen up their appearance. His companion is in a similar position, but with a watering can.

S205 – YOUNG NATURALIST and **COMPANION**
c.1878
Ht. 15in. (38.1cm)
Sculptor: R.J. Morris
Marks: R.J. Morris Sc.
Illus: Yes PP 493
Although both figures are attributed to the work of R.J. Morris, only the figure of the boy has been found so far with the sculptor's name marked.

It is thought that the title originally was 'Rustic Children of England'; this is based on an archival photograph of the girl with this title but scored through. The boy seems to be in the act of 'blowing an egg' which he has taken from the nest he has stolen. The girl is studying the butterfly which has settled upon her wrist. (As this is vulnerable, it is sometimes missing.) Both figures are illustrated in the catalogue of Silber and Fleming.

They are priced for the trade in c.1880 at 16/6 each and, in 1884, there is a choice of three prices!: 12/6 > 15/- > 17/6. It is not known what the meaning is of these varying prices in 1884. The making price was 2/8d each.

S206 – YOUTHFUL AFFECTION and **COMPANION**
c.1878
Ht. 6½in. (16.51cm)
Illus: Yes
Clearly intended as table decorations to hold small flowers, this pair of ornaments would make an ideal present for St. Valentine's Day. Of course, they could be used to hold sweets, chocolates or other delicacies.

In the c.1880 NPL they are priced at 10/6d each, falling to 6/- each in 1884. The making price was 1/2, but also there is a price of a 'new' model at only 8d. It is not known what this figure might be; perhaps it is the figure only without the bowl?

S206

PARIAN WARE BUSTS

Unidentified Subjects

Several portrait busts have been seen for which identifications are needed. *The Parian Phenomenon* includes four and one wrongly attributed.

Fig. 615, a bust by J. Sherwood Westmacott, 1852 – identified in June 2006 as John Masterman – see B47
Fig. 604, now identified as Matthew Noble, the sculptor
Fig. 605, a bust by H. Bourne
Fig. 614, now identified as Professor James Syme, surgeon
Fig. 622, stated as Duke of Wellington, but actually is William Taylor Copeland

From personal correspondents I have photographs of three portrait busts which remain unidentified, with no information about the sculptors.

Unidentified – ???

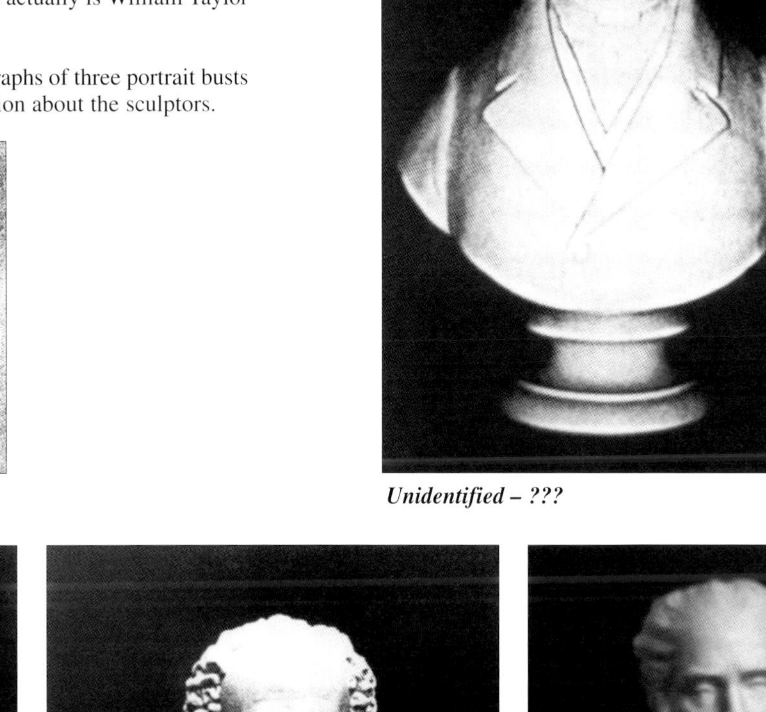

Unidentified – ???

Unidentified – PP 605

Unidentified – ???

PP 615 – John Masterman – see B47

B1

B1 – ACHILLES
c.1878
Ht. 24in. (60.96cm)
Sculptor: After the antique
Illus: Yes
A Greek legendary warrior, the son of Peleus and Thetis, chief of the Thessalian Myrmidon tribe, Achilles was the central figure of Homer's *Iliad,* which concerns his quarrel with Agamemnon, leader of the Greek hosts, and his martial exploits. Achilles was slain eventually by Paris before Troy was captured.

The only reference to this bust is a manuscript note in a copy of the c.1880 NPL where it gives for 1884 the price of 52/6 trade. Its date of publication is conjecture, but it may be two decades earlier.

B2 – APOLLO
1861
Ht. 13¼in. (33.66cm)
Sculptor: C. Delpech (reducit) from the antique
Sponsor: Art Union of London
Marks: Published Feb 1st 1861 Art Union of London 1861
Illus: Yes Shinn Fig. 30
One of the great Olympian gods of Greek mythology, Apollo was the son of Zeus and Leto. He represents light and life-giving influences, but also the god who punishes, the god who affords help and wards off evil, the god of prophecy, the god who protects flocks and cattle (he was once the shepherd boy of Admetus, see S6), the god who founded towns and civil constitutions. His attributes as god of the sun are not of Greek mythology but are of Egyptian influence. He was one of the muses and so was the god of healing, poetry and music. The common story is that he fathered Aesculapius, or Asclepius, the 'blameless physician'.

Delpech used as his source the beautiful representation in the Vatican known as the 'Apollo Belvedere', which is, in turn, a copy of a Greek original. Here he is portrayed as the god of youthful manliness.

Unfortunately, there is no reference to this bust in the Copeland archives. The author photographed the example which had been brought to him for this purpose. The quality of it suggested that it was from the Copeland manufactory.

B3 – ARIADNE
c.1858
Ht. 23in. (58.42cm)
Illus: Yes
In Greek mythology, Ariadne was the daughter of Minos, King of Crete, and Pasiphae. She fell in love with Theseus when he was sent to pay the tribute to the Minotaur and she gave him the thread by which he was able to escape from the labyrinth. Theseus promised to marry her and they went to the island of Dia (Naxos) where he deserted her. She was found by Dionysus who married her.

The SPB quotes 6 guineas trade and 9 guineas retail. These prices were held in the 1873 and 1876 lists, but in the c.1880 NPL it was £4.14.6, with a further reduction to 52/6 in 1884. The making price was 8/-, the highest making price of any bust except that of the life-sized

B2

B3

B4

B5

B3a

bust after the Venus de Milo at 9/-.

B4 – ASLEEP, companion to **Awake**
B5 – AWAKE, companion to **Asleep**
1860
Ht. 9in. (22.86cm)
Sculptor: J.S. Westmacott
Illus: Yes PP 584
This is a pair of small busts of typical Victorian sentimental appeal. 'Asleep' was also called 'Night', while 'Awake' was called 'Morning'.

They are recorded in the SPB at 6/6 trade and 10/6 retail; a version in 'Ivory col'd & gilt' was offered at 7/6 trade. In 1873 the trade price was 5/- and the retail price in 1876 was 7/6. By c.1880 the trade price was still 5/-, but it fell to 2/- in 1884. The making prices were: Asleep 8d, Awake 10d.

B6 – BARING'S BUST OF A LADY
The only reference to this enigmatic subject is the record in the SPB where a price of 31/6 is quoted for either trade or direct sale to a possible private commission.

B7 – BEACONSFIELD, Earl of,
1878
Ht. 12in. (30.48cm)
Sculptor: L.A. Malempré
Marks: BEACONSFIELD Protected Act 54 George III. L.C. & Co 9/9/78 L.A.MALEMPR Sc.
Illus. Yes PP 616
Benjamin Disraeli, English statesman and novelist, was born in London in 1804 and died there in 1881. He entered the House of Commons in 1837, becoming leader of the 'Young England' faction. In about 1845 Disraeli found himself the leader of the protectionist Tories who were opposed to the prime minister, Sir Robert Peel. He became Chancellor

B7

B8

of the Exchequer and Leader of the House in 1852 and again in 1858-9.

Disraeli carried through the Reform Bill of 1867 and was appointed prime minister in 1868, but resigned in the same year. He again became premier in 1874-80; he was created Earl of Beaconsfield in 1876.

The trade price quoted in the c.1880 list was 9/- which in 1884 had become 5/- > 9/-. The making price was 1/-.

B8 – BEECHER, Henry Ward
c.1887
Sponsor: probably private
Illus: Yes
Henry Ward Beecher was born in 1813 in Litchfield, Connecticut, USA. He died in Brooklyn, New York in 1887, so it is presumed that this bust was a private commission as a memorial. Beecher graduated at Amherst College in 1834 and studied theology at Lane Theological Seminary. He was a noted Congregationalist minister, author and reformer. He was the brother of Harriet Beecher-Stowe, the authoress of the anti-slavery novel *Uncle Tom's Cabin*..

The only record in the Copeland archives is the making price of 1/-.

B9 – BEETHOVEN, Ludwig van
1871
Ht. 10½in.(26.67cm)
Sculptor: A. Hays
Illus: Yes PP 612
Beethoven was born in Bonn, Prussia in 1770 and died in Vienna in 1827. A celebrated German composer of Dutch descent, he began his musical education at the age of four, under the tutelage of his father. In 1792 the Elector of Cologne sent him to Vienna. He made his last public appearance

B9

B10

B10a

on 16 April 1816, having become afflicted with total deafness.

The Copeland bust seems to be a reduced copy of one similar to that treasured by the Royal Philharmonic Society of London.

In the SPB it is at 8/- trade, so may have been commissioned about the centenary of his birth. The only other references are the price of 10/- trade in 1884 and the making price of 1/-.

B10 – BENTINCK, Lord George
1848
Ht. 8¼in. (20.96cm) unclothed, 9in. (22.86cm) clothed
Sculptor: Count D'Orsay
Marks: Count D'Orsay Sculp. 1848
Illus: Yes PP 605, unclothed, 617 clothed
Born William George Frederick Cavendish in 1802 at Welbeck Abbey, Nottinghamshire, he died there in 1848. An English politician and sportsman, he was the second son of the Fourth Duke of Portland. He led the opposition to the free-trade policies of Sir Robert Peel. A Statute of 1845 which restricted unlawful gaming and wagers became known as 'Lord George Bentinck's Act'. The parian bust was exhibited in the Great Exhibition of 1851.

It was priced in the SPB at 12/6 trade and 21/- retail, but it is not included in any other printed list. The making price was 10d, presumably for either version.

B11 – THE BRIDE, companion to **The Mother**
1861
Ht. 15in. (38.1cm)
Sculptor: Raffaele Monti
Sponsor: The Ceramic and Crystal Palace Art Union

B11

B12

B13

Marks: R. Monti 1861 Ceramic and Crystal Palace Art Union
Illus: Yes PP 586
The original marble sculpture of this subject was executed by Raffaele Monti for the Duke of Devonshire and was known as the 'Statue Voilee'. It was regarded by some as a splendid work of art, while others thought of it as mere 'technical trickery'. None the less it has become a well-known and eagerly collected bust.

The original bill for this piece is in the Copeland archive at the Spode factory. It states:

Alderman Copeland
To R.Monti, Sculptor
41 Gt.Marlboro' Street
To model of small veiled head representing 'The Bride', and copyright of it____
£10.0.0
October 11 1860
(signed over excise stamp) R Monti

The subject is priced at 21/- in the SPB and noted for the CPAU (the Art Union changed its name in 1861). In a c.1880 NPL there is a note added 'The Bride by Monti 1818-1881 14/-' in 1884. The making price was 3/-.

Some examples are known to have an inscription printed in brown on the back.

B12 – EDMUND BUCKLEY
1867
Ht. 12¼in. (31.12cm)
Sculptor: W. Theed
Marks: COPELAND'S CERAMIC STATUARY W.Theed Sculp. Published July 1867
Illus: Yes PP 604
It seems probable that this is Sir Edmund Buckley of Dinas Mawddwy, Merionethshire and of Grotton Hall, Saddleworth in the West Riding of Yorkshire. He was born on 16 April 1834, was MP for Newcastle-under-Lyme from 1865-1878 and was created baronet in 1868. He died in 1910.

The portrait bust is almost certain to have been commissioned privately.The only records are the price of 21/- in the SPB and the making price of 1/-.

B13 – ROBERT BURNS
c.1858
Ht. 4in .(10.16cm)
Illus: Yes
Robert Burns was born at Alloway in 1759. He died at Dumfries, Scotland in 1796. He was the eldest son of William Burness *(sic)*, a nurseryman, who went on to become a Scottish lyric poet.

Burns started by farming at Mossgiel with his brother Gilbert. He published a volume of poems at Kilmarnock in 1786, the year in which he changed his name to Burns.

By 1786 he was an established associate of the Scottish literati. A second edition of his poems appeared in 1787 and a third in 1793.

He married Jane Armour in 1788, having previously fathered several children by her. In addition to his farming enterprise, Robert Burns became an excise officer, in consequence of which he removed himself to Dumfries to devote himself to literature and his excise duties.

The SPB records a price of 2/- and it is marked 'small'. In 1873 it was 2/3 and the retail price in 1876 was 3/6. In the c.1880 NPL the price was 2/-. No mention is entered in 1884. The making price was 4d.

B14 – LORD BYRON
c.1848
Ht. large 17¼in. (43.82cm), small 7in. (17.78cm), life size (c.1878) 25in. (63.5cm)
Sculptor: possibly F. Chantrey
Illus: Yes PP 614
Born in London in 1788, Byron died at Missolonghi in 1824. He was the son of John Byron, a captain in the Guards. Byron inherited his title from his great uncle William, the fifth Lord Byron, in 1798, together with the estates including Newstead Abbey in Nottinghamshire. He went to Harrow School and Cambridge, becoming a Master of Arts in 1808.

A celebrated English poet, he travelled extensively throughout the continent of Europe where he indulged in several romantic affairs. Byron was something of a rebel and as such he joined the Greek insurgents at Cephalonia in 1823 against their Turkish overlords. He died of a fever in 1824.

Copeland produced a dinner and dessert service which depicted many of the places visited by Lord Byron; this is the pattern called 'Byron Views'.

The subject is included in the 1848 catalogue but no prices are quoted. However, the SPB does give prices of: Large 21/- and 31/6; Small 10/6 and 15/-. In the NPL of 1873 the prices were Large £1.4.0, Small 8/-. The retail prices in 1876 were Large £1.16.0, Small 12/-.

By c.1880 the prices were 18/6 and 6/6, which changed in 1884 to Large 13/6 > 18/6, and Small 5/- > 6/6. The making prices were 2/9 for the large one and 1/- for the small.

The life-size bust appears first in the c.1880 NPL as a handwritten note in 1884 at 35/- > 63/-. The making price was 7/-.

B15 – COLIN CAMPBELL, Lord Clyde
1858
Ht. large 10in. (25.4cm), small 9in. (22.86cm)
Sculptor: ? Morrison
Illus: Yes PP 623
Born in Glasgow in 1792, Colin Campbell died at Chatham in 1863. He

B14

B14a

B15

was a distinguished British Field Marshal who rendered outstanding service both in India and the Crimea. He was Commander-in-chief, Bengal, in 1857. Campbell rescued Havelock (q.v.) and Outram (q.v.) from Lucknow, he relieved Cawnpore, and subsequently re-captured Lucknow. He was made a Knight-Commander of the Bath in 1849 and elevated to the peerage in 1858, when he took the title Baron Clyde of Clydeside.

This bust is one of a series of three to honour British army commanders who served during the Indian Mutiny (see also Havelock and Outram). None of these subjects appears in the published price lists, so may be assumed to have been commissioned for private distribution.

There is some doubt about the attribution of sculptor; see the section on Sculptors.

The SPB quotes:

Lord Clyde Bust Campbell large	16/-	25/-
do. do. do. do. small	12/6	21/-

The making prices were 1/- and 8d respectively

See Colour Plate 35

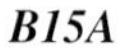

B15A

B15A

B15A – CANDLISH, Robert Smith
1874
Ht. 13¼in. (33.66cm)
Marks: COPELAND
Illus: Yes

Robert Smith Candlish DD. (1806-1873) was the Principal of New College, Edinburgh. He was one of the most eminent Scottish preachers of his day and, next to Chalmers, leader of the group of ministers who broke away from the established church and formed the Free Church in May 1843.

Although not recorded in the Copeland records, there is an example in the library of New College, the theological college of the Free Church. The identification of the bust is due to the recognition made by a librarian.

This bust was probably a private commission to commemorate Robert Candlish.

B16 – CLYTIE
1855
Ht. large 23in. (58.42cm), small 13½in.(34.29cm)
Sculptor: C. Delpech reducit. After the antique
Sponsor: Art Union of London (small size)
Marks: C.DELPECH REDT. ART UNION OF LONDON
Illus: Yes PP 610

Clytie was a sea nymph, daughter of Oceanus, who was changed into the plant heliotropium for unrequited love of Helios, the sun-god.

The marble bust first came to public notice after it was purchased by Charles Townley on 9 July 1772 from the Principe di Laurenzano of Naples. Townley stated in his notebook that it had been in that collection 'for many years'. The bust was Townley's favourite sculpture.

Some years ago, this bust was identified as that of the younger Antonia (36BC-AD38), daughter of Mark Antony and Octavia. She was the wife

B16

of Drusus, the brother of the emperor Tiberius, and mother of Germanicus, the father of the emperor Caligula, of Livia, and of the emperor Claudius. She was celebrated for her beauty, virtue and chastity. The marble bust has even been claimed to be an 18th century fake.

However, now it is thought to be of genuine Parian marble and therefore to have been quarried in antiquity. The Parian quarries were not re-opened until the 19th century. (Is it possible for an untouched chunk of ancient marble to have survived to be sculpted in the 1700s?) The bust shows evidence of great age in its present form and, after detailed scrutiny, no evidence of having been re-cut at a later date.

Dr Susan Walker of the Department of Greek and Roman Antiquities at the British Museum believes the sculpture to date from AD40-60. It may not be a portrait of Antonia Minor, however; its height is 57cm (nearly 22½in.) - almost the same as that of the large Copeland copy - and Dr Walker wonders if it might be meant to be of Ariadne or of a young woman as Ariadne. (See B3 for an account of Ariadne.)

Shinn states that the Copeland bust of 'Clytie' was exhibited in 1859 at their showroom at 160 New Bond Street, London, and was written about with acclaim in the *Art-Journal.*

The prices evidently remained the same from 1855 until 1876, at 6 guineas trade and 9 guineas retail for the large one; 25/- for the small one in 1855 to the Art Union of London; in 1878 this price was cut to 22/6 'see Mr.Battam's letter 18/1/78' (SPB). In c.1880 the trade price was £4.14.6, and down to 42/- in 1884. There may have been an 'ivory' one at 4 guineas.

B17 – RICHARD COBDEN
1865
Ht. 11in. (27.94cm)
Sculptor: Matthew Noble
Illus: Yes
Born in Sussex in 1804, Richard Cobden died in London in 1865. He was an English statesman and political economist who promoted the policies of free-trade and the pursuit of peace. He was the principal supporter of the Anti-Corn Law League of 1839-46.

Cobden was engaged in a calico printing business in 1831 and entered Parliament in 1841. He negotiated a trade agreement between England and France in 1859-60. His political pamphlets included *Political Writings* published in 1867 and *Speeches on Questions of Public Policy* in 1870.

The original marble bust is in the Reform Club, London.

The NPL of 1873 quotes 14/-, while the retail price in 1876 was £1.1.0. In c.1880 the price was 10/-, which fell to 6/- in 1884. The making price was 1/-.

B18 – COMEDY, one of the Muses
c.1878
Ht. 13¼in. (33.66cm)
Sculptor: possibly R.J. Morris
Illus: Yes
The Muses were the inspiring goddesses of song and regarded by some as presiding over the arts and sciences. They were the daughters of Zeus and Mnemosyne, born at the foot of Mount Olympus and, although originally there were only three, later they are considered to be nine.

1. Clio, the muse of history
2. Euterpe, the muse of lyric poetry
3. Thalia, the muse of comedy and of merry idyllic poetry
4. Melpomene, the muse of tragedy
5. Terpsichore, the muse of choral dance and song
6. Erato, the muse of erotic poetry and mimic imitation
7. Polymnia, the muse of the sublime hymn
8. Urania, the muse of astronomy
9. Calliope, the muse of epic poetry

In the c.1880 NPL she is quoted at 10/6d, with the price in 1884 of 7/6d. The making price was 1/6d.

B19 – TRAGEDY, One of the Muses
c.1878
Ht. 13½in. (34.29cm)
Illus: Yes
The trade price in c.1880 was 10/6d, falling to 6/6 in 1884. The making price was 1/3d.

B17

B18

B19

B20

B21

B20 – SAMUEL COOPER
1851
Ht. 10in. (25.4cm)
Sculptor: Timothy Butler
Sponsor: The Royal College of Surgeons
Marks: T BUTLER SCULPTOR 1851 SAMUEL COOPER FRS
Illus: Yes PP 606
Born in 1780 and died in 1848, Samuel Cooper entered St. Bartholomew's Hospital in 1800. He became a Member of the Royal College of Surgeons in 1803. In 1809 he published the first edition of his *Cooper's Surgical Dictionary* which was revised seven times during his lifetime. Cooper entered the army in 1813 and served at Waterloo. He was elected a Fellow of the Royal Society in 1846.

The price to the Royal College of Surgeons was 13/-, as recorded in the SPB. The making price in 1895 was 1/2d. There is no reference as to how long the bust was available; there is no evidence that it was a restricted or limited edition.

The portrait bust rests on a representation of his *Dictionary*.

B21 – WILLIAM TAYLOR COPELAND
1838, and onwards
Ht. 22½in. (57.15cm)
Sculptor: J. Birks
Illus: Yes
W.T. Copeland was born in London on 24 March 1797, the son of William Copeland, the partner of Josiah Spode II. Little is known of his early life and educational background, but in 1824 he became a partner with his father and Josiah Spode in the London business of Spode and Copeland. In the same year he was elected to the Livery of the Worshipful Company of Goldsmiths. On the death of his father in 1826, Copeland and Spode II formed a new partnership to run for seven years, each having two shares. On 29 April he married Sarah Yates, the daughter of John Yates, china manufacturer of Shelton. Copeland was interested in politics and in 1828 was elected Liberal Member of Parliament for Coleraine; also in 1828 he was elected Sheriff of London and Middlesex. In 1829 he was elected Alderman for the Bishopsgate Ward in the Corporation of the City of London. He was known as 'The Alderman' from that time onwards. Josiah Spode II had died in 1827 and his son, Spode III, had died two years later.

At the end of the seven years' partnership agreement in 1833, Copeland bought the remaining Spode shares in the London concern and most of the Stoke commercial and domestic property, including, of course, the factory in Stoke-upon-Trent. He took Thomas Garrett into partnership to oversee the affairs at Stoke, while Copeland himself supervised the London trade and was able to attend to his Corporation and political affairs.

In 1835 he was elected Lord Mayor of London at the age of thirty-eight, the third youngest person to be Lord Mayor of that great city. Two years later he was elected to be Prime Warden of the Goldsmiths' Company. He was also elected Conservative MP for Stoke-upon-Trent, a seat he retained until 1852. He was appointed a director of the London & Birmingham Railway Company in that same year. In 1846 he became a director of the North Staffordshire Railway. In the following year the partnership with Garrett ceased and the Copeland London business moved to the more fashionable area of Mayfair, where a showroom was opened at 160 New Bond Street.

Copeland was a real entrepreneur and first-class merchant; he made a substantial fortune, some of which he spent on his racehorses and much of which was robbed by unfaithful, yet trusted colleagues and servants.

He was a local Commissioner for the 1851 Great Exhibition of the Works of All Nations and was awarded a personal medal. He was re-elected MP for Stoke-upon-Trent in 1857, the year he installed the first filter-press in the pottery industry. In 1861 he was elected President of the Royal Hospital of Bridewell & Bethlem. The honour of being appointed China Manufacturer to H.R.H. the Prince of Wales occurred in 1866 and in 1867 he took into partnership his four sons, William, Alfred, Edward, and Richard.

William Taylor Copeland, 'The Alderman', died on 12 April 1868, highly respected as a London merchant, politician and pottery manufacturer.

This bust was not for sale

See Colour Plate 36

B22 – DAPHNE

1860

Ht. large 21in. (53.34cm), small 13½in. (34.29cm)

Sculptor: Marshall Wood

Illus: Yes PP 585

Daphne, a Greek mythological nymph, was the daughter of the river-god Peneus, in Thessaly. She was pursued by Apollo, who was charmed by her beauty. She was not so keen on being taken by him so, at the point of his reaching her, she prayed for aid and was metamorphosed into a laurel tree, which later became known as daphne.The bust portrays Daphne in the process of being transformed into the embrace of the laurel.

In April 1887, the firm received this letter:

J.A.& H.E.Farnfield 90, Lower Thames Street London EC 6th April 1887

Gentlemen,

Mr Percy Wood, Sculptor, the son, and successor of his late Father Mr Marshall Wood, is now with us in reference to a bust of 'Daphne' which he purchased a few days since from Messrs Storey & Son of King William Street and Cannon Street EC. and which he at once saw was a representation of his Father's work. It must be evident to you that to reproduce the work of a sculptor for the purpose of profit to Yourselves without in any way remunerating the person whose brain conceived the idea, or his Executors if he be deceased, cannot be permitted. In these circumstances we shall be glad to hear from you in the matter. Our client, and his Mother (who was the Executor of her late husband) have no wish to run into legal proceedings but at the same time it must be perfectly clear to you that the sale of the small models must materially damage that of the replicas. Awaiting your early reply with some explanation of the matter.

We are Gentlemen Yours truly

J.A.& H.E.Farnfield.

Messrs W.T.Copeland & Sons

12 Charterhouse Street, EC.

This letter was answered on 12 April:

Messrs Farnfield London

Gents.

We have not been able to reply earlier to your favor of the 6th inst. The contents of which amaze us. The late Alderman Copeland purchased from the late Mr M.Wood the model and right to produce the work in question which we have ever since made and sold.

Yours faithfully

W.T. Copeland & Sons.

B22

Not having photocopiers in those days this answer presumably must have ended the matter. If not , the respective firms were close enough for easy communication in person. However, here is the text of the receipt from Marshall Wood to demonstrate that Copeland did not sink to copying sculptors' works without permission and proper compensation.

London Nov.2.1860

Received of Wm.T.Copeland Esq. the sum of Fifteen pounds in payment for a reduced model of Bust of 'Daphne' (Size 15 inches) together with all Copyright and interest in the same or coming from the same.

(Signed over Excise Stamp) Marshall Wood

£15.0.0

The SPB quotes 6 guineas for the large bust; this is confirmed 8/3/61. The small bust was priced at 22/6 trade and 34/- retail. In the NPL of 1873 the prices were £5.15.6 and £1.5.0, while the retail prices in 1876 were £8.18.6. and £1.17.6. The trade prices in c.1880 were £4.14.6 and 18/-, while in 1884 they were 31/6 > 63/- and 10/6. The making prices were 5/6 and 2/- respectively.

B23 – DRYDEN et al.

There is a list of busts in the 1848 catalogue, only one of which, that of Daniel O'Connell by J.E. Jones, was printed in upper case letters and with a handwritten price of 15/- added. All the rest were printed in upper and lower case letters.

The complete list is:

BUSTS:

DANIEL O'CONNELL by J.E. Jones.

Shakespeare. Lord Eldon.

B24

B25

Sir Walter Scott. Lord Lyndhurst.
Lord Byron. Sir R.Peel.
Milton. George the Fourth.
Ben Jonson. Nelson.
Thompson. Wellington.
Dryden.

There is no further evidence at the moment that four of these subjects were actually produced. These are Dryden, Lord Eldon, Ben Jonson and Thompson. It seems that the 1848 list was a list of projected subjects and that the four above were never made. There is no archival evidence for a bust of George IV, but it is believed that one was bought at auction some few years ago. Small busts of George IV and Wellington, both marked COPELAND & GARRETT are known in Felspar Porcelain.

B24 – ELAINE, or Elein
c.1876
Ht. 13in. (33.02cm) including socle
Sculptor: L.A. Malempré
Sponsor: Ceramic and Crystal Palace Art Union
Marks: L.A.MALEMPRE SCULPT CERAMIC & CRYSTAL PALACE ART UNION PUB'D 1876 F 77
Illus: Yes

Elaine was a heroine from the Arthurian Legends. She is variously held to have been:

1. Half-sister of King Arthur, by whom she bore a son, Mordred.
2. The daughter of King Pelles and mother of Lancelot's son, Sir Galahad.
3. 'The Lily Maid of Astolat' who pined, and died, for Lancelot.
4. The daughter of King Brandegoris who bore a child to Sir Bors de Ganis. In Sir Thomas Malory's *Morte d'Arthur* Elaine also may have been the name of the daughter.
5. The wife of Ban of Benoie (Brittany) and mother of Sir Lancelot.

However, the bust was most likely inspired by Tennyson's 'Elaine' from his *Idylls of the King*.

The only price information is the stocktake figure of 10/6 in November 1881 when the Art Union ceased to trade; five busts were returned to Stoke on 10 November. The making price was 1/4d.

See Colour Plate 37

B25 – ENID (Oenid) The Fair and the Good
1861
Ht. 11in. (27.94cm)
Sculptor: F.M. Miller
Sponsor: Crystal Palace Art Union
Marks: ENID F.M.MILLER SCULP CRYSTAL PALACE ART UNION
Illus: Yes PP 592, 624

Enid appeared originally in Chrestien de Troye's (c.1140/50-c.1190) Arthurian romantic legend *Erec and Enide*, in which she is cast in the role of a damsel in distress whom Erec rescues and marries. The story re-appears in the *Mabinigion* of the Welsh people as 'Geraint, son of

B25a

B27

Erbin', and again in Tennyson's *Idylls of the King* (Geraint and Enid) and it is probably this which inspired Miller's work.

The SPB records a price to the CPAU of 10/-, or of 20/- on pedestal (the SPB enters this bust under the name spelt Oenid). The making price was 1/-.

Examples are known with surface tinting, white enamel and gilded highlights. These are not mentioned in the PB.

B26 – ETTA
1874
Ht. 10¼in. (26.04cm)
Marks: ETTA JBB COPYRIGHT RESERVED
Illus: Yes PP 610
There is no archival reference to this bust in the Copeland records. At present, also, the identity of the girl is not known.

B26

B27 – EVANGELINE
1861
Ht. 11in. (27.94cm)
Sculptor: F.M. Miller
Marks: EVANGELINE F.M.MILLER Sc. Pub Oct 1 1861
Illus: Yes PP 618, 624
The name Evangeline is from the Greek and means 'Bringer of Good News'. The portrayal is from Longfellow's idyllic poem *Evangeline*, published in 1847. This poem's inspiration stems from the tragic circumstances surrounding the romance of Evangeline and her lover Gabriel. The tragedy came about from the removal of the Acadians from Nova Scotia by the British in 1755. Evangeline and Gabriel become separated and spend the remainder of their lives seeking one another, but unsuccessfully.

The bust may have a printed inscription:
EVANGELINE
'DOWN THE LONG STREET SHE PASSED,
WITH HER CHAPLET OF PEARLS AND HER MISSAL,
WEARING HER NORMAN CAP.' LONGFELLOW

The SPB quotes 9/- and 18/- for the bust mounted on 'fluted pedestal'. There is a price also of 13/- if in 'ivory'. This is probably in ivory earthenware. The making price was 1/-

B28

B29

B30

B28 – EVENING STAR
c.1860
Ht. 10½in. (26.67cm)
Illus: Yes
A simple representation of Venus with a star upon her forehead.

Included in the SPB at 15/- trade and 21/- retail. In 1873 the NPL price was 12/- with the retail price in 1876 at 18/-. In the c.1880 NPL the price was 9/-; in 1884 it was 7/-. The making price was 1/4d.

B29 – FLORA
1848 or earlier
Ht. 10½in. (25.4cm)
Illus: Yes PP 600
Flora was the Roman goddess of flowers and spring; a festival, the Floralia, was held in her honour every year from 28 April to 3 May. It was an occasion for great merriment and lasciviousness!

This subject might be the 'delicate portrait-bust of a young woman' which was produced at the very commencement of the 'parian phenomenon'. It undoubtedly provided the inspiration for 'Evening Star'.

It is listed in the 1848 catalogue and priced at £1.0.0. It is priced in the SPB at 15/- and 21/-. By 1873 the trade price was 12/- and the retail price in 1876 was 18/-. In c.1880 the trade price was 9/- and in 1884 7/-. Although these prices run parallel with those for 'Evening Star', the making price was 2d more at 1/6d.

B30 – GLADSTONE, William Ewart
c.1884
Ht. 12in. (30.48cm)
Sculptor: Owen Hale
Illus: Yes
Born in Liverpool in 1809, Gladstone died at Hawarden Castle, North Wales, in 1898. The son of Sir John Gladstone Bt., a successful Liverpool merchant, Gladstone became an eminent statesman, financier and orator. His political career spanned the years 1832-1894, during which time he enjoyed high office on many occasions. He was prime minister four times for a total of fourteen years. Originally he was a Tory, but later he embraced liberalism. Despite offers of a peerage, he consistently declined, and thus became known as 'The Great Commoner'.

Gladstone found time for interests other than politics, one of which was a profound interest in ceramics. He was well known as a collector of Wedgwood ware and came to the Potteries to lay the foundation stone of the Wedgwood Institute in Burslem on 26 October 1863. In about 1865 he agreed to become President of the Ceramic and Crystal Palace Art Union.

Eliza Meteyard dedicated her *Life of Josiah Wedgwood* to Gladstone. In about the following year Wedgwood produced a portrait bust of Palmerston, sculpted by E.W. Wyon in 'Carrara', the white parian body, and made in two sizes.

Gladstone was given the cold shoulder at the time due, perhaps, to the personal antipathy of Francis Wedgwood. However, a bust of him was produced in 1879, sculpted by J.E. Boehm.

Only in 1884 is there a price mentioned in a Copeland price list; this was 5/- > 7/6. The making price was 1/-.

B31 – GRIEF, or **Sorrow**
B32 – JOY
c.1851
Ht. 5in. (12.7cm)
Sculptor: Raffaele Monti
Illus: Yes
These two small busts are included in the list of 'Additional works now ready' published in about 1851. The price then was 7/6 each. The SPB, which lists 'Grief' over half-way down the page, but still amongst the

B33

early subjects, quotes 2/6 trade and 4/- retail. 'Joy' is priced the same. The making price was 2d each.

B33 – HAPPY DREAM
1875
Ht. 12in. (30.48cm
Sculptor: L.A. Malempré
Sponsor: Ceramic and Crystal Palace Art Union
Marks: HAPPY DREAM L.A.MALEMPRE SCULPT CERAMIC AND CRYSTAL PALACE ART UNION

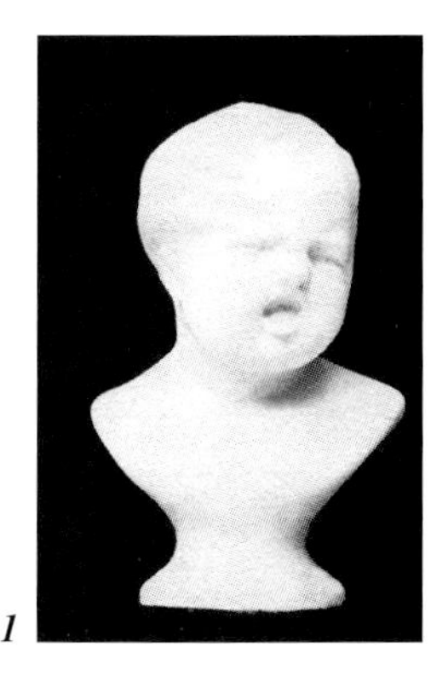

B31

B32

B34

Illus: Yes PP 595
This was, perhaps, one of the more disappointing subjects sponsored by the Union! She does not look very happy either!

At the stock take of 1881, when the Union ceased trading, forty busts of 'Happy Dream' were returned to Stoke! This was by far the largest number of any item which Copeland had to accept back. Not such a happy dream, more a nightmare! The price was 10/6 at valuation. The making price was 1/4d.

B34 – HAVELOCK
1858
Ht. 9½in. (24.13cm)
Sculptor: R. Morrison
Illus: Yes PP 623
A distinguished British general who served in India during the Indian Mutiny. A contemporary of Generals Campbell and Outram, he saw action with both at Lucknow and Cawnpore. His published notes on the First Afghan War were a commercial failure.

This is one of the three portrait busts issued to honour British army commanders of the Indian Mutiny, the others being Campbell and Outram. *The Parian Phenomenon* mentions 'Indian Heroes. A miniature series of busts depicting heroes of the Indian Mutiny. c.1858'. This must refer to the three busts of Campbell, Havelock and Outram.

Privately commissioned, the SPB quotes 12/6 trade and 21/- retail. The making price was 8d.

B35

B36

B35 – HOP QUEEN
1873
Ht. 14in. (35.56cm)
Sculptor: J. Durham
Sponsor: Ceramic and Crystal Palace Art Union
Marks: HOP QUEEN J DURHAM ARA PUB JANUARY 1873 CERAMIC AND CRYSTAL PALACE ART UNION
Illus: Yes PP 589
The 'Hop Queen' may have been intended as a companion bust to the 'May Queen' (q.v.). She may have her origins in an ancient fertility rite or festival to render thanks for a satisfactory harvest. The hop plant, *Humulus lupulus,* is a twining climber which bears male and female flowers on separate plants in autumn. The female flower spikes become drooping clusters of 'hops' which are gathered to act as a flavouring to beer.

An original terra cotta example is in the Royal Museum and Art Gallery, Canterbury, Kent.

In 1881 the price was 10/6; making price 1/6d.

B36 – JUNO, after the antique, large
c.1850
Ht. 25in. (63.5cm)
Sculptor: W. Theed
Illus: Yes
Juno was identified by the Romans with the Greek Hera. As Jupiter is the king of heaven and of the gods, so Juno is the queen of heaven and is the wife and sister of Jupiter. She was regarded as the protectress of marriage and the life-long guardian of 'womankind'. The month of June, originally called Junonius, was considered to be the most favourable period for marrying.

Juno is often portrayed dressed in a goatskin, bearing a shield and a spear, and sometimes accompanied by a sacred serpent. Like Saturn, she was the guardian of the finances and under the name Moneta (the origin of the English word 'money') she had a temple on the Capitoline Hill which contained the mint.

The original sculpture of this portrait bust is in the Museo Nazionale in Rome.

The Copeland bust was displayed at the Great Exhibition in 1851. The prices in the SPB are 6 guineas trade and 10 guineas retail; these prices were held in 1873 and 1876. In c.1880 the trade price fell to £4.14.6 and to 52/6 in 1884. The making price was 8/-.

B37 – JUNO, after the antique, small
1865
Ht. 12in. (30.48cm)
Sculptor: L.A. Malempré
Sponsor: Ceramic and Crystal Palace Art Union
Marks: MALEMPRE COPIO 1865 CERAMIC AND CRYSTAL PALACE ART UNION
Illus: Yes PP 588
There were a number of variations made of this bust. The SPB lists: Juno, small, CPAU 10/-; gilt & tinted (pale green and white enamel) 14/-; on tall fluted pedestal Gilt &c 20/; similar Gilt & chased & tinted light green (new style) 21/-. Making price 1/8 (bust only).

B38 – KILLICK
1854
The only evidence that Copeland may have made such a bust is the reference in the SPB to 'Killick 1/4/54'. No price.

B39

B39 – KOSSUTH
1860
Ht. 8in. (20.32cm)
Marks: KOSSUTH
Illus: Yes PP 611
Lajos, or Louis, Kossuth was born at Monok in Hungary in 1802 and died in Italy in 1894. He was a Hungarian patriot and political leader endowed with a keen perception of the power of the press. Despite the opposition, even persecution, of the Austrian authorities who seized his presses, Kossuth persisted in promulgating his beliefs by using the newly introduced lithographic process to continue his newspaper. In 1837 he was imprisoned for three years by the Austrians. Despite this, in 1848-49 he headed the Hungarian insurrection. It has been said that from 1837 to 1848 the history of Hungary is that of Kossuth. He was Minister of Finance in the independent Hungarian ministry, eventually becoming governor in 1849.

In 1851 Kossuth took up residence in England whither he had fled to escape further persecution in his homeland. By his presence he unwittingly caused a hiatus in Queen Victoria's relationship with her Foreign Secretary, Lord Palmerston. Palmerston incurred the Queen's wrath by agreeing to meet Kossuth. Lord John Russell was commanded to forbid such an occurrence. This he did with the consent and support of the Cabinet, but Palmerston reacted violently and the meeting appears to have taken place. Kossuth was popular. In addition to the bust by Copeland, he was commemorated by two transfer-printed plates: one shows a half-length portrait captioned 'Louis Kossuth', while the other shows a family group of his wife and three children.

Kossuth died in exile in Turin in 1894.

While Copeland produced a portrait bust of Gladstone, he did not make one of Palmerston.

The SPB lists 12/6 trade and 21/- retail, with a coloured and gilt version at 21/-. The making price was 1/-.

B40 – LESBIA, Companion to **Oenone**
1859
Ht. large 15in. (38.1cm), small 11in. (27.94cm)
Sculptor: W.C. Marshall
Sponsor: Ceramic and Crystal Palace Art Union
Marks: LESBIA W.C.MARSHALL RA SCULPT PUB SEPT 1 1859
Illus: Yes PP 587
According to Appuleius the real name of Lesbia was Clodia, the favourite of Catullus. He was the Roman poet, contemporary of Cicero, Caesar, Pollio, etc. Lesbia forms the theme of Catullus' amatory poems and is not, as is claimed sometimes, the sister of the demagogue Clodius, slain by Milo.

The bust was priced in the SPB at 10/6, reduced later to 10/-, and marked CPAU. There is also a version using the 15in. bust mounted on a fluted pedestal and gilded at 21/-; the pedestal for this was 7/6. The PP illustration shows this at Fig. 587. The making price for the bust was 1/.

Although the smaller bust exists, there is no reference to there being two sizes in the price records.

At the close of the Art Union, two busts were in stock at Stoke in November 1881, valued at £1.0.0.

On some busts a few lines of verse, printed in brown, are found.

B40

B41

B42

B41 – JENNY LIND
1847
Ht. 8¾in. (22.23cm)
Sculptor: J. Durham
Marks: MLLE.JENNY LIND 1847 JOSEPH DURHAM SC 1847 REDUCED BY B. CHEVERTON NOV 1847
Illus: Yes
Born in Stockholm, Sweden, in 1820, Jenny Lind died in Malvern, England, in 1887. A famous Swedish singer sometimes known as 'The Swedish Nightingale', she first appeared in Stockholm in 1838 and thereafter in France, Germany, England and America. She married Otto Goldschmidt, conductor and composer, in Boston, Mass. on 5 February 1852. She was professor of Singing at the Royal College of Music 1883-86.

This bust was included in the 1848 catalogue with the comment 'The following are just ready, BUST OF JENNY LIND, by J.Durham. 15/-'. (The price was written in pencil.)

In the SPB the trade price was 10/-, while the retail price was 15/-. The making price was 8d.

B42 – LOVE
1871
Ht. 13¼in. (33.66cm)
Sculptor: Raffaele Monti
Sponsor: Ceramic and Crystal Palace Art Union
Marks: R MONTI SEPT 1871 CERAMIC AND CRYSTAL PALACE ART UNION
Illus: Yes PP 618
The SPB quotes 10/-. There was a gilded and tinted version at 15/-. In 1881 the stock at Stoke was two busts valued at 10/- each. The making price was 1/6d.

B43 – LOW
1859
Sculptor:J. Critenden
Illus: Yes PP 485B
Sir John Low was born in 1788 and, after a distinguished career in the Indian Army, died in 1880. Low was an advocate of common sense and understanding of the Indian princes and the native problems. In April 1858, when the Indian Mutiny was almost suppressed, Low returned home and received the grateful thanks of the Indian Government. 'No man knew the temper of the natives better.'

There is a price of 10/6 trade quoted in the SPB.

B44 – LORD LYNDHURST
c.1850
Born John Singleton Copley at Boston, Mass. in 1772, the son of J.S. Copley, a distinguished Anglo-American portrait painter. He graduated from Trinity College, Cambridge, going on to become a noted English jurist. John Copley entered the English Parliament in 1818, rising to the

B43

B46

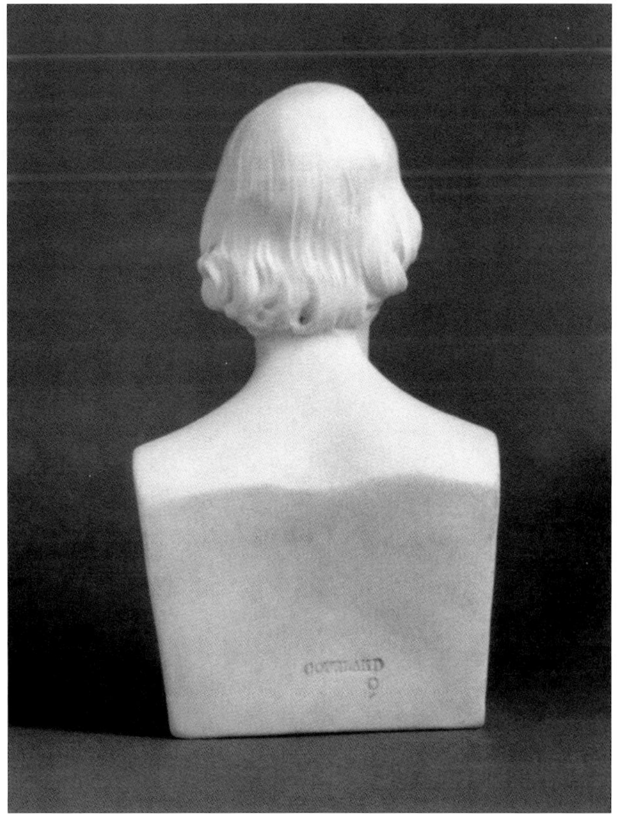

B46a

offices of Solicitor-General (1819), Attorney-General (1824-26), eventually becoming Lord Chancellor (1827-30, 1834, 1841-1845). He was created Baron Lyndhurst in 1827. He died in 1863.

The portrait bust is listed (in upper and lower case letters) in the 1848 catalogue. It is recorded in the SPB at 31/6 trade.

One of the 'unidentified gentlemen' may prove to be Lord Lyndhurst.

B45 – MARS
Life size
The only record is the making price of 6/-.

B46 – MARTIN
c.1860
Ht. 5¾in. (14.61cm)
Sponsor: possibly the National Choral Society
Marks: G.W. MARTIN
Illus: Yes
George William Martin was born in 1828 and died in 1881. He was Professor of Music at 'The Wormal College for Army Schoolmasters'. He conducted the National Schools Choral Festival, held at the Crystal Palace, in 1859. He established the National Choral Society in 1860. In 1864 Martin organised a choir of a thousand voices to sing the *Macbeth* music at Shakespeare's 300th anniversary.

The price of 3/6 (trade) is recorded in the SPB.

B48

B47 – MASTERMAN
1852
Sculptor: J. Sherwood Westmacott
Illus: Yes PP615
Previously unrecognised (see page 197), this has now been identified as John Masterman, a prominent banker in London and an MP for the City of London in 1847.
The SPB gives the prices as 12/6 trade and 21/- retail. The making price was 1/-.

B48 – MAY QUEEN
1868
Ht. 13in. (33.02cm)
Sculptor: J. Durham
Sponsor: Ceramic and Crystal Palace Art Union
Marks: J. DURHAM SC. PUB MAY 1 1868 CERAMIC AND CRYSTAL PALACE ART UNION
Illus: Yes PP 588
The 'May Queen', or 'Queen of the May', has been associated with the 'May Day' festival for centuries. The old Celtic year was divided into four parts, each beginning with a great celebration. The second one of these feasts was held on 1 May and was known as Beltane; it was dedicated to Belenus, god of herd and harvest, and was the origin of May Day. The maypole, which became the centre of local feasts, was an ancient symbol of fertility.

The Copeland busts present a conundrum. Two are listed in the SPB: 'May Queen Bust 15/- 25/-' (early in the list of 'M' subjects) and 'May Queen, new Bust 10/6, reduced to 10/-, and 15/-, raised on 17/1/74 to 16/6'. Also, 'May Queen Bust on fluted pedestal tinted & gilt 20/- C&CPAU'. The other prices for the earlier bust are: 1873, 12/-; 1876, 18/-; c.1880, 9/-; 1884, 7/-. The making price is 1/4d.

It must be the 'new' bust that was made for the C & CPAU because the only later price for that is the valuation of 10/- each for ten busts in stock at Stoke in 1881, with another four returned from London. In 1884 there is a hand-written note 'as CPAU 10/6'.

B49 – McCULLOCH
1860
Ht. 9¼in. (23.5cm)
Marks: I.R. McCULLOCH SP (in monogram)
Illus: Yes PP 606
A leading statistician and political economist, John Ramsey McCulloch was born at Whithorn, Wigtownshire in 1789. He wrote many articles, treatises, books, etc. including *A Dictionary, Practical, Theoretical, and Historical of Commerce and Commercial Navigation.* His works were translated into French, German and Italian. He died in 1864.

The price quoted in the SPB is 12/6. There is no other archival reference.

B49

B50

B50 – MILTON
1865
Ht. 13½in. (34.29cm)
Sculptor: M. Noble
Sponsor: Ceramic and Crystal Palace Art Union
Marks: M. NOBLE Sc. LONDON NOVEMBER 20 1865 CERAMIC AND CRYSTAL PALACE ART UNION
Illus: Yes PP 609
The celebrated English poet, son of John Milton, a scrivener, was born in 1608 and died in 1674. He entered Christ's College, Cambridge in 1624 and graduated in 1629. Most of his Latin poems were written during this period. He first married at the age of thirty-five, his wife being aged seventeen. She left him after one month but returned some years later to bear him three daughters. She died in 1652, the year in which Milton became totally blind. John Milton took a second wife (1656-8) and a third in 1663 who survived him. His universally acclaimed poem *Paradise Lost* was commenced in 1658 and published in 1667. *Paradise Re-gained* appeared in 1671.

A bust of Milton is included in the 1848 catalogue with the handwritten price of 15/-. This is illustrated in PP 611; its height is 7in. (17.78cm). An example is also known in COPELAND & GARRETT'S FELSPAR PORCELAIN. The SPB quotes 10/6 and 15/-; 1873, 7/6; 1876, 11/6; c.1880, 7/6; 1884, 5/-. Making price 8d.

The C&CPAU bust 10/-; making 1/6; 1884 7/6.

B50A – MINERVA
1857
The *Staffordshire Advertiser,* in its edition for 16 May 1857, while commenting on the most recent productions from Alderman Copeland's manufactory, noted 'a massive and beautiful column, of a new design, surmounted by a bust of Minerva, standing eight feet high, and said to be amongst the largest works in ceramic art.' No record of this bust has been found in the Copeland records.

Minerva is identified with the Greek goddess Athena. She was worshipped as the goddess of wisdom and the patroness of all the arts and trades. Minerva also guided men in the dangers of war, so she is represented wearing a helmet. There were many sculptures which Copeland might have copied and one could have been after the antique Athena Albani.

B51 – MIRANDA, partner to **Ophelia**
1859
Ht. 10¾in. (27.31cm)
Sculptor: W. Calder Marshall
Sponsor: Crystal Palace Art Union
Marks: MIRANDA W.C. MARSHALL RA SCULPT.
Illus: Yes PP 593
A character from William Shakespeare's *Tempest.* The daughter of Prospero, she was loved by Ferdinand. Her nature has been described as embodying the very elements of womanhood: beauty, modesty and tenderness. The Latin meaning of Miranda is 'admirable'.

The SPB quotes 10/6 reduced to 10/-, and a retail price of 17/- in 1881. There is also a version mounted on a fluted pedestal (no tinting) at 19/-. Making price of 1/4d.

A few lines of verse are printed on some early examples.

B51

B52

B53

B52 – THE MOTHER, companion to **The Bride**
1871
Ht. 15in. (38.1cm)
Sculptor: Raffaele Monti
Sponsor: Ceramic and Crystal Palace Art Union
Marks: R. MONTI 1871 CERAMIC AND CRYSTAL PALACE ART UNION
Illus: Yes PP 586
The price in the SPB is 21/-; this was still the valuation in 1881 for the two busts in stock at Stoke. In 1884 they were offered to the trade for 14/-. The making price was 3/-.

B53 – MUSIC, companion to **Poetry**
1874
Ht. 14in. (35.56cm)
Sculptor: L.A. Malempré
Marks: MUSIC L.A.MALEMPRE Sc 1874
The retail price in 1876 was £1.2.6. The trade price in c.1880 was 10/6, falling to 8/- in 1884. The making price was 1/8d.

B54 – NAPIER, Admiral Sir Charles
1854
Ht. 11⅜in. (28.89cm)
Sculptor: James Sherwood Westmacott
Marks: J. SHERWOOD WESTMACOTT SCULPT 1854
Illus: Yes PP 485A
Born near Falkirk in 1786, Sir Charles Napier died in 1860. He was the second son of Captain Charles Napier and cousin to Sir Charles James

B54

B55

B55a

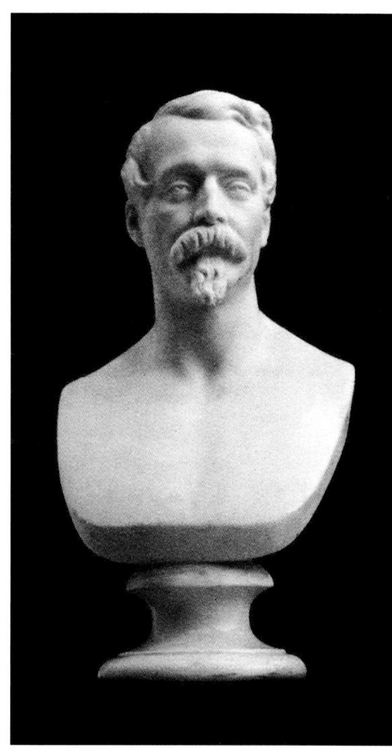

B56

Napier, a distinguished British general. He entered the navy in 1799, attaining the rank of admiral in 1858. During his career he served in the Potomac Expedition to America. He commanded the Portuguese fleet for a time for which he was created 'Count Cape St. Vincent'. Later he commanded the Baltic Fleet during the Crimean War and was severely criticised for refusing to storm Cronstadt. In 1842 he entered Parliament, and also wrote *War in Syria*.

The SPB quotes 16/- trade and 25/- retail. In 1873 the NPL quotes 14/-, with the retail price in 1876 of £1.1.0.The c.1880 price was 9/-, falling to 5/- in 1884. The making price was 1/-.

B55 – NAPOLEON the First, Bonaparte
1852
Ht. 11¾in.(29.85cm)
Sculptor: W. Theed
Illus: Yes PP 602
Napoleon Bonaparte, who became Napoleon 1st, Emperor of France, from 1804-1814, was born in Corsica in 1769 and died on the island of St. Helena in 1821. He was first commissioned in the French army in 1785 as a lieutenant, having spent the previous six years at various military schools. He proved to be a brilliant tactical commander who subdued most of Europe, Britain being the exception. His plan to attack India by way of Egypt was foiled by Nelson's outstanding victory at the Battle of the Nile (Aboukir Bay) on 1-2 August 1798. He concluded the Peace Treaty of Amiens between Great Britain, France and Spain in 1802, but his subsequent conduct provoked Britain into declaring war on France yet again in 1805. The failure of his projected invasion of England was followed by Nelson's victory at Trafalgar in 1805.

Napoleon's attack on Russia culminating in the enforced retreat from Moscow in 1812 saw the beginning of his decline. On his abdication in 1814 he retired to Elba. However, in an attempt to regain his former glory, Napoleon left Elba in February 1815 to lead an insurrection only to be vanquished finally at the Battle of Waterloo on 18 June 1815 by the Duke of Wellington's forces. Napoleon was banished for life to St. Helena, where he died. He had married Josephine de Beauharnais in 1796, divorced her in 1809 and married Maria Louisa of Austria in 1810.

Napoleon's activities caused considerable alarm in Britain and, in an attempt to give a boost to morale, a number of satirical prints lampooning Napoleon were issued. These were popular around the turn of the 18th/19th century and were used by potters to decorate jugs and mugs, a number of which emanated from the Spode factory. A later wall tile is recorded also which carries the mark of COPELAND & GARRETT, LATE SPODE. (See 'Politics on Pottery' by David Drakard, *Country Life* 6 December 1984. Also, *Spode Transfer-Printed Ware* by David Drakard and Paul Holdway, pp.130-145, Antique Collectors' Club 2002.)

The SPB has 16/- and 25/-. In 1873 £1.0.0; 1876 £1.0.0; c.1880 9/-; 1884 7/-. The making price was 1/4d.

B56 – EMPEROR NAPOLEON III
c.1878
Ht. 8½in. (21.59cm)
Sculptor: J.E. Jones
Illus: Yes PP 605
Born in Paris in 1808, he died at Chislehurst, Kent, in 1873. Charles Louis Napoleon Bonaparte was the son of Louis Bonaparte, King of Holland, and Hortense de Beauharnais. He was the nephew of Napoleon I. He served as Emperor of France from 1852 to 1870. A veritable firebrand, who appears to have spent his entire life trying to emulate his illustrious uncle, he indulged in a series of insurrections, mutinies, coup d'états and any other nefarious mischief that occurred to him. He took part in the Crimean War (1854-6) and waged war in Mexico (1862-7).

He was a complete despot. In 1870 he declared war on the King of Prussia in July and his forces were defeated totally at Sedan on 2 September. Two days later his regime was overthrown. He died in exile. The SPB quotes for two sorts:

Napoleon 3rd	Bust	10/6	18/-
" with drapery	"	12/6	21/-

In c.1880, the trade price was 8/-; in 1884, 5/-.

B57

B57 – NELSON, Horatio, First Viscount Nelson
1848
Ht. large 13in. (33.02cm), small 11in. (27.94cm)
Illus: Yes PP 613
Born in Norfolk in 1758, he died aboard HMS *Victory* at the Battle of Trafalgar on 21 October 1805. Horatio Nelson, Britain's most famous admiral, entered the navy in 1770, aged twelve years. He was made post-captain whilst serving in the American War of Independence. Throughout his twenty-five years' service in the Royal Navy, Nelson was present at many vital engagements. The most significant were Cape St. Vincent in 1797 (under Admiral Jervis, later Earl St. Vincent); the Battle of the Nile (Aboukir Bay) in 1798 as Commodore; Copenhagen in 1801 as Vice-Admiral. It was after Copenhagen that he was created Viscount, having been knighted in 1797. He had lost one eye on active service off Corsica and his right arm in an abortive attack on Teneriffe.

Nelson married Mrs Fanny Nesbitt, a widow with one son, on 12 March 1787, a marriage which foundered consequent upon the well-publicised attachment of Nelson to Emma, Lady Hamilton.

During the Spode period Nelson, as with Napoleon, was commemorated by way of transfer-printed pottery and bone china. (See 'Heroes, Trophies and Tea-cups' by David Drakard, *Country Life*, 6 March 1986. Also *Spode Transfer Printed Ware 1784-1833* by Drakard and Holdway, p.129, Antique Collectors' Club. 2002.)

The prices for the two sizes were:

	SPB	1873	1876	c.1882	1884
Large	21/- 31/6	£1.4.0	£1.16.0	18/6	10/6
Small	16/- 25/-	14/-	£1. 0.0	9/-	5/-

The making prices were 1/9 and 1/-.

B58 – EMPEROR NICHOLAS OF RUSSIA
1848
Ht. 8½in. (21.59cm)
Sculptor: Count D'Orsay
Illus: Yes
Born in 1796, Nicholas I, the third son of Paul I, succeeded his brother Alexander I as Czar of Russia in 1825. He engaged in war with Persia (1826-8), Turkey (1827-9) and suppressed a Polish insurrection in 1830-1. His war against Turkey in 1853 brought him into conflict with Britain and France and developed into the Crimean War (1854-6). He died in 1855.

The SPB quotes 10/6 trade and 15/- retail. The making price was 8d.

B58

B58A

B59

B58A – **MATTHEW NOBLE**
1876
Marks: 1876
Illus: Yes PP 604
The identity of this bust rests on its likeness to an illustration of Matthew Noble which appeared in the *Illustrated London News* of 8 July 1876, accompanied by his obituary. This coincides with Noble's death and the date on the back of the bust. There is no known reference in the Copeland archives to a bust of Noble having been made, but the evidence of the bust is from *The Parian Phenomenon* where it is stated 'Subject unknown'. So this attribution is tentative.

Matthew Noble (1817-1876) was born in Hackness, near Scarborough, Yorkshire. Having trained in London as a sculptor under J. Francis, he exhibited at the Royal Academy in the years between 1845 and 1869. He executed five items for Copeland. (See Sculptors.)

B59 – DANIEL O'CONNELL
1848
Ht. 9⅜in. (23.81cm)
Sculptor: John E. Jones
Marks: Danl. O'Connell J.E. JONES Sculp 1846
Reduced by B Cheverton COPELAND'S PORCELAIN STATUARY
Illus: Yes PP 617
Born in County Kerry, Ireland, in 1775, O'Connell was famous as an advocate. He founded the Catholic Association and led the cause of Catholic emancipation. In 1843 he was arrested for his political activities and convicted of conspiracy and sedition; this conviction was reversed in 1844.

The bust was listed in the 1848 catalogue at 15/- (retail). The date on the sculpture is probably that when Jones sculpted the marble.

This price appears also in the SPB with the trade price of 10/6. In 1873, the trade price was 8/- and the retail price was 12/- in 1876. The NPL for c.1880 shows 7/- and 4/- in 1884. The making price was 1/-.

The mark Danl O'Connell is in manuscript, with the 'l' raised above the line of the other letters.

A record of an engraved copper plate is in the Copeland Badge Book. A letter dated 14 May 1848 from O'Connell to Jones praises his sculpture.

> My dear Jones, The bust is admirable – as a work of art it does you the greatest credit and it is a most striking likeness – infinitely more like than any other bust attempted of me – My friends are unanimous in approving of it most highly both for execution and correct resemblance. Believe me to be Very faithfully yours, Daniel O'Connell.

B60 – OENONE
1861
Ht. 11½in. (29.21cm), on pedestal 16⅜in.(41.59cm)
Sculptor: W. Calder Marshall
Sponsor: Crystal Palace Art Union
Marks: OENONE. W.C.MARSHALL RA SCULPT. PUB. JAN 1 1860

B60

B61

BY W.T.COPELAND CRYSTAL PALACE ART UNION
Illus: Yes PP 587, 592
This bust may have been inspired by Tennyson's poem of that name and from which this extract is taken and printed on early busts:

OENONE
HITHER CAME AT NOON
MOURNFUL OENONE, WANDERING FORLORN
OF PARIS, ONCE HER PLAYMATE ON THE HILLS,
HER CHEEK HAD LOST THE ROSE, AND ROUND HER NECK
FLOATED HER HAIR OR SEEMED TO FLOAT IN REST.
TENNYSON

Oenone was the wife forsaken by Paris, a shepherd from the Mt. Ida region. Paris was chosen by the gods to adjudicate between the competing charms of Hera, Athena and Aphrodite. Paris signified his choice by presenting a golden apple inscribed 'To the most fair' to Aphrodite who promised him the fairest of women as a wife. He then forsook Oenone and, under Aphrodite's protection, he abducted Helen, the wife of Menelaus. This gave rise to the Trojan War, in which Paris was wounded. He returned to Oenone for succour, only to be rejected. Paris died of his wounds and in a fit of remorse Oenone killed herself.
The SPB quotes several versions:

Oenone		Bust	10/-
"	Slightly col'd & gilt	"	14/-
"	on pedestal " " "	"	20/-

The pedestal is fluted in Corinthian style. The making price was 1/4.
See Colour Plate 38

B61 – OPHELIA, partner to **Miranda**
1859
Ht. large 11¾in. (29.85cm), small 10½in. (26.67cm)
Sculptor: W. Calder Marshall
Sponsor: Crystal Palace Art Union
Marks: OPHELIA W.C.MARSHALL RA CRYSTAL PALACE ART UNION
Illus: Yes PP 591
Ophelia is the daughter of Polonius in Shakespeare's play *Hamlet.* She becomes unhinged when she is abandoned by Hamlet and is drowned when gathering flowers by the side of a stream. Ophelia was issued as a companion to Miranda.
The SPB lists several items:

CPAU	Ophelia	large	Bust	52/6
"	"	small	"	10/6
		reduced to		10/-
"	"	small slightly col'd & gilt		15/-
"	"	" on pedestal "	"	20/-

One bust at 10/- was returned to Stoke in 1881. The single making price of the bust was 1/4.

B62 – SIR JAMES OUTRAM
c.1858
Ht. probably about 10in. (25.4cm)
Sculptor: ? R. Morrison
Born in Derbyshire in 1803, Outram was an English general who

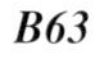

B63

B64

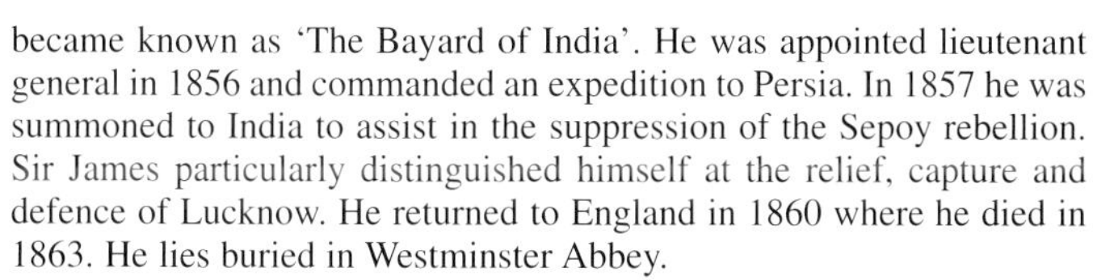

became known as 'The Bayard of India'. He was appointed lieutenant general in 1856 and commanded an expedition to Persia. In 1857 he was summoned to India to assist in the suppression of the Sepoy rebellion. Sir James particularly distinguished himself at the relief, capture and defence of Lucknow. He returned to England in 1860 where he died in 1863. He lies buried in Westminster Abbey.

The bust was issued to honour British Army commanders of the 'Indian Mutiny' – see also Campbell (B15) and Havelock (B34). Outram was appointed a KGCB in 1857 and created a Baronet in November 1858.

The price in the SPB gives 16/- trade and 25/- retail, which suggests that it is a companion to the large bust of Campbell. The making price was 10d.

B63 – SIR ROBERT PEEL
1850
Ht. 10¼in. (26.04cm)
Sculptor: J.S. Westmacott
Marks: JAMES S.WESTMACOTT Sculpt. PUBLISHED AUGT.13TH 1850
Illus: Yes PP 615
Born near Bury in Lancashire in 1788, the son of Sir Robert Peel, a successful calico printer. He was elected MP for Cashel in Ireland in 1809 and held the post of Secretary for Ireland from 1812-18. Peel initially opposed Catholic emancipation, but later changed his views and became a leading proponent of the cause. He is remembered for instituting the regular Irish Constabulary who became known as 'Peelers', a sobriquet later applied to the police generally. Sir Robert Peel held the post of prime minister from 1834-5, and again from 1841-6. He died in 1850.
The SPB lists:

Peel, large	Bust 21/- 1/6
" small	" 12/6 21/-

It is listed in the 1848 catalogue but without any handwritten price. It may be a partner to Lord Byron where the prices for the large 17in. (43.18cm) and small 7in. (17.78cm) are similar. The one making price was 10d, presumably for the smaller bust.
See Colour Plate 39

B64 – POETRY, companion to **Music**
1874
Ht. 14in. (35.56cm)
Sculptor: L.A. Malempré
Marks: L.A. MALEMPRE Sc. 1874
Illus: Yes PP 603
The retail price in 1876 was £1.2.6. The NPL of c.1880 quoted 10/6 and this had fallen to 8/6 in 1884. The making price was 1/8d.

B65 – PURITY
1860
Ht. 13¼in. (33.66cm)
Sculptor: M. Noble

B65

B68

B69

Sponsor: Crystal Palace Art Union
Marks: CERAMIC AND CRYSTAL PALACE ART UNION PUB. NOVEMBER 1860
Illus: Yes PP 595
The bust is taken from the full length statuette of Purity. An engraving of this subject appeared in the *Art-Journal* of 1859.

The prices given in the SPB are 10/- and 15/- 'col'd & Gilt'. The valuation of the remainder stock in 1881 also was 10/- each, but in 1884 the wholesale price was 7/6 to 15/-. The making price was 1/8d.

There does not appear to be any evidence that this figure might have been intended to have portrayed the Greek goddess Aphrodite.

B66 – JAMES RAMSDEN
The entry 'Ramsden, Jas Esq.' occurs in the SPB at 16/6d trade. It will have been a private commission. The making price was 10d.

There was a Reverend Henry James Ramsden, born 1837, died 8 December 1862.

B67 – ROUSSEAU
A bust of Rousseau, with a Copeland & Garrett mark, has been seen by G. Fisk, a member of the Spode Society. There is no reference to it in any Copeland archival material known to the author.

B68 – RUSSELL, LORD JOHN
1854
Ht. 11¼in.(28.58cm)
Marks: PUBLISHED MARCH 1 1854
Illus: Yes
Born in London in 1792, the third son of the sixth Duke of Bedford, Lord John Russell became an eminent statesman, orator and author. He entered Parliament as a Whig in 1813, after having first studied at Edinburgh, and he rapidly established a reputation as a great 19th century reformer. His most illustrious cause was the Reform Bill which was passed in 1832. Throughout Lord Russell's parliamentary career he held most of the major governmental offices culminating in that of prime minister from 1865-66. He was created Earl Russell in 1861 and died in 1878. Perhaps because of his involvement with the Reform Bill he is the most widely featured politician on ceramic commemorative items.

The SPB quotes 16/- and 25/-. In the NPL of 1873 the price was 14/-, while the retail price in 1876 was £1.0.0. In c.1880 the net price was 10/6 dropping to 6/6 in 1884.

B69 – LORD SALISBURY
1878
Ht. 12in. (30.48cm)
Sculptor: L.A. Malempré
Marks: SALISBURY. PROTECTED ACT 54 GEO III L.G.& CO 9/9/78 L.A.MALEMPRE Sc.
Illus: Yes PP 616
Born in 1830 as Robert Arthur Talbot Gascoyne Cecil, the second son of the second Marquis of Salisbury, he was first known as Lord Robert Cecil and later by the courtesy title of Viscount Cranborne. He succeeded his father in 1868. He entered Parliament in 1854 as Tory M.P. for Stamford, in Lincolnshire, and subsequently held a number of eminent public offices including the Chancellorship of Oxford University. During the years 1885-1902 he was prime minister on four occasions, playing the dual role of premier and foreign secretary for much of the time. He died in 1903.

In the NPL of c.1880 this bust was offered at 9/-, falling to 5/- in 1884. The making price was 1/-.

B70

B70 – SIR WALTER SCOTT

The records suggest that five different busts of Sir Walter Scott were made, and it is not absolutely certain which is which, and so it is difficult to state a date when each was introduced.

The SPB lists the following:

				Making price
Scott to match	large Byron	21/-	31/6	2/9
"	small	10/6	15/-	9d
"	new 24in.	31/6	52/6	7/-
"	Extra Large Fictile Marble	7 Gns	-	
C&CPAU Scott Sir W. Bust c.Feb 1870		10/-	1/2	

It looks as if the prices of 31/6 and 52/6 for a 24in. (60.96cm) bust are much too low and it may be that this item is the same as the 'Extra Large' one; this would relate to the making price of 7/- and to the trade price of 7 guineas. The individual entries, therefore, will be presented on this basis.

Walter Scott was born in Edinburgh in 1771 and died at Abbotsford in 1832. He was a very famous Scottish novelist and poet. He read for the Bar at Edinburgh University and was admitted a member of the Faculty of Advocates in 1792. He was appointed Sheriff of Selkirkshire in 1799. He married a Miss Carpenter, a French refugee's daughter, in 1797.

His interest in German romantic literature led him to translate and publish works by Burger and Goethe. His own early works from 1802 onwards were printed and published by Messrs. Ballantyne's with whom Scott formed a secret partnership. This partnership was not successful, so Scott sold his copyrights to Messrs. Constable who failed also, leaving Scott with considerable debts.

He was created a baronet in 1820 by George IV, being the first recipient of an honour under that monarch.

The Busts

		1873	1876	c.1880	1884
Large to match Byron	Ht. 17in. (43.18cm)	£1.4.0.	£1.16.0	18/6	13/6
Small	Ht. not known	7/6	11/6	6/6	5/-
Life Size, by Chantrey	Ht. 26in. (66.04cm)			4Gns	35/-
C&CPAU	Ht. 14in. (35.56cm)	10/-			

It may be that John Steell, RSA sculpted the 'Large bust to match Byron', and that this was adapted from the one which was exhibited at the 1851 Exhibition.

It is reported that Chantrey considered the life size bust to be one of his finest sculptures. The 1881 NPL gives its height as 26in.

The only bust of which an illustration is available is that which measures 17in.

A bust of Sir Walter Scott is included among the list of busts published in the 1848 catalogue; it is not known which, if any, of the above early ones may be this, but it is most likely to be that described as 'small'.

See Colour Plate 40

B70

B71a

B71 – THE SEASONS
1881
Ht. 17½in. (44.45cm)
Sculptor: Owen Hale
Marks: OWEN HALE Sc 1881
Illus: Yes PP 586, 625, 626
The four seasons of Spring, Summer, Autumn and Winter were popular 19th century subjects for artistic expression. They attracted the attention and talents of many sculptors

B71b

B71c

B71d

of whom those by Owen Hale must rank among the finest.

In the NPL of c.1880 (it may now be seen that this must date from 1883) the price was £1.5.0.each; in 1884 it was 16/6 to 21/-. The making price was 3/3 each.

See Colour Plate 41

B72 – WILLIAM SHAKESPEARE
c.1848
Ht. 8in. (20.32cm)
Sculptor: probably J. Durham
Illus: Yes PP 611

B72

William Shakespeare was born at Stratford-on-Avon in 1564 and died there in 1616. He was the first son and third child of John Shakespeare, a glover, and Mary Arden. He has become Britain's most illustrious dramatist and poet. Little is known of his boyhood or where he was educated. In 1582 he married Ann Hathaway, who bore him three children, two of whom were twins. Much of Shakespeare's life was spent on and around the London stage where he was a contemporary of Alleyne, Kempe and Pope, all gifted actors of considerable note.

Shakespeare's works, as playwright and poet, are too numerous to list here. Since the middle of the 19th century there has been much controversy about the actual author of the works attributed to him, but that is for others to discuss.

This bust is listed in the 1848 catalogue with a handwritten price of 15/- against it. The SPB quotes 10/6 and 15/-, which were reduced to 7/- and 10/6 at some later, unspecified, date. In 1873 it was 7/6; the retail price in 1876 was 11/6. In 1881 it was 7/6, falling to 5/- in 1884. The making price was 8d.

B73

B73 – WILLIAM SHAKESPEARE
1861
Ht. 13½in. (34.29cm)
Sculptor: R. Monti
Sponsor: Crystal Palace Art Union
Marks: R.MONTI Sc. PUBLISHED MARCH 1 1861 CRYSTAL PALACE ART UNION
Illus: Yes PP 609

A receipt, dated 'December 24 1863' states 'Received of Alderman Copeland the Sum of twenty Pounds Sterling for the Model of a Bust of Shakespere executed to his order and the Copyright of which remains with him – £20.0.0. R. Monti'.

The price in the SPB for this exclusive issue was 10/-, and it was at this price that the three busts returned to Stoke in 1881 were valued. In 1884, when trying to sell them off, the trade price was reduced to 7/6.

B74 – SHENTON
The only reference to this subject is an entry in the SPB 'Shenton Bust 15/-'. Clearly this was a private commission.

B75 – NEGRO SLAVE
1861
Ht. 10in. (25.4cm)
Marks: PUB.MAY 1861
Illus: Yes PP 621

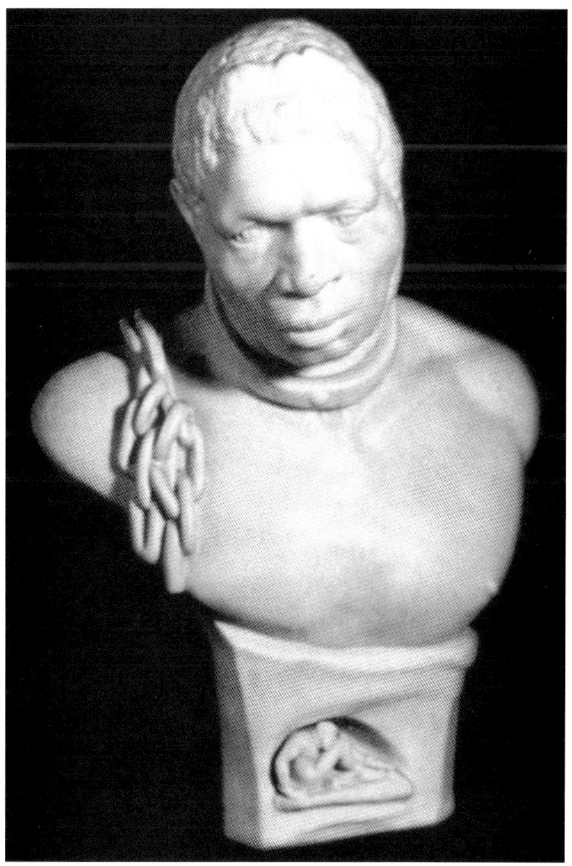

B75

B78

B79

This may have been published to promote the sale of *Uncle Tom's Cabin* by Harriet Beecher-Stowe who visited Britain in 1853. To publicise her book ceramic items were issued at that time to support the promotion. Also some were issued later on the occasion of theatrical productions.

An Act for the Abolition of Slavery in all the British Dominions was passed in 1833. The English nation had to pay £20 million as compensation to the owners who had lost their slaves.

A price of 12/6 is recorded in the SPB with the date 17/6/64 and the other price is £1.0.0 retail in 1876. No making price is recorded.

B76 – CAPTAIN SMITH

This is probably the notorious self-styled Captain John Smith who was among the colonists sent out by the London Company in 1606. They landed at Chesapeake Bay in 1607 and John Smith, after a lot of bickering and indecision, decided to adopt the role of leader. He forced everyone to work on the Biblical principle of 'He that will not work neither shall he eat'. This idea rooted itself in the American consciousness for two centuries.

The only reference to this item is in the SPB where it records: 'Smith, Captain, Bust 15/-'.

B77 – SPARROW

This is recorded in the SPB: 'Sparrow Bust 12/6'. The making price was 1/-.

The identity of the person remains to be found.

B78 – SPRING, companion to **Summer**
B79 – SUMMER, companion to **Spring**
1870
Busts Ht. 12in. (30.48cm)
Sculptor: L.A. Malempré
Marks: PUB. APRIL 1870
Illus: Yes PP 594

These busts were issued also on pedestals of different heights, usually gilded and tinted. They are not simply the heads taken from the statuettes of Spring and Autumn, although the facial characteristics are similar. The statuettes were sculpted in 1872.

	SPB	1873	1876	1882	1884	Making
Bust	12/6:18/-			14/-	£1.0.0	10/6
7/6	1/4					
" gilt & tinted	14/-	20/-				
Corinthian Pedestal 8in.	6/-	6/-	10/-	6/-	3/6	
" " 10in.	11/-	11/-	17/6	10/6	5/-	

B80 – SPURGEON

c.1882

Born at Kelvedon, Essex, in 1834, Charles Haddon Spurgeon died at Mentone, France in 1892. He was an English Baptist preacher and founded 'The Tabernacle' in Newington, London, in 1861. He was also a founder of a theological college, schools, almshouses and an orphanage. In addition to editing a monthly magazine, *The Sword and the Trowel*, he wrote and published many religious books together with volumes of sermons.

The only reference in the Copeland records is the hand-written price in 1884 of 15/- in a copy of the 1881 NPL.

B81 – GEORGE STEPHENSON
before 1873
Ht. 8in.(20.32cm)
Illus: Yes PP 605
George Stephenson was born in 1781 and died in 1848. He was the son of, and later assistant to, Robert Stephenson, the fireman of a colliery engine at Wylam, near Newcastle-on-Tyne. He furthered his education in engineering by attending night schools. It was while working as an engineer for a colliery that Stephenson constructed a 'travelling engine', worked by steam, for use between the colliery and the local port. Successful trials were conducted in 1814.

B81

He became the engineer of the Stockton and Darlington Railway which opened in September 1825; this was the first steam railway to carry both passengers and goods. The Liverpool and Manchester Railway line, opened in 1830, was constructed under his direction.

His son, Robert, built the famous 'Rocket' steam railway engine in 1829. Portrait busts of both George and Robert, sculpted by E.W. Wyon, were produced and issued by Wedgwood in 1858.

The SPB quotes 10/6 and 15/-. In 1873 the trade price was 7/6, while the retail price in 1876 was 11/6. In 1881 the trade price had fallen to 5/- and to 3/6 in 1884. The making price was 8d.

B82 – SUTHERLAND, DUKE OF
1850
Ht. 7½in. (19.1cm)
Sculptor: John Francis
Born 8 August 1786, George Granville Leveson-Gower of Trentham Park, Staffordshire, he died 28 February 1861. He succeeded to the title in 1833 as the 2nd Duke, was a member of Parliament (as Baron Gower), High Steward of Stafford, Lord Lieutenant of the County of Sutherland and Custos Rotulorum of Staffordshire.

His place in the Parian story is assured because in the early 1840s he was shown and purchased the first piece of Statuary Porcelain offered for sale by Copeland and Garrett. This was a reduced copy of R.J. Wyatt's marble statue of Apollo as the shepherd boy of Admetus. The original stood in the grounds of Trentham Park.

B82

B83

His duchess encouraged the work of the Afro-American sculptor Eugene Warburg, from whom she commissioned a series of bas-reliefs based on the story of *Uncle Tom's Cabin* by Harriet Beecher-Stowe; one of these may have been the source of Uncle Tiff and the Negro Slave.

The bust illustrated was bought at auction by a collector who stated that it was one of three busts, all of members of the Sutherland family. He has made a study of the Sutherland family and is convinced that this bust is of the second duke. The quality of it is certainly consistent with Copeland's quality.

Shinn lists the bust and suggested the date of 1850. It is listed among the items exhibited at the 1851 Great Exhibition and may have been produced as a private commission to be given as gifts by the Duke to his friends.

The SPB records the price of 25/- trade and 42/- retail. This suggests that the bust was of a size about 18in. (45.72cm) tall, but the actual example belies this suggestion. The making price in 1895 was 1/6, although there is no other reference in the Copeland records.
See Colour Plate 42

B83 – SYME, PROFESSOR JAMES
1870
Sculptor: William Brodie
Marks: WM. BRODIE RSA 1870
Illus: Yes
Born at Edinburgh in 1799, he died in 1870. Professor Syme was a noted Scottish surgeon. He published *Excision of Diseased Joints* in 1831, and *Principles of Surgery* in 1832.

There are entries in the Making Price Book where there are two references: 'Professor Sime (Private op.) 1/9d' and 'Scotch Professor 1/10d'. This presumes that the bust was a private commission.

B84

B85 THE ROYAL COLLECTION ©2006 HER MAJESTY QUEEN ELIZABETH II

THOMPSON
See reference at Dryden, B23. The bust may be of Thomas Perronet Thompson (1783-1869), an English politician and mathematician.

TRAGEDY
Companion to **Comedy**, where the details will be found, B18, B19.

B84 – UNA
1863
Ht.11½in. (29.21cm
Sculptor: John Hancock
Marks: UNA. JOHN HANCOCK Sc.1863
Illus: Yes PP 591
Una is regarded as the personification of truth, 'a lovely ladie' taken from Spenser's *Faerie Queene*. St. George, the Red Cross knight, with whom she became united, slew the dragon on her behalf.

Una is sometimes portrayed accompanied by a lion whom she has tamed with the impact of her personality. Minton produced a famous figure of 'Una and the Lion' in parian in 1847.

Listed in the SPB at 12/6 trade and 21/- retail, it was 14/- in 1873 and £1.0.0.retail in 1876. By 1881 it was 9/- and in 1884 5/-. The making price was 1/2d.

B85 – VAN DE WEYER, BARON SYLVAIN
1874
Ht. 14½in. (36.83cm)
Sculptor: W. Theed
Illus: Yes PP 619
Born at Louvain in Belgium in 1802, he died in 1874. Van de Weyer was a diplomat, politician and doctor of law. He began his career as a journalist on the *Courrier des Pays Bas*. A qualified lawyer, he became a member of the Belgian provisional Government and, later, served in the national Congress as the Brussels representative. He was a negotiator for Belgian independence. Appointed Minister for Foreign Affairs in 1831, he then came to the Court of St. James as Ambassador to Great Britain. He held this post for his entire career except for a short period between 1845-1846 when King Leopold I asked him to return to preside over a cabinet of national unity. Baron Van de Weyer was much loved and respected by Queen Victoria and the Copeland portrait bust in parian which she bought remains at Osborne House in the Isle of Wight.

There is no reference to this bust in the Copeland archival records.

B86 – VENUS DE MILO
c.1884
Ht. 25in. (63.5cm)
Sculptor: F.M. Miller, after the antique
Illus: Yes
The Roman mythological goddess of beauty and sensual love was of little importance until she was identified with the Greek goddess Aphrodite. A favourite subject with poets, artists and sculptors, she was portrayed in diverse manners, often accompanied by Cupid.

The bust by Copeland is derived from the Greek statue in the Louvre in Paris, considered by many authorities to be the finest existing single work of antiquity. The original marble statue was found on the Greek island of Melos in 1820 and is dated to about 400BC. Perhaps the correct title should be 'Venus of Melos'.

B86

B88

It has been suggested that this may have been intended as a companion to Mars, but there are several large busts after the antique or of mythological subjects: Achilles, Ariadne, Clytie, Daphne, Juno, Mars.

There is a handwritten note of 52/6 in the 1881 NPL for 1884. The making price was 9/-.

B87
VILLIERS, LADY CLEMENTINA
c.1846
Sculptor: Lawrence MacDonald, reduced by B. Cheverton
This bust was exhibited at the Great Exhibition in 1851. The subject may be the wife of the 4th Earl of Clarendon

The SPB records prices of 10/6 trade and 15/- retail. The making price was 8d.

B88 – VIOLA SANS CHAPEAU
1862
Ht. 11in. (27.94cm)
Sculptor: F.M. Miller
Sponsor: Crystal Palace Art Union
Marks: VIOLA F.M. MILLER Sc. PUB.MARCH 1862
Illus: Yes PP 593
The principal female character in Shakespeare's *Twelfth Night.* Viola is the sister of Sebastian; they are both shipwrecked on the coast of Illyria, but separated. Viola, disguised as a boy named Cesario, encounters Orsino, Duke of Illyria, whose heart she succeeds in winning.

Sponsored by the Crystal Palace Art Union the trade price recorded in the SPB is 10/-. The making price was 1/-.
See Colour Plate 43

B89 – WAR, companion to **Peace**
The Parian Phenomenon includes this bust as a companion to Peace, stating that it was sculpted by Joseph Durham in 1861.

No documentary evidence has been found so far in the Copeland archives that these subjects were made.

B90 – GEORGE WASHINGTON
1863
Ht. 10½in. (26.67cm)
Marks: *Washington Copyright Reserved*
Illus: Yes PP 613
Born in 1732 and died in 1799. Washington was the eminent American statesman and general who played such an important part in the War of Independence. He became the first President of the United States of America by unanimous acclaim in 1789 and remained so until 1797.

A quiet, dignified but determined man, Washington was respected by the American people for his prowess as an administrator and military commander.

The SPB records 15/- trade and 25/- retail. The NPL of 1873 quotes 11/- and the retail price in 1876 was 17/6. In 1881 the trade price was 9/-, falling to 5/- in 1884. The making price was 1/-.

Although *The Parian Phenomenon* states that two sizes, 10½ and 8½in. (26.67 and 21.59cm), were made, no corroboration of this has been found in the archives.

B91 – DANIEL WEBSTER
before 1873
Ht. 18in. (45.72cm)
Illus: Yes
Daniel Webster (1782-1852) became an eminent American lawyer and statesman. He was a member of congress and of the Senate for various

B90

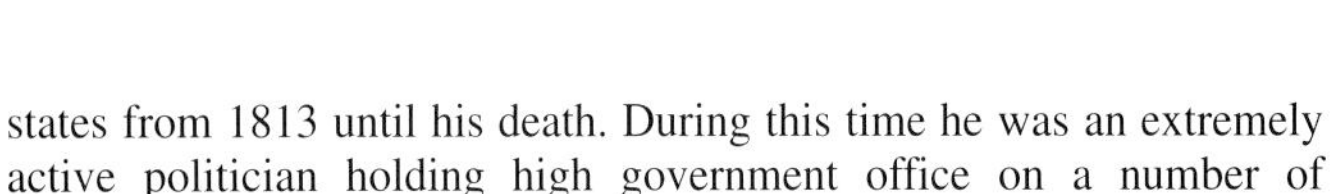

B91

states from 1813 until his death. During this time he was an extremely active politician holding high government office on a number of occasions. He was three times an unsuccessful candidate for the Whig Presidential nomination.

The SPB quotes 42/- trade and 63/- retail. By 1873 the NPL had £2.5.0 and in 1876 the retail price was £3.7.6. In 1881 the trade price was down to £1.11.0 and fell further to 12/6 in 1884. The making price was 2/6.

B92 – WELLINGTON, DUKE OF
1852
Ht. 7½in. (19.05cm), 11¾in. (29.85cm)
Sculptor: Count D'Orsay
Marks: *Comte d'Orsay. Sc.1852*
Illus: Yes PP 602,611
Arthur Wellesley (1769-1852) was the son of the First Earl of Mornington. He entered the army as an ensign in 1787, reaching the ranks of colonel in 1796, major-general in 1802 and lieutenant-general in 1808. His military career was pursued in parallel with political activities. He was knighted in 1805, elevated to the viscountcy of Wellington in 1809, becoming Earl and Marquis of Wellington in 1812. In 1814 he was made Duke of Wellington. His victory, with his ally Blucher, over Napoleon at Waterloo gave rise to the idiom 'to meet one's Waterloo'. An old Etonian, he received his military instruction at the French University of Angers.

In the catalogue to the Great Exhibition it lists: 'Duke of Wellington, by the Count D'Orsay'. This is listed with the busts, but the statuette of the Duke is also possibly by D'Orsay and that was shown in the 1845 Manchester Exhibition (see S193). It is probable that it was the statuette that was shown.

It is said that D'Orsay offered the bust to Minton's in exchange for a royalty of £1 per bust sold, claiming that on the Duke's death sales would generate great profit. Mintons refused but it seems that Summerly's Art Manufactures accepted. That business failed, however, and the bust was issued by Copeland in 1852. Two sizes are recorded. The prices are as follows:

	SPB		1873	1876	1881	1884	Making
large 11¾in.	16/-	25/-	14/-	£1.1.0.	9/-	5/-	1/-
small 7½in.	10/6	15/-	7/6	11/6	6/-	3/6	8d

Another bust of Wellington was produced in 1846 by Copeland & Garrett in Felspar Porcelain (see illustration B92a). It is 8½in. (21.59cm) high.

The Parian Phenomenon illustrates another bust said to be of the Duke of Wellington at Fig. 622, one that is dated 1891. This is incorrect. The bust is of William Taylor Copeland, sculpted in 1838 (see B21).

B93 – JOHN WESLEY
c.1860
Ht. 9¼in. (23.5cm)
Illus: Yes PP 600

B92

B92a

B93

Born in 1703, died in 1791. John Wesley was the son of Samuel Wesley, a clergyman of the Church of England. John became a curate to his father after completing his education at Charterhouse School and Christ Church College, Oxford. He became a Fellow of Lincoln College, Oxford in 1726 and settled in Oxford. By 1729 he was leading a religious group known as 'Methodists', due to both their fervour and their strict moral code. Against this background Wesley was to found the Methodist Church. In addition to his ecclesiastical pursuits, Wesley was something of a physician and published a handbook on the diagnosis and treatment of a whole plethora of diseases; it went into many editions. Wesley visited the Staffordshire Potteries several times; at first he was roughly treated, but his teaching bore results. He met Josiah Wedgwood, of whom he was to comment later 'He was small and he was lame, but his soul was near to God'.

The only record is the making price of 7d.

B94 – YOUAVE
Sculptor: W. Theed
Little is known of this bust, in fact the only record is in the SPB where it records:

Youave, bust	large	8d	1/-	1/3 col'd & gilt
" "	small	6d	10d	

B95 – VICTORY, by Hale, is listed in the Making Price Book at 3/3. No other information is known.

ROYAL BUSTS AND STATUETTES

In a book devoted to recording one factory's production of parian ware it seems both fitting and convenient to set aside one section entirely to those busts and seated figures pertaining to Queen Victoria and members of her family, because parian was essentially a child of the Victorian era. Conceived in the early years of Queen Victoria's reign, its steep decline commenced, coincidentally, with the Queen's death in 1901.

The sovereign became an accomplished artist in her formative years, her education in the arts having begun in 1827, at the age of eight, under the tutelage of Richard Westall, RA and continuing until his death in 1836. His role was later to be filled by Edwin (later Sir Edwin) Landseer.

Victoria took as consort a man who also possessed an absorbing interest in the visual arts, accompanied by a talent for painting and sculpture. Much of Albert's work is to be found at Osborne House, amongst which is a sculpture of 'EOS', his favourite greyhound. In the execution of this work he was assisted by John Francis, RA, who later cast the statue in bronze.

Thus the new ceramic medium, by which artists' works could be easily and inexpensively reproduced to be distributed throughout the British Empire, was bound to attract royal attention and support. This is evidenced by the readiness of both Queen and Consort to permit likenesses of themselves and their children to be used by the potters for commercial purposes.

Strangely, of the Queen's nine children only six were featured by Copelands in their parian productions. Of these six, five appeared as themselves; the sixth, Victoria, the Princess Royal, appeared only as 'Summer' in the set of Royal Seasons.

Very few details of prices are recorded in the Copeland archives, and the existence of many items is known only from actual examples. All models are portrait busts unless stated otherwise

R1 – QUEEN ADELAIDE
Princess Amelia Adelaide Louise Theresa of Saxe-Coburg-Meiningen was born on 13 August 1792. On 18 July 1818 she married HRH the Duke of Clarence, later to be crowned King William IV. She died on 2 December 1849.

There are two references in the Copeland records to this subject. The SPB lists 'Queen Adelaide 10/6 15/-'. The making price was 8d. No dates are known.

R2 – ALBERT, Prince
1855
Sculptor: Joseph Durham
Sponsor: Crystal Palace Art Union
For biographical details see R5, Albert, The Prince Consort Seated figure. He was created Consort on 25 June 1857.

No price information available.

R3 – ALBERT, The Prince Consort
1864
Ht. 12¼in. (31.12cm)
Sculptor: W. Theed
Sponsor: Crystal Palace Art Union
Marks: W. THEED Sc. PUBd.AUG 1 1864
Illus: Yes PP 96
This bust was issued as a companion to that of Queen Victoria and executed on behalf of the Crystal Palace Art Union, who issued them as prizes in 1865. See R5 for biographical details.

R4 – ALBERT, Prince
1853
Ht. 11½in. (29.21cm)
Sculptor: J.S. Westmacott

R3

R4

Marks: J.S. WESTMACOTT Sc 1853
Illus: Yes PP 599
Issued together with the youthful portrait bust of Her Majesty Queen Victoria. The Prince is wearing the insignia of the Most Noble Order of the Bath. See R5 for biographical details.

The SPB records that it was offered at 16/- trade and 25/- retail. In 1873 the NPL has it at 14/- and at £1.1.0 retail in 1876. In 1881 the trade price was 10/6 and this fell to 6/6 in 1884. The making price was 1/-.

R5 – ALBERT, The Prince Consort, Seated
1862
Ht. 10⅝in. (26.99 cm)
Sculptor: G. Abbott
Sponsor: Richard McMichael & Co.
Marks: PUBLISHED MAY 1ST 1862 BY RICHARD McMICHAEL AND CO 5 ADAM ST, EAST PORTMAN SQUARE LONDON. G.ABBOTT FECIT. LONDON.
Illus: Yes
Richard Albert Francis Augustus Charles Emmanuel of Saxe-Coburg-Gotha was born at the Rosenau, near Coburg, Germany, on 26 August 1819. He was the second son of the Duke of Saxe-Coburg-Gotha. The Queen proposed marriage to him in October 1839 and they were married on 10 February 1840. As the Prince Consort of Queen Victoria, he died at Windsor Castle on 14 December 1861.

The sponsors were printsellers.

The trade price in 1873 was £2.5.0 and the retail price in 1876 was £3.7.6. In 1881 the trade price was £2.2.0 and in 1884 it was 18/6.

R6 – ALBERT EDWARD, Prince of Wales
1863-64
Ht. 14½in. (36.83cm)
Sculptor: Morton Edwards
Sponsor: Art Union of London
Illus: Yes
Albert Edward was born on 9 November 1841, the second child and eldest son of Queen Victoria. He married Princess Alexandra of Denmark on 10 March 1863. He toured Egypt and Palestine (1862), British India (1875-6) and the USA and Canada (1880). He ascended the throne as King Edward VII on 22 January 1901. Until his accession he was known popularly as 'Prince Edward', to distinguish him from his father, Prince Albert, the Prince Consort. He died on 6 May 1910.

There is no price information on this bust.

In 1848 a statuette of the young prince was sculpted by Mary Thornycroft to represent 'Winter'. See The Royal Seasons.

R7 – ALBERT EDWARD, Prince of Wales
1876
Ht. 16½in. (41.91cm)
Sculptor: L.A. Malempré
Marks: W.T.COPELAND & SONS PUBd. MAY 1876 L.A. MALEMPRE

R5

R6

R7

Illus: Yes PP 607
The bust shows the Prince wearing the following Masonic regalia:
Around the neck: The jewel (medal) of the 11th Degree of the Rite of Freemasonry (Swedish).
Chain: The chain and jewel of the Grand Master of the United Grand Lodge of England.
Breast Jewels: Left – member's jewel Prince of Wales Lodge No.259. Right – member's jewel Royal Alpha Lodge No.16. (This has the appearance of a miniature Star of the Order of the Garter.)

The Prince was initiated into Freemasonry in December 1868 by King Oscar II of Sweden and Norway in the Lodge Den Nordiska Forsta, in Stockholm. A year later, in December 1869, he was invested as an honorary Past Grand Master of the United Grand Lodge of England. In October and August 1870 he was invested, respectively, as Grand Patron of the Order in Scotland and Ireland. On 28 April 1875, at the Royal Albert Hall, he was installed in the high office of Grand Master of the United Grand Lodge (UGL) of England, an office he continued to hold until becoming King in 1901. Thereafter he was proclaimed 'Protector of the Craft in England, Ireland and Scotland'.

There is little doubt that this bust was issued to mark the occasion of his installation as Grand Master. The bust was priced at £2.15.0, delivered free to members of the different lodges throughout England.

In addition to a parian bust there is also a marble bust by Malempré in the Library and Museum of the UGL, Freemason's Hall, Queen Street, London.

The bust is included in the NPL of 1881 at £1.1.0 and at 15/- to 18/- in 1884. The making price was 3/6d.

R8

R9

R10

R8 – ALBERT EDWARD, Prince of Wales
1863
Ht. 12½in. (31.75cm)
Sculptor: Marshall Wood
Sponsor: Crystal Palace Art Union
Marks: MARSHALL WOOD SCULP 1863 PUBD AUG 1 1863 CRYSTAL PALACE ART UNION
Illus: Yes PP 601
The mark above is recorded on a bust exhibited by Richard Dennis in his exhibition of December 1984 entitled *The Parian Phenomenon,* item number 190. C. and D. Shinn in their *Victorian Parian China*, Plate 32, show a bust in their collection which they describe as 'After Marshall Wood. Parian model by F.M. Miller. Marked 'Crystal Palace Art Union. F.M. Miller, Sculpt. Pubd.Feb 1st, 1863' PUBd Feb. 1st 1863'. It will be observed that the 'Miller' bust was published six months before the 'Marshall Wood' version. The pair was issued to mark the engagement of Edward and Alexandra.

The few references in the Copeland records are the price of 10/- for the four busts returned to Stoke from the Art Union in 1881 and the making price of 1/4d.

See Colour Plate 44

R9 – ALEXANDRA, Princess of Wales
1863
Ht. 12⅛in. (30.8cm)
Sculptor: F.M. Miller
Sponsor: Crystal Palace Art Union
Marks: PUBD. FEBY 1st 1863 CRYSTAL PALACE ART UNION F.M.MILLER SCULP.
Illus: Yes PP 597
Alexandra Caroline Marie Charlotte Louise Julie was born in Copenhagen on 1 December 1844, the daughter of King Christian IX of Denmark. She married Edward, Prince of Wales, on 10 March 1863 and became Queen Alexandra upon the Prince's accession in 1901. She died in November 1925. The bust was issued as a pair to Marshall Wood's bust of Prince Edward.

Two versions of the bust were issued at different dates, the earlier one (12in., 30.48cm) being adorned with ear-rings, and representing Alexandra as Princess of Denmark, and the later one, without ear-rings, after her marriage.

In the Copeland papers at Spode Limited is the invoice and receipt for this portrait bust:

Mr. Aldn, Copeland To F.M.Miller
1862
Dec. For modelling a small Bust of the Princess of
Denmark including copyright 12.0.0
Recd. on acct. Dec. 6 5.0.0
£ 7.0.0

T Battam
Received Dec 20th 1862
F.M.Miller.

The price in the SPB is 10/-, with 18/- for 'Gilt & tinted with Orange wreath'. No example with this treatment has come to the author's attention. Only one bust was returned to Stoke in 1881 and this, like the Prince, was valued at 10/-. The making price, however, was 1/10d.

A statuette of the Princess dressed as Queen Mary, Queen of Scots,

R12

R14

was produced in 1879 and is featured in the Statuette Section, S103.
See Colour Plate 45

R10 – ALEXANDRA, Princess of Wales
1863
Ht. 15in. (38.1cm)
Sculptor: Mary Thornycroft
Sponsor: Art Union of London
Marks: ART UNION OF LONDON MARY THORNYCROFT Sc.Facsimile signature: W.T.Copeland
Illus: Yes PP 590
The making price was 1/4d.

R11 – ALFRED, Prince, Duke of Edinburgh. Figure
1848
Ht. 17in. (43.18)
Sculptor: Mary Thornycroft
Marks: MARY THORNYCROFT Sc.1848
Illus: Yes PP 543
See under ROYAL SEASONS

Born on 6 August 1844, Prince Alfred, Queen Victoria's fourth child and second son, was accorded the title of Duke of Edinburgh. He became the Duke of Saxe-Coburg and Gotha in 1893, having been elected King of Greece in 1862, an honour which he saw fit to decline, mainly because of the plans that his parents had for him. Commissioned into the Royal Navy, Prince Alfred served in HMS *Euralyus*, a fifty-gun screw-propeller frigate. In January 1874 he married, in St. Petersburg, the Grand Duchess Marie Alexandrovnia, the only daughter of Czar Alexander II. He died on 30 July 1900.

R12 – ALICE, Princess
1879
Ht. 15in. (38.1cm)
Sculptor: Mary Thornycroft
Sponsor: Art Union of London
Marks: MARY THORNYCROFT Sc ART UNION OF LONDON
Illus: Yes PP 590
Born on 25 April 1843, Princess Alice Maud Mary was the third child and second daughter of Queen Victoria. In 1862, she married Louis IV, Prince of Hesse-Darmstadt (1837-92) and she died from diphtheria on 14 November 1878 at the age of thirty-five years.* Thereafter thirty

copies of the portrait bust were issued as prizes by the Art Union of London.

The making price was 1/10d.

See Colour Plate 46

*One of her daughters, Princess Victoria of Hesse, married Prince Louis of Battenberg in April 1884; another daughter, Alix, married Csar Nicholas II in 1894. Princess Alice was the founder of the Women's Union for Nursing Sick and Wounded in War.

R13 – HELENA, Princess

1851

Sculptor: Mary Thornycroft

Princess Helena (family name 'Lenchen') was born on 25 May 1846, the fifth child and third daughter of Queen Victoria. She died in 1923, the widow of Prince Christian of Schleswig-Holstein-Sonderburg-Augustenburg (1831-1917), by whom she had five children. She was one of the three children who were present at the death of Prince Albert.

The SPB quotes 15/- trade and 21/- retail.

R14 – LOUISE, Princess

1871

Ht. 15½in. (39.37cm)

Sculptor: Mary Thornycroft

Sponsor: Art Union of London

Marks: ART UNION OF LONDON APRIL 1 1871

MARY THORNYCROFT Sc.

Illus: Yes PP 590

Born in 1848, Princess Louise was the sixth child and fourth daughter of Queen Victoria. The portrait bust was issued to commemorate her wedding to a Liberal MP, the Marquis of Lorne, later to succeed to the Dukedom of Argyll in 1900. There was no issue of the marriage which was the first to break the custom of members of the Royal Family only marrying members of other royal families. This custom was supported by the Prince of Wales, who opposed the marriage, but, happily, the Queen did not.

Princess Louise was, for a time, a pupil in the studio of the sculptress Miss Susan D. Durant (1830-73), who was much favoured by members of the Royal Family for whom she prepared busts and medallions.

Princess Louise died in 1939.

The price recorded in the SPB was 13/6 to the Art Union of London. The making price was 1/10d.

R15 – VICTORIA, The Princess Royal, Figure

1848

Sculptor: Mary Thornycroft

Illus: Yes

Born on 21 November 1840, 'Vicky' was the first child of Queen Victoria and christened Victoria Adelaide Mary Louise. She was wet nursed by Mrs Southey, from Cowes! She married Prince Frederick William of Prussia on 25 January 1858.

The SPB quotes 57/6 trade and 73/6 retail. The making price was 2/6d. See ROYAL SEASONS.

A statuette of Prince Friedrich Wilhelm was offered on eBay during 2001. It showed the prince with his pet dog. It was marked COPELAND but no mention has been found in the Copeland records. It must have been a private commission. See R26.

THE ROYAL SEASONS

1848

Prince Edward, Ht. 17in. (43.18cm), Prince Alfred, Ht. 17¼in. (43.82cm)

Sculptor: Mary Thornycroft

Marks: MARY THORNYCROFT Sc.1848 COPELAND'S PORCELAIN STATUARY on the figure of Edward, Prince of Wales.

Illus: Yes PP 542-544A, the two above of parian, the other two reproduced from the *Art-Journal* of 1848.

A set of four statuettes, portraying the four seasons, were sculpted for Queen Victoria. They are:

Spring	Princess Alice – for short biography see R12
Summer	Princess Victoria, Princess Royal – see R15
Autumn	Prince Alfred – see R11
Winter	Prince Edward, Prince of Wales – see R6

W.T.Copeland negotiated for and obtained the copyright to reproduce these in Statuary Porcelain.

A letter dated Sept 2 from S.C. Hall to Alderman Copeland:

My Dear Sir,

I wish you would contrive to drive up to Mrs Thorneycroft *[sic]* to see the 4 statues.

They are exceedingly beautiful, and apart from their interest as the children of the Queen, would make a more charming set of statuettes.

Mrs Thorneycroft speaks of making small copies of them - for sale.

I think you will do a wise thing to purchase the copyright before she goes any further, for I am sure they will be eagerly grasped at the moment they are seen: and think you have no time to lose.

I received Her Majesty's direct command to engrave them – large steel plates – for the Art Union.

Truly Yours ever, S.C. Hall

Mrs Thornycroft having considered the proposal of Mr Copeland regarding the production of reduced copies in porcelain of her statues of the Royal Children; is willing, with the consent of Her Majesty the Queen, for their publication, to furnish Mr Copeland with a half size model of each of the four statues, and liberty to make porcelain copies of the same: for the sum of two hundred pounds. Mrs Thornycroft would also require that her name should be legibly inscribed on each copy.

39 Stanhope Street Septr/3/47

Royal Seasons. left to right, Winter, Autumn and Summer ©BLAIR CASTLE

Winter, Prince Edward

Spring, Princess Alice

Autumn, Prince Alfred

Copeland's letter, dated 8 September 1847, from 37 Lincoln's Inn Fields reads:

To Mrs Thornycroft
Madam
The indisposition of a near and dear relative and my absence from town must plead my apology for not replying earlier to your letter of the 3rd inst. I will accept your terms save that the amt. must be £150 one hundred & fifty pounds paid in … of the fourth as last figure is delivered. And should success attend the sale, I will give the other fifty pounds (£50) I am, Your faithful Servant.
W.T.Copeland
P.S. My son will deliver this.

The SPB only gives prices for Princess Victoria and the Prince of Wales; these were 57/6 trade and 73/6 retail. A making price of 2/6 seems to have applied to each of the four figures.

The original marbles are at Osborne House and the bronze copies are in Buckingham Palace. A complete set is at Blair Castle.

The parian reproductions were shown at the 1849 exhibition in Birmingham and at the Great Exhibition in 1851.

See Colour Plate 47.

R16 – DUCHESS OF KENT
1874
Ht. 15in. (38.1cm)
Sculptor: W. Theed
Marks: W. THEED Sc. LONDON 1874
Illus: Yes PP 608

Born in 1786, Victoria Mary Louisa of Saxe-Coburg-Saalfield was the sister of King Leopold I of Belgium and the widow of Emich Charles, Prince of Lenigen-Dachsburg-Hardenburg, to whom she bore a son, Charles, and a daughter, Princess Feodore (q.v.).

On 29 May 1818, in Coburg, she married Edward Augustus, Duke of Kent, the fourth son of King George III. The only issue of the marriage was a daughter, Victoria, later to become Queen of England (q.v.).

The Duchess was widowed for the second, and last, time on 23 January 1820. It was to the Duchess that Queen Victoria owed her undeniably fine education, an attribute which never has been fully acknowledged.

The Duchess was much under the influence of her 'confidential secretary', Sir John Conroy, and this association was to bring much unhappiness to the young Princess Victoria. Gossip insinuated that the Duchess was Conroy's mistress, but of this there is no proof. She died in March 1861.

There is no mention in any of the Copeland records of either this or the following royal portrait bust. Their provenance is that they are in the Royal Collection at Osborne House.

R16 THE ROYAL COLLECTION ©2006 HER MAJESTY QUEEN ELIZABETH II

R17 THE ROYAL COLLECTION ©2006 HER MAJESTY QUEEN ELIZABETH II

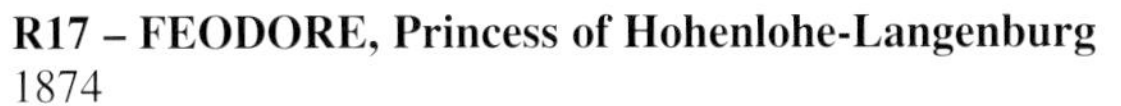

R17 – FEODORE, Princess of Hohenlohe-Langenburg
1874
Ht. 15in. (38.1cm)
Sculptor: W. Theed
Illus: Yes PP 620
Queen Victoria's older step-sister by twelve years, Princess Feodore was the daughter of the Duchess of Kent by her first husband. She and Victoria were devoted to each other. She married Emich Charles, Prince of Leiningen in 1828. She died in 1872.

R18 – GEORGE IV
c.1847
Ht. 8¾in. (22.23cm)
Marks: COPELAND & GARRETT LATE SPODE
Illus: Yes
The only bust known to the authors is not of parian but is of Felspar Porcelain. However, it is included here because this subject is included in the list of busts in the 1848 catalogue. It may be that a parian bust was made from the same mould.

George was born in London in 1762 and died at Windsor in 1830, the son of King George III of Great Britain and Ireland. He contracted an illegal marriage with Mrs Fitzherbert in 1785, but in 1795 he entered into a legal marriage with his cousin, Princess Caroline of Brunswick. Both extravagant and dissolute in habit, he was, nevertheless, appointed Regent in 1811 because of his father's illness, which, at the time, was thought to be insanity. His flamboyant passion for the exotic is immortalised in the Brighton Pavilion, in which there were several objects specially produced by Spode in about 1818.

Originally an ardent supporter of the Whig party, he later allied

R18

R20

R20a Marble

himself with the Tories. In 1820 he petitioned the House of Lords for a divorce, but was unsuccessful. The main administrative event of his reign was the passage of the Catholic Emancipation Act in 1829, during the ministry of the Duke of Wellington.

As Prince of Wales he visited the Spode factory in Stoke-upon-Trent in 1806, and appointed Josiah Spode 'Potter and English Porcelain Manufacturer to His Royal Highness the Prince of Wales'. He renewed the Warrant of Appointment when he ascended the throne.

R19 – QUEEN VICTORIA
1855
Sculptor: J. Durham
Sponsor: Crystal Palace Art Union
This bust is listed in C. and D.Shinn's book *The Illustrated Guide to Victorian Parian China*, on page 72, but there are no other references known to the author at present.

R20 – QUEEN VICTORIA
1848
Ht. 10¼in. (26.04cm)
Sculptor: J. Francis
Marks: VICTORIA J. FRANCIS Sc. LONDON 1848
Illus: Yes PP 600
A trade price of 5/- is noted in 1884

R21 – QUEEN VICTORIA
1887
Ht. 13½in. (34.29cm)
Sculptor: Owen Hale
Marks: OWEN HALE Sc. PUB. FEB.1887
Illus: Yes PP 610
This bust of the 'old' queen was issued to celebrate the Golden Jubilee of her reign. It is reported that a glazed example, dated 1901, exists; this may have been produced to mark the death of the queen.

R21

R22

The SPB records several busts of the Queen and it is not exactly clear which one is which, but the Hale bust is probably that recorded as 'new model 12/6 21/-'. A price of 7/- is recorded for 1884, but this price probably does not apply to this bust because of the date. The Making Book records: 'Queen by Hale No.1 1/9d; No.2 1/4d'. There was also a 'Pedestal to Jubilee Bust of Queen 1'.

R22 – QUEEN VICTORIA, Seated Figure
1887
Ht. 10½in.(26.67cm)
Sculptor: L.A. Malempré
Sponsor: F. Battam
Marks: L.A.MALEMPRE SCULP. 1887 M PUB. BY F.BATTAM 87
Illus: Yes
Published by Frederick Battam to commemorate Queen Victoria's Golden Jubilee.

R23 – QUEEN VICTORIA
1856
Ht. life size 25in. (63.5cm), smaller
Sculptor: M. Noble
Marks: VICTORIA M.NOBLE Sc. LONDON 1856
Illus: Yes
The larger bust shows the Queen wearing the 'Garter Star', also a tiara with larger jewels. These jewels were supplied loose and fitted into sockets in the tiara.

The SPB quotes:
Queen large 6 gns 10 gns
Ivory 4 gns 6 gns

In 1873 the trade price was £5.15.6, retail in 1876 was £8.18.6. In 1881 the price was £4.14.6 and in 1884 42/-. The making price was 7/-, with 1/- extra for the jewels.

R23

R23a

R24

R25

R26

R24 – QUEEN VICTORIA
1864
Ht. 13in. (33.02cm)
Sculptor: W. Theed
Sponsor: Crystal Palace Art Union
Marks: W.THEED Sc. PUBd. AUG 1 1864
Illus: Yes PP 596
Theed's portrait bust of the Queen was issued as a pair to his bust of Albert, Prince Consort, both of which were issued as prizes by the Crystal Palace Art Union in 1865.

This item seems to have been available with the 'coronet' gilded, for a manuscript note gives a price in 1884 of '5/6 and 10/- gilt'.

The SPB gives a price of 10/- and this was the valuation in November 1881 when one bust was returned to Stoke.

See Colour Plate 48

R25 – QUEEN VICTORIA
1853
Ht. 11in. (27.94 cm)
Sculptor: J.S. Westmacott
Marks: J. SHERWOOD WESTMACOTT Sc 1853
Illus: Yes PP 599
This portrait bust was issued as the companion to the sculptor's bust of Prince Albert.

Victoria was born on 24 May 1819, the daughter of the Duke and Duchess of Kent. She ascended the throne on 20 June 1837, on the death of the King, William IV, and her coronation took place a year later on 28 June 1838. She married Prince Albert (see R5) on 10 February 1840 and bore him nine children: Victoria (1840), Edward (1841), Alice (1843), Alfred (1844), Helena (1846), Louise (1848), Arthur (1850), Leopold (1853), Beatrice (1857).

Queen Victoria died on 22 January 1901, having reigned for sixty-three years.

The SPB quotes 15/- and 21/-. The NPL of 1873 gives 14/- and the retail price in 1876 was £1.1.0. By 1881 the trade price had fallen to 10/6 and to 6/6 in 1884. The making price was 1/-.

R26 – FRIEDRICH WILHELM, Prince
c.1858
Ht. 14in. (35.56cm)
Sculptor: Gensihow Berlon
Marks: COPELAND
Illus: Yes
Born in Potsdam on 18 October 1831, he was the son of William and Augusta of Saxe-Weimar-Eisenach. He was the first Prussian prince to attend a university and also received a military education. He married Princess Victoria, Queen Victoria's eldest daughter, on 25 January 1858. He became Emperor as Frederick III on 9 March 1888 but survived for only ninety-nine days. He died from throat cancer.

No reference to this figure has been found in the Copeland records, so it is assumed that, like the busts of the Duchess of Kent and of Princess Feodore, it was a private commission from the Palace.

It was offered on eBay in July 2001.

MISCELLANY

During the fifty or so years during which parian was popular several hundred objects other than groups, statuettes and busts were produced by Copeland. The names of many of these have been taken from price lists or from photographic records. The size of this book does not permit a pictorial survey of these but many of them are listed here.

The most precise information comes from actual examples; some are found in collections, some in auctions or offered for sale at fairs. *The Parian Phenomenon* illustrated a number of examples.

ANIMALS

The Net Price List of c.1882, under the heading 'Copeland's Statuary Porcelain', includes the following animals:

- Bear Extinguisher and Stand
- Bear Match Box
- Begging Dog, large & small
- Begging Dog Extinguisher and Stand
- Belgian Lion
- Bloodhound
- Bone Picker Dog
- Boy with Begging Dog, Vesta-holder
- Bride of Lammermoor Dog
- Cat, small
- Cow on plinth, small
- Deer
- Donkey and Panniers
- Ducks, group
- Elephant, *Jumbo**
- Faun
- Fowls, toys
- Fox
- Fox's head
- Greyhound, large& small
- Hooded Rat*
- Owl
- Pointer on plinth
- Pointers, group of with dead game
- Rabbit, small
- Rabbits, group
- Sentinel Dog, large & small
- Setter Dog
- Sheep
- Spaniels, King Charles group
- Squirrels, group
- Stag, large
- Stag, wounded

* examples are known coloured

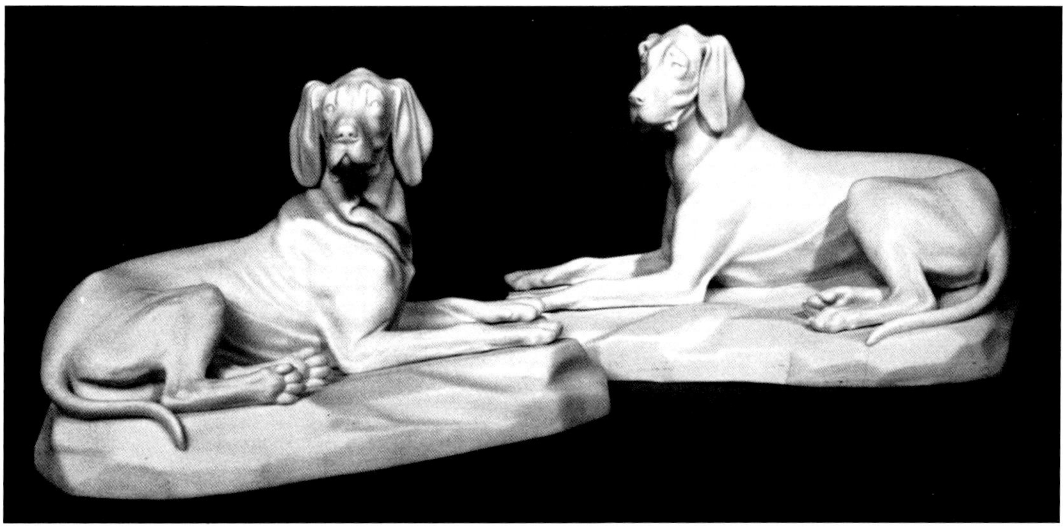

Bloodhounds, a pair

There may be other subjects which were not listed and may come to light after the publication of this book.

The Spode Museum photographic records (SPR) together with known examples which are illustrated in *The Parian Phenomenon* (PP) show the following:

Cow, on plinth. A Copeland & Garrett example has been seen but is thought to be smear-glazed earthenware
Bloodhound, PP 581, SPR
Bloodhounds, a pair, SPR
Greyhounds, a pair, SPR
Sentinel Dog (Irish Wolfhound), PP 581
King Charles Spaniels, Cavalier's Pets, PP 583, SPR
Pointers, on plinth, SPR
Pointers with Dead Game, Dogs Group, PP 578
Setter Dog, SPR. An example with a broken leg in the Spode Museum Collection
Spaniel, SPR
Group of Terriers, PP 579, SPR
Boy with Terriers, PP 578, SPR
Bone Picker, PP 582
Begging Dog;PP 583
Death of the Fox, SPR
Dog, Hen and Chickens, SPR
Lion, after the original by Sir Edwin Landseer for the Nelson Column memorial, PP 80
Other subjects include:
Donkey and Panniers; SPR, Norwich Museum
Deer Browsing, Spode Museum Collection
Fowl, Private Collection
Hooded Rat, Private Collection
Elephant, *Jumbo,* Spode Museum Collection
Rabbit, Private Collection
Group of Rabbits, PP 582

OBJECTS FOR USE OR AS ORNAMENTS

The same observation that is made about animals applies to these items. The Spode Museum photographic records (SPR) illustrate large numbers of objects which might well have been in the parian body. Equally, many of them are known to have been produced in white bone china and also some were decorated with majolica glazes on earthenware.

The following items are known to have been made in parian:

Alhambra Vase, PP 574, SPR, Manchester Museum
Candlestick, 9in. (48.26cm), PP 576
Centrepiece, 'Return from the Vintage', PP 567 (incomplete) and 1851 Catalogue, SPR
Comport, 'Abundance', 19½in. (49.53cm), PP fig 567, female figures representing Joyfulness, Abundance and Gratitude
Comport, 'The Three Graces', 30½in. (77.47cm), PP 567
Basket, 'The Three Graces', Private Collection
Cupid with Shell, 11½in. (29.21cm), PP 576
Dolphin Flower Holder, 9in. (22.86cm), PP 576
Chamber Candlestick and Extinguisher, 7½in. (19.05cm), PP 577
Gothic Pierced Flower Vase, 13½in., PP 575, SPR, 1851 Catalogue
Kneeling Lurline with Shell Dishes, PP 577
Angel Front Ewer, PP 575, SPR
Renaissance Two-handled Vase, PP 575, SPR
Renaissance Style Bottle, with gilding, PP 576
Wall Bracket, 7½in. (19.05cm), PP 577
Wedding Cake Plate, diam. 15in. (38.1cm), PP 573, Spode Museum Collection

Also items not illustrated in *The Parian Phenomenon* in private collections unless stated otherwise

Vintage Garden Pot, Ottawa Museum Collection
Vintage Jugs, three sizes, with hinged covers, Spode Museum Collection
Renaissance Butter Dish, Cover and Stand, coloured, Spode Museum Collection
Cream Jug, Lily of the Valley, 3¼in. (8.26cm)
Cream Jug, Strawberry, 3¼in. (8.26cm)
Corinthian Wall Brackets, in pink parian
Vase, with Dancing Hours, gilded, 8½in. (21.59cm)
Vase, with wedding vows, gilded, 9½in. (24.13cm)
Shell on foot, 2in. (5.08cm)
Crocus Bowl with loose pierced centre, 8½in. (21.59cm)
Winchester Font, Spode Museum Collection
Warwick Vase, 4½in. (11.43cm)
Convolvulus Vase, 6in. (15.24cm)
Great Vases, 33in. (83.82cm), after antique examples in the British Museum; one was exhibited in 1845
Beauvais Jug
Water Bottles, handled and unhandled, coloured and gilded. Two in Spode Museum Collection
Sandon Vase, glazed parian with colour, Spode Museum Collection
Shell on Dolphins, glazed parian, Spode Museum Collection
Shakespeare's House

THE REPRODUCTIONS FROM THE ASSYRIAN SCULPTURES

Great excitement was caused when Henry Layard discovered the site of the ancient Assyrian city of Nimrud between 1845 and 1851 and, later, the cities of Nineveh and Khorsabad. It was the name Nineveh which most people recognised, probably because it was familiar from the stories in the Holy Bible.

Aaron Hays worked at the British Museum whither some of the great finds had been taken. Although not renowned as a sculptor, in 1871 he did execute a portrait bust of Beethoven (see B9). In about 1859 he saw a commercial opportunity in promoting these Assyrian sculptures. In the February 1860 issue of *The Art-Journal* (see Figure 35) there is a footnote to an article on Assyrian antiquities:

> It may not be out of place to mention here, that very truthful miniature copies of these objects, and of the celebrated Lion, also in the Museum, have been modelled by Mr. A Hays, of Elizabeth Street, Hans Place, Chelsea, who has had them executed in statuary-porcelain by Messrs. Copeland and Co., as ornamental works of a singular but interesting character.

This is the first reference to Copeland producing these items. It is not known if they were marketed in 1860 because one item, a figure of Sennacherib, is marked: 'A HAYS PUB.MARCH 1868.REGd.FEB 25th 1868'.

Of a complete set in the Bolton Museum, the three figures of Sardanapalus and the Queen of Sardanapalus and of Sennacherib are date-marked for August 1878 and the Winged Lion is date-marked March 1882.

All prices quoted are for the nineteenth century, e.g.1881, unless given in full, i.e. 1913.

These same three figures are included in the Statuary Price Book (SPB) at a price of 12/6; this was reduced on 23/7/81, but raised back to 12/6 on 21/12/91 for twenty-five copies. The making price was 2/- each.

The original price for the **Nineveh Lion Weight** was 3/-, reduced to 1/9 on 29/11/81, and raised to 2/6 on 13/11/93.

The original price for **Nimrod's Head** was 4/-, reduced to 2/6 on 29/11/81 and raised to 3/9 on 13/11/93. The price changes on 29/11/81 were authorised by Richard Pirie Copeland and quoted to Alf Jarvis, 43 Willes Road, Kentish Town, London. NW.

The original price for the **Winged Lion** and **Winged Bull** was 21/- each; this was reduced on 23/7/81 by R.P. Copeland to 12/6 and this was re-confirmed on 21/12/93, with a further proviso for twenty-five copies, but small quantities were to be charged at 16/6 in 1893; this, in turn, was raised to 20/- on 2/9/1913.

The **Garden Scene Panel**, 22 x 8in. (55.88 x 20.32cm) was charged 22/6 on 2/9/1913.

Another panel, which has come to be called the '**Tribute Panel'**, measuring 20 x 11in. (50.8 x 27.94cm) is inscribed with Sanskrit characters, and is marked: 'OWEN HALE Sc. COPELAND COPYRIGHT RESERVED REGISTERED and ALFRED JARVIS, WILLES ROAD, LONDON NW.'

The pricing in 1913 suggests that the demand for these reproductions was greater than their non-appearance in collections or the market today might have led one to assume.

The story of the excavations and the parian reproductions have been researched by L.A. Compton who has tried to unravel the various strands and present them along the lines of a theatrical production. He points out that there were so many people tearing up and down the banks of the River Tigris that he found it difficult to grasp who precisely was doing what, where and when. At any moment, night or day, they would leap astride a horse and gallop off to investigate the latest whisper or rumour of a discovery.

ASSYRIA REVIVED
A NINETEENTH CENTURY MASQUE

Episode 1. The Scenario
Episode 2. The Thespians
Episode 3. The Proscenium
Episode 4. The Plot
Episode 5. The Impresarios – Entrances and Exits
Curtain Call

Episode 1. The Scenario

In the mid-1840s three seemingly unrelated events took place which culminated in the issue by W.T. Copeland of a series of parian figures inspired by Assyrian artefacts of the period 500-900 BC.

First, 'Assyria Revived' attempts to give an encapsulated

account of the archaeological excavations of the ancient cities of Khorsabad, Nimrud and Nineveh which were located along the eastern bank of the River Tigris roughly one thousand miles north of the present port of Basra in the Persian Gulf (see map, Figure 6). Brief details of those taking part are also given.

Secondly, it notes the concurrent events taking place in far-off Stoke-upon-Trent between Messrs. Copeland and Minton regarding the development of the parian body; these have been discussed earlier in this book.

Thirdly, in the interests of ceramic history, it places on record the story of a remarkably gifted servant of the British Museum.

It might be observed here that whereas this book is about the parian wares of the Copeland manufactory, 'Assyria Revived' is also, in part, a very considerable part, the story concerning the British Museum, for it was from the Museum that sprang Britain's interest in Mesopotamia. It not only supplied substantial funding for the expeditions but, of the nine characters appearing in this narrative, seven were directly employed by the British Museum. Portraits of these nine persons are illustrated in Episode 2, together with brief supporting biographies.

Episode 2. The Thespians

In 1820 **Claudius Rich** (Figure 1), the British Resident in Baghdad from 1808 to 1821, took it upon himself to prepare a map of Babylon and, at the same time, to make a serious study

Figure 1. Claudius Rich. From *Uncovering the Ancient World* by H.V.F. Winstone

Figure 2. Paul-Emile Botta. From *Uncovering the Ancient World*

of the antiquities which were to be found along the banks of the River Tigris.

The principal areas of investigation were the sites of the ancient cities of Nimrud, Nineveh and Khorsabad. During his visit Rich learned much of Assyrian history and culture as disclosed by sculptures, frescos, bas-reliefs and other artefacts dating back some two thousand years.

As mementos of his survey he recovered fragments of carved stone, etc., which included clay tablets and cylinders inscribed with cuneiform characters; these he presented to the British Museum in 1821, together with his report, where they languished without recognition until 1836, when the report was published, having been edited by his widow, Mary.

Born in 1787, Rich died from cholera while visiting Persia in 1822. His contributions to the British Museum were to be his enduring memorial, for from them grew the finest collection of Assyrian sculpture in the western world.

Little further activity in the area appears to have taken place until 1842, when **Paul-Emile Botta** (Figure 2), the French Consul in Mosul, carried out excavations at Khorsabad. These excavations proved to be a startling success because Botta unearthed a palace of the Assyrian King Sargon, built about 710 BC. Much of the structure was decorated with panels carved in low relief and bearing cuneiform inscriptions. Such was the interest aroused by this discovery that the French Government

Figure 3. Major Sir Henry Creswicke Rawlinson. From *Uncovering the Ancient World*

Figure 4. Austen Henry Layard as a young man. Courtesy National Portrait Gallery, London

funded further research until October 1844, when it was felt that the site had become barren. The French chose to keep many of the finer sculptures from the Khorsabad site and now, housed in the Louvre, they form the most outstanding Khorsabad Collection in Europe.

Transportation of the heavy sculptures to France was fraught with difficulty and eventually the site was abandoned. Sadly, Botta became addicted to drugs and, with failing health, he became of little account.

An accomplished botanist, Botta was held to be the first human of modern times to view the Assyrian ruins in situ.

Henry Creswicke Rawlinson (Figure 3) came next to the forefront of the scene when, in 1849, he bought from the French two Human-Headed Winged Bulls which they had abandoned at Khorsabad. Rawlinson (1810-1895), the British Resident in Baghdad, was an archaeologist as well as a diplomat who went on to become an outstanding expert at de-ciphering the cuneiform inscriptions on which he published important works. After his retirement from Baghdad in 1855, he pursued a political and diplomatic career until 1861, when he became increasingly preoccupied with Assyriology. From that time onwards until his death he enjoyed the privilege of a private room at the British Museum where he continued to employ himself in translating the myriad cuneiform artefacts arriving from Assyria.

Figure 5. Layard in later life. Photograph by Fradelle and Young. Wallace & Cockerell

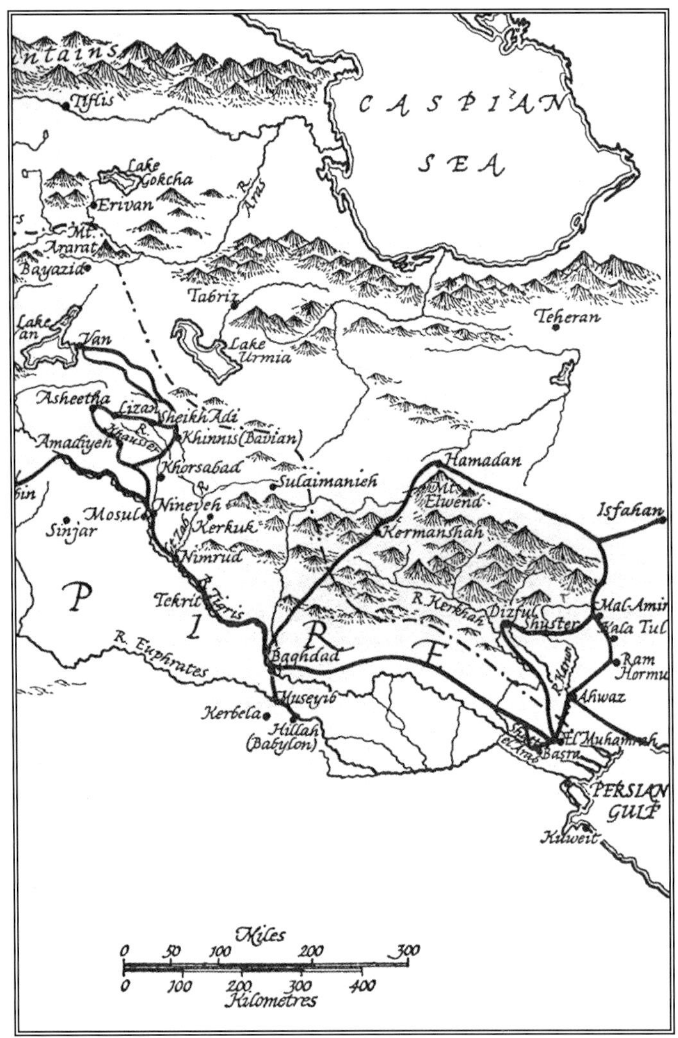

Figure 6. Map showing the journeys of Sir Henry Layard in Mesopotamia (Iraq) 1839-1854. From *Layard of Nineveh* by G. Waterfield

Undoubtedly the best known of the Mesopotamian archaeologists was **Austen Henry Layard** (Figures 4 and 5). Born in Paris in 1817, he was of Huguenot descent on his father's side, his mother being the daughter of Nathaniel Austen, a banker of Ramsgate, Kent. Her brother, Benjamin, a London lawyer and Layard's godfather, promised the boy patronage provided that he was named as 'Austen Henry'. This was done but without enthusiasm and Layard was generally known as Henry (later as Sir Henry) Layard. The offer of patronage, however, proved to be little more than legal training in his uncle's office with the prospect of very uncertain reward.

Although the position was taken up, it was not to young Henry's liking and soon he relinquished it so that he might pursue his deep and abiding interest in all forms of art together with an unquenchable thirst for adventure. These twin interests, stimulated by a chance discovery of the Rich 'Collection and Report', eventually led him, in the mid-1840s, to the ancient cities.

His first discovery was Nimrud. He believed it to be Nineveh, but further discoveries made it clear that he was mistaken. The whole area became home to Layard for the next decade (Figure 6).

However, by 1860 he felt that he had sojourned long enough and sought a more settled existence. He returned to England where he married a daughter of Lady Charlotte Elizabeth Schreiber, a lady whose name is well known to students of ceramics for her collection which is now in the Victoria & Albert Museum. He became Member of Parliament for the London Borough of Southwick.

After a somewhat inauspicious beginning, Henry Layard became an outstanding scholar, archaeologist and diplomat who rendered many important services to his country, not the least of which were his discoveries which now form such a major part of the National Collection.

Figure 7. Hormuzd Rassam. From *Uncovering the Ancient World*

Figure 8. William Kennet Loftus. From *Uncovering the Ancient World*

Figure 9. George Smith (1840-1876). From *Uncovering the Ancient World*

Queen Victoria, on 27 May 1878, bestowed upon Layard the Grand Cross of the Order of the Bath; he had been honoured already in March 1853 by being granted the Freedom of the City of London. Layard died in 1894 at the age of seventy-seven.

As his assistant, Layard was fortunate to obtain the services of a literate Chaldean Christian, named **Hormuzd Rassam** (Figure 7), a younger brother of Christian Rassam, British Vice-Consul at Mosul. He joined Layard in 1846 at the age of twenty and remained with him until Layard's final departure for England in 1851. Thereafter, except for one brief interlude, he continued to excavate the sites on behalf of the British Museum, until he, too, left for England in 1882, where he spent his closing years in comfortable and uneventful circumstance with his English wife and family.

Although Rassam was to make his career in the shadow of Henry Layard, nevertheless he made important and essential contributions to the national collections; his work continued long after Layard's had ended. Of all the sculptures which he sent to the Museum, the reliefs carrying hunting scenes, taken from the walls of Ashurbanipal's Palace are held, generally, to be of the greatest importance. He is remembered also for his published memoirs and the book *Ashur and the Land of Nimrud.*

Rassam was followed as Layard's assistant by **William Kennet Loftus** (Figure 8), a professional geologist employed by the Assyrian Exploration Fund, an organisation fostered by Layard with support from, among others, HRH Prince Albert and Lord John Russell (Prime Minister 1846-52 and 1865-66). The aim of the Fund was to maintain pressure on the British Museum to continue exploring Mesopotamia. Loftus' role appears to be of little significance because, sadly, he died at an early age in 1858. He lies buried in Aleppo.

George Smith (Figure 9) did not visit the Assyrian sites until 1876, where, sadly, he fell sick and died. However, no biographical summary of the participants would be complete

Figure 10. The Black Obelisk

Figure 11. Procession of the Bull from Nimrud. (Radio Times Hulton Library). From *Monuments of Nineveh* by A.H. Layard

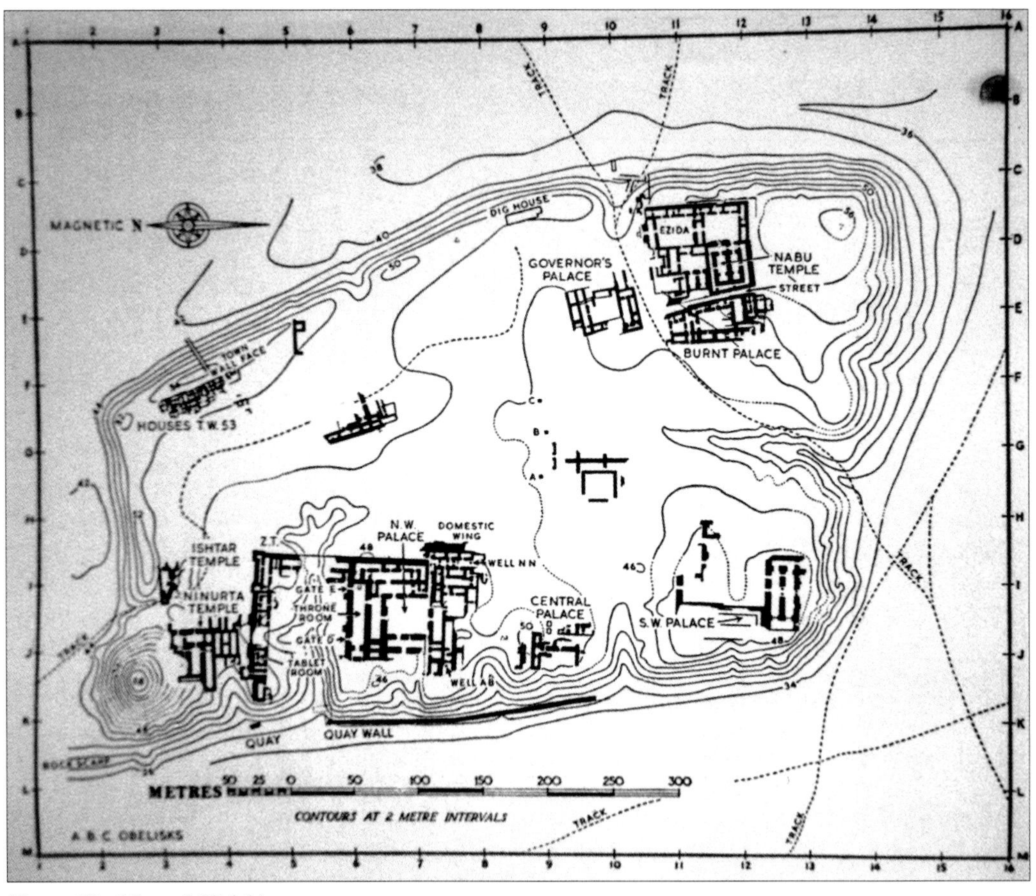

Figure 12a. Nimrud (Calah)

without his inclusion. He was an engraver of banknotes by trade, but discovered that he had a gift for deciphering ancient scripts, especially cuneiform. He became an employee of the British Museum through the influence of Sir Henry Rawlinson, whose confidence in him was soon justified when Smith translated the inscriptions from a panel of the Black Obelisk (Figure 10) showing Shalmaneser III receiving the payment of tribute from Jehu, King of Israel. Among Smith's notable achievements, besides the translation mentioned above, was the identification of the Assyrian version of the Story of Noah and the Flood; at last biblical legend was becoming proved as fact!

The parts played by others appearing in this account are detailed later in considerable depth.

Episode 3. The Proscenium

By the mid-nineteenth century the only remaining visible evidence of a bygone civilisation along the banks of the River Tigris was a number of carbuncular mounds of earth dotted about the countryside and, although the detritus of earlier habitations lay strewn around in the form of masonry, household utensils and other artefacts, the local populations for centuries had shown little interest in these mounds other than as a casual source of building materials.

Of nowhere was this more true than the sites of Khorsabad, Nimrud and Nineveh; they are listed and discussed here, briefly, in the chronological order of their discovery.

KHORSABAD. The Palace of Sargon (721-705 BC), the most northerly of the sites, was investigated first in 1843 by the Frenchman Paul-Emile Botta. It yielded the Human-Headed Winged Bulls, two of which were purchased by Henry Rawlinson from the French in 1849. They can be seen now in Room 16 of the British Museum. Later, a Bull from Khorsabad was to inspire one of the bookends in the Copeland series of parian miniatures.

NIMRUD (Figures 11 and 12a). The most southerly of the three sites was the location of the Palaces of both Ashurnasirpal II (883-859 BC) and Shalmaneser III (858-824 BC). Here were found a Human-Headed Winged Lion in the Palace of the former and the Black Obelisk in the Palace of the latter. The Lion was used to form a pair with the Bull, while from the Obelisk came the plaque known as the 'Tribute Panel'.

NINEVEH (Figure 12b). This site is situated mid-way between the other two and was the Palace of Ashurbanipal (668-627 BC). Nineveh was the last site to be investigated. When, initially, Layard discovered Nimrud he believed mistakenly that it was Nineveh and only later realised his error. For some strange, unknown reason it was the name Nineveh that caught the public's attention. Perhaps because of its biblical references it was the generic term to be applied to the whole of the Assyrian ventures, both archaeological and commercial.

It was from here that came the 'Beautiful Garden Scene' panel, of which the Copeland plaque is a faithful copy, and the basis for which, in turn, furnished the figures of Sennacherib and of Sardanapalus and his Queen.

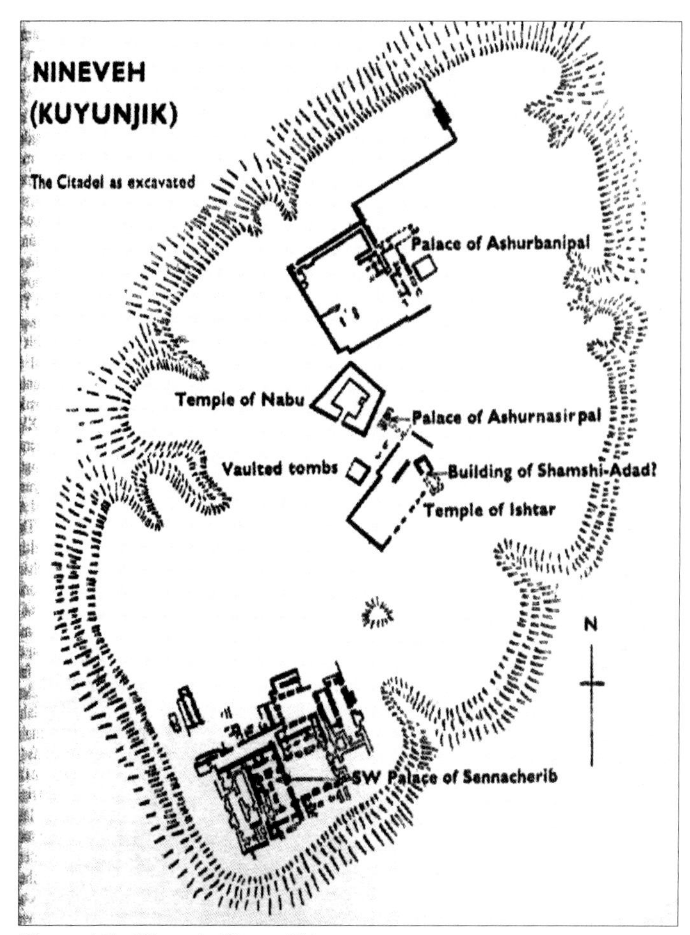

Figure 12b. Nineveh (Kuyunjik)

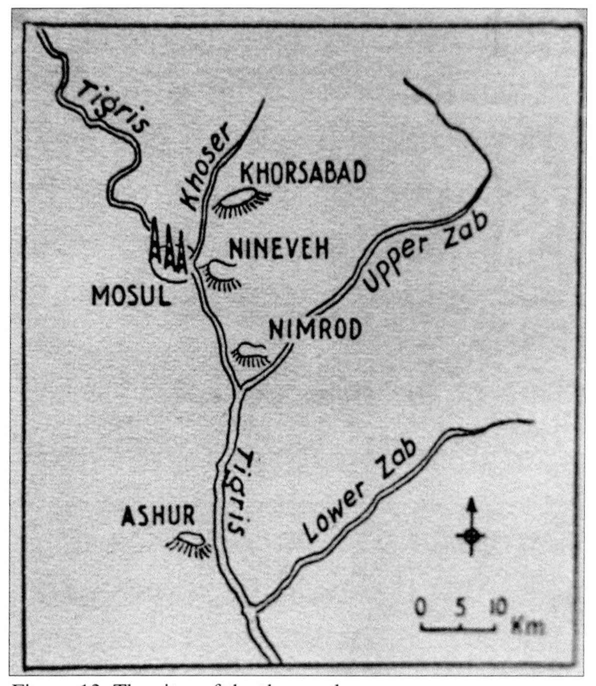

Figure 13. The sites of the three palaces

Figure 14. Reconstruction of Ashurnasirpal's throne room at Nimrud. From *Assyrian Sculpture* by J. Reade

That the name 'Nineveh' was used in a general sense when referring to matters Assyrian is evidenced by two examples:

First, Henry Layard invariably incorporated the name into the many descriptive books which he published, regardless of their contents. Indeed, his *Monuments of Nineveh* had nothing to do with that place! It had everything to do with Nimrud!

Secondly, when the Crystal Palace was moved from Hyde Park to Sydenham in 1854, the Nimrud reliefs, the Winged Bulls and Lions, etc., were all exhibited in a so-called 'Nineveh Court' for which Layard wrote a descriptive pamphlet. The 'Court', designed by the architect James Ferguson, was decorated with casts of the Colossal Winged Bulls and palace reliefs from Nimrud. The various halls comprising the court were painted according to remains of the original colours to give a finished effect similar to the reconstructions of the 9th century BC Palace of Ashurnasirpal which had been published in Layard's celebrated *Monuments of Nineveh*, Volume I, of 1849 (Figure 14). Julian Reade, in his *Assyrian Sculpture*, fig. 22, p.21, makes the comment that 'details are wrong, but the scene as a whole carries conviction'.

Nineveh was named after Nin, a goddess of Mesopotamia. The king of Assyria, Sennacherib, who reigned from 706-681 BC, made Nineveh his capital. In his magnificent 'palace without a rival' were sculptured walls with narrative scenes from his life to impress visitors of the invincibility of the conqueror and the folly of resistance. Sennacherib was at war for most of his reign in an attempt to extend the kingdom and was eventually murdered by his sons. Nineveh reached the height of its fame under Ashurbanipal (668-637 BC). It became the political, economic, cultural and artistic centre of Assyria, but it was destroyed finally in 612 BC by the Medes.

Episode 4. The Plot

Whereas documentary information regarding Assyrian-style jewellery over the period AD 1850-80 is readily available, examples of Assyrian-style ceramics are less well recorded. The firm of Doulton produced Assyrian relief-moulded vases in the 1870s and an expatriate English potter, Frederick Hurten Rhead, produced copies of the Khorsabad Lion in the United States of America. However, nothing, for curiosity or enterprise, was to compare with the unique series of Assyrian style parian figures produced by Messrs. W.T. Copeland. These are now discussed in some detail.

Wherever possible the original sculpture(s) from which a reproduction was derived is illustrated. Therefore it may be asked how such large blocks of masonry were moved around in what were virtual wastelands in which there were very few suitable amenities. For example, the Winged Human-Headed Bulls from Khorsabad each weigh approximately sixteen tons and had to be moved some twenty miles overland to Mosul for onward movement to Basra, and thence shipped to London. The Assyrian sculptures, wall panels, etc., were executed normally in

Figure 15. Lowering the Bull. From *A popular account of the Discoveries at Nineveh* by A.H. Layard. The figure atop the right-hand stonework is that of Layard himself. (J.W. Whymper. Sc.)

the water-soluble, stone-like mineral hydrated calcium sulphate, commonly known as 'gypsum'; exceptionally, the dark hued, igneous rock, basalt, was used also (see Figure 10).

The French had experienced considerable problems when attempting to move each of their statues in one piece. Rawlinson solved this problem with remarkable success by sawing the Bulls into manageable sections, the joins now being barely discernible as they stand in Room 16 in the British Museum.

Overland transport was by means of crude home-made carts or sledges, mostly drawn by human beings; numbers of 500-600 have been mentioned. This was the same system which had been used for over two millennia, and was probably the very same method used to transport these loads from the quarries where they were cut. On one occasion Henry Layard, reporting on the movement of a Bull and Lion each weighing some fourteen tons, reveals that he tried to use a team of oxen. However the dumb, intractable beasts proved to be rather more intractable than dumb, for, upon feeling the great weight behind them, they refused to move. They were replaced by several hundred men whose flexible ingenuity completed the operation successfully.

All water-borne traffic was carried downstream from Mosul to Basra on disposable rafts, known as 'keleks'. For a graphic description of this mode of transport one can do little better than to quote from Herodotus' account of his passage through Mesopotamia in 450 BC:

> What surprised me most was the popular means of transport from north to south. The boats which come down the river to Babylon are circular and made of skins; the frames, which are of willow, are cut in the country of the Armenians above Assyria, and on these, which serve for hulls, a covering of skins is stretched outside, and thus the boats are made, without either stem or stern, quite round like a shield. They are then entirely filled with straw, and their other cargo is put on board after which they are suffered to float down the stream. They are managed by two men who stand upright in them, each plying an oar – one pulling and the other pushing. When they reach their destination the cargo is landed and offered for sale; after which the men break up their boats and sell the straw and the frames. The current is too strong to allow a boat to return upstream, for which reason they make their boats of skins rather than wood.

The distance from Mosul to Basra is almost 1,000 miles. The return journey for the crew, either on foot or mounted, was certainly a long and, no doubt, arduous one.

The experience Layard gained in moving large masses of stone proved to be invaluable when it came to move a Bull from Khorsabad to Nimrud, for the distance of twenty-five miles was covered in a mere two days (Figure 15). At Nimrud he caused to be built two large keleks, each constructed from six hundred inflated sheep and goat skins, and on these both the Bull and the Lion were floated safely downstream to the mouth of the River Tigris.

Figure 16. The reception of the Nineveh sculptures at the British Museum. From *The Illustrated London News* 28 Feb. 1852

A1 – SENNACHERIB
c.1860
Ht.13½in. (34.29cm)
Sculptor: A. Hays
Publisher: A. Hays
Marks: on front of plinth, SENNACHERIB B.C.721 COPELAND COPYRIGHT RESERVED impressed inside plinth, printed in blue ALFRED JARVIS, WILLES RD. LONDON NW.
Illus: Yes PP 568 (Figure 17)

Sennacherib, King of Assyria from 705-681 BC, was similar in outlook to his father, Sargon II; ruthless in war, but caring and socially responsible in peacetime. He it was who re-habilitated the City of Nineveh.

The Copeland figure (Figure 17) shows Sennacherib attired as King of Assyria and High Priest of Nineveh. The bow in his left hand is sacred to his position, having been presented to the kings of Assyria by Ishtar, the Assyro-Babylonian goddess of both love and war. She was known as 'Mistress of the Bow', 'Archeress of the gods', and 'Lady of War and Battle'. Possession of the bow was believed to ensure victory. Sennacherib eventually met his death by being murdered by two of his sons whilst at his devotions.

Hays derived the body of the figure from a sculptured wall-relief unearthed from Sennacherib's palace at Nineveh. Sadly, the head had suffered damage, possibly by mutilation (Figure 18), a defect which Hays overcame rather neatly by using a 'transplant' of the headdress of Sennacherib's grandson, Sardanapalus (or Ashurbanipal) (Figure 19), as shown in bas-reliefs discovered in his palace, also at Nineveh.

Rather surprisingly, in view of Hays' workplace, the date shown on the figure refers to Sennacherib's father, Sargon II. The error is corrected in the text of the sales leaflet published by Hays' promoter, Alfred Jarvis, where he quotes the correct dates of 705-681 BC.

The figure of Sennacherib is listed in the SPB originally at 12/6 (date unrecorded). On 23 July 1881 the price was reduced 'for quantity' to 7/-, but was returned to 12/6 on 21 December 1891 for twenty-five copies. On 13 November 1893 the price was 9/- for small quantities, and this was raised on 2 September 1913 to 12/6. All these prices were ex-works. The making price was 2/-.

Figure 17. Copeland parian figure of Sennacherib

(Top right) Figure 18. Bas-relief of Sennacherib inspecting the booty from Lachish. Detail from a wall-relief in Sennacherib's palace

(Right) Figure 19. Bas-relief of the head of Ashurbanipal. Detail from a wall-relief of a lion hunt from Ashurbanipal's palace, Nineveh

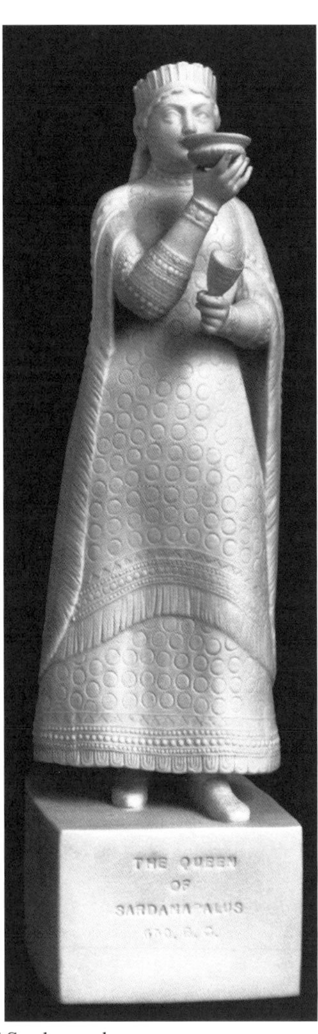

Figure 20. Copeland parian figure of Sardanapalus

Figure 21. Copeland figure of the Queen of Sardanapalus

A2 – SARDANAPALUS
c.1860
Ht. 12in. (30.48cm)
Sculptor: A. Hays
Publisher: A. Hays
Marks: on front of plinth: SARDANAPALUS 662 B.C. on sides and back of plinth: COPELAND COPYRIGHT RESERVED. BY A. HAYS. All marks impressed.
Illus: Yes PP 568 (Figure 20)

Sardanapalus (668-627 BC) was the Grecian form of the Assyrian name Ashurbanipal. He was the son of Esarhaddon (680-669) and the grandson of Sennacherib. He was the last of the great kings coming from the Sargonide dynasty. He is referred to in the Old Testament as 'Asnapper the Great and Noble' (Ezra Ch.IV v.10). He is reported as being both a homosexual and a transvestite. His reign was marked not only by many uprisings, which he put down with a fierce cruelty, but also by great prosperity in which art and literature flourished. Sardanapalus described himself as 'endowed with attentive ears' and 'interested in all inscribed tablets'. He collected, documented and re-edited the whole cuneiform literature then known to mankind. He deposited his collection in the library of his palace at Kuyunjik, in the environs of Nineveh, where the great bulk of it was re-discovered in the 1840s by Henry Layard. Now housed in the British Museum, it plays an important role in the understanding of biblical and Assyrian history.

The Copeland figure is derived from one of the Lion-hunt bas-reliefs found so abundantly among the Assyrian discoveries. In translating a figure in relief to one in the round Hays has copied many details with great accuracy, but he failed signally with the stance which he has depicted as a typically Victorian 'heroic' one, that is, Victorian heads with Roman drapes, in place of the mechanical Assyrian style.

In 1821 Lord Byron published a tragedy *Sardanapalus* for production by the eminent tragedian W.C. Macready

The prices for this figure were exactly the same as those for Sennacherib.

A3 – THE QUEEN OF SARDANAPALUS
c.1860
Ht. 12in. (30.48cm)
Sculptor: A. Hays
Publisher: A. Hays
Marks: on the front of plinth: THE QUEEN OF SARDANAPALUS 650

Figure 22. Bas-relief detail from The Beautiful Garden showing the Queen of Assyria

Figure 23. Copeland parian model of the Winged Human-headed Bull

Figure 24. The Bull sculpture from the palace of Sargon II at Khorsabad, in the British Museum

B.C. on sides and back of plinth: COPELAND COPYRIGHT RESERVED N93. All impressed (N93 is the date mark for November 1893). Printed in blue inside the plinth: ALFRED JARVIS, WILLES RD.LONDON NW.
Illus: Yes PP 568 (Figure 21)
The lady represented here is probably the most important of King Sardanapalus' many wives. It was his practice to marry the daughters of the kings whom he conquered, thus creating a harem of considerable size.

Once again, Hays found his inspiration in a wall sculpture of about 645 BC from the Kuyunjik Palace of Sardanapalus at Nineveh (Figure 22). In this sculpture the queen can be seen, centre stage, drinking from a bowl held in her right hand while music is played in a garden attached to the palace. This same panel was reproduced by Owen Hale and is known as 'The Beautiful Garden Scene' plaque.(q.v.)

The prices were identical to those for Sardanapalus and Sennacherib.

TWO DECORATIVE ORNAMENTS

A4 – WINGED HUMAN-HEADED BULL

A5 – WINGED HUMAN-HEADED LION

c.1872
Ht. 8⅜in. (21.27cm), L.10⅜in. (26.35cm)
Sculptor: A. Hays
Publisher: A. Hays
Marks: COPELAND COPYRIGHT RESERVED M82 (March 1882)
Illus: Yes PP 569 (Figures 23 and 25)
The ornaments represent the winged colossi ('Shedii' or 'Spirit Guardians') which were placed at the doorways of Assyrian palaces to protect the King, upon his entrance and exit, from evil influences. They were a popular adornment of all Assyrian palaces while the countryside appeared to teem with herds of bulls and prides of lions in varying sizes and guises.

The Winged Human-Headed Bull (Figure 23). The bull was sacred to Anu, god of heaven, the supreme god of the Assyro-Babylonian Pantheon. The source for this example is taken from a sculpture unearthed at the palace of Sargon II (721-705 BC) at Khorsabad, Mesopotamia, in 1842 by Paul-Emile Botta, the French Consul in Mosul. It was purchased from the French in 1849 for the British Museum by Henry Rawlinson, the British Resident in Baghdad. It is now in Room 16 in that Museum (Figure 24); it will be seen that the headdress of this example is truncated.

Figure 25. Copeland parian model of the Winged Human-headed Lion from the palace of Ashurbanipal II at Nimrud

The Winged Human-Headed Lion (Figure 25). The lion is the emblem of Nergal, god of war and death, and one of the great Assyro-Babylonian gods. He is mentioned in the Second Book of Kings, Chapter XVII, verse 30, as the deity of the men of Cuthah, confirmation of which is to be found in the cuneiform inscriptions. It emanated from the Palace of Ashurbanipal II (883-859 BC) at Nimrud and was discovered by Henry Layard in 1845/6. It is now in Room 26 in the British Museum.

Whereas both the bull and the lion were sculpted as bas-reliefs, and therefore one-sided, Hays modelled his reproductions as double-sided figures and they have been dubbed 'book-ends' as a result. As such they would, perhaps, have been bought as a pair, although they were priced singly at £2.2.0 each, retail.

Both figures have a curious physical appearance in that, when viewed from the three-quarter aspect, they reveal five legs! Viewed from the side, the animal is moving forward, while the front view is that of an animal standing still. No firm reason for this peculiarity has been established yet, but later examples of these artefacts are equipped with the standard issue of four legs.

The SPB records: 'Winged Lion/Winged Bull printed on front & back 21/-.(no date). RP 12/6 23/7/81. And again for 25 copies 21/12/93. But small qtys are 16/6 Each 13/11/93'. This was increased to 20/- each on 2/9/1913.

A6 – BEAUTIFUL GARDEN SCENE PANEL
c.1886
22 x 8½in.(55.88 x 21.59cm)
Sculptor: Owen Hale
Publisher: Alfred Jarvis, London
Marks: COPELAND REGISTERED 1886
Illus: Yes PP 570 (Figure 26)
The scene shows King Sardanapalus (q.v.) drinking wine in his garden after returning from a lion hunt. He is resting in the company of one of his many queens together with her harem attendants. Upon one of the trees hangs the head of his enemy Te-umman, the King of Elam. The banquet seems to parallel those described in the Book of Esther, Chapter I, verses 5 and 6 (the feast at the Palace of Shushan) and Chapter VII verses 7 and 8 (a banquet of wine in the palace garden). The source for this panel (Figure 27) is one removed from the Palace of Ashurbanipal at Kuyunjik, outside Nineveh, which shows the royal couple drinking to the sound of music. It was from this panel that Hays derived the statue of the Queen of Sardanapalus.

It is not known why Hays chose to use the Greek version of the King's

Figure 26. Copeland parian panel of The Beautiful Garden

Figure 27. Original panel of The Beautiful Garden, c.645 BC, in the British Museum

(Right) Figure 29 Original panel of The Tribute of Jehu on one side of the Black Obelisk, British Museum

Figure 28. Copeland parian panel of The Tribute of Jehu

name instead of that used by the British Museum, the owner of the source of his material.

The only price mentioned in the SPB for this 'Garden Scene Panel' is 22/6 on 2/9/1913.

A7 – THE TRIBUTE OF JEHU PANEL
c.1886
20⅜ x 11in. (51.75 x 27.94cm)
Sculptor: Owen Hale
Publisher: Alfred Jarvis, London
Marks: COPELAND COPYRIGHT RESERVED REGISTERED MAY 1886 OWEN HALE Sc. at lower left front ALFRED JARVIS WILLES RD LONDON NW
Illus: Yes (Figure 28)
The panel is derived from a scene featured on 'the Black Obelisk' (c.825 BC), fashioned from a type of basalt rock (see Figure 10), which was found at Nimrud by Henry Layard in 1847 in the Palace of Shalmaneser III (858-824 BC), King of Assyria, who is seen receiving the tribute of Jehu, King of Israel (845-813 BC) (Figure 29). The scene is one of a series embellishing the Black Obelisk. The figure shaded by the parasol is King Shalmaneser III, who is seen holding a cup in his right hand whilst he rests his left hand upon his sword. The kneeling figure is either King Jehu or his representative, volunteering his tribute as an ally (he was not a conquered enemy). The style of his dress distinguishes him as a foreigner, in this case an Israelite; it is the earliest known illustration of a person of that particular race. Another panel, not reproduced by Copeland, shows Assyrian attendants bearing some of the gifts brought by Jehu. The Black Obelisk may be seen in Room 19 in the British Museum.

No price is recorded in the SPB, nor in the promotional material published by Alfred Jarvis.

Figure 30. Copeland parian Nimrod's head vase

A8 – NIMROD'S HEAD VASE
c.1872
Ht.6½in. (16.51cm)
Sculptor: A. Hays (attributed)
Publisher: A. Hays (presumed)
Marks: J82
Illus: Yes PP 569 (Figure 30)
This vase is based on the head of a colossal bull taken from the Palace of King Esarhaddon (680-669 BC) at Nimrud. It is difficult to determine whether the vase is intended to portray the bust of Nimrod 'the mighty hunter' of Genesis Chapter X verses 8 and 9, or is simply a reproduction of the head of a mighty bull in Esarhaddon's Palace at Nimrud. At the time it was excavated the local people were convinced that it was a representation of Nimrod, the son of Cush himself, and joyfully spread the news in the city of Mosul.

There seems to be confusion over the spelling of the name. 'Nimrod' is the spelling of the son of Cush and of the mighty hunter of the Holy Bible, whereas 'Nimrud' is the accepted spelling of the Assyrian city. In the book of Micah, Chapter V, verse 6, the land of Assyria is referred to as 'the land of Nimrod'.

Nimrod's name is perpetuated in several place names, including Birs-Nimrud south-west of Babylon and Nimrud in Assyria. This city, also called Calah, was founded by Asshur, a follower of Nimrod, moving from Shinar: 'And Cush begat Nimrod: he began to be a mighty one in the earth. He was a mighty hunter before the Lord...And the beginning of his kingdom was Babel, and Erech and Accad, and Calneh, in the land of Shinar. Out of that land went forth Asshur, and builded Nineveh, and the city Rehoboth, and Calah, and Resen between Nineveh and Calah: the same is a great city' (Genesis Chapter 10, verses 8-12). Some scholars identify Nimrod with Sargon I of Agade, c.2300 BC, who was a great warrior and hunter and ruler of Assyria. No certain identification has been made so far.

The prices recorded in the SPB show that the original price, wholesale, was 4/-. This was reduced to 2/6 on 26/11/1881, being 'quoted by R.P Copeland to Alfd. Jarvis, 43 Willes Road, Kentish Town London NW'. The price was raised on 13/11/1893 to 3/9d each.

LION PAPERWEIGHT
c.1872
length 4⅜in.(11.11cm)
Sculptor: A. Hays (attributed)
Publisher: A. Hays (presumed)
Marks: COPELAND (printed, or impressed J82)
Illus: Yes PP 569 (Figure 31)
This paperweight was inspired by a lion couchant, in bronze, brought to England from the south-west palace at Nimrud by Henry Layard. Inscribed on the back, in Assyrian cuneiform characters, is the name of Sennacherib, and on the side, in Phoenician, another inscription which reads '3 mana of the country'. The inscription provides interesting evidence of a commercial activity between the countries of Assyria and Phoenicia.

The SPB records 'Nineveh Lion 3/-, reduced to 1/9 RP on 29/11/81.' The price for 'Small qtys are charged Nineveh Lion Weights 2/-; increased to 2/6 on 13/11/93'.

Note. The photographs of the Copeland parian examples were taken in the Bolton Museum by Robert Copeland, with the exception of the Tribute panel which is in the Spode Museum Trust Collection. The illustrations of the original statues and panels are of examples to be found in the British Museum.

Marks

All parian items bear the impressed or printed mark of COPELAND. Other markings may vary and do not appear on each and every piece; moreover the date marks will vary and may not be present at all. Sizes, too, may vary a little from those quoted due to variations in firing over the years.

Figure 31. Copeland parian lion paper weight

5. The Impresarios – Entrances and Exits

The activities and biographies of those involved with the Assyrian discoveries who had any association with the British Museum have been given in various amount of detail in the many books which have been published on the subject.

Hitherto, however, little mention has been made of two significant contributors to the Museum's story; significant because, in a way, their association was the closest of all for they were servants who were employed by the Museum in a humble capacity and were wholly dependant upon it for their livelihoods. The more important of the two has already received brief recognition in some of the earlier sections. Their names were Aaron Hays and Alfred Jarvis. Here, then, is given the first full account of their contribution to the history of 'Assyria Revived' together with their biographies which ran consecutively.

Aaron Hays

Decorative art in the third quarter of the nineteenth century which arose from the Assyrian discoveries was to be found in various materials and forms, the most prized of which was jewellery fashioned from gold or silver, or a combination of both; other examples were bronze statuettes for mantelpieces, clock ornaments, book-ends, etc.

Aaron Hays, together with Messrs Copeland, made his own contribution to decorative art by way of a number of statuettes which were executed in Statuary Porcelain, and these were to form the basis of the unique series manufactured by W.T. Copeland & Sons of Stoke-upon-Trent.

The rate records for 1861 reveal that Hays was born at St. Michael's, Dorset in 1814. Nothing further is known of him until 1830 when, from his curriculum vitae of 1830-1845, we learn that he earned a living in domestic service.

1830.

I beg to certify, that during the time AARON HAYS lived in my service, (which I believe was about a year and-a-half) I found him perfectly steady, sober, honest, and perfectly civil and obliging.

MARY FRYER.
Wenbourne, March 5th., 1845.

1834.

Aaron Hays was in my service about Five Months, and I believe him to be perfectly honest, sober, industrious, and well behaved ; he came to me from Miss Fryer, who gave him a good character.

B. LENTHORNE, ESQ.
High Hall, March 18th., 1835.

1835.

I hereby certify, that AARON HAYS lived in my service in the capacity of Footman and Groom, or general Servant, more than 2 years, viz. from the end of March 1835, to the beginning of April, 1837, and I here readily subscribe to the satisfaction he gave me, by his honesty, sobriety, and general good conduct during the said period. As witness my hand and seal at Bilkerne, near Southampton.

CHARLES WM. DAVY, ESQ.
January 28th., 1844.

1837.

To RICHARD WHITE, ESQ.

Sir,

In reply to the Letter I have just received from you, respecting AARON HAYS, I am happy to be able to state, that (though I did not know his age) I always believed him to be unmarried, that he lived with me 3 years and left me in April, for the reason as he then told me, that he assigned to you. I think him thoroughly trustworthy, sober, active, and cleanly, and very willing, and have always considered him peculiarly steady. Of wine, in my family, he would not have much to do with a cellar of wines, but I have every reason to think he would act conscientiously ; and I shall be glad to think that he is so fortunate as to enter into your service.

I have the honor be be, Sir,
your humble Servant,
Twickenham, May 20th.
FRANCES CLAYTON

I have omitted to say, that his memory is good, as also his health and temper.

1840.

Sir,

I had an excellent character with AARON HAYS from the lady he last served. During the time he was in my service, I found him honest, sober, and willing to make himself useful, and I parted with him for no fault. I send, inclosed, the character I received from Mrs. Clayton—the reason which he gave for leaving her service was, to "better himself".

I am, Sir, your obedient Servant,
Acton Hill, July 11th, 1840.
RICHARD WHITE.

1840.

Dear Sir,

I beg to say in reply to your letter, that my knowledge of HAY's abilities as an Upper Servant is very limited, as I only keep 1 Man Servant, and from the short time he lived in my service, should say, that he was better suited to a situation in which he had some assistance, than in a single-handed place ; but the inclosed notes will, I hope, satisfy you better respecting his character than I can possibly do ; I found him honest and sober, nor did I part from him for any fault, as he gave me warning, in consequence of some misunderstanding between him and my son.

I beg to remain, dear Sir, very truly yours,
Woodhall, Feb. 15th, 1841.
MARY ANN JONES.

FROM HARRY EDGELL, ESQ.

I hereby certify, that AARON HAYS has lived in my service as Butler, the last 4 years without any intermission, during which time he has uniformly conducted himself steadily, and with great propriety. I consider him a very honest, sober, diligent, careful, trusty, and attentive Servant, a good Waiter at table, and a good cleaner of Plate, and fully qualified for the situation ; he is anxious to obtain as third Butler in the Honourable Society of Gray's Inn. He came into my service from that of Mrs. Jones, the Widow of the late Marshall, of the Queen's Bench Prison.

21, Cadogan Place.
[7 May 1845]

The above Original Testimonials are now in the hands of me, HARRY EDGELL.

The curriculum, together with a letter of recommendation from the architect Richard Westmacott junior was submitted to the Trustees of the British Museum in late 1845, when Hays applied for a vacancy in the Department of Antiquities; Westmacott was the designer of the Façade of the British Museum and the son-in-law of Harry Edgell from whom Hays obtained his final testimony:

> Wilton Place Nov 20/45
> Dear Mr Henry,
> I take the liberty to write to you at the request of a person of whom I have every reason to think well – from the excellent testimonials he has – & from his having lived for some time/ with perfect satisfaction to his master/ as butler to my wife's father – he is most desirous of obtaining the employment of an attendant in the British Museum and he has just heard from one of your staff – a servant formerly of Col. Leake – that there is a vacancy for one in the Department of Antiquities etc.
> I have no doubt you are persecuted by applications for such situations and I apologise for adding to your trouble, but I assure you I believe I am recommending to your notice a very worthy and superior person. At any rate pardon this intrusion and believe me, Dear Mr Henry,
>
> Yr. Obliged & faithful
>
> Rich'd Westmacott
> His name is Aaron Hays and he is now butler to Harry Edgell Esq (a bencher* of Gray's Inn).
>
> Note by Mr Henry: Aged 31, writes a good hand. Produces fair testimonials. Has lived five years with Mr Edgell. Married 6 years. No family.

* A bencher is a senior member of any of the Inns of Court, London.

Hays' application was successful, and on 2 December 1845, aged thirty-one, he was appointed Attendant Third Class in the Department of Antiquities; by this time he was married but without issue. In December 1856 he became an Attendant Second Class and in April 1864 was promoted to Attendant First Class in the Oriental Antiquities Department, which had been formed in 1860.

As evidence of his burgeoning skills as a sculptor, or perhaps modeller is a better description, Hays had submitted a number of sketches of an architectural sculpture nature with his application and, while the sketches are of no relevance to this work, they did forewarn the Trustees of his artistic aspirations, of which they were to be reminded later.

There is circumstantial evidence that as early as 1858 Hays had commenced to occupy himself with producing reproductions of the Assyrian artefacts for, on 17 April of that year, he, together with two other attendants, were reprimanded by the Trustees for allowing photography to be carried out in the galleries without permission. Further, he had permitted the illumination of antiquities by the use of a lighted candle in the room in which the photographs were being taken.

Hays was to cleverly transform his models of the Assyrian Royalty, the Winged Human-Headed Bull and Lion into the 'round' from basso-relievo. To achieve his purpose without the Museum, he would have needed some form of visual aid and what better aid than that from a camera? It almost beggars belief that there was no connection between this incident and his modelling interests.

The first statuettes were being offered for sale in February 1860 from Hays' home address at 9 Elizabeth Street, Hans Place, Chelsea (see footnote to the *Art-Journal* article on page 266) where, according to local rate records and the 1861 Census, he lived with his wife, Selina, his daughter Francis *(sic)* and an American lodger working at the War Office. The premises were rented, as were those at No.3 Elizabeth Street. Hays paid the rates on both properties; No.3 is listed as a dwelling-house, outbuildings and premises, but there is no mention of any business use.

Aaron Hays was no sluggard for, in addition to his museum duties and indulging his sculptural skills, he also found time to play a leading role in the 37th Middlesex Volunteer Rifle Corps. In 1860 he requested leave of absence from the Trustees to participate in a prestigious shooting competition; his request was granted.

> Gallery of Antiquities
> British Museum
> June 27th 1860
>
> Sir,
> I humbly trust you will pardon me again trespassing upon your time but I beg most respectfully to say my Commanding Officer Captain Jenkes has selected me to compete for the Prize given by Her Majesty the Queen to be shot for on Monday next the 2nd of July on Wimbledon Common by the Volunteer Rifle Corps. I respectfully beg to say, I am most anxious to get 2 days practise Rifle Shooting at the Target at Aldershot previous to Monday next. I humbly solicit the great favour of you to kindly grant me leave of absence for Friday, and Saturday, next for the practise at Aldershot. Also Monday, and Tuesday, next, to go to Wimbledon to shoot for the Prize.
> I have the honour to remain
> Sir
> Your obedient & humble Servant
> (signed) A Hays
> Sergeant of the 37th Middlesex VRC

In 1861 he repeated the request, but this time without success. It will be noted that by this time he had progressed from Sergeant to Quarter-Master Sergeant.

> To the Right Hon The Trustees of the British Museum
> My Lords and Gentlemen,
> I humbly trust you will be pleased to pardon me in venturing to trespass upon your valuable time, but I beg most respectfully to say I am a member and Quarter Master Sergeant of the 37th Middlesex Volunteer Rifle Corps. The Corps of the Parish, now numbering six hundred effective members, and out of the above number they are only allowed to send three to compete for the Prize and to represent the Corps at Wimbledon and having been successfull in shooting into my class – I was entitled as one of the three to go to Wimbledon, for which I was obliged to take four days, I beg most respectfully, my Lords and Gentlemen to solicit the very great favour of you, to be so

kind as to grant me the 4 days extra so as not to be deducted from my holiday.

I have the honour to remain
My Lords & Gentlemen
Your most obedient & humble Servant
(signed) A Hays
Attendant in the Gallery of Antiquities

British Museum records show that Hays had periods of sickness lasting for two years – in 1864, in 1866 for two months, and again in 1868 for six weeks. The nature of his illnesses is not known.

Hays retired from the Museum's service on 21 December 1876 with a 'retired allowance' of £62 per annum, a sum which would be equivalent to about £3,000 in 2006.

B.M. January 1 1877

The Assistant Secretary of the British Museum is directed to inform Aaron Hays that the Lords Commissioners of Her Majesty's Treasury have been pleased to award him a retired allowance of £62 (sixty-two pounds) per annum; and that the Paymaster General has been instructed to pay the allowance from the 21st of December, 1876, inclusive.

Mr Aaron Hays
30, Clarence Road
Kentish Town,

He was sixty-two years of age and had removed to Kentish Town. His only other known sculptural work is a portrait bust of Beethoven (see B9) which he produced in 1871 and which is in the possession of the London Philharmonic Orchestra.

Alfred Jarvis

Alfred Jarvis was born in 1841 at Catford, Kent, where he attended 'The National School'. He joined the staff of the British Museum in September 1869 at the age of twenty-seven, having previously been employed as a waiter at the Burlington Hotel, Cork Street, London, and as butler to William Harrison Esq. of Salmesbury Hall, Blackburn, from where he seemingly forwarded his application to the Museum. His testimonials as to his conduct and deportment were both many and impeccable.

By deduction it seems possible that he could have been related to Hays, either by blood or marriage, whom he joined when he became an Attendant Second Class in the Museum's Department of British and Medieval Antiquities; he was then a married man. There is little more to record of Jarvis's personal life.

As was the case with Hays, he was found guilty at some point of an act of 'grave misconduct'. This time it remains unspecified, but for this fall from grace Jarvis suffered a reduction in his pension when he retired in 1900, aged sixty.

According to an announcement in *The Athenaeum* in July 1878, Jarvis had by then acquired all rights to Hays' interests in the manufacture and sale of the Assyrian reproductions. The terms and conditions of the transfer are not known, but he would surely have been aware of all details and have deemed the acquisition to be a rewarding one. By reference to the details quoted for the Nimrod's Head Vase it will be seen that he was still buying from Copelands in 1893, and perhaps still in 1913, assuming that he retained the rights in the reproductions.

Alfred Jarvis' son, also named Alfred, was also to become a servant of the British Museum. There is no evidence that he ever became involved in the Hays-Jarvis enterprise.

Curtain Call

Funding and Promotion

The few references to Hays which have appeared in various publications give rise to speculation over the means by which Hays, a man of apparently humble circumstances, could fund and promote his trading interests. He would not have been familiar with the doggerel:

He who whispers down a well
about the goods he has to sell
will never reap the golden dollars
like he who climbs a tree and hollers!

He may not have heard it but certainly he understood it!

Since commercial motivation requires money, it is sensible first to consider the fund-raising avenues available at the time. There were banks, of course, but it seems unlikely that in the mid-nineteenth century a prudent lender would advance money to a man who had little collateral to offer.

Perhaps someone of substance with a close connection to the Assyrian sculptures might have helped. Here Layard's name springs to mind, but there is no evidence amongst his papers at the British Museum of any arrangement with Hays. Richard Westmacott junior is a possibility; he and Hays were well acquainted and he himself was a sculptor. But so far the authors have failed to locate his papers and are therefore unable to make further comment.

No information is found in the Copeland archives.

So the most plausible explanation occurring to the authors is that the venture was, in fact, self-financing and for the following reason: it was the practice of pottery manufacturers, such as Copeland, to purchase models, manufacturing and distribution rights from sculptors. For example, Copeland paid £200 to Mary Thornycroft for the rights to her sculptures of the four royal children dressed to represent the Four Seasons; this sum, equal to about £20,000 in 2006, was exceptionally high, however.

It may well be that Hays chose to take his payment, in whole or in part, as finished goods in lieu of cash and, by so doing, would obtain an initial stock. But so deeply buried are the questions that the true answers may never be dug out.

Unless Hays' abilities as an entrepreneur are to be grossly underestimated, a guiding hand can be discerned in the quality and ambition of his promotional campaign, which appears to have commenced as a footnote to an article in the *Art-Journal* of February 1860 (see Figure 35, centre panel at foot of page 266). Nothing else is recorded of Hays' activities until 13 January 1865 when a receipt was issued by him for two statuettes sold to HM Queen Victoria (Figure 34, Sardanapalus and his Queen). The present whereabouts of these two items are not known.

Figure 32. Logotype from A. Hays' notepaper

Figure 33. Device from the 'Triumphal March' panel in the British Museum which acted as the idea for the logotype

The logotype, or badge, on Hays' notepaper

The logotype (Figure 32) which Hays chose for his notepaper was taken from the 'Triumphal March' panel in the British Museum (Figure 33). Dating from c.865-860 BC, it shows the Assyrian king, Ashurnasirpal II, accompanied by the god in the winged disc, returning in triumph to camp. A horseman follows with a spare horse for the use of the king (see *Monuments of Nineveh*).

The 'Sun-Disc' also appears on the casket presented to Henry Layard on the occasion of his being granted the Freedom of the City of London in 1853. This was some twelve years before the invoice to Queen Victoria and so may have been the inspiration for Hays to adopt the disc as his badge. (See *The Louvre Catalogue De Khorsabad à Paris. La découverte des Assyriens,* 1994.) The receipt (Figure 34) supports the claim, made later in Jarvis' sales brochure, naming the Queen (Victoria) as a patron of the reproductions.

No further examples of promotional activity are known until Alfred Jarvis made what could have been a final push to clear remaining stocks before his forthcoming retirement; in this respect, the year 1893 has some significance.

Figure 36 shows the descriptive brochure, issued by Jarvis, giving full details and retail prices of the complete series with the rather strange exception of the 'Tribute of Jehu' panel from the

9 - Elizabeth Street Hans Place

B. B. Woodward Esqr

To A. Hays

2 Statuettes

Sardanapalus & his Queen

£2:10:0

INLAND REVENUE
ONE PENNY

Received the above

A. Hays

Jany 13 1865

Figure 34. Copy of invoice to H.M. Queen Victoria 1865.

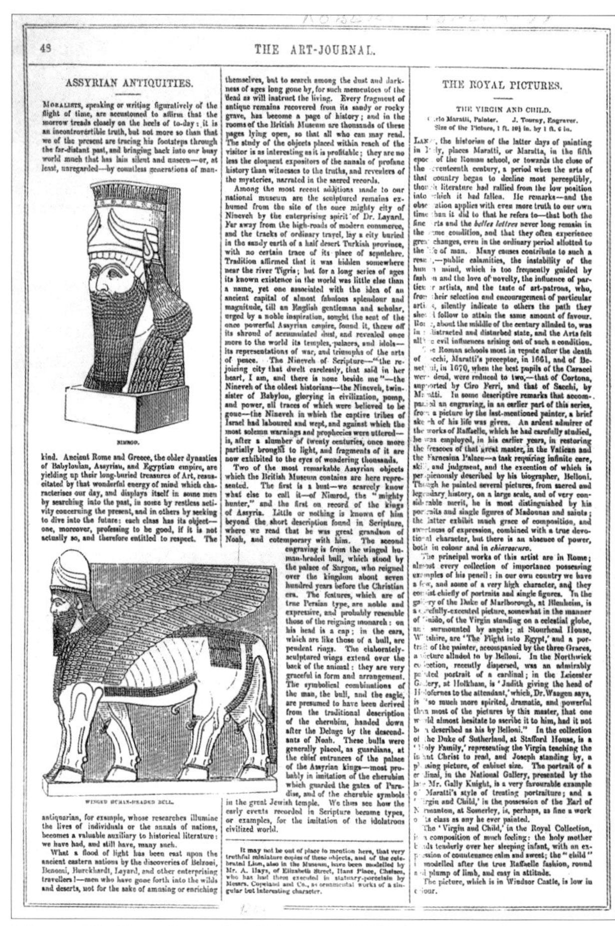

48 THE ART-JOURNAL.

ASSYRIAN ANTIQUITIES.

MORALISTS, speaking or writing figuratively of the flight of time, are accustomed to affirm that the morrow treads closely on the heels of to-day: it is an incontrovertible truth, but not more so than that we of the present are tracing his footsteps through the far-distant past, and bringing back into our busy world much that has lain silent and unseen—or, at least, unregarded—by countless generations of mankind. Ancient Rome and Greece, the older dynasties of Babylonian, Assyrian, and Egyptian empire, are yielding up their long-buried treasures of Art, resuscitated by that wonderful energy of mind which characterises our day, and displays itself in some men by searching into the past, in some by restless activity concerning the present, and in others by seeking to dive into the future; each class has its object—one, moreover, professing to be good, if it is not actually so, and therefore entitled to respect. The antiquarian, for example, whose researches illumine the lives of individuals or the annals of nations, becomes a valuable auxiliary to historical literature: we have had, and still have, many such.

NIMROD.

WINGED HUMAN-HEADED BULL.

What a flood of light has been cast upon the ancient eastern nations by the discoveries of Belzoni, Benomi, Burckhardt, Layard, and other enterprising travellers!—men who have gone forth into the wilds and deserts, not for the sake of amusing or enriching themselves, but to search among the dust and darkness of ages long gone by, for such mementoes of the dead as will instruct the living. Every fragment of antique remains recovered from its sandy or rocky grave, has become a page of history; and in the rooms of the British Museum are thousands of these pages lying open, so that all who can may read. The study of the objects placed within reach of the visitor is as interesting as it is profitable; they are no less the eloquent expositors of the annals of profane history than witnesses to the truths, and revealers of the mysteries, narrated in the sacred records.

Among the most recent additions made to our national museum are the sculptured remains exhumed from the site of the once mighty city of Nineveh by the enterprising spirit of Dr. Layard. Far away from the high-roads of modern commerce, and the tracks of ordinary travel, lay a city buried in the sandy earth of a half desert Turkish province, with no certain trace of its place of sepulchre. Tradition affirmed that it was hidden somewhere near the river Tigris; but for a long series of ages its known existence in the world was little else than a name, yet one associated with the idea of an ancient capital of almost fabulous splendour and magnitude, till an English gentleman and scholar, urged by a noble inspiration, sought the seat of the once powerful Assyrian empire, found it, threw off its shroud of accumulated dust, and revealed once more to the world its temples, palaces, and idols—its representations of war, and triumphs of the arts of peace. The Nineveh of Scripture—"the rejoicing city that dwelt carelessly, that said in her heart, I am, and there is none beside me"—the Nineveh of the oldest historians—the Nineveh, twin-sister of Babylon, glorying in civilization, pomp, and power, all traces of which were believed to be gone—the Nineveh in which the captive tribes of Israel had laboured and wept, and against which the most solemn warnings and prophecies were uttered—is, after a slumber of twenty centuries, once more partially brought to light, and fragments of it are now exhibited to the eyes of wondering thousands.

Two of the most remarkable Assyrian objects which the British Museum contains are here represented. The first is a bust—we scarcely know what else to call it—of Nimrod, the "mighty hunter," and the first on record of the kings of Assyria. Little or nothing is known of him beyond the short description found in Scripture, where we read that he was great grandson of Noah, and cotemporary with him. The second engraving is from the winged human-headed bull, which stood by the palace of Sargon, who reigned over the kingdom about seven hundred years before the Christian era. The features, which are of true Persian type, are noble and expressive, and probably resemble those of the reigning monarch: on his head is a cap; in the ears, which are like those of a bull, are pendent rings. The elaborately-sculptured wings extend over the back of the animal: they are very graceful in form and arrangement. The symbolical combinations of the man, the bull, and the eagle, are presumed to have been derived from the traditional description of the cherubim, handed down after the Deluge by the descendants of Noah. These bulls were generally placed, as guardians, at the chief entrances of the palace of the Assyrian kings—most probably in imitation of the cherubim which guarded the gates of Paradise, and of the cherubic symbols in the great Jewish temple. We thus see how the early events recorded in Scripture became types, or examples, for the imitation of the idolatrous civilized world.

It may not be out of place to mention here, that very truthful miniature copies of these objects, and of the celebrated Lion, also in the Museum, have been modelled by Mr. A. Hays, of Elizabeth Street, Hans Place, Chelsea, who has had them executed in statuary-porcelain by Messrs. Copeland and Co., as ornamental works of a singular but interesting character.

THE ROYAL PICTURES.

THE VIRGIN AND CHILD.

Carlo Maratti, Painter. J. Tourny, Engraver.

Size of the Picture, 1 ft. 10½ in. by 1 ft. 6 in.

LANZI, the historian of the latter days of painting in Italy, places Maratti, or Maratta, in the fifth epoch of the Roman school, or towards the close of the seventeenth century, a period when the arts of that country began to decline most perceptibly, though literature had rallied from the low position into which it had fallen. He remarks—and the observation applies with even more truth to our own time than it did to that he refers to—that both the fine arts and the *belles lettres* never long remain in the same condition, and that they often experience great changes, even in the ordinary period allotted to the life of man. Many causes contribute to such a result,—public calamities, the instability of the human mind, which is too frequently guided by fashion and the love of novelty, the influence of particular artists, and the taste of art-patrons, who, from their selection and encouragement of particular artists, silently indicate to others the path they should follow to attain the same amount of favour. Rome, about the middle of the century alluded to, was in a distracted and disturbed state, and the Arts felt all the evil influences arising out of such a condition.

The Roman schools most in repute after the death of Sacchi, Maratti's preceptor, in 1661, and of Benedetti, in 1670, when the best pupils of the Caracci were dead, were reduced to two,—that of Cortona, supported by Ciro Ferri, and that of Sacchi, by Maratti. In some descriptive remarks that accompanied an engraving, in an earlier part of this series, from a picture by the last-mentioned painter, a brief sketch of his life was given. An ardent admirer of the works of Raffaelle, which he had carefully studied, he was employed, in his earlier years, in restoring the frescoes of that great master, in the Vatican and the Farnesina Palace—a task requiring infinite care, skill, and judgment, and the execution of which is perspicuously described by his biographer, Belloni. Though he painted several pictures, from sacred and legendary history, on a large scale, and of very considerable merit, he is most distinguished by his portraits and single figures of Madonnas and saints; the latter exhibit much grace of composition, and sweetness of expression, combined with a true devotional character, but there is an absence of power, both in colour and in *chiaroscuro*.

The principal works of this artist are in Rome; almost every collection of importance possessing examples of his pencil: in our own country we have a few, and some of a very high character, and they consist chiefly of portraits and single figures. In the gallery of the Duke of Marlborough, at Blenheim, is a carefully-executed picture, somewhat in the manner of Guido, of the Virgin standing on a celestial globe, and surmounted by angels; at Stourhead House, Wiltshire, are 'The Flight into Egypt,' and a portrait of the painter, accompanied by the three Graces, a picture alluded to by Belloni. In the Northwick collection, recently dispersed, was an admirably painted portrait of a cardinal; in the Leicester Gallery, at Holkham, is 'Judith giving the head of Holofernes to the attendant,' which, Dr. Waagen says, is "so much more spirited, dramatic, and powerful than most of the pictures by this master, that one would almost hesitate to ascribe it to him, had it not been described as his by Belloni." In the collection of the Duke of Sutherland, at Stafford House, is a 'Holy Family,' representing the Virgin teaching the infant Christ to read, and Joseph standing by, a pleasing picture, of cabinet size. The portrait of a cardinal, in the National Gallery, presented by the late Mr. Gally Knight, is a very favourable example of Maratti's style of treating portraiture; and a 'Virgin and Child,' in the possession of the Earl of Normanton, at Somerley, is, perhaps, as fine a work of its class as any he ever painted.

The 'Virgin and Child,' in the Royal Collection, is a composition of much feeling: the holy mother bends tenderly over her sleeping infant, with an expression of countenance calm and sweet; the "child" is modelled after the true Raffaelle fashion, round and plump of limb, and easy in attitude.

The picture, which is in Windsor Castle, is low in colour.

Figure 35. Page from the February 1860 *Art-Journal*

Nineveh

REPRODUCTIONS
FROM THE
ASSYRIAN SCULPTURES
(BRITISH MUSEUM).

Under the Patronage of—

HER MAJESTY THE QUEEN;
SCIENCE AND ART MUSEUM, DUBLIN;
CHADWICK MUSEUM, BOLTON;
ASTOR LIBRARY, NEW YORK;
H.I.H. THE GRAND DUKE CONSTANTINE OF RUSSIA,
SHEFFIELD MUSEUM;
SMITHSONIAN INSTITUTION, U.S.A.; AND
VARIOUS OTHER PUBLIC INSTITUTIONS.

THREE STATUETTES
OF
Sennacherib,
Assurbanipal (Sardanapalus) and his Queen
(B.C. 705-625).

The Beautiful Garden-Scene
(From the Palace of Assurbanipal).

Winged Human-headed Lion and Bull,
Nimrod's Head, and Lion Weight.

* * * * * * * * * * * * * * * * * *

THE great revival of interest in Oriental Antiquities, and especially in the Sculptures of Ancient Nineveh, has induced me to re-issue the series of careful reproductions of the best examples of Assyrian art, which were modelled by the late Mr. A. Hays, who was for many years employed in the Oriental Department of the British Museum.

The statuettes and bas-reliefs in this series are carefully modelled from the originals in the British Museum, every detail of costume and ornament being accurately reproduced. Neither pains nor expense have been spared to make them perfect. They are made in the beautiful porcelain biscuit known as Parian, from its resemblance to the marble of that name, of the finest quality and of a delicate tone of colour.

The relationship between Assyrian, Phœnician, and Greek art is now so clearly established, that all students of classical art know that a knowledge of the art of ancient Assyria must form a preface to their studies. Such a knowledge could only be acquired by a visit to the Assyrian Galleries of the British Museum, but the reproductions which I now issue are so accurate in detail as to enable students in Schools of Art, and others, to obtain a knowledge of the richness and finish of Assyrian sculpture at its best period.

The reproduction of the "Garden-Scene" from the palace of Assurbanipal, which is now issued for the first time, is of special interest, as it is one of the few sculptures which afford us a glimpse of the private life of the king; the subjects usually being derived from the war or the chase. Taking the figures in the chronological order, or the reigns of the monarchs represented, we have :—

[2]

SENNACHERIB (B.C. 705-681).

THE statuette (13½ inches high) of Sennacherib, the opponent of Hezekiah, represents him as clad in the robes of the dual office of King and High-priest. The drapery is most richly embroidered and fringed, and the long under-robe extends nearly to his feet. Over the shoulders falls a richly fringed and decorated cape. The King wears the tiara, so commonly represented on the monuments, and carries in his hand the sacred bow of office. This bow, which was handed down from king to king, was the gift of the goddess Ishtar, or Ashtareth, who had the name of "Mistress of the bow," "Archeress of the Gods," "Lady of War and Battle," and the possession of it was supposed to ensure victory. His arms, which are bare, are encircled by rich bracelets, similar to those figured on the sculptures of Nineveh.

The whole bearing of the figure serves fully to convey the character of a king who styled himself "the father of the people of Assyria."

* * * * * * * * * * * * * * * *

ASSURBANIPAL or SARDANAPALUS (B.C. 668-625).

(Modelled from the figure in the Lion Hunt Sculptures.)

THE labours of Assyriologists have enabled us to recognise in the warlike and yet luxurious monarch Assurbanipal, the Sardanapalus whom Ctesias and Byron have rendered so familiar to students of what was once considered Oriental history.

In the statuette, which is 12 inches high, we seem to see the true king of Assyria, as he appeared on the fatal night when Nineveh fell; clad in his robes of battle, and wearing on his head a richly jewelled diadem, below which fall his long locks of hair. The king is clothed in a close-fitting robe, reaching to the knees in front, and somewhat longer behind, the groundwork of which is richly spotted with a handsome lozenge pattern; the lower part being decorated with two rows of braiding and a rich tasselled fringe. Over the right shoulder and crossing the breast is a broad belt. The waist is bound by a wide band of cloth, over which is a narrow girdle of richly worked metal. The breast and short sleeves of this robe are most elaborately treated. On the arms are a pair of gold bracelets, and the knees are encircled by garters. The king wears boots of the Median style, and leather greaves reaching nearly to the knee, bound with thongs of that material. In the left hand the king carries negligently a sword of light make.

In the free and athletic bearing of the figure before us we seem to see a man such as might well be styled "the warrior of the gods, the beloved of Ishtar (Aphrodite)," a conqueror and a king.

* * * * * * * * * * * * * * * *

QUEEN OF SARDANAPALUS.

IN this figure (11¼ inches high) we have an exact reproduction, in the round, of the figure of the Queen of Assurbanipal as represented on a bas-relief obtained from Kouyunjik. The queen wears long garments of a less ornate character than those of the king. In her right hand she holds a wine cup of Cyprian workmanship.

Assurbanipal had many wives, as he made it the custom to marry the daughters of conquered kings; and his large harem was no doubt the cause of the numerous conspiracies among rival princes, which broke out upon his death.

* * * * * * * * * * * * * * * *

GARDEN-SCENE.

(From the Palace of Assurbanipal at Kouyunjik.)

ALL the Assyrian palaces had gardens attached to the harem apartments. There were in most cases several wives, and each establishment had its garden. In this sculpture we see the king resting in the garden of one of his queens, probably after the fatigues of the lion hunt.

The garden here is a veritable Oriental paradise planted with the choicest trees and flowers taken from the lands under the rule of the Assyrian empire, which then extended from the Tigris to the Nile. The king reclines upon a rich couch, probably one of the ivory couches the tribute of Egypt; while

(Above and overleaf) Figure 36. Four page brochure of 'Reproductions from the Assyrian Sculptures' (British Museum)

Black Obelisk (Figure 28). It will be seen from the four press opinions quoted under 'Re-issue' that they are all dated 1893, as is also a press cutting from the *Independent.*

Also in 1893 Jarvis wrote on his personal notepaper to Dublin Museum as follows:

> 43, Willes Road,
> London. N.W.,
> ENGLAND. 25 October 1893
> Sir,
> I beg to inform you that I am re-issuing my reproductions from the Assyrian sculptures of the British Museum; and I enclose a proof of my new prospectus – now in the press.
> You will notice that I have added the famous 'Garden Scene' to the Original series; and I beg to offer a copy of this work at a reduction of 25 per cent off list price, and also a copy of the Lion-weight – which I do not think you have – I was not publishing it when you purchased your set.
> I am, sir,
> Your obedient servant,
> Alfred Jarvis
>
> The Director,
> Science & Art Museum,
> Dublin.

Once more, the 'Tribute of Jehu' panel is ignored.

Amusingly, but not to Jarvis, on the relevant museum file (A & I File) the Keeper of the Division advised the Director "We have quite enough of this!"

There is little reason to doubt the claims of 'Patronage', for, in addition to Queen Victoria and the Dublin Museum, both Bolton and Sheffield Museums have provided proof of purchase. No dates of acquisition are to be had from Bolton, but it is suggested that the figures may have been donated in the Museum's formative year, c.1880. A full set minus the 'Tribute of Jehu' panel is to be found there and they were photographed by the author.

The City Museum, Weston Park, Sheffield, has a complete set of nine items which were purchased over the period 1885-1896.

No further information is available regarding Alfred Jarvis's sales campaign and so it seems that 1896 saw his final sales effort.

The complete series of nine reproductions (A1-A9) evolved over a period of approximately thirty years, during which time no London institution appears to have shown any interest until 1985-1989, when six pieces were purchased by the British Museum. They are:

Sennacherib purchased 1985

[3]

opposite him the queen is seated, clad in a "rich embroidered robe," while around are the various harem attendants. The banquet is evidently one similar to that described in the book of Esther (v. 6), "a banquet of wine" in the palace garden (Esther vii. 7). The parallel is all the more close when we notice that in the branches of one of the trees a head hangs, the head no doubt of some rival whose removal the queen is celebrating by a banquet to the king, though some authorities consider this head to be that of Te-umman, King of Elam.

Here the scene is particularly Eastern, and illustrates the luxurious, sensual life of the king. Attendants are employed in bringing in trays laden with fruits and sweets, while a band of musicians and singers discourse soft, sweet music. The whole sculpture illustrates the luxury of court life at the grandest period of the Assyrian empire.

The size of this bas-relief is 22 inches by 8½ inches.

* * * * * * * * * * * * * * * * *

WINGED HUMAN-HEADED LION AND BULL.

THE winged bulls and lions of the Assyrian palaces are, perhaps, the most popularly known of the Assyrian sculptures. These winged colossi were known as *shedii*, or spirit guardians, and were placed at the doorways to protect "the goings out and comings in of the king." The winged bull was sacred to the god Anu, the god of heaven. The winged lion was the emblem of Nergal, the god of "War and Death," in his character of the "Great Eater" (*Irkalla*). Compare Judges xiv. 14: "Out of the eater came forth meat." The winged figures were really a species of Cherubim guarding the royal presence, and their appearance exactly agrees with that of the Cherubim of Ezekiel's visions.

The height of these reproductions is 9 inches and the length 10¾ inches.

* * * * * * * * * * * * * * * *

NIMROD'S HEAD.

THIS is a reproduction of the head of one of those monsters who guarded the portals of the palaces of the Kings of Nations. It well represents the conventional treatment of animal life by the artists of Assyria. When the head of one of these monsters was first unearthed, the Arabs rushed to tell the people of Mosul they had found Nimrod.

The reproduction is 6½ inches high.

* * * * * * * * * * * * * * * * *

A LION WEIGHT.

THIS is the figure of a lion couchant, and is a model of one of the pretty bronze weights obtained by Sir Henry Layard from the South West Palace at Nimroud. On the back of the figure is inscribed, in Assyrian, the name of Sennacherib (B.C. 702), and on the side of the figure a Phœnician inscription which reads "3 Mana of the Country." This weight, which is very accurately copied, is an interesting monument of the commercial contact between Assyria and Phœnicia.

The reproduction is 4½ inches long.

List of Prices.

	£	s.	d.		£	s.	d.
Sennacherib ...	1	10	0	Winged Human-headed Lion ...	2	2	0
Assurbanipal ...	1	10	0	Winged Human-headed Bull ...	2	2	0
Queen of Assurbanipal ...	1	10	0	Nimrod's Head ...	0	10	0
Garden-Scene ...	2	2	0	Lion Weight ...	0	7	6

The Complete Series of Eight Works, £11 : 0 : 0

43, Willes Road,
London: N.W.

Alfred Jarvis,
Sole Publisher.

PRESS OPINIONS.

RE-ISSUE.

"The Athenæum," of October 7, 1893, says:—"In the *Athenæum* for July 6, 1878, we called attention to the issue of a small series of reproductions of Assyrian bas-reliefs, &c., in Parian porcelain. The objects selected for modelling were a winged human-headed Lion and Bull from Nimroud; a colossal head, formerly said to be that of Nimrod, also from Nimroud (the Biblical Calah); figures of the Assyrian kings Sennacherib, and Assurbanipal and his queen; and of a lion-weight with bilingual inscription in Phœnician and Assyrian. These interesting and faithful reproductions attracted much notice at the time, and the numerous enquiries which have been made for them since the first edition was exhausted have induced Mr. Jarvis to re-issue the series, which has since been increased by the addition of the famous scene in which Assurbanipal is drinking wine with his queen in a garden, upon one of the trees of which hangs the head of his enemy, the King of Elam."

"The Irish Times," Sept. 30, 1893:—"The beauty of Assyrian art has been practically illustrated by Mr. Jarvis, who has finished an interesting series of small reproductions of the Assyrian sculptures and bas-reliefs. These reproductions are exact copies. Among the best are the small portrait statues of the two great kings, Sennacherib and Assurbanipal. . . ."

"The Daily Graphic," Sept. 30, 1893:—" . . . An interesting series of reproductions, and, though reduced in scale, exact copies. . . ."

"The Manchester Guardian," Sept. 29, 1893:—" . . . Really accurate in representing the execution of the Assyrian work. . . ."

FIRST ISSUE.

"The Art Journal" thus reviews the statuettes of Sardanapalus and his Queen:—" . . . Two statuettes of Sardanapalus and his Queen have been recently modelled from one of the Nineveh Marbles. The forms, the features, the attitudes, and the draperies have all been rendered with scrupulous fidelity. The result is a pair of figures of much and singular interest, valuable as fac-similes from the remotest antique of art, and desirable as among the most agreeable of ornaments for the drawing-room and the boudoir. The date of the original bas-relief is, as we know, some six hundred and fifty years before the Christian era, yet they are of great merit as art works—such as the sculptor has scarcely surpassed in two thousand years. . . ."

"The Academy," June 1, 1878:—" . . . Mr. A. Hays has executed a pair of statuettes representing the two Assyrian Kings, Sennacherib and Assurbanipal or Sardanapalus. These statues, which are exact reproductions from the figures in the bas-reliefs, are now supplemented by a female figure representing the Queen of Sardanapalus. The forms and features and the elaborate embroidered drapery are rendered with most scrupulous fidelity. In addition to these statuettes there are two small reproductions of the head of a Winged Bull and one of the lion-weights, which are most faithful in their rendering, and form interesting examples of the conventional treatment of animal life which is so marked a feature in the art of the Assyrian Empire."

"The American Antiquarian," Oct. 1883:—" . . . For the benefit of those who wish to compare the art of the golden age of Assyria with that of other nations, Mr. Jarvis has prepared a series of reduced reproductions of the most typical examples. History is represented by two statuettes of Sennacherib and Sardanapalus. Court life by a picture of the Queen of Sardanapalus. Symbolical art by figures of the Winged Lion and Bull. These interesting figures are most faithful reproductions of Assyrian art, and may be safely used by lecturers and teachers. The statuette of Sennacherib serves thoroughly to convey to us the idea of the king who styled himself the 'Father of the people of Assyria,' and that of Assurbanipal, which is modelled with great care, places before us a true portrait of the Sardanapalus whom Ctesias and Byron have made so familiar to us. The figure of the Queen of Assurbanipal is an exact reproduction, and extremely intersting. These statues are truthful and accurate in detail."

Mr. Hormuzd Rassam says:—"I have much pleasure in recommending Mr. Jarvis's Assyrian Statuettes to those who wish to possess unique representations in porcelain of the renowned Assyrian monarchs, Sennacherib, Sardanapalus, and other objects, more especially the well-known Nineveh human-headed Lion and Bull. They reflect great credit upon the designer's skill and good taste for the work of art, and above all the moderate price he has set upon them."

Sardanapalus	1985
Queen of Sardanapalus	1989
Winged Human-Headed Bull	1987
Winged Human-Headed Lion	1987
Nimrod Vase	1986

Marks

As is so often the case the marking of the pieces is haphazard. However, it can be said that of the nine items in the series seven came from the hand of Aaron Hays and two from that of Owen Hale, details of whom may be found among the list of sculptors.

All are impressed with the manufacturer's name, COPELAND, and many have the date mark which consists of a letter, signifying the month, and two numbers, being the last two digits of the year in which the object was made in clay.

So ends the story of a unique and interesting series of ceramic commemorative objects born of the absorbing events of the River Tigris.

Bibliography

Anon. *Assyrian Antiquities*. *The Art-Journal*, February 1860. London.

The Nineteenth Century. A Monthly Review, Vol. 15 April 1884. London: Keegan Paul Trench & Co. 1884.

The Century Cyclopedia of Names (1905.) London: *The Times*.

Atterbury, P. ed. (1989).*The Parian Phenomenon*. Shepton Beauchamp: Richard Dennis.

Brackman, A.C. (1980). *The Luck of Nineveh*. London: Eyre Methuen.

Copeland, R. (1997). *Spode and Copeland Marks and other Relevant Intelligence*. London: Studio Vista/Cassell.

Douglas, J.D. (1962). *The New Bible Dictionary*. London: The Inter-Varsity Fellowship.

Gunnis, R. (1957). *The Dictionary of British Sculptors 1660-1851*. London.

Keller, W. (1963). *The Bible as History. Archaeology confirms the Book of Books*. Translation from the German by W. Neil. London: Hodder & Stoughton.

Layard, A.H. (1903). *Autobiography and Letters from Childhood, etc.* Edited by the Hon. William Bruce. London: John Murray.

(1849). *Monuments of Nineveh*. Volumes I and II. London: John Murray.

(1861). *A Popular Account of the Discoveries at Nineveh*. London: Murray.

Reade, Dr. J. (1983). *Assyrian Sculpture*. London: British Museum.

Rudoe, J. (1989). 'Assyrian Style Jewellery'. *The Antique Collector Magazine*.

(1991). *Decorative Art 1850-1950. A Catalogue of the British Museum Collection*. London: British Museum.

(1993). *Henry Layard et les Arts Décoratifs du Style 'Nineveh' en Angleterre*. Paris: The Louvre.

Saggs, H.W.F. (1984). *The Might that was Assyria*. London: Sidgwick & Jackson.

Waterfield, G. (1963). *Layard of Nineveh*. London: John Murray.

Winstone, H.V.F. (1985). *Uncovering the Ancient World*. London: Constable.

GLOSSARY OF TERMS

Backstamp. Mark carrying the manufacturer's name, trade mark and perhaps pattern details stamped on the base of an article. May be impressed into the clay, or printed.

Ball clay. A sedimentary kaolinitic clay that fires to a pale buff colour and, because of its fine particle size, is very plastic.

Bedding. A method of placing porcelainous ware on or in powdered flint (after 1934 in powdered alumina) to support it during the biscuit fire.

Biscuit. Unglazed fired ceramic ware.

Body. 1) The mixture of raw materials comprising the clay used by the potters.
2) That part of a piece of ware on which glaze may be applied: e.g., The parian *body* is unglazed, but translucent.

Bone china. A hard, vitreous body renowned for its strength, whiteness and translucency and the richness of enamel colours obtainable.

Burnishing *see* Gilding.

Bust. A sculpture of a person's head, shoulders and chest, a portrait bust.

Calcine. To heat to a temperature which will render a substance easier to crush or refine.

Casting slip. A clay and water mixture of a creamy consistency. After about 1923 sodium compounds (silicate and carbonate) were added to increase the clay:water ratio. The casting process involves pouring the slip into moulds of plaster of Paris which absorb the water to yield a deposit of clay on the inner surface.

Ceramic. The term derived from the Greek word *Keramos* to apply to the range of products based on high temperature treatment of silica compounds.

Chasing. Using a pointed agate stone to burnish lines on the matt surface of gilding.

China clay. White burning clay consisting mainly of kaolinite, an alumino-silicate.

Cornish stone. Partly decomposed granite consisting of feldspathic minerals and quartz. Also called China stone. Comparable to Chinese pet-un-tse.

Embossed. Referring to marks which have been made in a separate mould and applied to an object like a jug, or marks formed in the actual mould of the item.

Feldspar. Minerals consisting of alumino-silicates of potassium, sodium or calcium. Potash feldspars are usually used in parian manufacture. Used to be spelled *felspar.*

Fettling. Removing rough edges, seams and excrescences in the clay state caused in the making process.

Figure. A single statuette.

Firing. The process by which clay ware is subjected to heat which transforms it into a hard substance by irreversible reactions.

Flint. Nodular silica from chalk deposits. Flints are calcined to about 900-1000°C then ground in water to a creamy consistency and dried. Used in most ceramic bodies. Before 1930s used for bedding bone china flatware.

Flux. A material which lowers the temperature at which a mixture of ceramic substances melts.

Frit. A ceramic composition that has been fused, melted, then quenched in water to form a glass-like substance that is then ground for use in body composition.

Gilding. Application of gold to add richness to an object, perhaps to a bangle or trimming to the edge of a garment. Best gold fires to a matt surface and needs to be burnished with a 'bloodstone' to render it shiny. Bloodstone is made from haematite, a naturally occurring solid iron oxide. Agate stone is used for very delicate work.

Glaze. A prepared mixture of glass-forming materials which, when applied to a ceramic object and fired, will form a thin glassy layer on the surface.

Glost. Glazed.

Green. Unfired clay state.

Group. A sculpture consisting of more than one subject. e.g., mother and child, girl and rabbit.

Impressed. A mark which has been pressed into damp clay by a marker with letters/ numbers.

Kiln. An oven specially constructed to fire ceramic ware to high temperatures.

Modelling. The craft of producing an original model, usually in clay, for reproduction.

Mould making. The process of making plaster of Paris moulds from a model for reproduction in clay.

Parian. A pale cream coloured vitreous porcelain principally made from feldspar and china clay. The name derives from the island of Paros, the source of marble used by the Greeks. This name was first adopted by Minton in 1847. Copeland & Garrett, who first introduced the body material in 1845, called it Statuary Porcelain. Wedgwood adopted the name Carrara, after the marble quarried in north-west Tuscany.

Placing. Setting ware ready for firing in a kiln.

Porcelain. A vitreous, translucent ceramic usually pale grey in colour. Early artificial, or soft paste, porcelains contained glassy substances and, while very lovely, were difficult to manufacture. True, or hard paste, porcelain originated in China in the 10th century, and is made of kao-lin (china clay) and pet-un-tse (feldspathic stone); it was fired at 1400°C.

Pottery. General term covering domestic ceramic wares made with clays, flint and stone.

Pressing. Press moulding: making an object, like a figure, using plastic clay and pressing the clay to the mould rather than using clay slip, as in casting.

Print. A single colour decoration or backstamp (mark) obtained from an engraved copper plate.

Prop. A length of clay, tipped with flint, to secure protruding parts of a figure (like arms) during the firing process, saving them from drooping or collapsing.

Saggar. A box made of fireclay in which clayware or glost ware is placed in the kiln. It protects the ware from direct contact with flames and smoke, and enables huge amounts of ware to be stacked in 'bungs' (columns).

Slip. Casting slip; clay and water.

Statuary. Porcelain statuary, a name for figures, groups and animals to distinguish items from ornamental and functional objects.

Stopping. Filling up of any cracks in a biscuit figure before it is glost fired.

Tinting. Term used to describe the colouring of parian, usually in pale colours and often restricted to delicately printed or painted borders on the hems of garments.

BIBLIOGRAPHY

Anon. (1905). *Cyclopaedia of Names.* New York: The Century Co.

Dictionary of National Biography.

(1968). *British Sculpture 1850-1914.* Exhibition Catalogue. London: The Fine Art Society.

(1970). *The Royal Academy of Arts. A Complete Dictionary of Contributors and their Work from its Foundation in 1769 to 1904.* Reprint of Volumes 1-4. London: Royal Academy.

(1914). *British Art. Catalogue with Descriptions, Historical Notes and Lives of Deceased Artists.* London: National Gallery.

(1916). *Descriptive Catalogue to the Pictures, Busts and Statues in Trinity College, Dublin (and the Provost's House).*

Archival material at the Spode Factory, Courtesy of the Spode Museum Trust:

Correspondence with private persons from 1977 to 1994.

Lists of Stock Returned to Stoke from 160 New Bond Street, London, and items 'waiting', and so charged, to Ceramic and Crystal Palace Art Union August 1881, from 12 Charterhouse Street.

Making Price Books of 1895 and 1928. Hand written.

Photographs of subjects c.1870s and after.

Recipe books.

Statuary Price Book. Hand written.

Art-Journal, 1849-1866, including the Catalogues to the 1851 and 1862 International Exhibitions

Art-Union, 1845-1848

Aslin, E. & Atterbury, P. (1976). *Minton 1798-1910.* Catalogue to the Exhibition at the Victoria & Albert Museum and sponsored jointly by the Museum and Thomas Goode & Company.

Atterbury, P. ed. (1980). *English Pottery and Porcelain.* Chapter VI.

Victorian and Later Pottery & Porcelain, articles from *Antiques Magazine* (New York). London: Peter Owen.

ed. (1989). *The Parian Phenomenon.* Shepton Beauchamp: Richard Dennis. Contributions from Maureen Batkin, Martin Greenwood, Benedict Read, Dr. Roger Smith, Dr. Philip Ward-Jackson, and G.D.V. Glynn.

Barker, D. (1985). *Parian Ware.* Princes Risborough: Shire Album 142.

Batkin, M. (1982). *Wedgwood Ceramics 1846-1959.* London: Richard Dennis.

Battie, D. & Turner, M. (1975). *Price Guide to 19th & 20th Century Porcelain.* Woodbridge: Antique Collectors' Club.

Busse-Joachim Busse Compendium (1977). *International Directory of Painters and Sculptors of the 19th Century.* London: George Prior.

Catalogue, Official, to the Exhibition of the Works of all Nations, 1851

Catalogues of Copeland's Statuary Porcelain:

1848. *A List of Groups, Statuettes, Vases, etc. executed in Statuary Porcelain, from models by the following eminent artists: Gibson, RA., Wyatt, Foley, Durham, Cumberworth, &c.; also copies from the works of Cellini, Fiamingo, Marochetti, Pradier, &c. (hand written 'List of Prices 24th May 1848').* Courtesy Josiah Wedgwood & Sons Ltd.

1851. Similar to 1848 with the addition of the names of Marshall, Theed, Jones, & Francis.

1873, January. *Net Price List of Groups, Figures, Vases, &c., in Statuary Porcelain.* (For the Trade only.) Courtesy The Dyson Perrins Museum Trust.

1876, January. *Price List of Groups, Figures, Vases, &c., in Ceramic Statuary.* Illustrated with photographs.

1883, with MSS additions in 1884. *Net Price List of Groups Figures, Vases, &c., in Statuary Porcelain.* For the Trade only. Undated, but date estimated from actual objects.

Collard, E. (1968). Parian Statuettes. *Canadian Antiques Collector.* July.
(1984). *Nineteenth Century Pottery and Porcelain in Canada.* 2nd edition. Montreal: McGill-Queens University Press. pp. 177-187.
Copeland, R. (1986). 'Parian Porcelain Statuary: Sculpture for the Many'. New York: American Ceramic Circle *Bulletin* Number 5.
(1993). *Spode and Copeland Marks and other Relevant Intelligence.* London: Studio Vista.
Cudden, J.A. (1980). *Dictionary of Sport and Games.* London: Macmillan.
Daiches, D. (1966). *Robert Burns.* London: André Deutsch.
Dennis, R. 1984). *The Parian Phenomenon.* Catalogue to the Exhibition in Chelsea Town Hall, London. December.
Drakard, D. (1984). 'Politics on Pottery.' London: *Country Life.* 6 December.
(1986). 'Heroes, Trophies and Tea-cups.' London: *Country Life.* 6 March.
Frangopulo, N.J. ed. (1962). *A Guide to the History of Manchester.* Manchester Education Committee.
Garner, R. (1860). *Supplement to the Natural History of the County of Stafford, comprising its Geology, Zoology, Botany, and Meteorology, also its Antiquities, Topography, Manufactures, etc.* London: John van Voorst.
Godden, G.A. (1961). *Victorian Porcelain.* Chapter 7. The Parian Body. London: Barrie & Jenkins.
Godley, A.D. (1910). *The Poetical Works of Thomas Moore.* London: Henry Frowde.
Groce, G. & Wallace, D. *Dictionary of Artists in America.* Yale University Press.
Gunnis, R. (1964). *Dictionary of British Sculptors 1660-1851.* London: The Abbey Library. New Revised Edition.
Haslem, J. (1876). *The Old Derby China Factory.* London: George Bell.
Hughes, G.B. (1950). 'English Statuary Porcelain Ware.' London: *Country Life.* 8 December. pp.1986-7.
(1964). 'Parian Statuary for Victorian Homes.' London: *Country Life.* 2 January. pp.30-31.
Huxley, E. (1975). *Florence Nightingale.* London: Weidenfeld & Nicolson.
Jewitt, L. (1883). *The Ceramic Art of Great Britain.* London: J.S. Virtue. pp.384-5,389-395. Note: the captions to Figs.1119-1128 should read 'Messrs.Copelands' productions' and not Minton's.
Landale, C. (1977). 'Parian Ware.' London: *Antique Collector.* May.pp.53-55.
Loch, M.L. (1986). '19th Century Parian Identified.' USA: *Antiques & Collecting.* June.
Macht, C. (1950). *Classical Wedgwood Designs.* New York: Gramercy Publishing Company.
Mackay, J. (1977). *Dictionary of Western Sculptors in Bronze.* Woodbridge: Antique Collectors' Club.
May, J. (1983). *Victoria Remembered.* London: Heinemann.
May, J. & J. (1972). *Commemorative Pottery 1780-1900.* London: Heinemann.
Mullen, R.& Munson, J. (1987). *Victoria. Portrait of a Queen.* London: BBC.
Palgrave, F.T. (1862). *Introduction to, and catalogue of, the Sculpture section, British Division of the Fine Art Department at the International Exhibition of 1862 and Handbook to same.*
Raines, F.R. & Sutton, C.W. ed. (1903). *The Life of Humphrey Chetham.* 2 vols. Manchester Chetham Society: NS 50.
Read, B. (1982). *Victorian Sculpture.* Yale University.
Reilly, R. & Savage, G. (1980). *The Dictionary of Wedgwood.* Woodbridge: Antique Collectors' Club.
Robertson, J.L. (1958). *The Poetical Works of Robert Burns.* Oxford University Press.
Shinn, C. & D. (1971). *The Illustrated Guide to Victorian Parian China.* London: Barrie & Jenkins.
Souchal, F. (1981). *French Sculptors of the 17th and 18th Centuries.* London & Oxford.
Spielman, M.H. (1901). *British Sculpture and Sculptors of Today.* London.
Staffordshire Advertiser 1846 onwards, as quoted.
Strickland, W.G. (1913). *Dictionary of Irish Artists.* 2 Volumes.
Warrington, J. (1961). *Everyman's Classical Dictionary.* London: Dent.
Watkyn, G.G. (1967). *The Liverpool Blue Coat School Past and Present.* Liverpool: Illustrated Liverpool News.
Woodham-Smith, C. (1950). *Florence Nightingale.* London: Constable.

SUBJECT INDEX

B=Bust; S=Statuette; GP=Group; R=Royalty

Assyrian Subjects

GENERAL INDEX

LOVE
16½ IN. 7IN. 10½ IN.
HIGH WIDE LONG
THE RIVER SIDE
18½ IN. 6IN. 6IN.
THE SISTERS
23IN. 8IN. 8IN.
NEW FRIENDS
17½ IN. 6½ IN. 6½ IN.
LOVE
16½ IN. 7IN. 11½ IN.
HIGH WIDE LONG
STUDIES FROM LIFE
20IN. 7½ IN. 10½ IN.
HIGH WIDE LONG
CLYTIE
23 IN. 15 IN.
STUDIES FROM LIFE
20IN. 7½ IN. 10½ IN.
HIGH WIDE LONG
PROSPERITY
20IN. 6IN. 7IN.
BEATRICE
22IN. 6IN. 7IN.
PATIENCE
23IN. 13IN. 13IN.
MAIDENHOOD
21½ IN. 6½ IN. 6IN.
ADVERSITY
19½ IN. 7IN. 7IN.